THE UNWANTED

THE
UNWANTED

America, Auschwitz, and a Village Caught In Between

Michael Dobbs

United States Holocaust Memorial Museum

ALFRED A. KNOPF | NEW YORK | 2019

THIS IS A BORZOI BOOK
PUBLISHED BY ALFRED A. KNOPF

Copyright © 2019 by United States Holocaust Memorial Museum

Published in the United States by Alfred A. Knopf, a division
of Penguin Random House LLC, New York, and distributed
in Canada by Random House of Canada, a division
of Penguin Random House Canada Limited, Toronto.

www.aaknopf.com

Knopf, Borzoi Books, and the colophon
are registered trademarks of Penguin Random House LLC.

Library of Congress Cataloging-in-Publication Data
Names: Dobbs, Michael, [date] author.
Title: The unwanted: America, Auschwitz, and a village caught in between / by Michael Dobbs.
Description: First edition. | New York: Alfred A. Knopf, [2019] | Borzoi book. |
Includes bibliographical references and index.
Identifiers: LCCN 2018024784 (print) | LCCN 2018025652 (ebook) |
ISBN 9781524733209 (e-book) | ISBN 9781524733193 (hardcover)
Subjects: LCSH: Holocaust, Jewish (1939–1945) | Roosevelt, Franklin D. (Franklin Delano),
1882–1945—Relations with Jews. | Roosevelt, Franklin D. (Franklin Delano), 1882–1945—
Political and social views. | Jews, European—Government policy—United States—
History—20th century. | United States—Emigration and immigration—Government policy—
20th century. | Jews—Persecutions—Europe—History—20th century. |
World War, 1939–1945—Jews—Rescue.
Classification: LCC D804.3 (ebook) | LCC D804.3 .D63 2019 (print) |
DDC 940.53/18142—dc23
LC record available at https://lccn.loc.gov/2018024784

Jacket photograph courtesy of Dianne Lee / Hedy Epstein Estate
Spine-of-jacket images: (top) Max and Fanny Valfer, on vacation in Bad Neuenahr, Germany,
August 1934. Doris Bergman; (middle) Hedy Wachenheimer, age 14. Dianne Lee/Hedy Epstein
Estate; (bottom) Siegfried and Charlotte Maier, with sons Kurt and Heinz. Kurt S. Maier
collection, edited by John Robert Bauer
Jacket design by Tyler Comrie
Maps by Gene Thorp

Manufactured in the United States of America
First Edition

For the Victims

It is a fantastic commentary on the inhumanity of our times that for thousands and thousands of people a piece of paper with a stamp on it is the difference between life and death.

—DOROTHY THOMPSON, American journalist, 1938

It was the season of Light, it was the season of Darkness, it was the spring of hope, it was the winter of despair, we had everything before us, we had nothing before us, we were all going direct to Heaven, we were all going direct the other way.

—CHARLES DICKENS, *A Tale of Two Cities*

Contents

Foreword

Sara Bloomfield, Director
United States Holocaust Memorial Museum

At the beginning of this book, fourteen-year-old Hedy Wachenheimer rides her bike to school through the foothills of the Black Forest on November 10, 1938, unaware that her life is about to change forever. That same morning, U.S. diplomats and consuls in Nazi Germany struggle to make sense of the burning of synagogues, the destruction of Jewish shops and homes, and the arrest of thirty thousand Jewish men and boys. What did these attacks portend? Should the United States respond? If so, how?

What we now term "the Holocaust" changed our world, shattering our assumptions about human nature, the character of "Western civilization," and the very notion of progress. At the time of Kristallnacht this was all in the future.

We need to keep reminding ourselves that the Holocaust was not inevitable. With the benefit of hindsight and scholarship, we can now identify the various factors that led to the rise of Nazism and the genocide of the Jews. We can see the bad decisions, fecklessness, and missed opportunities all around—motivated by ideological beliefs and hate but also by fear, greed, resentment, indifference, and wishful thinking.

Adolf Hitler was appointed chancellor of Germany in January 1933, in the midst of a serious economic depression and widespread fears of Communism. Conservative elites found his extremism and propensity for violence distasteful, but thought they could control him. He would soon eliminate their power as he transformed Germany from a democracy to a dictatorship, enabling the implementation of his vision of a racially pure nation.

Over the course of the 1930s, the Nazi regime instituted laws stripping Jews of their German citizenship and removing them from all aspects of German society—its economy, government, and the media as well as educational, social, and cultural institutions. During this period, Nazi policy regarding the Jews was to encourage emigration. But the forced impoverishment of the Jews and strong antisemitic views worldwide made it hard for the Jews to find places of refuge willing to accept them.

In September 1939, with the invasion of Poland and the beginning of World War II, things would change dramatically. Jewish communities were targeted for exclusion, persecution, and violence in all the Nazi-occupied lands. After the surprise German invasion of the Soviet Union in June 1941, the regime started systematic mass shootings and later turned to industrialized murder by gassing.

Americans could read accurate information about the Nazi persecution of German Jews as early as 1933. Front-page articles about newly inaugurated President Franklin Roosevelt and his New Deal sat next to reports of the German boycott of Jewish businesses and the burning of books by Jews and other "unacceptable" authors.

In response to this news, some Americans held rallies and protests, and started a boycott movement against stores that carried German goods. Hundreds of petitions from all over the country urged government officials to protest Nazi Germany's treatment of Jews. Yet in 1933 the United States, and other nations, considered diplomatic protest to be violations of Germany's national sovereignty and accepted international norms. It was not against the law for a country to attack its own citizens.

Meanwhile, polls showed that Americans were consistently unwilling to expand the United States' restrictive 1924 immigration quotas to allow more immigrants to enter the country. Between 1933 and 1938, the German quota went unfilled. By early 1939, more than 240,000 Germans, mostly Jews, had applied for U.S. immigration visas, creating a multiyear backlog. Although Americans did not know that the Holocaust would happen, they did know that something terribly wrong was happening in Nazi Germany, and that it was getting worse. Yet, save for a few courageous individuals, Americans did not take a stand.

.   .   .

In *The Unwanted,* Michael Dobbs reconstructs the German village of Kippenheim, and the members of the Jewish community who lived there. It's a world like any other—full of dreams and ambitions, friendships and families. Dobbs can bring us into their daily life because of the extraordinary amount of archival material, photographs, and oral histories available. For most communities, especially in eastern Europe, where the vast majority of the victims of the Holocaust lived, such records, if they survived at all, are much more fragmentary. The well-documented story of Kippenheim is a painful reminder that this is just one of approximately four thousand Jewish communities across Europe that were destroyed.

Some Kippenheimers were able to navigate the United States' increasingly restrictive immigration process, which required applicants to find an American financial sponsor, pre-purchase a ticket for one of the few ships crossing the Atlantic, and prove beyond doubt that they were not a security threat. East European Jews, whose communities were occupied by Nazi Germany through wartime conquest, did not have the same hope of escape.

No amount of studying or writing or memorializing can bring back those who were murdered in the Holocaust. But it can help us remember them as people who lived, not just victims who died. By doing so, we begin to realize the magnitude of what was lost: the millions of worlds that vanished, the generations never to be born, long-standing communities totally obliterated, complete families that ceased to exist. And above all, the individuals.

The world failed to save them. We must not fail in remembering them. We must also not fail in trying to do for victims of genocide today what was not done for the Jews of Europe. As Mark Twain is credited with saying, "History does not repeat itself, but it rhymes." We study history to help us imagine the unimaginable, to appreciate the power of individuals, and to remind ourselves to be vigilant. In the words of Holocaust scholar Peter Hayes, "Beware the beginnings."

THE UNWANTED

ONE

November 1938

H EDY WACHENHEIMER cycled down Adolf-Hitler-Strasse on her way
to school. It was a bitterly cold morning. The whitewashed two-
story brick houses on either side of the road were shrouded in predawn
gloom. Dim lights flickered behind the still drawn shutters.

When Hedy reached the edge of the village, near the sign reading
JEWS ARE UNWANTED HERE, she dismounted. There was a steep incline
ahead. Lacking the strength to pedal uphill, she pushed the bike into
the open countryside.

The sun soon began to rise. Often at this time of year, in the late fall,
a thick mist settled over the fields and vineyards of the upper Rhine
valley, making it difficult to see more than a few feet ahead. But today
the frosted meadows and trees sparkled in the early morning light.
The road was slick from the fallen leaves of the aspens and birches that
mingled with the firs and pines of the forest.

Shivering in the frigid air, Hedy thought about the strange behavior
of her parents the previous evening. They seemed unusually nervous
and preoccupied. Her father had told her to hide inside the wardrobe
if woken by "loud noises" during the night. Her parents refused to
explain the reason for their concern. This was unlike them. An only
child, Hedy was accustomed to sharing their joys and sorrows.[1]

The talk of trouble seemed connected somehow to a report, on the
radio, that a German diplomat in Paris had been murdered by a crazed
Jewish refugee. Why that had anything to do with the Wachenheimer

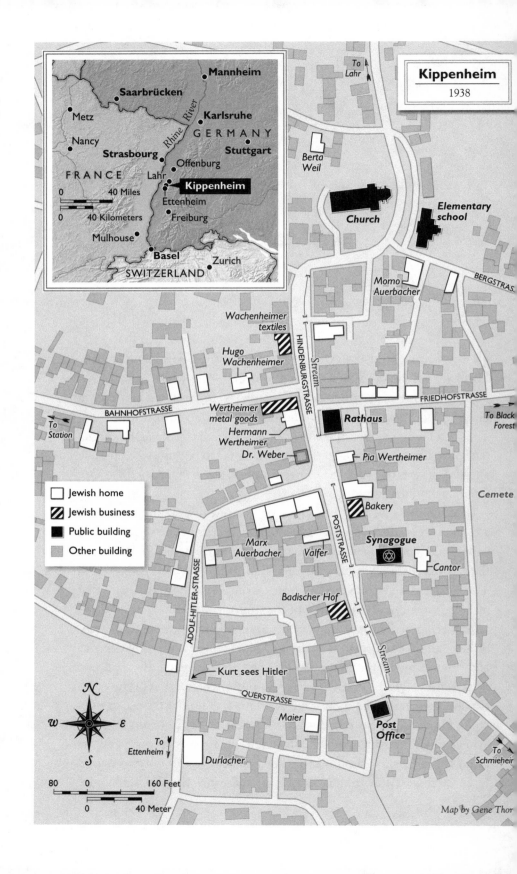

Kippenheim
1938

To Lahr

Berta Weil

Church

Elementary school

BERGSTRAS

Momo Auerbacher

Wachenheimer textiles

HINDENBURGSTRASSE

Stream

FRIEDHOFSTRASSE

Hugo Wachenheimer

To Black Forest

BAHNHOFSTRASSE

Wertheimer metal goods

Rathaus

To Station

Hermann Wertheimer

Dr. Weber

Pia Wertheimer

Cemete

Bakery

Jewish home

Jewish business

Public building

Other building

POSTSTRASSE

Synagogue

Marx Auerbacher

Valfer

Cantor

Badischer Hof

ADOLF-HITLER-STRASSE

Kurt sees Hitler

QUERSTRASSE

Maier

Post Office

To Schmieheir

N

W   *E*

S

To Ettenheim

Durlacher

80   0   160 Feet

0   40 Meter

Map by Gene Thor

Inset map:

Mannheim

Saarbrücken

Metz

Rhine River

Karlsruhe

Nancy

GERMANY

Strasbourg

Offenburg

Stuttgart

FRANCE

Lahr

Kippenheim

0   40 Miles

Ettenheim

0   40 Kilometers

Freiburg

Mulhouse

Basel

Zurich

SWITZERLAND

family, living hundreds of miles away in Kippenheim, an obscure village, in the Baden region of southwest Germany, the fourteen-year-old did not understand. In the end, Hedy and her parents had slept undisturbed.

It took Hedy roughly forty minutes to make the three-mile trek to school, half walking, half pedaling. With just eighteen hundred inhabitants, Kippenheim was not big enough to have its own high school, so Hedy was obliged to commute to nearby Ettenheim. The winding country road took her through the foothills of the Black Forest, beloved by generations of Germans for its picture-perfect villages, hiking trails, and gorgeous scenery. To her right was a castle, atop a hill, with a commanding view of the Rhine River. The mountains of eastern France formed a dark bluish blur in the distance, on the other side of the wide river plain.

Back in the seventeenth century, when Jews first settled in the area, the Mahlberg Schloss had been part of the defenses of the Holy Roman Empire. It had been built by the rulers of Baden, known by their aristocratic title of "margrave." The margraves had relied on Jewish bankers and wealthy businessmen to provision their armies. These "court Jews" relied in turn on a network of rural Jewish traders willing to do business on more favorable terms than Christian merchants in big towns like Freiburg that were off-limits to Jews.[2] Protected by the margraves, Jews had been living in the strategically important border region ever since.

Hidden in the hills on the opposite side of the road from the castle was the Jewish cemetery at Schmieheim, where three generations of Wachenheimers lay buried. It was a heritage that meant little to Hedy, who did not even know she was Jewish until the age of six, when her elementary school teacher insisted she attend Torah class. The strong-willed Hedy told the teacher she did not want to be Jewish. If she was required to have a religion, she preferred to be Catholic or Lutheran, like the other children. The teacher made it clear she had no say in the matter. Her parents, aunts, uncles, cousins, and all the distant Wachenheimer relatives were Jewish. That meant she was Jewish as well.

Her anxiety grew as she cycled past a dentist's office on the outskirts of Ettenheim. All the windows in the house had been smashed. The violence seemed inexplicable and arbitrary—no other house in the street had been attacked—but Hedy was sure it had something to do with the fact that the dentist was also Jewish.

Hedy parked her bike outside an imposing neoclassical building with the word GYMNASIUM and 1875 inscribed across the entrance. Small groups of teachers and students were engaged in excited conversations. They glanced at her out of the corner of their eyes, but did not speak to her. She made her way as usual to her classroom on the second floor, overlooking the schoolyard. She was used to being treated like a pariah. During breaks, she would stand by herself on the front steps of the school while the other children played tag in the yard. Never invited to join their games, she was left with nothing to do but nervously finger a reddish-brown sandstone column until the break was over. After three years standing in the same spot, she had worn a small indentation in the stone.

Most of the teachers behaved correctly, if distantly, toward her. The exception was the math teacher, Hermann Herbstreith, a sergeant in the Nazi Party "protection squad," or Schutzstaffel, known more familiarly as the SS. Herbstreith enjoyed humiliating his Jewish students. He came to class in a black SS uniform, with a revolver thrust into his right boot. When he asked Hedy a math question, he would gesture at the gun. Sometimes, he even pulled the revolver out of his boot and pointed it directly at Hedy, towering over his terrified, diminutive pupil. It did not matter how Hedy answered the question. As far as Herbstreith was concerned, her answers were always wrong.

"That's a Jewish answer," he would sneer, as her classmates snickered. "And we all know that Jewish answers are no good."[3]

Hedy dealt with the ostracism of her peers by focusing on her studies. She received top marks in all her subjects with the exception of math, which she failed repeatedly.[4]

The Gymnasium was an elite secondary school, reserved for students with an excellent academic record. After the Nazis came to power in 1933, they had switched the emphasis from academic studies to "German studies," including physical education and the glorious antecedents of the Third Reich. When Hedy's parents first tried to enroll her in the school, back in 1935, she had been rejected as a non-Aryan. The principal, Walter Klein, made an exception for the young Jewish girl on the grounds that her father had fought for the Fatherland in the Great War, and had even been wounded in battle.

Classes started punctually at eight o'clock. On this particular day—Thursday, November 10, 1938—the moon-faced Dr. Klein entered Hedy's classroom half an hour later. He made a speech, dictated to him earlier by the mayor, about the "justified wrath of the German people," before pointing his finger directly at Hedy.

"Get out, you dirty Jew," he screamed, his usually smiling face contorted with rage.[5]

Hedy could not comprehend the transformation that had overcome the principal, a gentle man with a bald pate and trim mustache, in the space of a few seconds. Even though she had seen the broken windows of the Jewish dentist's office, she found it difficult to grasp the reason for Dr. Klein's anger. Previously, he had seemed well disposed to her and had even praised her "aptitude for languages."[6] She thought she was somehow at fault. Perhaps she had yawned in class, or failed to pay attention to one of her teachers. She worried about how to explain herself to her parents when she got home.

Mystified by what she had done wrong, and how she might make amends, Hedy asked the principal to repeat himself. He not only repeated the words *"Raus mit dir, du Dreckjude!"* but grabbed her by the elbow and pushed her out the door. He then instructed the remaining students to join a demonstration against the Jews that was being organized outside the village hall. Minutes later, the students streamed out of the classroom, yelling "dirty Jew" as they rushed past Hedy, and headed up the street toward the Baroque town hall, the Rathaus.[7]

Unsure what to do, Hedy crept back into the empty classroom. She sat down at her desk and took out a schoolbook. After a few minutes, there was a timid knock at the door. It was Hans Durlacher, also from Kippenheim, the only other Jewish student left in the school for the fall 1938 term. Hans was in the grade below Hedy. He told Hedy that the principal had screamed at him as well. He was frightened. Reluctantly, Hedy said he could stay with her as long as he did not disturb her studies.

Hans sat by the window overlooking the schoolyard and Adolf-Hitler-Strasse, the name given to the most important street in every German village. After an hour peering out the window, he beckoned urgently to Hedy to join him. Together, they watched SS men herd dozens of disheveled prisoners down the street with whips and sticks, shouting at them to go faster. The men and boys, some not much older than Hedy, were chained together at the ankles in rows of four. Bringing up the rear was a gang of hoodlums from the local furniture factory armed with chair legs that they used to smash the windows of Jewish homes. Draped around their necks were strings of sausages looted from a Jewish butcher.[8]

The terrified students decided they should call home to find out what was happening. They went to a nearby store to find a telephone. When Hedy tried to reach her mother, a strange voice answered. *"Der Anschluss ist nicht mehr in Betrieb,"* the voice announced. "The connection is no longer in operation." Next she tried her father's office and the Kippenheim home of her aunt. Everywhere the result was the same. "The connection is no longer in operation."[9] Hans got the same answer at his house.

The school day was not yet over but the building was deserted. Everybody else in the Gymnasium was either taking part in the demonstrations or had gone home in disgust. There was nothing for Hedy and Hans to do except go home themselves. When Hedy reached her apartment on Bahnhofstrasse, she noticed that the blue shutters on the second floor were closed. The front door was locked. This was odd, as her mother was normally at home during the day and always left the shutters open.

Hedy rang the doorbell but nobody answered. Trying to hold back her tears as she stood in front of the empty apartment, Hedy noticed one of the village's most prominent Nazis walking down the street. Normally she would have done anything to avoid the man, who was notorious for his hostility to Jews, but she was desperate to find her parents. She crossed the street and asked the Nazi if he knew what had happened to her mother.

"I don't know where the goddamn bitch is," he snarled. "But if I find her, I will kill her."[10]

. . .

Less than three months before, at the end of August, Kippenheim had received a surprise visit from the man after whom so many German streets were named. Adolf Hitler had passed through the village on an inspection tour of the "West Wall," the defense system better known abroad as "the Siegfried Line." The visit was organized so hastily that villages along the route did not have time to put out all the usual Nazi bunting. As his motorcade approached Kippenheim, there were excited whispers of *"Hitler kommt"*—"Hitler is coming." Soon afterward, Kippenheimers caught a fleeting glimpse of the Führer standing in the front of his open Mercedes in a long beige raincoat. A limousine crammed with eight generals in full uniform with glistening medals followed on behind. Hitler acknowledged the frenzied *Sieg Heils* of the crowd with a dismissive wave of his upturned right hand.[11]

After touring the hastily built fortifications along the Rhine, Hitler used a giant telescope to peer into France. In his autobiography, *Mein Kampf,* he had dubbed France "the mortal enemy of our nation" and called for its destruction as a prelude to Germany's expansion to the east.[12]

"Hitler Inspects Nazi Forts on French Border; Führer at Rhine 1st Time Since War" ran the headline in *The Washington Post* the following day. "German Army Massed at French Border," reported the *Los Angeles Times.* "War or Peace?" asked *The New York Times.* "Europe Waits in Hope."[13]

That particular war scare had faded after France and Britain agreed to Hitler's demands for the dismemberment of Czechoslovakia. But the respite granted by the appeasement of Hitler at the Munich conference in late September did not last long. Sated on the international front, the dictator turned his attention to a domestic obsession: his war with the Jews.

In early November, Hitler ordered the expulsion from Germany of some twelve thousand east European Jews. Although they had been born in Poland, virtually all of them had been living in Germany perfectly legally for decades. Yet they were chased out of their homes overnight, taken to the nearest railroad stations, and dumped on the Polish border, without any money or property. Even by Nazi standards, the operation was unusually brutal. The American consul in Berlin, Raymond Geist, described the mass arrests and expulsions as "one of the cruelest acts on record in modern times."[14]

Reports of misery and suicides on the Polish frontier reached the seventeen-year-old son of one of the deportees, Herschel Grynszpan, who was living in Paris illegally, hoping to travel to Palestine. On November 2, Grynszpan received a letter from his sister describing the family's expulsion from Germany, after twenty-seven years living in Hannover. "No one told us what was up, but we realized this was going to be the end," Berta wrote. "We haven't a penny. Could you send us something?"

The destitute Grynszpan had little money to send. On November 7, he spent his remaining francs on a pistol, and took the Metro to the German embassy. After telling the doorman that he had "an important document" to deliver to the ambassador, he was ushered into the room of a junior aide, Ernst vom Rath. When vom Rath asked him to produce his document, he pulled out his pistol, shouting, "You are a filthy *boche* and here, in the name of twelve thousand persecuted Jews, is your document."[15] He then fired five shots at the diplomat, hitting him in the stomach and spleen.

Vom Rath died of his wounds two days later, on November 9. His murder gave Hitler the perfect pretext for unleashing nationwide violence against the Jews. The Nazi press had already pinned responsibility for the attack in Paris on the entire Jewish people, who were collectively branded as "murderers." The propaganda chief, Joseph Goebbels, informed Hitler that anti-Jewish protests had erupted in several German cities, including Berlin. Goebbels recorded the Führer's reaction in his diary: "He decides: demonstrations should be allowed to continue. The police should be withdrawn. For once the Jews should feel the wrath of the people."[16]

According to the Nazi propaganda machine, the German people erupted in a "spontaneous outburst" against the remaining 320,000 Jews in Germany—down from more than half a million in 1933— on the night of November 9–10.[17] In fact, the savagery was carefully orchestrated. Shortly after his meeting with Hitler, Goebbels ordered regional Nazi Party offices to stage "spontaneous" protests, beginning that same night. Several hours later, at 1:20 a.m. on November 10, a top Nazi security official, Reinhard Heydrich, sent an urgent teletype message to Gestapo offices and police stations throughout Germany. The message included detailed instructions on how to respond to demonstrations:

- *Only such measures should be taken which do not involve danger to German life or property. (For instance synagogues are to be burned down only when there is no danger of fire to the surroundings.)*
- *Business and private apartments of Jews may be destroyed but not looted.*
- *The demonstrations that are going to take place should not be hindered by the police.*
- *As many Jews, especially rich ones, are to be arrested as can be accommodated in the existing prisons.*[18]

The attacks on synagogues and Jewish homes and businesses began almost immediately in cities like Munich and Stuttgart. By contrast, it took several hours for the instructions to percolate down to smaller towns and villages. The orders did not reach SS and Nazi Party headquarters in Lahr, five miles north of Kippenheim, until after four a.m. The police chiefs held a hurried meeting with Nazi officials to divide up the work. The SS and the police would round up the Jewish men. Party activists would organize "additional measures," to include attacks on Jewish homes and businesses. The Nazi leader in Lahr, Richard Burk, instructed local mayors to hold rallies and make anti-Jewish speeches. He also mobilized members of the local Hitler Youth movement to spearhead the destruction of synagogues.

The senior SS man in the district was a former concentration camp commander named Heinrich Remmert, who had been banished to Lahr for incompetence. His superiors regarded him as a man of very limited intelligence who had trouble understanding "the simplest concepts." He was the SS equivalent of a lieutenant colonel but, according to his personnel file, would have been better suited to a post of *Sturmführer*—the lowest commissioned officer rank—in a "remote rural area."[19] Charged with arresting all the Jewish men in his district, and dispatching them to concentration camps, Remmert seized the opportunity to impress the doubters with his ideological zeal.

Shortly after Hedy left for school on the morning of November 10, the observant Jewish men of Kippenheim assembled outside the Moorish-style synagogue on Poststrasse for Thursday morning minyan. Their numbers had been depleted by illness, death, and emigration, both abroad and to German cities where they could be more anonymous. But they were still able to muster the necessary quorum of ten adult males to say Kaddish for their loved ones.

Those present included the tobacco and cigar distributor Max Val-fer, who lived across the street with his large, rambunctious family, the dry goods dealer Siegfried Maier, and the cattle dealer Marx Auer-bacher, known for his ribald stories. An assortment of Wertheimers and Auerbachers and Weils, the leading Jewish families in the village, made up the rest of the congregation. Since there were not enough Jews in Kippenheim for the synagogue to have its own rabbi, the services were led by the cantor, Gottfried Schwab.[20]

The worshippers were awaiting the arrival of the most prominent member of the Kippenheim Jewish community before filing into the synagogue. As the richest man in the village, Hermann Wertheimer was respected and resented by Jews and Christians alike. Some Kippen-heimers referred to him sarcastically as "the Grand Mogul" because of his business empire.[21] His metal equipment company was one of the most successful in the region, with an annual turnover of around half a million reichsmarks. Hermann employed twenty workers, including four traveling salesmen, each with his own company car.[22] He took his duties as parnass, or elected leader, of the Kippenheim congregation, very seriously. It was most unusual for him to be late for a service.

The other Jewish men were still wondering what to do when Her-mann's nineteen-year-old daughter, Ilse, arrived on her bicycle. Ner-vous and out of breath, she recounted the events of the night. Her father had been woken by the Gestapo after midnight, taken to the synagogue, and ordered to open the safe where valuables and sacred objects were stored. He was allowed to go back to bed, but only for a couple of hours. There was another loud hammering at the door at 5:30 in the morning. The Gestapo official now informed him that he was under arrest. Still in his dressing gown, he was taken to the Rathaus, a four-hundred-year-old building with overhanging windows and high pedimented roof, almost directly opposite his house. The family was provided with no explanation for his sudden arrest.[23]

Alarmed by these developments, the men decided to cancel the prayer meeting and return home. As they left the synagogue, they were intercepted by municipal officials. They were marched up Poststrasse to the Rathaus, where they were detained in the village council chamber. The lone prison cell in the Rathaus was occupied by Hermann Wertheimer.

Several truckloads of Hitler Youth arrived in Kippenheim from Lahr soon after the arrest of the Jewish men. They were joined by local Nazi activists, including the postmaster, Camill Link, who had a long history of harassing Jews. Link routinely opened the letters of Jewish residents and berated them when they visited the Post Office to pick up their mail. He had once greeted a meek little man who wanted to buy stamps with a slap in the face and a curse, "How dare you come in here, you Jewish bastard."[24] The Nazi thugs marched up and down Poststrasse, looking for Jewish homes and businesses. Women and children cowered in terror at the back of the Valfer cigar business and the Auerbacher clothing store as stones and rocks flew through the display windows in front.

A squad of Hitler Youth members, dressed in combat fatigues and armed with axes on long poles, entered the synagogue. They climbed up to the balcony where the women and girls traditionally sat. After smashing a hole in the wooden railings, they tossed pews and wooden paneling through the gap, creating a pile of broken furniture in the hall below. They used a fireman's ladder to smash the chandeliers, scattering shards of glass all around.

The young Nazi fanatics wanted to burn the building down, but the Christian neighbors objected, because of the risk to the adjoining "German property."[25] They contented themselves instead with pulling the sacred Torah scrolls out of their lovingly embroidered cloth mantles and scattering them across the floor. They threw some of the

Kippenheim synagogue, November 1938.
Boys gathering crystal fragments can be seen on the left of the photograph.

rolls into the little stream that ran through the village, together with piles of religious books.

After destroying the interior of the synagogue, two of the Hitler Youth posed for a celebratory photograph with an SS officer, their axes slung across their shoulders. Their faces bore huge grins. Attracted by the excitement, local children scurried through the wreckage, searching for pieces of crystal to take home as souvenirs. The local Nazi Party leader arrived in Kippenheim later in the day to inspect the damage. Unsatisfied with the partial destruction of the synagogue, Burk ordered a local stonemason to pull down the tablets of the Ten Commandments from the roof. As the stone tablets hit the pavement below, they splintered into fragments.[26]

Even though Kippenheim Jews did not know what was happening inside the synagogue, they could hear the sounds of destruction. The yells and whistles of the Hitler Youth were clearly audible to eight-year-old Kurt Maier around the corner on Querstrasse. Minutes later, an angry crowd appeared in front of the Maier home. They began throwing stones through the windows of the two-story building. The troublemakers included a mentally infirm teenage boy by the name of Wewe, who had previously shown no ill will toward the Jews. He obviously did not understand what was happening, but was egged on by the rest of the crowd.

During the tense period leading up to that dreadful morning, Kurt had brought smiles to his parents' worried faces with an uncanny Adolf Hitler imitation. He caught the screeching cadences of the dictator's voice perfectly, marching up and down the living room with a comb under his nose and hair slicked across his forehead.[27] The time when it was possible to laugh about Hitler, at least in a private family setting, had vanished in a flash.

Kurt's previous experiences of antisemitism had been largely confined to nasty encounters with the teenage son of the postmaster. The brute had once attempted to run Kurt down with his bicycle, before slapping him in the face. This was much more terrifying. As the mob threw stones through the windows, his mother pulled him up to the top floor, where they crawled beneath an upturned bathtub. They sat together underneath the protective metal cover, listening to the sound of breaking glass. They had no idea what had happened to Kurt's father, who had not returned from the synagogue, or his brother, who was still at school.

In the meantime, forlorn groups of Jewish men were arriving at the Kippenheim Rathaus from neighboring villages like Ettenheim and Schmieheim. They, too, were detained in the council chamber, where they were obliged to listen to the mocking taunts of the crowds outside. The SS men confiscated their belts, ties, and prayer books.

Some unfortunates were singled out for especially severe treatment. An apprentice baker from Schmieheim, Siegbert Bloch, and his father had avoided the first wave of arrests thanks to a Christian neighbor who protected them. Unfortunately, their names were on a pre-prepared list. When they failed to show up at the Rathaus in Kippenheim, a brown-shirted storm trooper was dispatched to find them. The storm trooper ordered them both into the sidecar of his motorcycle, but refused to allow the eighteen-year-old Siegbert to sit on his father's lap. Instead, he grabbed him by the hair, yanking him violently from side to side as they careened around the country lanes. When they reached the synagogue, the storm trooper told Siegbert to get out and walk, even though he had broken his leg just a short time before and could only hobble.

The Hitler Youth who had wrecked the synagogue wrapped Siegbert in fragments of Torah scrolls. They filled his cap with cow dung and marched him to the Rathaus. The storm trooper then attempted to ram the back of his leg with his sidecar, only to be stopped by a stern voice from a window across the street.

"Leave that man alone. He is my patient. He has suffered enough."[28]

The voice belonged to the village doctor, Bernhard Weber, who was dressed in a familiar black uniform. As a reserve SS officer, Weber outranked the brown-shirted street brawler from the rival Sturmabteilung, or SA.[29] Even though he was a Nazi Party member of long standing, Weber had continued to treat his Jewish patients. He lived opposite the Rathaus, close to the Wertheimer family. They were still on good terms. When it looked as if the people looting the Wertheimer business would break into the Wertheimer home, the doctor had yelled at them to stop.

Inside the house, Ilse Wertheimer was cowering behind the curtains with her mother after returning from the synagogue, where she had raised the alarm about her father's arrest. Listening to the hailstorm of stones striking the windows, she wondered how long it would take for the looters to "break the door down and kill us."[30] Miraculously, the mob backed off.

After the threatening encounter with the Nazi villager outside her house, Hedy ran to the home of her uncle and aunt. They lived around the corner, next to the family textile business. Along the way, she passed the Wertheimer metal goods store. Looters had used the cast-iron beams and machines outside to smash the glass display windows. They were now helping themselves to the equipment inside. The mood was gay, and people were laughing, which Hedy also did not understand. The menacing but relatively peaceful world with which she was familiar had suddenly turned upside down.

Hedy found her mother at Aunt Käthe's house on Hindenburg-strasse. Relieved to see that her daughter was safe, Bella Wachenheimer described the tumultuous events of the morning, as she had experienced them. The local Nazis had come to the apartment on Bahn-hofstrasse about ten minutes after Hedy left for school. Hedy's father, Hugo, was still at home, in his pajamas. Unlike most of the other Jews, he attended synagogue only on High Holy Days. The Nazis told Hugo he was under arrest. They would not let him put on a coat, even though it was a very cold day.

"Find Hedy, stay together" were Hugo's last words as he was chased onto the street.[31]

A couple of Nazis stayed behind in the apartment to smash the windows and the furniture in the dining room, which included a table and chairs made out of walnut imported from Russia. After they left, Bella closed the shutters to protect the apartment as best she could from the winter air. Forgetting that she was dressed only in her nightclothes, she ran to her sister-in-law's house.

When Hedy finally arrived, Bella and Käthe were staring out of an upper-story window. They were trying to figure out what was going on at the Rathaus, a block and a half away, and possibly catch a glimpse of their husbands. Bella looked grotesque. She was wearing Käthe's clothes, which did not fit her, as Bella was taller and slimmer than her sister-in-law.

Hedy joined the two older women in their watch at the window. Finally, after about an hour, they saw the men coming out of the Rathaus, escorted by the SS. It was a pitiful sight. Nazi thugs were humiliating the Jews in every way possible. Some were wrapped in fragments of Torah scrolls, ripped out of the synagogue. Others had been drenched in water. Several men wore hats full of cow dung that dripped down onto their faces. There must have been sixty or seventy men altogether, not just from Kippenheim, but from Jewish communities all around, including Ettenheim and Schmieheim. The Kippen-heim village hall had been used as a collection point for Jewish males from the entire area.

The Jewish men were divided into two groups. A few elderly men and invalids were loaded onto a truck and driven to Lahr, the district capital, five miles away. SS officers with whips herded the remaining "healthy Jews" up the street like cattle, under Aunt Käthe's window. As Hugo passed in front of the house, still in his pajamas, Bella pushed Hedy's head out of the window. She wanted him to know that their daughter was safe.

"We have Hedy," she yelled. "We are together."[32]

The sad procession headed up the street and around the corner, past the church. Outside the village primary school, they had to pass through a barrage of students who had been mobilized to hurl insults at the Jews and spit at them.

After watching her father and the other men disappear from sight, Hedy returned to the living room with her mother and aunt. Suddenly, there was a loud banging at the door and shouts to open up. Bella had already experienced Nazi thugs invading her own apartment around the corner. Terrified of facing them again, the women retreated to the attic. They found an old armoire that they turned around so that the door faced the high sloping roof. Then, one by one, they crept inside, keeping as quiet as they could.

The banging and yelling continued for a few minutes—only to fade away as suddenly as it had begun. They had no way of knowing that the "spontaneous" demonstrations against the Jews had been officially called off at noon. All they knew was that their men had been taken away, and they themselves were possibly in mortal danger. They remained in the wardrobe for a long time, huddled together for comfort and warmth. Hedy refused to let her mother out of her sight. She kept repeating, over and over again, "I want to get out of here."[33]

She did not mean "out of the wardrobe" or even "out of Kippenheim." She meant "out of Germany." Tens of thousands of Jews squeezed into cupboards in attics and basements, or cowering under beds and bathtubs, in villages and towns across the Third Reich had precisely the same thought. Any doubts about what they should do were swept away in an instant. A single hope remained: emigration.

TWO

Visa Lines

T HE UNITED STATES CONSULATE GENERAL in Stuttgart was housed
in a six-story Art Nouveau building on the Königstrasse, the city's
main shopping street. Topped with neoclassical statues gazing down at
the throngs of asylum seekers below, the building expressed the confident romanticism felt by many Europeans and Americans on the eve
of World War I, before the dreams turned to despair in the trenches of
Ypres and Verdun. The elegant, rigidly symmetrical façade reflected
the American consular service's idea of itself as the guardian of the
immigration laws of a powerful and generous country. The Stars and
Stripes fluttering above the ornately decorated second-floor balcony
contrasted with the Nazi banners and swastikas on the buildings all
around.

Each day, a hundred or so would-be immigrants to the United States
and their families were summoned to the consulate for long-awaited
interviews to determine their fate. They came from all over western
and southern Germany, from Münster to Munich. The Stuttgart consulate served more than half the country, making it one of the busiest
visa-issuing facilities in the world, along with Naples and Montreal. In
addition to those with appointments, hundreds more people stood in a
different line, hoping for answers to questions on American immigration law or simply seeking protection from their Nazi tormentors. Both
lines included "babies, small children, old people," many of whom had
been waiting since early morning.[1]

By the time of the events that would come to be known as Kristall-nacht, the "Night of Broken Glass," any semblance of efficient organization had vanished. Exhausted consular officials were overwhelmed by the flood of desperate people, most of whom they were unable to help. The visa section consisted of a few rooms on the third floor of the six-story building, designed to handle no more than thirty to forty visa applicants a day. Successive consul generals had pleaded with Washington for extra space and extra help as the refugee crisis deepened, in direct proportion to Nazi persecution of German Jews. The State Department had allowed the consulate to hire extra clerks to handle the increased demand for visas, but stalled on the requests for larger premises. An upsurge of immigration applications in the middle of 1938, in response to the mounting anti-Jewish campaign, had created a vast bureaucratic backlog. Unanswered correspondence piled up in great stacks around the office. A Foreign Service inspector remarked on the chaos shortly after Kristallnacht:

> My first impressions of the consulate were 200 visa applicants squeezed into a single reception room, and 32 officers and employees crowded into 8 diminutive rooms. Under such circumstances working conditions were almost intolerable. Face to face, back to back, or elbow to elbow, the employees were huddled around desks which seemed to have been dropped indiscriminately into any vacant spaces. Into this "hodge-podge," clerks weaved their way, or pushed, or realizing the futility of making further progress, stood still and shouted to the employees they could not reach. Upon desks, chairs, and even window sills, there were piled high documents of all descriptions.[2]

Typically, the line outside the visa section started on the third floor, ran all the way down the sweeping Jugendstil staircase, out into the street, and around the block. But Thursday, November 10, 1938, was not a typical day. The overnight roundups of Jews had prevented most of the visa applicants from keeping their scheduled appointments. While the men were being marched off to concentration camps, the women and children were cowering inside their homes. The consulate, and the street outside, was virtually deserted.

One of the few visa seekers to make it to Stuttgart this Thursday morning was twenty-seven-year-old Erich Sonnemann from Mannheim. Fired from his job as an apprentice pharmacist, Erich had applied for a U.S. immigration visa back in 1937. A wealthy relative from Nashville, Tennessee, had agreed to serve as his sponsor after being contacted out of the blue by his mother. The long-forgotten but now vitally important relative signed a piece of paper, known as an affidavit, certifying that Erich would not become "a public charge" if admitted to the United States. Finding a suitable sponsor was key to the emigration prospects of German Jews prohibited by Nazi edict from taking their savings with them to America.

It had taken Erich more than a year to assemble the required forms and submit them to the American consulate. He also underwent a medical examination, designed to ensure that he did not belong to a class of alien "that shall be excluded from the United States" under the 1917 Immigration Act. In addition to prostitutes, polygamists, anarchists, and those plotting to "overthrow by force or violence the Government of the United States," the long list of banned aliens included "imbeciles," "epileptics," "professional beggars," "persons afflicted with tuberculosis in any form," and others deemed unable "to earn a living."[3]

Shortly before Kristallnacht, the Sonnemann family had changed apartments. Their new address was not yet registered with the police: this enabled them to avoid the Gestapo dragnet. Erich spent the night with his parents in the attic, waiting for a knock on the door that never came. That morning, he made his way to the Mannheim railway station, a route that took him past the still smoldering synagogue. He stopped to rescue a Torah from the ruins, hiding it in a secure place. He then took a local train to Stuttgart, knowing that the SS always checked the express trains.

Arriving in Stuttgart after his seventy-mile train trip, Erich walked the five blocks from the main railway station to the consulate at Königstrasse 19A. There was nobody in sight, except for two SS men standing by the entrance. He marched straight past the two Black Shirts, up the staircase at the back of the building, to the almost empty third-floor waiting room. Here he breathed a huge sigh of relief, happy that fortune was finally smiling on him.

Erich spent the next couple of hours being shuttled from office to office. His papers all appeared to be in order. In determining whether to grant an immigration visa, consular officials paid particular attention to the bona fides of the sponsor. They were likely to refuse a visa if they suspected that the relationship between sponsor and would-be immigrant was tenuous. If a sponsor had signed affidavits for too many potential immigrants, that was also grounds for refusal, particularly at Stuttgart, where the consul had the reputation of being "a strict constructionist respecting visa procedure."[4]

On this occasion, however, the consul did not have a problem with Erich's distant relative in Tennessee. Instead, he pointed to a report from the examining surgeon. An X-ray had revealed a hernia on his left side. The visa applicant was classified as "physically defective."

"I am sorry, but I cannot let you go to America in this condition."[5]

The consul told Erich that he could undergo an operation to remove the hernia and return in six weeks' time. No amount of pleading would induce him to change his mind. The consul did, however, allow the terrified asylum seeker to leave by the back door, to avoid the further attentions of the Gestapo.

The consulate general was closed the following day, Friday, November 11, in honor of the veterans who had died in World War I. The Great War, as it was then known, had ended "at the eleventh hour of the eleventh day of the eleventh month" of 1918. Armistice Day was a public holiday in the United States, France, and Britain, but not in Nazi Germany, where it was viewed as a reminder of a shameful defeat.

By the time the consulate reopened for business on Saturday morning, the street outside was packed with thousands of desperate visa seekers. The wrought-iron entrance gates had barely cracked open when "a mass of seething, panic-stricken humanity" surged into the six-story building.[6] "Jews from all sections of Germany thronged into the office until it was overflowing," reported Consul General Samuel Honaker. "Women over sixty years of age pleaded on behalf of husbands imprisoned in some unknown place. American mothers of German sons invoked the sympathy of the Consulate. Jewish fathers and mothers with children in their arms were afraid to return to their homes." Everybody in the crowd seemed to have a relative in America. They all wanted an immediate visa, or at least a piece of paper to show to the Gestapo proving their intent to leave Germany at the earliest possible date.

From his office on the second floor, directly below the visa section, Consul General Honaker described the heart-rending scene in a dispatch to the American ambassador in Berlin. "Sir, I have the honor to report," he began, in the formal style required by the Foreign Service, "that the Jews of Southwest Germany have suffered vicissitudes during the last three days which would seem unreal to one living in an enlightened country during the twentieth century if one had not actually been a witness of their dreadful experiences." He went on to describe "the horror of midnight arrests, of hurried departures in a half-dressed state from their homes in the company of police officers, of the wailing of wives and children suddenly left behind, of imprisonment in crowded cells."[7]

Like other foreign observers, Honaker had no doubt that the anti-Jewish violence was centrally planned and directed. His staff had observed a new Mercedes packed with "high S.S. officials" cruising slowly through the center of Stuttgart while Jewish shops were being smashed and plundered. "These men made an inspection of what was going on, and apparently after giving their approval, drove pompously away while the destruction continued."[8] Honaker reported that it was "easy to recognize . . . trained and disciplined S.A. or S.S. men" under the civilian clothes of many of the rioters. According to the consul general, most ordinary Germans were "in complete disagreement with these violent demonstrations against the Jews. Many people, in fact, are hanging their heads with shame." Honaker estimated that "possibly 20 per cent of the population" approved "the application of radical measures."

A twenty-five-year veteran of the Foreign Service, Samuel Honaker had arrived in Germany in June 1934, just as Hitler was consolidating his totalitarian regime with the Night of the Long Knives. The ruthless bloodletting targeted potential Nazi rivals like the storm trooper leader Ernst Röhm, who was shot after declining the option of suicide. It was accompanied by a purge of officials considered politically unreliable, including the conservative politicians who had helped bring Hitler to power. The largest opposition parties, the Social Democrats and the Communists, had already been outlawed. The armed forces had sworn allegiance to Hitler. There was no longer anyone who could, or would, stand up to the Führer.

When Honaker assumed his duties in Stuttgart, the flow of immigrants to the United States had been perfectly manageable. The consulate issued 200 to 250 immigration visas a month, only half of them to "members of the Hebrew race."[9] Many German Jews viewed the Hitler government as a temporary phenomenon that would crumble once their compatriots returned to their senses. But Hitler did not go away. The demand for visas became a mighty clamor. By the middle of 1938, the Stuttgart consulate was approving more than 1,500 immigration visas a month, 90 percent of them to Jews.[10]

Even larger numbers of would-be immigrants were turned away. Out of 23,000 people who applied for visas at Stuttgart during the twelve months ending June 1938, more than 14,000 were denied a formal appointment with the consulate because of "unsatisfactory" documentation. A further 1,200 were rejected at the interview stage, either for medical reasons or because there was something wrong with their affidavits. The overall refusal rate, in other words, was well over 60 percent.[11]

While Honaker drew praise for his political reporting, including several dispatches on the Nazi persecution of Jews, he was generally considered a poor administrator. He showed little interest in the details of consular work. State Department inspectors described Honaker as a moody, unsociable officer, given to "violent personal likes and dislikes." He complained about infrequent promotions and undesirable postings. As a young man, Honaker had been a star quarterback for the University of Virginia, but his health had sharply deteriorated. "He does not give the impression of being an entirely well man—either physically or mentally," reported one superior. Another detected signs of an incipient persecution complex, depicting the diminutive former athlete as "a psychological case" who "casts a gloom over everybody and everything in his vicinity."[12]

Honaker's tenure as consul general at Stuttgart had been marred by controversy. Jewish groups headed by the banker Felix Warburg had complained about long waiting lines and hostile officials. Some alleged that an adverse medical decision could be reversed upon payment of a large sum of money, around $5,000. A January 1937 investigation by a State Department inspector showed that the Stuttgart consulate was rejecting visa applicants on the grounds of tuberculosis at nearly ten times the rate of the consulates in Berlin and Hamburg. The inspector conceded that the medical examiner might have been "slightly over-zealous" in many tuberculosis diagnoses. He nevertheless attributed most of the discrepancy to an influenza and bronchitis epidemic in the Stuttgart region, "which diseases, I am told, often present symptoms similar to those of tuberculosis."[13]

Honaker and his consuls and vice consuls had been officially exonerated—for now.

To the throngs of asylum seekers lined up on the sidewalk, the American consul was the representative of a distant potentate. He operated on the basis of mysterious laws that were difficult for ordinary human beings to comprehend. As America's gatekeepers, the consuls were guided by a thick red volume that contained the "Code of Laws of the United States of America." The well-thumbed law book included a long section entitled "Aliens and Nationality" that was further divided into chapters on immigration and visas which every consul could recite almost by heart.

"I wracked my brains for a way to strike a spark of understanding in that consular brain," mused the German Jewish writer Anna Seghers in her novel *Transit*, a classic account of the nightmarish refugee experience. "Nothing useful came to mind except the realization that I'd never before come up against such an incorruptible official. In his own way, he was a just man. He carried out his difficult duties as a Roman official might once have done, in that same place, listening to the emissaries of foreign tribes with their dark and to him ridiculous demands."

Interview questions that seemed pertinent to consuls determined to proceed "by the book" sounded arbitrary, even crazy, to asylum seekers. In order to test the mental faculties of visa applicants, the

Stuttgart consul peppered them with queries like "What is the difference between a horse and an ox?" A young man from Mannheim was ruled "mentally defective" in the weeks after Kristallnacht because he had trouble estimating the height of a door and interpreting various traffic signs during a two-hour examination.[14]

The 1924 immigration law, passed by a bipartisan Congress during the wave of xenophobic nationalism that followed World War I, established rigid country-by-country quotas for immigrants. Ostensibly these quotas were designed to reflect the "national origins" of the United States, but the process by which they were derived was "closer to mysticism than social science," in the phrase of a future immigration historian.[15] The final selection was a more accurate reflection of the makeup of the American ruling class, with a heavy bias toward white Anglo-Saxon Protestants, than the way America actually looked in the early twentieth century.

Vast populations, including all Chinese, Japanese, and most South Asians, were deemed racially "ineligible" for American citizenship, and therefore inadmissible as immigrants. The descendants of "slave immigrants" and "American aborigines" were similarly excluded, although independent African nations, such as Ethiopia and Liberia, were each granted a token one hundred quota spots. International protectorates like Palestine and Iraq also received symbolic quotas that were mainly reserved for European settlers. More than three quarters of roughly 150,000 quota places were assigned to the "Nordic countries" of northern and western Europe deemed to have contributed the bulk of America's original settler stock.[16] (The Western Hemisphere was excluded from the quota system due to the need for cheap agricultural labor.)

The most generous quota allocation went to the United Kingdom, which was permitted to send 65,721 immigrants a year to the United States under revised rules issued in 1929. Next came Germany, which was assigned a quota of 25,957 immigrants. This was increased to 27,370 following Hitler's annexation of Austria in March 1938. Nations of southern and eastern Europe, including Poland and Russia, fared much less well. A former census chief complained that these countries were inhabited largely by "beaten men from beaten races" and "vast masses of peasantry, degraded below our utmost conceptions."[17] The perceived merits of each nationality were reflected in a State Department chart that showed how the quota system favored Anglo-Saxon and Nordic countries. An Englishman had more than three times the chance to immigrate to the United States of a German, ten times the chance of an Italian, and nearly sixty times the chance of a Russian. The most favored nationality of all was the Irish; least favored were Spaniards, Turks, and Romanians.[18]

Officially, religion played no part in the calculation of the quotas, or in the application of U.S. immigration law. On paper at least, a German Jew had the same chance to immigrate to the United States as a German Christian. On the other hand, Congress's decision to favor the "Nordic" populations of northern Europe came against the background of public protests against the arrival of hundreds of thousands of Jews from central and eastern Europe. The chief author of the 1924 law, Congressman Albert Johnson of Washington State, argued that America was in danger of being swamped by "unassimilable" Jews, who were "filthy, un-American," and often "dangerous in their habits." Johnson believed that America's "cherished institutions" were being compromised by "a stream of alien blood."[19]

The new immigration laws were an atavistic response to changing demographics. By 1910, the proportion of foreign-born residents of the United States had reached a near high of 14.7 percent, a level it would not approach again until more than a century later.[20] (See chart on page 293.) "The myth of the melting pot has been discredited," Johnson crowed in 1927, as the immigrant share of the overall population began to decline dramatically. "The United States is our land.... We intend to maintain it so. The day of indiscriminate acceptance of all races has definitely ended."[21]

Up until 1938, the German quota had been sufficient to meet the demand from "eligible" immigrants.[22] Applicants for an immigration visa to the United States could typically expect to wait no more than three or four months before being summoned for an interview. If the consul determined that they were "admissible" under the immigration laws, and they passed the medical exam, they were issued a visa. If not, their applications were either deferred or rejected. By the time of Kristallnacht, however, what had been a manageable stream of asylum

"*I sit here sadly in Amsterdam because I was told in the consulate that my papers have still not arrived.*" *Lisl Weil self-portrait, September 1938.*

seekers had turned into an uncontrollable flood. Even fully qualified applicants faced a two- or three-year wait for an appointment at an American consulate.

In response, visa applicants devised ever more creative ways of jumping to the front of the line. Some waylaid consulate employees in the street, or approached them at social events, such as the annual winter carnival. Others inundated American diplomats with letters, drawings, and even poems entreating their help, some desperate, others humorous. The consulate general in Vienna maintained a special file, labeled "freak letters," that it forwarded to State Department officials for their amusement.[23] A cartoon drawn by an artist named Lisl Weil showed her sitting forlornly in front of a consulate, waiting for news on her case.

The cafés around the Stuttgart consulate were filled with people exchanging tips on which consulate clerk was willing to be "helpful" if approached informally. It became apparent that the aura of incorruptibility that initially impressed refugees like the writer Anna Seghers was a façade. Supposedly sacrosanct waiting lists were not so sacrosanct after all. Rigid immigration laws could be bent and stretched for those with the right connections.

For Jews seeking to escape from Nazi Germany, money was often the least important consideration. As Honaker reported in a January 1939 dispatch, "German Jews were willing to pay practically any price to expedite their departure from Germany." Would-be emigrants preferred to spend any remaining reichsmarks on ship tickets, affidavits, and bribes rather than pay extortionate foreign currency fees to the German state. In Honaker's words, "Money had lost a great part of its relative value" for German Jews.[24]

One of the German clerks who gave way to temptation was a ten-year veteran of the Stuttgart visa section named Emil Friesch. As the waiting lists grew, Friesch began accepting large bribes from visa applicants with high registration numbers. One such "client" was a traveling salesman from the Düsseldorf area, Siegfried Spier, who had registered with the Stuttgart consulate in August 1938. After assembling the necessary affidavits, he visited the consulate in October, only to learn that his case would not be reviewed until the middle of 1940. He learned from the gossip circuit that there was a clerk in the consulate with the initial "F" who could help facilitate matters. Through an intermediary, he put down an initial "deposit" of 1,200 reichsmarks, nearly $500 at the official rate of exchange and the equivalent of roughly $9,000 in 2019.[25]

Nothing happened until after Kristallnacht when Spier was sent to the Dachau concentration camp. In desperation, his wife, Hedwig, arranged to meet "Herr Friesch" in a side street near the consulate. He agreed to give her a "preliminary examination" certificate stating that affidavits submitted by her husband "appear to be satisfactory, as far as can be determined at the present time."[26] She was able to use the certificate to convince the Gestapo that Siegfried was taking the necessary steps to leave Germany. This was sufficient to get him released from Dachau in early December. Soon after his release, Spier paid Friesch a further 1,800 reichsmarks to "expedite" his immigration case. By inserting bogus correspondence into the file, Friesch was able to backdate Spier's visa application by a year, from August 1938 to August 1937.[27]

By November 1938, such operations had become a "highly profitable source of revenue" for the German clerks of the consulate. An informal sliding scale developed for various services. A visa applicant might pay a hundred reichsmarks for an introductory "interview" with Friesch at his home and two hundred reichsmarks for a document search in the piles of unanswered correspondence. Alteration of an asylum seeker's priority status—a matter of life or death in many cases—cost the equivalent of a year's salary for a consular clerk or middle-class German.

If there was one American diplomat in Germany who deserved the epithet "indispensable," it was the Berlin consul, Raymond Geist. A slightly pudgy man of medium height and brushed-back hair, Geist spoke German fluently. He was a descendant of a so-called Forty-Eighter, a supporter of the 1848 German revolution who fled to the United States after its suppression by Prussian troops. Fiercely anti-Nazi, Geist had built an unrivaled network of high-level Nazi contacts during his nine years looking after American interests in Germany. At the same time, he was liked and trusted by Jewish groups, refugee advocates, and American journalists stationed in Berlin.

Geist's reputation as the embassy's top troubleshooter was partly attributable to his length of service and formidable language skills.[28] But it was also testimony to his charm, tact, and understanding of the Nazi mind-set. He knew instinctively "where and when to strike, where and when to be aggressive and where and when to use more gentle methods."[29] A Shakespearean stage actor in his youth, he had learned how to conceal his emotions behind a mask of amiable politeness.

Geist had entered the Foreign Service late, at the age of thirty-six, following an eclectic academic career that included studies in medieval French, Gothic, and Anglo-Saxon, in addition to a PhD from Harvard. He had served in the office of the chief naval censor during the war, attended the Versailles Peace Conference as a translator, and organized a relief network in Austria that fed hundreds of thousands of children in five hundred soup kitchens.[30] His progress up the diplomatic ranks had been held back by rigid seniority rules, despite his "excellent" ratings. His responsibilities, which included administration of the German immigration quota, greatly exceeded his mid-ranking titles of "first secretary" of the embassy and "acting" consul general. As the senior consular official in Berlin, Geist was responsible for supervising the work of Honaker and eight other full consul generals, all of whom formally outranked him.[31]

During his early years in Berlin, Geist had made frequent bicycle trips into the surrounding countryside, passing himself off as a local. These excursions had enabled him to observe the rapid military buildup that followed Hitler's rise to power in 1933. As he later recalled, he discovered numerous "new large military establishments, including training fields, airports, barracks, proving grounds, anti-aircraft stations," while taking care to avoid battalions of Hitler Youth staging mock attacks through the woods. His wide range of contacts included the German army chief of staff, General Franz Halder, who warned him that Germany was prepared to "go to war" with the "Western powers" if they opposed the Nazi program of expansion toward the east. When Geist objected that such a war would inevitably bring in the United States, the general had replied laconically, "That is a pity."[32]

Geist's responsibility for protecting U.S. citizens put him in regular touch with the Gestapo. He was a frequent visitor to Gestapo headquarters on Prinz-Albrecht-Strasse, a few blocks away from the United States consulate on the corner of Bellevuestrasse and the Tiergarten. He had even escorted American Jewish delegations through the great iron doors of the dreaded building, striding confidently past the sign that read *Juden haben keinen Zutritt* ("No Entry for Jews"). He often served as negotiator-translator on these occasions, staring into the "beady button eyes" of the top Nazi security official Heinrich Himmler while his intimidated companions looked on. To the Americans, Himmler had the appearance of "an experienced title searcher" in some county clerk's office. His assistant, the six-foot-three-inch Reinhard Heydrich, resembled a tackle on a professional football team. "He was a blond gorilla—big shoulders, long arms, powerful legs."[33]

Geist referred to his Gestapo interlocutors as "my devils." He understood that he needed their cooperation in order to distribute relief to destitute Jews.[34] One of his Gestapo contacts was the official in charge of the "Jewish problem," Karl Hasselbacher, whom "I came to know very well." In late 1938, around the time of Kristallnacht, Hasselbacher told Geist that Germany would be made *judenrein*—"clean of Jews"—and that "all the Jews who failed to leave Germany would be exterminated."[35]

"It has been necessary for me to keep on good relations with this crowd," Geist informed Assistant Secretary of State George Messersmith in October 1938, referring to the Gestapo. "Otherwise, I could have little influence on the gates of the concentration camps, which now and then I manage to pry open."[36]

For all his sympathy with the plight of German Jews, Geist was obliged to operate within the narrow constraints of U.S. immigration law. Early in his tour of duty in Germany, in December 1932, he had been involved in the Albert Einstein case, which turned into a black comedy of misunderstanding. The father of the theory of relativity had accepted a visiting professorship in California. A group of American "women patriots" was opposed to granting him a visa. Their leader, the splendidly named Mrs. Randolph Frothingham, informed the FBI that Einstein was "affiliated with more anarchistic and Communist groups than Joseph Stalin himself."[37] The charge was ludicrous, but the State Department was obliged to show that it was upholding a ban on political subversives.

The task of interviewing Einstein fell to Geist, who was in charge of the consulate during the temporary absence of the consul general, George Messersmith. Both men knew it was impossible to "keep ideas out of a country and that no wall can be built by the law or by any other means high enough to keep them out."[38] Geist guided Einstein through a long questionnaire that all visitors to the United States were required to fill out. As he ran through the list of obligatory topics, Einstein began to suspect that he was the victim of an elaborate "practical joke." He was particularly irritated by questions seeking information on his "political activities and affiliations."

"Are you trying to kid me?" Einstein asked, reaching for his hat and coat. "Are you doing this to please yourselves or are you acting upon orders from above?"[39]

Reports of the "humiliating" treatment of the world's most celebrated scientist, relayed to journalists by his wife Elsa, caused outrage in progressive circles in the United States. The controversy was defused somewhat the following day when Geist informed Einstein that he would be granted a visa after all. Messersmith vigorously defended his deputy, insisting that the Einsteins had been treated "with every courtesy and consideration." The questioning had been entirely routine, in order to observe "the formalities of the law."[40]

Einstein sailed for America shortly afterward, laughing at the zeal of Mrs. Randolph Frothingham and other "watchful citizenesses."[41]

As the lines of Jews besieging American consulates grew ever longer in the fall of 1938, Geist tried to approve as many visas as possible. By juggling the numbers of visas available to various consulates, he was able to make full use of the 27,370 slots in the annual German quota for the first time ever. He was prepared to bend the rules in his attempt to "find ways to save the existence of decent people." At the same time, he confessed to Messersmith, who had since been promoted to assistant secretary of state, that the psychological strain was "pretty heavy . . . I am forced to go ahead a great deal on my own responsibility."[42]

Any hope of keeping pace with the ever rising demand for U.S. immigration visas vanished after Kristallnacht. On the following Monday, November 14, Geist informed Washington that fifteen hundred visa seekers were lined up on the street outside the consulate "as result of present antisemitic measures."[43] A few days later, the *New York Herald Tribune* reported that 160,000 Germans wanted to immigrate to the United States. This translated into a minimum three-year wait for fully qualified visa seekers, even after ineligible applicants were weeded out.[44]

The crowds of "terrified Jews" swarming into the Berlin consulate opposite the Tiergarten included "some of the oldest and most famous names" in the city—Kempinskis, Wertheims, Rosenthals. A Geist assistant reported that the Jews "trembled in front of our desks, pleading for visas and passports—anything to save them from the madness" outside. At night, the homes of consular officials were "crammed with Jewish families seeking refuge until the storm subsided." American diplomats watched horrified as Nazi thugs looted Jewish stores and invaded Jewish apartments, "tossing their occupants into the streets where more thugs were waiting to greet them with clubs." A friend of one of the consuls reported seeing a small boy pushed from a second-story window into a "forest of kicking black boots." At the Wertheim department store, one of the largest in Berlin, the mob rolled grand pianos out of the gallery, laughing gleefully as they crashed into pieces six floors below.[45]

Geist had come to think of himself as "a mother chick" responsible for protecting "the scared ones under my wings."[46] In some cases, he was able to get Jewish men released from concentration camps by telling the Gestapo that they would eventually be given American visas. He made several visits to the Sachsenhausen camp north of Berlin to plead the cases of consulate employees or prominent Jews, like the banker Fritz Warburg, who were interned there. Writing to George Messersmith, he described how a Jewish couple had "gone to pieces" in his office and threatened to commit suicide. "They declared I was their last hope," he told Messersmith. "Needless to say, I promised to get them out of the country."[47]

For many years, Geist had advised his rich Jewish friends against leaving Germany if it meant abandoning all their wealth. But "the Geist optimism" had been dealt a crushing blow by events of the past few months. It was now obvious to everybody that flight was the only option. Physically exhausted, and sick with a recurring bladder complaint, he went to the office every day "with a heavy step because I know the tragedies that await me there."

As a student of medieval history, Geist had marveled how men could be "so cruel, benighted, and murderous during those dark ages." He was now witnessing similar horrors in the heart of Europe in the middle of the twentieth century. The terror campaign against a defenseless minority was being carried out with "a relentlessness unparalleled in history since the days of Nero." It seemed to Geist that not "even a thousand years of decent conduct"—a sarcastic reference to Hitler's promise of a "thousand-year Reich"—would be sufficient to wipe out the "ineradicable stain" on the land of his ancestors.[48]

In the weeks after Kristallnacht, the Berlin consul came to believe that Hitler was determined to remove the Jewish race from Germany. Flush with their victories in Austria and Czechoslovakia, the Germans had lost all sense of restraint. "They have embarked on a program of annihilation of the Jews," Geist wrote Messersmith on December 5. "We shall be allowed to save the remnants if we choose."[49]

While Washington dithered, Geist tried to persuade other foreign consuls to issue temporary visas to Jews with pending U.S. immigration applications. His principal ally in these efforts was the British passport officer Frank Foley, who was working undercover for the intelligence agency MI6. A small, mild-mannered man who had studied to be a priest, Foley regarded Hitler as the "devil on earth." Together he and Geist devised a plan to permit "persons in desperate circumstances," including former concentration camp inmates, to spend their "waiting time" in England.[50]

The plan soon ran into bureaucratic obstacles back in Washington. Assistant Secretary of State Messersmith objected to any arrangement that implied the promise of a U.S. visa at some future date. Messersmith feared that this would be a violation of U.S. immigration law and cause a political outcry in Congress. "We cannot give promissory notes on the quotas," he instructed the State Department visa section.[51] Under pressure from Washington, Geist was obliged to clarify the situation with his British counterpart. He told Foley that at least half the people on the American waiting list were unlikely ever to receive U.S. immigration visas. It would be "grossly unfair" to the British government to leave the impression that they would "be admitted to the U.S.A. almost automatically."[52]

British officials took care not to publicize the State Department warning. They had presented their refugee program to British public opinion as a humanitarian gesture designed to help persecuted German Jews in transit to another country. If word leaked out that Britain would be permanently saddled with tens of thousands of refugees deemed "inadmissible" by the United States, political support for the program would quickly unravel. In that event, the British government would have to reconsider its position.

For the time being, the British escape route remained at least semi-open. In January 1939, Geist reported, Foley was still handing out visas to "large numbers" of German Jews on the basis of their American "waiting list" numbers.[53] How long his rescue operation could continue was a different matter.

.   .   .

As American diplomats observing the rise of Hitler, George Messersmith and Raymond Geist had become exceptionally close. In many ways, their relationship resembled that of teacher and favorite pupil. "I have always tried to be an apt scholar," Geist wrote his mentor in 1934, soon after Messersmith left Berlin to become minister in Vienna.[54] Although Geist was only two years younger than Messersmith, he never dreamed of addressing him as "George." It was always "Mr. Messersmith" and "Raymond." For his part, the feisty, sometimes caustic Messersmith went out of his way to praise Geist for his ability "to foresee developments [in Germany] surely and clearly."[55] He fought to win promotions for his protégé, clashing with the State Department bureaucracy over seniority rules.

In their lengthy correspondence, the two career diplomats grappled with one of the greatest challenges that can confront a democracy: how to deal with a totalitarian regime that employs "gangster methods" to get its way. The two German Americans saw eye to eye on the evil of Nazism, which they identified as a major threat to the United States much earlier than any of their colleagues. They both warned of the dangers of appeasement and the risks of being seduced by the Nazi propaganda façade. Like Messersmith, Geist was convinced that war with Germany was inevitable, sooner or later.

There was, however, one matter on which they sharply disagreed: the feasibility, or even desirability, of a massive rescue effort for German Jews. Their different perspectives reflected their different vantage points. Messersmith had spent many years in Germany and Austria but was now back in Washington, sitting in a grand office next to the White House. Geist, by contrast, witnessed the horrors of Nazism on a daily basis.

Surrounded by human misery in Berlin, Geist had come to believe that America had a duty to do everything in its power to assist the persecuted. If it was necessary to mute American criticism of the German government to facilitate an agreement on Jewish emigration, that was a price he was prepared to pay. Geist wanted to act "as fast as possible before the situation of the half million potential refugees"—not only in Germany, but also in Austria and Czechoslovakia—"becomes so desperate that salvation will be beyond recall." At some point, the United States would have to "break off relations" with Germany and "join in a war" against the Nazis. Until that moment came, however:

> I would suggest that we do nothing to aggravate the position of the victims, but avail ourselves quickly of any chance to approach the Germans and endeavor to halt this cruel process. . . . One must always count on a certain measure of deceit and double-crossing, but even that should not discourage us. This is a struggle to save the lives of innocent people.[56]

Looking for ways to help the victims, Geist saw a glimmer of hope in a proposal floated by Reichsbank president Hjalmar Schacht. The so-called Schacht plan provided for the "orderly" emigration of 150,000 Jewish men plus their families over a three-year period. There was, however, a significant catch. The refugees would be required to leave a large chunk of their wealth behind in Germany in a "trust fund" as "collateral" for a bond issue to be financed by "international Jewry." The bond issue would be used to support the resettlement of German Jews in foreign countries. Repayment of the bonds by Germany would be linked to a future increase in German export revenues.

The highest priority for Messersmith, from his Washington vantage point, was maintaining maximum economic pressure on Nazi Germany, even at the expense of assisting the persecuted. In his view, the Schacht plan was a crude "blackmail" attempt designed to undermine the economic sanctions on Nazi Germany that the FDR administration was working so hard to enforce.[57] Hitler would undoubtedly use any funds generated by Schacht's financial wizardry to further build up his war machine. If the Nazis achieved their *judenrein* goal, other countries with large Jewish minorities, such as Poland, would be tempted to follow suit.

Messersmith suggested that Geist was too "close to the situation" to have a complete understanding of U.S. policy. "You see these horrible things happen and you see more horrible ones still in the offing," he wrote Geist on December 20, in a "personal and confidential" letter delivered by diplomatic courier. Washington-based officials were also repulsed by Nazi atrocities, Messersmith wrote, but were convinced it was impossible to prevent "further action against the Jews."[58]

"Fundamental issues are at stake," the assistant secretary lectured. "These issues are greater than any individual or any individual suffering."

Messersmith had another, purely domestic, reason for opposing the Schacht plan. He feared that a flood of Jewish refugees into the United States would exacerbate American antisemitism. Just a few days earlier, he had explained to Geist that there was "a real feeling in the country that with our own problems of unemployment, et cetera, we are not in a position to become a haven for all the distressed people in the world." Any attempt to increase American immigration quotas would likely lead to an anti-Jewish backlash that would in turn result in even more restrictive immigration policies.

Beyond the difference in perspective, the dispute reflected sharply differing views on the durability of the Nazi regime. Messersmith believed that Kristallnacht was a sign of desperation on Hitler's part, concealing a crumbling of Nazi power that could be hastened by tough American policies. Geist agreed that Hitler was facing a growing economic crisis but emphasized his ability to use "terroristic methods . . . to crush any sort of opposition." He predicted that the Führer would seek a solution to his problems in the form of a military "offensive toward the East" in pursuit of grain and oil.[59] Even before Kristallnacht, he had come to the depressing conclusion that "the dictators have won," at least in the short term.[60] He wanted to save as many people as he could, while it was still possible.

Berlin was awash with rumors about high-level splits within the Nazi regime. The "moderates" were said to be clustered around Hermann Göring, Hitler's designated successor. In a confidential talk with the British chargé d'affaires, the corpulent field marshal had stated flatly that "the Jews must be eliminated from Germany." He added, however, that he was "much disturbed" by the level of violence against them. Holding back the "extremist elements" from "further physical attacks on the Jews" was very difficult.[61] The only way out was an emigration deal along the lines proposed by Schacht.

According to Geist's informants, the hard-liners were led by propaganda minister Joseph Goebbels, who favored draconian measures against the Jews. On this question above all, Goebbels had Hitler's ear. Göring's aides believed that Germany was headed toward a disastrous war that could only be averted if Goebbels was "eliminated," together with the radicals who supported him. The problem, they told Geist, was that Göring was "so much tied up with Hitler that he cannot act against him."[62]

Into this atmosphere of murderous intrigue stumbled an unlikely American delegation. The Religious Society of Friends was committed to the belief that there was good in everybody and no man was beyond redemption. After Kristallnacht, they decided to send three senior Quakers led by the theologian Rufus Jones to Berlin to see what could be done to alleviate the plight of the Jews. To assure the best chance of success, the mission would be conducted "without any publicity."

Unfortunately, word leaked to the American press as Jones and his companions were crossing the Atlantic on the *Queen Mary*. By the time the delegation arrived in Berlin on December 8, Goebbels's propaganda sheets were already making fun of the "three wise men" from Philadelphia. "They are to investigate us, for bad things are told in Pennsylvania about Germans who relieve poor Jewish millionaires of a little of their swindled money," editorialized the Berlin newspaper *Der Angriff*.[63]

The Quakers had been hoping to see Hitler. When this proved impossible, they got in touch with Geist, who introduced them to his "devils" in the Gestapo. Rufus Jones later described how the consul ("if ever there was a good man, he was one") went out into a blizzard on the coldest day of the year to track down Reinhard Heydrich after failing to reach him on the phone. The police chief declined to see the Quakers, but they spoke to two of his aides. Jones detected "a softening effect" on the "iron-natured" faces of the Gestapo officers as he requested permission to distribute relief to German Jews. After Heydrich's aides retired to consult their boss, Jones proposed a moment of "quiet meditation and prayer—the only Quaker meeting ever held in the Gestapo."[64] The Gestapo officials returned half an hour later to announce that they would cooperate with a Quaker relief effort. As they helped the Quakers on with their winter coats, Rufus Jones was convinced that he had witnessed "a miracle wrought by the way of love."

Others took a bleaker view of the likely course of events. Before they left Germany, the Quakers had a meeting with Hjalmar Schacht, the man behind the Jewish emigration plan. Schacht urged them to act quickly because "nobody knows what happens in this country tomorrow."[65]

Support for Geist's policy of rescue through emigration was hardly universal, even among the Quakers. Some worried that the United States might end up facilitating a Nazi program of ethnic cleansing. In the aftermath of Kristallnacht, the Quaker representative in Berlin, Howard Elkinton, described Nazi policy as "childishly simple: the Jew must get out." Whether this happened through emigration or forced labor camps or even "gas" was of little concern to the Nazis. (Elkinton employed the term "gas" as a metaphor for mass killing.) Writing to Quaker leader Clarence Pickett, Elkinton argued that it might be salutary for ordinary Germans "to witness a slaughter of a fraction of their own people." Such an outcome would be "horrible for the Jews," but could have the effect of rousing the rest of the population from their shameful passivity. The alternative—a mass emigration of German Jews—would be perceived as "another German (Hitler) triumph."

"Thee understands me, of course," Elkinton wrote Pickett, using the intimate form of address favored by Quakers in talking to each other. "I wonder sometimes whether in our humanity we may not be rushing into this situation a little head-long, furnished as we are with Jewish money."[66]

In Stuttgart, meanwhile, the steady flow of "members of the Jewish race" to the apartment of consular clerk Emil Friesch had attracted the attention of his neighbors. Nazi dogma prohibited Aryans from "business or social intercourse" with Jews unless absolutely necessary, as in the case of the forced sale of Jewish businesses. One particularly zealous neighbor had denounced Friesch to the Office for Customs Offenses. Customs inspectors suspected that Friesch might be "conniving with Jews to get money out of Germany" in violation of the exchange controls.[67] They watched his apartment and opened his mail.

The net soon widened to include other German consular clerks and Jewish visa seekers who had been observed meeting with Friesch. Customs officials arrested the Spier couple and forced them to make a full confession. They then arrested Friesch in his apartment, as "several Jewish callers" waited outside. Since the offense had nothing to do with customs regulations, he was turned over to the Gestapo.

Concerned that the integrity of United States immigration law had been compromised, Consul General Honaker ordered a review of six months of immigration cases. Regular consular work ground to a halt as his investigators pored over back files to determine who might have been able to jump the line. Half a dozen German clerks were dismissed on the spot after confessing to accepting bribes. Two of Honaker's American vice consuls also came under suspicion, but the allegations were never proven.[68] Honaker's investigation into the registration records of Jewish visa applicants was similarly inconclusive. The consul general told the State Department that he had ended the trafficking in bogus documents and certificates at the very moment that it was "assuming the proportions of a racket."[69]

What was clear was that huge sums of money had changed hands for services either rendered or promised. The Gestapo informed Honaker that they had searched the home of one of his consular clerks and found an envelope containing 25,000 reichsmarks. The money was evidently payment "for favors or assistance extended to prospective Jewish immigrants to the United States." A search, this time by the consulate, of another clerk's personal files turned up an envelope with 19,500 reichsmarks. How the clerks had managed to accumulate such wealth on an annual salary of around 2,000 reichsmarks the consul general could only surmise.[70]

THREE

FDR

A N EVEN LARGER THAN USUAL crowd of journalists had gathered in the White House on the afternoon of Tuesday, November 15, 1938, for what they fondly called "the greatest show in town." Franklin Delano Roosevelt was giving one of his twice weekly press conferences. News had broken earlier that day that he was recalling his ambassador to Nazi Germany for "report and consultation," signaling a deepening international crisis. The president's press secretary, Steve Early, had alerted reporters that FDR would have "something to say" on the subject of Germany.[1]

An usher withdrew the red cord outside the Oval Office at precisely four p.m. The journalists surged forward, led by the wire service men, followed by correspondents for the major national newspapers, radio commentators, magazine writers, and finally representatives of far-flung local newspapers. The senior reporters gathered fanwise around FDR's desk, as less favored colleagues jostled for places at the back. By the time an aide stationed by the door let out the traditional cry "All in!" some two hundred press men (and a scattering of women) were crowded into a room that could barely hold them.[2]

The thirty-second president of the United States leaned back in his reclining chair, a ceramic cigarette holder with a lit cigarette clenched between his teeth. FDR took full advantage of the rule that the president was the only person permitted to smoke in the Oval Office. As he waited to go onstage, he exchanged joking remarks with the men in the front row, whom he treated as friends. He knew the names of their wives and how they got on with their bosses. He had nicknames for many of them, invited them to social functions, congratulated them on their successes, and gently scolded them for their failings. Occasionally, only half in jest, he even offered to write their stories for them. A former editor of the *Harvard Crimson,* Roosevelt would often preface his remarks with the phrase, "If I was writing your stories today, I should say ..."

Like no president before him, Roosevelt understood how to use the media to grab the nation's attention and speak directly to the American people. An admiring newspaper editor once told him that he was "the most interesting person" in the land. "For box office attraction, you leave Clark Gable gasping for breath."[3] The presidency became an inexhaustible source of news. "He talked in headline phrases," an Associated Press man observed. "He was sensible, he was unreasonable, he was benevolent, he was malicious. He was satirical, he was soothing; he was funny, he was gloomy. He was exciting. He was human. He was copy."[4]

The spectacle apart, the primary function of the press conferences was to shape the news. Unless FDR agreed to be quoted directly, everything he said was for background purposes only. In the words of one reporter, the president "was like a friendly, informal schoolmaster conducting a free-for-all seminar."[5] He used the press to educate the American people on the challenges facing the nation, patiently laying the groundwork for future shifts in policy.

The president batted aside the first two questions, which reflected the parochial concerns of the day. The banter seemed designed to reinforce the mood of conspiratorial intimacy that characterized his relations with the fourth estate. One journalist inquired, in a jocular vein, about the difficulty in obtaining planning permission for a new national airport outside Washington. Another raised the vexed matter of "The Cherry Tree Rebellion." Roosevelt critics were protesting his plans to create a memorial to one of his most distinguished predecessors, Thomas Jefferson, a step that would require the transplanting of hundreds of Japanese cherry trees planted around the

Tidal Basin. A group of prominent women, led by Eleanor "Cissy" Patterson, the fiercely isolationist owner of the Washington *Times Herald,* had threatened to chain themselves to the trees to prevent their removal.[6]

"Let us come down to more serious things than cherry tree campaigns," interjected a suddenly impatient FDR. He picked up a piece of paper from a desk cluttered with ashtrays, books, ornamental paperweights, and political memorabilia. He had made some handwritten annotations on the typewritten statement, which he proceeded to read out in a "cold, serious voice new to many of his listeners."[7] His statement would be on the record.

The reporters scribbled furiously as the president denounced the anti-Jewish pogroms in Germany, which, he said, had "deeply shocked public opinion in the United States." He put special emphasis on a sentence he had written himself, strengthening the more anodyne language prepared by his aides. "I myself could scarcely believe that such things could occur in a twentieth century civilization."[8]

By summoning his ambassador back from Berlin, Roosevelt had gone further than any other world leader in condemning the atrocities in Germany. But obvious questions remained about what his government was prepared to do to alleviate the suffering of hundreds of thousands of Jews on the other side of the ocean. Here the president was caught in a bind. While he sympathized with the victims of Nazi persecution, he was also very aware of a xenophobic strain in American public opinion. He felt it would be political suicide to propose major changes to the restrictive immigration laws, even supposing that he could push them through the anti-immigrant Congress.

Up until now, FDR's solution to this conundrum had been to share responsibility for helping the refugees with the Western democracies. After Germany annexed Austria in March 1938, subjecting a further 200,000 Jews to Nazi racial laws, he came up with the idea of an international conference to deal with a rapidly growing refugee crisis. Two hundred delegates from thirty-two countries had duly assembled in the French spa town of Évian-les-Bains in July. Beyond expressions of sympathy, however, the Évian conference produced few concrete results. Nazi propagandists gloated that the "democracies" were quick to criticize Germany but were unwilling to open their own doors to Jews.

A reporter asked the president if he had given "any thought" to finding some other part of the world that "could take care of mass emigration of the Jews from Germany."

"I have given a great deal of thought to it."

"Can you tell us any place particularly desirable?"

"No, the time is not ripe for that."

Another reporter wanted to know if he would "recommend a relaxation of our immigration restrictions so that the Jewish refugees could be received in this country."

"That is not in contemplation. We have the quota system."

The press conference had veered into dangerous territory. FDR had no desire to ignite a national debate about immigration that could lead to demands for even greater restrictions. The so-called national origins system had produced a result that was relatively favorable to German Jews, at least compared to southern and eastern Europeans, let alone Asians and Africans. Prior to 1937, the German quota had been less than one third filled.[9] As Roosevelt saw it, filling the quotas to capacity was a more effective way of helping the refugees than proposing significant changes in the quota system that would risk a public backlash. By combining the German and Austrian quotas, he had made it possible for up to 27,370 predominantly Jewish refugees to enter the United States every year from German-speaking countries. It was up to other countries to do their part as well, in his view.

As a diligent student of American public opinion, Roosevelt was certainly well aware of a poll published in the July edition of *Fortune* magazine, around the time of the Évian conference. The poll showed a 55 percent approval rating for the president against a 34 percent disapproval rating. That was satisfactory but he was skating on thin ice on the refugee issue. Only 5 percent of Americans were in favor of "raising our immigration quotas" to admit more refugees into the United States. Just over 18 percent were willing to allow refugees into the country "but not raise immigration quotas." Two out of every three Americans wanted to "keep them out."[10]

The journalists showed no interest in pressing FDR on immigration quotas. For the first time in weeks, they had big news to report from a presidential press conference. *The New York Times* used a four-column, multiple-deck headline at the top of the front page to describe the president's unprecedented condemnation of Nazi Germany:

ROOSEVELT CONDEMNS NAZI OUTBREAK:
'COULD SCARCELY BELIEVE' IT, HE SAYS;
LONDON STUDIES JEWISH COLONIZATION

—

STATEMENT SHARP

—

Language Is as Strong as
a President Ever Used
to a Friendly Nation

—

OPINION 'DEEPLY SHOCKED'

"Not in years has so much come out of a 30-minute talk between Mr. Roosevelt and those who seek to keep the world informed of his every action," reported *The Washington Post.*

In FDR's mind, the problem of Jewish refugees was closely connected to a much larger problem: how to deal with the crazed demagogue who was moving into one European country after another in flagrant violation of all international treaties. Hitler had followed up on the annexation of Austria by sending troops into the Sudetenland region of Czechoslovakia, which was mainly inhabited by ethnic German speakers. He had insisted that the Sudetenland was "the last territorial demand I have to make in Europe," but there was no reason to trust him.[11] The European democracies led by Britain and France had proved unable, or unwilling, to stand up to the Führer. "Peace for our time," the British prime minister, Neville Chamberlain, had declared in his reedy voice on September 30, after agreeing to the dismemberment of Czechoslovakia at the Munich conference. Public opinion polls suggested that Americans, by a large majority, did not want to get dragged into another European quarrel, just two decades after the carnage of "the war to end all wars." Letters of protest poured into the White House whenever the president took even a small step toward interfering in the affairs of Europe.

In the weeks after Munich, Roosevelt had held a series of meetings with his foreign policy advisors on how to respond to Hitler. They assembled in the president's bedroom on the second floor of the White House as he ate his breakfast. Covered by a blue flannel cape, he would peruse the alarming State Department cables spread out in front of him on the bed as his aides offered suggestions.[12] The conclusion that emerged from these meetings was that appeasement would almost certainly fail. A new world war was becoming increasingly likely. America's best hope of avoiding direct involvement in the coming conflict lay in using her vast industrial resources to bolster the armies of Britain and France. That would mean repealing, or at least amending, the Neutrality Acts that banned the shipment of military matériel to belligerent countries.

The president knew he had to proceed very carefully to push such a program through Congress. Just a year before, he had been forced to retreat after delivering a hard-hitting speech calling for the "quarantine" of Nazi Germany. He had been taken aback by the strength of popular opposition to his proposals. "If you want peace, keep the peace," read a typical telegram. "No one is coming over here to attack us." According to his speechwriter, Samuel Rosenman, FDR quickly realized that he "had made a mistake that he seldom made—the mistake of trying to lead the people of the United States too quickly, and before they had been adequately informed of the facts."

"It's a terrible thing," Roosevelt told Rosenman, one of several Jews on his staff, "to look over your shoulder when you are trying to lead—and to find no one there."[13]

FDR concluded that he had to educate Americans about the dangers confronting them. In recent days, he had been amused by a quote attributed to a Greek peanut vendor. Steve Vasilakos had been hawking his wares outside the White House for so long that reporters came to regard him as a popular oracle. His latest pronouncement, faithfully recorded for posterity, concerned the international situation. "All the world is yelling and pushing at each other except here. Over there are guns. Here there are squirrels on the lawn. Ain't it wonderful?" In a November 15 letter to a writer friend, FDR complained that the peanut man overlooked "the unfortunate fact that the fuss and pushing and guns on the other side are coming closer to our country all the time."[14] He had to find some way to counter the depiction of an American idyll sheltered from the crises of Europe.

FDR prided himself on his knowledge of German culture and history and his understanding of the German character. He had made several extended visits to Germany with his parents as a youth to improve his German and take the mineral baths at Bad Nauheim before being packed off to prep school at Groton. He had cycled through the German countryside with his tutor, staying overnight with farmers. As a special treat, at the end of his final German stay in 1896, his parents had taken him to the Bayreuth festival for the Wagner Ring Cycle, where he had sat through all fifteen hours of rousing nationalistic opera. He was fourteen at the time, but was "most attentive and rapt during the long acts and always sorry to leave, never for a moment bored or tired," his mother recorded.[15]

Even though FDR and Hitler never met, their careers intersected at key points. Roosevelt's inauguration as president in March 1933 came just five weeks after Hitler's appointment as chancellor of Germany. Their leadership approaches represented polar opposite ways of responding to the economic crisis and upheaval in the international order that followed World War I. Roosevelt's "New Deal" was the democratic, American alternative to Hitler's "New Order." The relationship between president and Führer was almost personal in its intensity. In many ways, they were reverse mirror images of each other. Roosevelt referred to Hitler in private as "that madman"; the Nazi leader raged about "the imbecile" in the White House. FDR had no illusions about Hitler and the danger he represented. He observed that the English edition of Hitler's autobiography, *Mein Kampf,* omitted many of the more inflammatory passages from the original German. "This translation is so expurgated as to give a wholly false view of what Hitler really is or says," he noted on the flyleaf of his copy of the book.[16]

Roosevelt's aristocratic sensibilities were offended by the screaming at Nazi rallies and the crudeness of German propaganda. He was horrified when he listened to Hitler's triumphant speeches after Munich. "Did you hear Hitler today?" he asked his cousin Margaret Suckley, after one such rant by the Führer. "His shrieks, his histrionics, and the effect on the huge audience. They did not applaud—they made noises like animals."[17] At the same time, FDR instructed his secretary of the interior, Harold Ickes, to remove any direct references to Hitler and other Nazi leaders in an otherwise scathing radio speech denouncing Kristallnacht.[18] He despised Hitler, but he also had to deal with him.

The president had attempted to exploit the most recent outrages in Germany to emphasize the need for the United States to build up its depleted defenses. At the November 15 press conference, he described the possibility of an attack on the American homeland as "infinitely closer than it had been as recently as five years ago." He had gone on to call for a new national defense program "to make the entire continent impregnable from the air." Nevertheless, he refused to explicitly name Germany as the most likely aggressor, leaving it to the reporters to draw the obvious inference.

There were several reasons for his restraint. He had just suffered a major political setback in the midterm elections of November 1938, which resulted in the defeat of several key allies. This came on top of the collapse of his "court packing" plan in 1937. Buoyed by his reelection in the biggest landslide in American history in 1936, he had attempted to overcome judicial resistance to the New Deal by expanding the Supreme Court. The move triggered a firestorm of public criticism and accusations of "dictatorship." Congressional Democrats joined in the attacks on their own president. The Supreme Court fight was soon transformed into a much larger battle between the executive and legislative branches that ended in a humiliating defeat for Roosevelt.

The lesson FDR drew from these setbacks was that he must proceed by stealth and sleight of hand. For his every step forward, he would have to take a half step back, and several steps to the side. As an assiduous reader of the *Congressional Record,* the daily transcript of debates on Capitol Hill, he was fully aware of the isolationist mood of the country. While he had succeeded in charming the White House press corps, he was opposed by most of the editorial writers, who took instructions from conservative newspaper owners such as Robert McCormick and William Randolph Hearst. Roosevelt became accustomed to hearing himself described as a "warmonger" and "saber-rattler." He had to convince Congress and the American people that his rearmament program represented the best hope of avoiding another European war.

Underlying FDR's caution were memories of the ordeal undergone by his political mentor, Woodrow Wilson, after the last war. As Wilson's assistant secretary of the navy, Roosevelt had watched the idealistic president battle a recalcitrant Congress over his vision for a new international order. Taking its lead from a war-weary country, an isolationist Senate had refused to ratify the treaty establishing the League of Nations in 1920, dooming the project from the start. Roosevelt believed that Wilson had made a huge political error by failing to include Republican senators in the preliminary negotiations. Wilson never recovered from the setback. Shortly after the rejection of the Treaty of Versailles, he suffered a massive stroke.

FDR was determined to avoid the mistakes of his predecessor, which he had witnessed firsthand. "While I learned much of what to do [from President Wilson], I also learned much of what not to do," he told Rosenman.[19] It was clear to him that idealism and good intentions were not by themselves sufficient to bring order to the chaos of world affairs. Hardheaded political realism was equally important. On occasion, the times called for dramatic action; at other times, it was necessary to fudge and dodge. In a democracy, the lack of bipartisan consensus could undermine the most vigorous and imaginative of foreign policies. In order to win over Congress, he first had to win over the American people.

The secretary of the treasury, Henry Morgenthau Jr., telephoned FDR at 9:45 a.m. on November 16. He wanted to congratulate the president on the press conference the previous day, which was front-page news in all the papers.[20] The decision to recall the ambassador from Berlin had been generally well received, even in quarters not usually favorable to Roosevelt. The president had succeeded in tapping into the outrage felt by the vast majority of his fellow countrymen over the barbaric events in Germany.

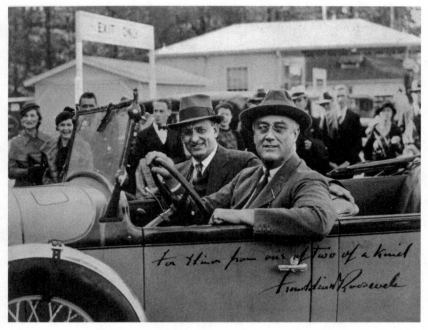

Henry Morgenthau Jr. and FDR, "two of a kind"

Morgenthau was one of Roosevelt's oldest friends. They lived not far from each other in Hyde Park, in upstate New York, sharing a common interest in forestry as gentlemen farmers. "From one of two of a kind," FDR had scrawled across a photograph of him and Morgenthau sitting in an open automobile with almost identical jaunty smiles on their faces. When Roosevelt ran for governor of New York back in 1928, Morgenthau had served as his confidant, driving the candidate thousands of miles around the state in an old Buick. The son of a prominent businessman and former ambassador, Morgenthau was the only Jew in the cabinet. Aware of the prejudices of the time, he preferred to describe himself as "one hundred per cent American." Roosevelt valued him for his loyalty and blunt talk. When the economy veered back into recession in 1937, it was Morgenthau who had warned the president about America being "headed right into another depression."[21]

Like Roosevelt, Morgenthau had been giving much thought to the problem of resettling European Jews. In public, both men took care to talk about "political refugees" rather than "Jewish refugees," to avoid stirring up latent antisemitism. In private, however, they acknowledged that Hitler had unleashed nationalist demons across Europe that were directed primarily against the Jews. The situation was likely to worsen sharply as Germany expanded its power and influence toward the east. The problems presented by the persecution of half a million German Jews were "trivial in comparison" to the forced emigration of "some seven million persons" from eastern Europe.

In FDR's view, the only possible long-term solution to the refugee crisis was the "creation of a new Jewish homeland capable of absorbing substantially unlimited Jewish immigration."[22] After the breakup of the Ottoman Empire, the United States had agreed to a League of Nations proposal for the establishment in Palestine of "a national home for the Jewish people" under British tutelage. But Roosevelt was skeptical that Palestine alone could absorb millions of refugees, even supposing that the political obstacles, including vehement Arab opposition to Jewish settlers, could be overcome. He turned to Morgenthau to help him in the search for an alternative place of refuge.

"I have got the first concrete suggestion to make for the Jewish refugees," said Morgenthau, after reaching the president in his bedroom.[23]

"Well, for heaven's sake, what is it?"

The place that Morgenthau had in mind was Guinea, a territory on the west coast of Africa administered by Britain and France. He outlined a complicated plan that would forgive the colonial powers a portion of their war debts in exchange for opening the territory to Jewish immigrants.

"It's no good," snapped FDR, who had spent hours poring over relief maps of Africa and South America complete with temperature charts and markings showing areas of possible "white settlement."[24] "It would take the Jews twenty-five to fifty years to overcome the fever there."

The president thought much more highly of the Cameroons, a former German colony that now belonged to France. He had heard that the Cameroons had some "wonderful high land" and were "very thinly populated." An alternative was the Portuguese-administered territory of Angola, farther to the south, which was also suitable for large-scale European colonization. FDR was soon dreaming up ways to convince the Portuguese dictator, António de Oliveira Salazar, to support the project. He ordered his diplomats to tell Salazar that the "creation of a new Jewish homeland in Angola" would prove an economic boon for Portugal and make the Portuguese strongman "one of the greatest figures in the history of his country and our times."[25]

Such grand schemes appealed to Roosevelt's fertile imagination. The treasury secretary felt he had a duty to assist the president, who seemed alone in his determination to think big. "Nobody is helping him," he recorded in his diary that night. "I am going at least to do the spadework."[26] Over one of their regular working lunches a few weeks later, Morgenthau indulged his boss by talking about the possibility of raising $500 million to finance the orderly departure from Europe of half a million Jews. "Nothing ventured, nothing gained" was Morgenthau's motto. Thinking out loud with his friend, Roosevelt thought it might be possible for the United States to take twenty thousand Jews a year, if other countries could be persuaded to make room for eighty thousand a year.[27]

Whatever the long-term feasibility of FDR's grand resettlement vision, in the short term he was boxed in by domestic constraints. The quota system established by Congress accorded no priority to refugees fleeing racial or political persecution. Unless the president was prepared for a bruising fight he would probably lose, he had to limit himself to small steps that would help at least a few of the refugees. The most important step was to make sure that the quotas were actually filled.

His labor secretary, Frances Perkins, wanted to extend the visitor permits of some fifteen thousand German Jews temporarily admitted to the United States. Since Perkins also oversaw the Immigration Service, her views were important. But the State Department was strongly opposed. Assistant Secretary Messersmith argued that the proposal would violate the law, "mean a complete breakdown of our whole visa practice," and provoke "an overwhelmingly unfavorable reaction throughout our country."[28] Roosevelt sided with Perkins, saying it would be cruel to put the Jews "on a ship and send them back to Germany under the present conditions." The visitors would be given renewable six-month extensions of their visas.

"I cannot, in any decent humanity, throw them out," FDR told journalists at a November 18 press conference.[29]

Even minor changes to U.S. immigration policy risked provoking a public backlash. After Kristallnacht, telegrams and letters poured into the White House and State Department protesting the entry of refugees. A telegram signed by "a fed up American gentile" from New Jersey accused FDR of "going too far.... You may face either a revolution or an impeachment if you continue [to be] a catspaw for Washington Jewish minorities."[30] A bank president from Ohio wrote to say that he would willingly donate money to "help buy the Jews a home country," but did not want them in "this country." A textile salesman from New York said he felt "very sorry for the Jew in Germany" but worried they would compete for jobs with "many of our own citizens who should be given first consideration."

"Don't we have enough unemployment, people on relief?" the salesman wrote, striking a theme common to many of the letter writers.[31]

If many Americans were alarmed by the prospect of hordes of refugees flooding into America in the weeks after Kristallnacht, others searched for practical ways to help the persecuted. On the evening of December 18, prominent philanthropists and social workers gathered in a Fifth Avenue apartment opposite Central Park in New York to launch a campaign for the rescue of Jewish children. The twenty-eight attendees included the Chicago department store magnate Marshall Field, the owner of *The Washington Post,* Eugene Meyer, and the Quaker leader, Clarence Pickett. They quickly sketched out a plan for placing up to twenty thousand refugee children in foster homes across the United States with the help of local churches. By focusing their efforts on children, they hoped to avoid the complaint that the refugees would compete for jobs with American workers. The vital question was "how to get the children over here."[32]

The earnest men and women who crowded into the living room of the eminent child psychiatrist Marion Kenworthy were inspired by the Kindertransport program in Britain. Galvanized into action by harrowing newspaper stories from Germany, refugee advocates had persuaded the British government to permit the temporary entry of children persecuted by the Nazis. The foreign secretary, Lord Halifax, hoped that "an act of generosity might have a knock-on effect and cause the United States to open its doors wider."[33]

No firm limit was placed on the number of children who would be admitted to Britain under the plan, but ten thousand was believed to be a feasible target. Refugee organizations pledged to raise £50 a child (roughly $1,500 in 2019) as a guarantee that the children would "re-emigrate" as soon as possible. By mid-December, trainloads of Jewish children were arriving at Liverpool Street station in London from cities like Berlin, Vienna, and Frankfurt, following an overnight journey across the North Sea via the Hook of Holland.

Persuading the U.S. government to adopt a similar scheme was likely to prove considerably more difficult. Kenworthy and her colleagues believed that FDR was "sympathetic" to their initiative but knew that he was not the final arbiter on immigration matters. A British prime minister could normally rely on his parliamentary majority in the House of Commons. In the system designed by the American founders, the legislature served as a permanent counterbalance to the power of the executive.

Roosevelt had made no effort to change American immigration practices after succeeding Herbert Hoover as president of the United States in 1933. His predecessor had taken steps to further slash immigration following the onset of the Great Depression. In September 1930, less than a year after the stock market crash, Hoover ordered the State Department to ensure that immigrants would not compete for jobs with Americans or become a financial burden on the government.[34]

Prior to 1930, the "likely to become a public charge" clause had been used mainly to exclude the chronically sick and mentally unstable. The clause was now interpreted to apply to all those unable to support themselves as soon as they stepped off the boat. In the fiscal year ending June 1931, for the first time in American history, more people left the United States than arrived. The number of German immigrants admitted to the United States declined precipitously from 27,119 in 1930 to 10,100 in 1931 to 2,086 in 1932.[35]

Preoccupied with the domestic unemployment crisis, FDR did little to address the immigration question until the beginning of his second term. In January 1937, two months after he was swept back to the White

House, the State Department quietly relaxed the "public charge" provision. Rather than reject anyone who might "possibly" become a public charge, consuls were now told to reject only those applicants who would "probably" constitute a long-term burden. Visa applicants were no longer required to produce financial guarantees from immediate family members already living in the United States. Nonbinding affidavits of support from more distant relatives were deemed satisfactory under the new regulations.[36]

Such tweaks in the interpretation of the immigration law led to an immediate increase in the granting of visas during Roosevelt's second term. The granting of immigrant visas to Jewish applicants tripled between 1936 and 1938. It was not until the middle of 1938, however, that consuls began using all the slots in the German and Austrian quotas.[37] (See chart on page 296.) Admissions to the United States rose sharply, but failed to keep pace with the ever increasing demand for German quota visas. The tumultuous events of 1938, beginning with the annexation of Austria and ending with Kristallnacht, created a refugee crisis of entirely new dimensions.

While a president enjoyed some latitude in interpreting the immigration laws, he could not waive the quota limits unilaterally. Admitting twenty thousand refugee children into the country outside the quota system would require an act of Congress. FDR had to carefully consider how much political capital he was prepared to invest in the passage of new immigration legislation at the expense of other priorities.

The generous souls in Marion Kenworthy's living room had an excellent connection to the White House: Eleanor Roosevelt. The activist First Lady had worked with many of them on a wide variety of humanitarian causes. During the Spanish Civil War, she had been moved by the plight of Basque children forced to flee their homes by the Nationalist forces of General Francisco Franco. "The Spanish children are weighing more and more heavily on my mind," she wrote in a May 1937 newspaper column. "I hope very much that those of us who can in this country will contribute money so that these children may be taken to safety, fed and clothed and educated adequately." She donated to a Quaker relief committee for the children, brushing aside critics on the right who claimed that she was "abetting communism."[38]

Eleanor promised to talk to her husband about the proposal to bring tens of thousands of children to the United States. FDR stopped short of endorsing the initiative himself, but had some encouraging words for the child refugee advocates that they interpreted as a green light to proceed. Eleanor relayed his views to her friends in New York:

> My husband says that you had better go to work at once and get two people of opposite parties in the House and in the Senate and have them jointly get agreement on the legislation which you want for bringing in children. The State Department is only afraid of what Congress will say to them and, therefore, if you remove that fear, the State Department will make no objections. He advises that you choose your people rather carefully and, if possible, get all the Catholic support you can.[39]

Kenworthy and her colleagues followed the president's advice. They enlisted Senator Robert F. Wagner of New York, a prominent New Deal Democrat who also happened to be a Catholic and first-generation German immigrant, to sponsor their proposed legislation in the Senate. On the House side, they recruited Edith Nourse Rogers, a liberal Republican congresswoman from Massachusetts.

The Wagner-Rogers bill was endorsed by many religious leaders, despite a stream of anti-Jewish invective from the renegade Catholic "radio priest," Father Charles Coughlin. In his weekly broadcasts, Coughlin depicted Kristallnacht as a justified response to Jewish persecution of Christians. He identified Jews with the "communistic government of Russia" that had "murdered more than twenty million Christians" and stolen "forty billion dollars" of Christian property.[40] The Catholic archbishop of New York, Francis Spellman, was opposed to Coughlin, but did not want his name attached to the children's bill. It was left to the archbishop of Chicago to represent the Catholic Church on the non-sectarian Committee for German Refugee Children.[41]

As the *annus horribilis* of 1938 gave way to what everybody hoped would be a more peaceful new year, powerful forces lined up on either side of the refugee children debate. Led by Catholic and Protestant clerics, the great and the good of the land defended the ideals symbolized by the Statue of Liberty. Supporters of the children's bill included the former president, Herbert Hoover, who had tightened immigration restrictions at the start of the Great Depression. Hoover was an acknowledged authority on refugee problems: he supervised the delivery of relief to Europe after the Great War, helping to save millions of lives. A Quaker, Hoover now urged Americans to "receive its proportionate share of refugee children from Europe and settle them in American homes."[42]

Leading newspapers also endorsed the bill. *The New York Times* reminded readers that America had "gladly given aid" to the children of war-torn Europe in the past. "Though we no longer open our gates to all the earth's oppressed, it is in our tradition, in keeping with the warm-heartedness on which we pride ourselves, to open them to these children."[43]

The opposition was also mobilizing. For every bill submitted to Congress relaxing the immigration quotas, three or four bills called for even greater restrictions. A Democratic senator from North Carolina, Robert Reynolds, wanted a ban on all immigration for the next ten years along with the deportation of "all alien criminals and undesirables." Other demands included keeping America "out of war," the fingerprinting of all aliens, and the banishment of "all foreign isms."[44]

The State Department, meanwhile, feared that attempts to liberalize the immigration laws would backfire politically. George Messersmith reported that the anti-immigrant lobby was trying to collect and publicize information on the high percentage of Jews admitted under the quota system. In a January 1939 memorandum, the assistant secretary predicted a surge of antisemitism if the children's bill was passed. "It is quite obvious that under the surface a good deal is brewing which can have very undesirable effects," he warned. It was better to avoid any changes in immigration law, given that the United States already had "the most liberal immigration practice of any country today." Messersmith claimed that "thoughtful and informed Jews" agreed with him.[45]

Most troubling for the champions of the children, American public opinion remained deeply hostile to the admission of refugees. While most Americans were appalled by the violence of Kristallnacht, this did not translate into a greater willingness to allow victims of Nazi persecution into the country. In January 1939, the Gallup organization asked Americans whether they supported the plan for "refugee children from Germany to be brought into this country and taken care of in American homes." Two thirds of those questioned were opposed; only one quarter were in favor. When the wording of the question was altered slightly to specify that the refugee children were "mostly Jewish," support for their admission actually increased from 26 to 30 percent. Opposition declined from 66 to 61 percent.[46] Americans, it seemed, were against any kind of immigration, not just Jewish immigration.

As he neared the end of his sixth year in the presidency, Franklin Roosevelt felt increasingly tired and listless. While he still projected an image of indomitable energy in public, he could not disguise his condition from those around him. A paralyzing illness, diagnosed as polio back in 1921, had confined him to a wheelchair. He was dependent on other people for the normal routines of everyday life. Those who saw him up close were often shocked by his condition, which was kept secret from ordinary Americans. "There was a great weariness in his eyes, and I could see he was very fatigued," the visiting Canadian prime minister, Mackenzie King, confided to his diary at the time of Kristallnacht.[47] Interior Secretary Harold Ickes "could not but notice at Cabinet meetings that his face showed, perhaps more than ever, the terrific strain under which he has been working." The president's normally upbeat physician, Admiral Ross McIntire, was "more anxious" about his patient than ever before.[48]

FDR's antidote to fatigue and illness was to escape from Washington as often as he could. He received jolts of energy from these trips, which were a respite from the endless stream of visitors to the Oval Office. In spring and summer, he liked to visit his childhood home in upstate New York, but in winter he preferred to head south, toward the sunshine. At the end of November, he made a two-week trip to Warm

Springs, Georgia, where he had founded a recuperative spa for polio patients. The mineralized water that gushed out of a nearby mountain relaxed his wasted muscles and invigorated his spirits.

He derived a similar psychological boost from the sea. An accomplished sailor, he loved nothing more than to stand (even with support) on the deck of an American battleship, his blue navy cape flying behind him in the wind. By immersing himself in the details of seafaring, he could momentarily put aside the burdens of the presidency.

Roosevelt had planned a two-week Caribbean cruise on his favorite warship, the USS *Houston,* for the end of February. His ostensible goal was to observe naval maneuvers that included a mock battle between a "White Fleet" and a "Black Fleet." The maneuvers would send a signal to the dictators over in Europe that the United States was fully prepared to defend its two-thousand-mile Atlantic coastline. But the real purpose of the trip was to give the president a much needed break. McIntire considered canceling the cruise after FDR came down with a bad case of flu, but eventually decided that his patient would benefit from getting "away from Washington."[49]

Roosevelt's health began to revive as soon as he was ceremonially piped aboard the nine-thousand-ton cruiser anchored off Key West. As the ship sailed over the horizon with its huge guns, *The New York Times* reported (from the shore) that the president was living his boyhood fantasies. "He will sail on a secret course, he will have a rolling deck under his feet, a tropical sun and stars shining on the bluest of blue water around him, and the caressing touch of the trade winds fanning his face day and night."[50] Communications with Washington were restricted to daily drops of mail and a coded wireless channel for urgent messages.

Among the problems that FDR had left behind in the White House was the child refugee bill. Eleanor Roosevelt had already told journalists (with "permission to quote") that she favored the legislation for "humanitarian" reasons. "Other nations take their share of the child refugees, and it seems a fair thing to do."[51] The First Lady sent a message to the *Houston* from New York asking whether her husband would also support the measure. She signed off by wishing him "a grand time" at sea.

The president was in a quandary. While he privately welcomed the refugee bill, his advisors were urging him not to express his support publicly. Under Secretary of State Sumner Welles complained about being overwhelmed with protests about Jews entering the country "under various pretenses."[52] Some members of Congress wanted to cut the quotas by 90 percent or more. In the meantime, the isolationists were mounting daily assaults on FDR, accusing him of embroiling the country in foreign wars. Defeat on a major piece of legislation that he personally had endorsed would seriously undermine his authority.

It did not take long for Franklin to weigh the pros and cons. Happily ensconced in the admiral's cabin of the *Houston,* he dictated his reply to Eleanor:

ALL WELL ON BOARD FINE WEATHER HERE KEEPING TO SCHEDULE PERIOD IT IS ALL RIGHT FOR YOU TO SUPPORT CHILD REFUGEE BILL BUT IT IS BEST FOR ME TO SAY NOTHING TILL I GET BACK MUCH LOVE FDR[53]

FOUR

Kippenheim

I N THE DAYS AFTER KRISTALLNACHT, Hedy Wachenheimer felt "paralyzed with fear." The feeling persisted even after she ventured out of the attic wardrobe where she hid with her mother and aunt to escape the howling mob in the street below. Hedy had no idea where the Nazis had taken her father or whether she would see him again. She panicked whenever her mother was out of her sight.[1]

The fate of the men remained mysterious for two weeks. Nobody knew if their loved ones were alive or dead. On the day after the men were arrested, Postmaster Link appeared at the synagogue with a huge ball of ties and belts. The sight of the confiscated clothing items alarmed Fanny Valfer, a member of the extended Wertheimer clan, who lived opposite the synagogue. In addition to her husband, Max, the tobacco and cigar man, several of her brothers and cousins had been taken away.

"My God, did they kill the men?" she screamed.

"Maybe," smirked Link.[2]

After two weeks, postcards began arriving from Dachau, site of the first SS-run concentration camp. The postcards bore a few reassuring words from the prisoners in their own handwriting, along with a pre-printed message stating they were forbidden to receive visits.[3]

There was clearly no point going to Dachau, which was a day's journey from Kippenheim, close to Munich. Bella Wachenheimer instead decided to plead her husband's case at the provincial Gestapo headquarters in Karlsruhe, sixty miles to the north. Hedy begged her mother not to go, fearing that she, too, would be arrested, but Bella insisted. She left home early in the morning by train and returned late at night. The Gestapo officials made clear that the release of the Jewish prisoners was linked to their emigration from Germany. If their families could show they were taking active steps to leave the country, they would be freed. Bella provided the Gestapo with a note from the United States consulate in Stuttgart stating that Hugo was number 20,753 on its "waiting list" for a U.S. visa.[4]

On the Monday of the fourth week, Bella made a final trip to Karlsruhe. This time, the Gestapo official told her that Hugo would probably be released soon, but added an ominous warning. "If he does not come back by Friday, it means he is no longer alive."

The first men from Dachau began arriving back in the village that same day, walking from the train station, twenty minutes away. Their heads were completely shaved. They all looked dazed and emaciated. None of them was willing to talk about his experiences. There was no sign of Hugo on Tuesday, or Wednesday, or Thursday. By Friday, December 9, Bella had given up hope. Grieving for her husband, she refused to get out of bed. "He's dead," she kept repeating. "He's never coming home."

There was a knock at the door. Bella was convinced that the Nazi ruffians had returned. She tried to stop Hedy from going to see who was knocking. The fourteen-year-old tore herself away, ran downstairs, and opened the door. It was her father. He took off his hat.

"They shaved your hair," screamed Hedy.

Bella barely recognized Hugo when he came up the stairs. He was wearing an overcoat, which he did not want to take off, even though it was warm in the apartment. He refused to undress or change his clothes. They offered him breakfast, but he did not want to eat. His hands were covered with a mixture of frostbite and burns from carrying great kettles of soup for the other prisoners. He did not want to get undressed because his arms were swollen from beatings. Bella had to use scissors to cut him out of his clothes, revealing still more burns and bruises. From his daughter's perspective, Hugo had left Kippenheim in the prime of life—aged forty-nine—and returned a "broken old man."

Later that morning, Bella and Hedy heard a thud from the bathroom where Hugo was shaving. He was crumpled on the floor. There were no Jewish doctors in Kippenheim and Christian doctors were no longer allowed to treat Jews. The family doctor, Bernhard Weber, was the reserve SS officer who had restrained the storm troopers from even worse excesses on Kristallnacht. Weber came secretly that night to treat Hugo, who had suffered a light heart attack. Over subsequent nights, he nursed his patient back to health.

The prisoners had been instructed not to discuss their experiences with anyone. But the horror of what had happened to the men seeped out slowly in whispered conversations with their wives and adult children. The long walk from the train station to iron gates emblazoned with the words *Arbeit Macht Frei,* "Work Sets You Free." Cold showers, beatings for imaginary offenses, hundreds of men crammed together in flimsy wooden bunks. The shouts of *Raus, raus, raus,* "Out, out, out." The whipping stool in the detention building. Counting aloud the lashes from the SS man's bullwhip until you fainted or forgot the number, in which case the torture resumed from the beginning. The bitter wind blowing off the Bavarian Alps. Freezing temperatures that prevented sleep and caused previously strong men to die from pneumonia.

Early morning roll call was a particularly terrible ordeal. Every day, twenty thousand prisoners would gather on a vast parade ground, the *Appelplatz,* beneath the searchlights. In their striped pants and white shirts, they resembled an army of shaven mutes. They were not permitted to move or even cough. They had to keep their eyes to the ground at all times. If there was the slightest noise, the commandant would refuse to inspect the parade. If the numbers did not tally, the counting would begin all over again. Sometimes the torture lasted for many hours, as sick prisoners collapsed and were dragged away.[5]

The cruel punishments had the intended effect. After their release from Dachau, the Jewish men and boys from Kippenheim became even more determined to leave Germany, as soon as possible, to any country willing to accept them.

Nazi leaders had been working for many months to force the Jews to emigrate. The tempo of persecution had picked up in early 1938 after the annexation of Austria. In April, Jews were required to register all property in excess of 5,000 reichsmarks. In June, security forces carried out the first mass arrests of Jews as part of a nationwide roundup of alleged work shirkers dubbed "Operation Work Shy." That same month, the government ordered the registration of all Jewish-owned businesses, an apparent prelude to their confiscation. In August, Jews were instructed to adopt an additional name: "Sara" for women, "Israel" for men. In October, they were forced to apply for new passports, stamped with the letter "J" for *Jude*.

The stream of discriminatory decrees became a flood in the days after Kristallnacht. Field Marshal Hermann Göring summoned senior Nazi officials to a conference on November 12 to discuss further measures against the Jews. As "atonement" for the murder of the German diplomat, he ordered a one-billion-reichsmark fine on the Jewish community. Instead of receiving compensation for their losses, Jews would themselves pay for the damage they had "provoked." Insurance payments for the destruction of Jewish property—including 7,500 businesses and 267 synagogues—went directly into state coffers. A "Decree on the Elimination of Jews from Economic Life" closed all Jewish-owned businesses, including retail stores. Other decrees forbade Jews from attending state schools and universities and froze most Jewish assets.[6] "I would not like to be a Jew in Germany today," gloated Göring at the end of the meeting.[7]

Implementation of the new decrees began immediately. Individual "atonement fines" amounted to around 20 percent of the value of the property that Jews had been required to register a few months previously. Richer families were given twenty-four hours to pay the fine or face arrest. Subsequent decrees prohibited Jews from frequenting places of entertainment, operating automobiles, and owning carrier pigeons. There was even talk of confining Jews to ghettos or requiring them to wear a yellow star on their clothing, although this suggestion was rejected for the time being.[8]

In Kippenheim, where there were many Jewish businesses, the decrees served as a green light to predators. As the richest man in the village, Hermann Wertheimer was already the object of much jealousy and resentment. Business rivals had accused him of "corrupt trading practices" stemming from his domination of the metal business in the surrounding area. They now had an opportunity to put him out of business entirely. Without waiting for Hermann to come home from Dachau, local officials ordered his wife, Zerline, to sell the company for a fraction of its true value. The purchasers were two "Aryan" business-men from Freiburg. The attorney who arranged the sale received one of the company cars as payment.[9]

As the elected leader of Kippenheim's Jewish community, Hermann Wertheimer was also made responsible for repairing the damage to the synagogue. Since he was now impoverished, he was obliged to sell the building to the municipality to cover the cost of repairs. Village officials turned the former place of worship into an agricultural ware-house, but overlooked an inscription etched into the stone in Hebrew. Taken from the Book of Genesis, it read, "This is none other than the house of God."

Some Jewish-owned companies in Kippenheim, including the tex-tile business founded by Hugo Wachenheimer's grandfather in 1857, were sold to Aryan employees for nominal sums. Others, such as Max Valfer's wholesale tobacco business, were liquidated outright. Jewish businessmen were obliged to write off the debts of their Aryan custom-ers. After returning home from Dachau, Siegfried Maier spent much of his time compiling long, handwritten lists of his creditors, none of whom ever repaid him.

After losing their businesses, Jews were ordered to turn over many of their remaining valuables to state-operated pawn shops. (They were allowed to keep two pieces of cutlery per person, a plain gold wedding band, and a watch.) Radios were also confiscated, even without a gov-ernment decree, on the grounds that Jews had no right to participate in "German culture."[10] Jews were forbidden to subscribe to newspapers, with the exception of a single Nazi-controlled propaganda sheet for Jews alone.

The overall effect of the decrees was to make paupers out of once prosperous, middle-class families, prior to hounding them out of Ger-many. In addition to the "atonement fine," even moderately well-off Jews were forced to pay a 25 percent "Reich flight tax," and a 100 per-cent tax on all personal belongings purchased after 1933. Any remaining funds were declared "blocked," meaning that they could not be taken out of the country.

"Nazi Restrictions, Special Taxes Strip Jews of Wealth" ran the headline of a December 23, 1938, report from Berlin by the Jewish Telegraphic Agency, which had managed to retain a correspondent in the German capital with the help of Consul Geist.[11]

Prior to Hitler's appointment as chancellor of Germany on January 30, 1933, there had been little open friction between Jews and Christians in Kippenheim. Although they rarely intermarried, Germans of different faiths had walked to school arm in arm, attended each other's funerals and weddings, and wished each other well on religious holidays. The Lutheran pastor often attended Jewish seders. Catholics welcomed Jewish participation in the Corpus Christi Day procession. At Passover, Jewish children visited their Christian neighbors with gifts of matza, and received Easter eggs and bunnies in return.[12] It took less than six years for relations between the two communities to deteriorate to the point where there was no longer a place for the Jews.

Kippenheim Jews had benefited from the relatively liberal atmosphere in Baden, long regarded as one of the more progressive regions of Germany. Before being absorbed into the German Empire in 1871, the boomerang-shaped sliver of territory along the Rhine valley was a sovereign state ruled by a margrave, and later a grand duke. (See map on page 150.) The ideas of the French Revolution—"Liberty, Equality, Fraternity"—had accompanied Napoleon's armies across the river from Alsace. The inspiration for a comic opera by Jacques Offenbach, *La Grande-Duchesse de Gérolstein,* the grand duchy had its own currency, postage stamps, and miniature army. It had diplomatic relations with several dozen foreign countries, including the United States. The aristocrats of Europe flocked to the mineral baths at Baden-Baden. The grand duke was the first German ruler (in 1808) to offer his Jewish subjects the promise of civil and religious equality—provided they conformed to German cultural and educational practices. It was a bargain that most Jews were happy to accept.

"I am a German and cannot be anything else," wrote the Jewish writer Berthold Auerbach after participating in the liberal revolution of 1848, which was put down by Prussian troops. "I am a Swabian and

I don't want to be anything else. I am a Jew. Together all this produces the right mixture."[13] Born in a remote village on the other side of the Black Forest from Kippenheim, Auerbach was the most popular German writer of his time. His *Village Tales from the Black Forest* depicts a simple, peaceful world in which Jewish peddlers and Catholic farmers lived side by side, tolerating each other's foibles and traditions.

While Auerbach's "village tales" were certainly idealized, they were not too far off the mark in describing relations between the different religious communities in Kippenheim in the second half of the nineteenth century. Kippenheim Jews would look back on the period as a golden age, when they were able to establish successful businesses. In 1852, they built a grand new sandstone synagogue in the center of the village in the Moorish style then in fashion. Full emancipation followed a decade later. By the end of the century, there were three hundred Jews living in Kippenheim. When Grand Duke Frederick celebrated the golden jubilee of his reign in 1906, the Jews of Kippenheim proudly joined in the festivities. The entire village was bedecked in portraits of the grand duke and the yellow-red-yellow triband of Baden. Children at the village school were taught a "Kippenheim song" that included the line "Jews and Christians live together in cozy groups, appreciating the sweet calm."[14]

Not all was peace and harmony. Every few decades, a spasm of antisemitism would convulse the land, often coinciding with periods of political upheaval. During the 1848 revolution, Auerbach himself witnessed riots in Heidelberg directed against a Jewish manufacturer of ready-to-wear clothes accused of taking business away from local tailors. The trauma of those events may have contributed to the death of Auerbach's beloved wife, Auguste, after she gave birth prematurely. For the most part, however, the anti-Jewish disturbances were confined to towns and cities, bypassing villages like Kippenheim.

Kippenheim Jews demonstrated their loyalty to the German state by marching enthusiastically to war alongside their Christian neighbors in August 1914. They erected a memorial in the Jewish cemetery in nearby Schmieheim to eight Kippenheim Jews killed during the war. THESE SONS FELL FOR THEIR FATHERLAND read the inscription etched in the granite in German and Hebrew, PEACE, PEACE TO THOSE FAR AND NEAR. ISAIAH 57:19."[15]

Jews had begun migrating away from villages like Kippenheim to cities like Karlsruhe and Mannheim in search of greater economic opportunity even before World War I. The outward migration continued after the war, causing the Jewish population to decline to 144 in 1933, when Hitler came to power, from a high point of 323 just sixty years earlier.[16] In the years that followed the war, the renamed "Republic of Baden" became a breeding ground for economic discontent. The region was particularly badly hit by the punitive measures in the Treaty of Versailles. Unemployment was higher than elsewhere because of the severing of economic ties with Alsace, which had been ceded back to France. The German side of the Rhine was declared a demilitarized zone, discouraging industrial investment. The Nazis exploited the toxic political mix by accusing the Jews of "a stab in the back."

The Nazis, or National Socialists, did very well in Protestant villages, sometimes capturing more than 90 percent of the vote. But they had difficulty establishing themselves in Kippenheim, which was 58 percent Catholic and 33 percent Lutheran, according to the 1925 census. The Catholics were a more cohesive political force than the Lutherans, who did not have their own political party. Only three Kippenheimers voted for Hitler in the Reichstag election of 1928. By July 1932, the Nazis had increased their share of the Kippenheim vote to 36 percent, but still trailed the Catholic-dominated Center Party with 42 percent.[17] In order to block the Nazis, many Kippenheim Jews gave their votes to Catholic candidates rather than the more liberal political party they had traditionally supported.

During the early period of Nazi rule in 1933, Kippenheim Jews had not been too worried. They viewed Hitler as "a madman" and doubted the staying power of his regime. The village council adopted a resolution by majority vote in March, refusing to display the swastika flag over the Rathaus for fear of provoking disorders.[18] A harbinger of the new order came on April 1, when the Nazis organized a nationwide boycott of Jewish businesses. Hedy Wachenheimer would long remember the brown-shirted storm trooper standing outside her father's textile store, hands behind his back, legs spread apart, looking into the distance. He had been stationed there to stop Christians from entering the store. Other storm troopers stood outside the Jewish bakery, the butcher, the hardware store, the winery, and the tobacco wholesaler.

"Don't worry. They will go away," her father remarked confidently, after she asked what the storm troopers were doing in the previously peaceful village.[19] The storm troopers did go away: the official boycott lasted for only one day. But from that moment on, Christians ran the risk of being termed "Jewish lackeys" if they continued to shop in Jewish stores. Christian businessmen who worked closely with Jews were subjected to "preventive detention."

It took almost ten months following the shift of power in Berlin for the Nazis to install their own supporters in positions of authority in Kippenheim and fly the swastika over the Rathaus. The pro-Nazi faction in the village quickly made up for lost time with a slew of anti-Jewish decrees. The village Nazis turned out to be even more extreme than the urban Nazis. In March 1935, they passed a resolution demanding that no more Jews be allowed to settle in Kippenheim. The resolution described Jews as the "mortal enemy" of the Nazi Party and urged Kippenheimers to "eradicate any foreign elements that pose a threat to German culture." Even though the unsanctioned resolution had no legal force, signs declaring *Juden sind hier unerwünscht* appeared at the entryway to the village. "Jews are unwanted here."[20]

The Kippenheim Nazis were quick to denounce any signs of fraternization between Christians and Jews. They threatened to unmask "our fellow Germans" who continued to do business with Jews. Such "dishonorable conduct," the March 1935 resolution warned, would not be tolerated.[21] Despite this edict, many Christians maintained good relations with their Jewish neighbors in private, while keeping their distance in public.

At the national level, discrimination against the Jews was formally enshrined in German law by the Nuremberg decrees of September 1935. Since it was often difficult to distinguish a Jew from a non-Jew, the law defined a Jew as someone with at least three Jewish grandparents, whether or not they had converted to another religion. Jews were not considered citizens of Germany, but rather "subjects of the state." Another law made sexual relations between Jews and Aryans a criminal offense. "Race defilement"—*Rassenschande*—was punishable by prison terms of up to fifteen years.

Hugo Wachenheimer attempted to maintain a positive outlook for as long as possible. Like many Kippenheim Jews, he shared the cultural interests of middle-class Germans. His bookcases were crammed with works by Goethe, Schiller, and other classic German writers. He liked to listen to Beethoven and Schubert on the gramophone in the evening. A wounded war veteran, Hugo refused to believe that such a civilized country would allow the Nazis to get their way. But even his confidence was shaken when a glass display case appeared on a wall near his store with the latest edition of the antisemitic rag *Der Stürmer*. Hugo told his daughter to ignore the display case. She did her best to obey him, but could not help noticing the caricatures of hunchbacked Jews with hooked noses counting bags of money that often stared her in the face.

The local Nazis were constantly dreaming up new ways to torment the Jewish villagers. One day, they announced the expulsion of Jews from the volunteer fire brigade. This was followed by the exclusion of Jewish cattle traders from the village hay auction. Then came news that Jewish residents would no longer receive their share of wood felled from the village forest. Jews were also accused of sexual assault. A lurid story in the local Nazi newspaper *Der Führer* from 1934 accused an unnamed Jewish dentist in Kippenheim of "using his professional position to take advantage of his patients." The newspaper claimed that female patients of "the Jew X" frequently "fled from his operating room with drilled teeth in order to spare themselves from being defiled. No girl was safe from this beast."[22]

Living next to the Rathaus, the family of Richard Wertheimer became accustomed to Nazi parades through the swastika-bedecked streets. On one occasion, they woke up to discover that the entire front of their house had been covered in a giant Nazi flag, drenching the living room in a menacing blood-red hue. The processions and demonstrations produced a deep impression on Richard's fourteen-year-old daughter, Pia. At first she enjoyed the rousing music. As she listened to some of the lyrics, she was horrified. One song in particular, "Once There Was a Young Storm Trooper," made her retreat back to bed and hide her head in the blankets. "When Jewish blood flows from the knife, then life will be twice as nice."[23] *Wenn das Judenblut vom Messer spritzt, dann geht's noch mal so gut.*

The antisemitic madness extended even to pets. Pia's family had a dachshund named Waldi who loved to follow funeral processions. Waldi was welcomed at Jewish funerals, but chased away from Christian funerals as a "Jewish dog."

There were also moments of quiet solidarity between Jew and Christian. Pia was a good friend of the Lutheran pastor's daughter, Annemarie Kaiser, who rode with her every day by bicycle to the Gymnasium in Ettenheim. Adam Kaiser had been a pastor in Switzerland before returning to his native Baden in 1929. He was influenced by the teachings of the Swiss reform theologian Karl Barth, an outspoken critic of the Nazis. "The whole family was very courageous," Pia recalled decades later. "Pastor Kaiser was demonstrative in his anti-Nazi sentiments."[24] Pia's piano teacher, Frau Bergmann, also made no secret of her anti-Nazi views.

Pastor Kaiser belonged to a dissident minority known as the "Confessing Church" that was opposed to the Nazi takeover of religion. He resisted Nazi attempts to establish a pro-regime church that would incorporate various different strands of Protestantism. He ran afoul of the village postmaster, who also served as an *Überwachungsleiter,* or "surveillance supervisor," for the Nazi Party. Postmaster Link informed his Nazi superiors that the dissident preacher had been overheard telling his parishioners, "We would rather be dead than lose our religion." In an October 1934 report, he accused Kaiser of using his pulpit to spread "a spirit of agitation and insurrection in an otherwise quiet Protestant community."[25]

Another parishioner complained that Kaiser showed "much more understanding and Christian love" for "Catholics and Jews" than "he did for us, his fellow believers, and the Third Reich." "We need a pastor who stands by his Führer," the parishioner concluded.[26] Kaiser was transferred to another parish shortly afterward.

It was difficult for even the most principled Germans to indefinitely resist the power of the totalitarian state. The archives of the Lutheran Church reveal that Pastor Kaiser also had his breaking point. It came in the summer of 1941 following the German invasion of the Soviet Union. The pressure to renounce his dissident views became intense at a time when the entire nation was being mobilized to fight the Red menace, which was conflated, at least in Hitler's mind, with the Jewish menace. As the German army advanced toward Moscow, the pastor who had stood up for Kippenheim Jews signed a statement pledging his loyalty "to the Führer and to the Third Reich."[27]

For many Christian Kippenheimers, antisemitism was more a matter of class resentment than racial hatred. Barred for centuries from owning land, Jews became peddlers and cattle traders. The farmers viewed the cattle dealers with suspicion, even though they were in daily contact. "In the opinion of the farmers, trading and money-lending did not have the same value as physical labor on the land," said Ulrich Baumann, the author of a sociological study of Catholics, Protestants, and Jews in rural Baden. "The farmers did not appreciate the work the cattle dealers did. For them, receiving money for buying and selling a cow was not work."[28] A cultural and psychological gulf developed between the Christian farmers and the Jewish tradesmen.

By long-standing tradition, Kippenheim farmers divided their land among all their children, leaving each generation poorer than before. By contrast, the Wertheimers and the Wachenheimers and the Valfers had built their itinerant peddling businesses into successful companies, with cars and full-time employees. They aspired to urban standards of living and insisted on the best education for their children. According to Baumann, Jewish villagers "bought the first cars, the first radios, the first prams and baby-strollers. The farmers did not see the need for a baby-stroller. They carried their babies in their arms." The leading Jewish families of Kippenheim employed Christian maids.

The social differences were exacerbated by different religious traditions. The farmers went to church on Sundays; the Jews observed Sabbath on Saturdays and socialized with each other after synagogue. "My father and other Jews wore high silk hats, like Abraham Lincoln, when they went to synagogue," recalled Kurt Maier. "When the farmers came through with their goats and hay wagons, they would see the Jews all dressed up in their best clothes. To the farmers, it seemed that Jewish holidays were going on all the time. It was a clash of two different cultures. Even in the peaceful times, there was always antagonism."[29]

Prior to Kristallnacht, young children like Kurt were largely sheltered from the *Rischus,* the Yiddish term for antisemitic actions. The occasional incidents of hostility left a deep impression, however. Kurt would long remember the time when his mother sent him to a neighbor's house to buy some parsley with a ten-pfennig coin in his hand. As he was standing in the doorway waiting for the parsley, he heard a male voice grumbling in the background. "They send a Jew boy here with ten pfennigs. We are supposed to live on that, while they are rich."[30]

The eight-year-old boy's sense of himself as an unwanted outsider was confirmed in August 1938 when Hitler passed through the village. His parents, along with other Jewish adults, had been instructed to shutter their windows and remain indoors. But nobody paid attention to "the Jew boy with ten pfennigs" as he crept out of his house, walked to the end of the street, and stood quietly on the corner. All around him, villagers were cheering the Führer with excited *Sieg Heils.*

As the motorcade rolled past, it seemed to Kurt as if Hitler "looked right at me" with his burning, hypnotic eyes. Kurt was the only person in the crowd who did not have his right arm raised in the Nazi salute. As a Jew, he knew that he was not permitted to "greet the leader of the German nation." He could merely stand in silence and impassively observe the spectacle. Never had he felt so alone and out of place.

Kippenheim at this time consisted of just a dozen streets, four of which converged on the Renaissance-style Rathaus and nearby fountain. The old Jewish quarter, and the original synagogue, lay behind the Rathaus in the twisting lanes that climbed into the forest. The sleepy community of eighteen hundred people blended naturally into the surrounding countryside. A little stream ran down the main street; farmers led cows past the church and synagogue; cattle dealers kept animals in the yards behind their houses. The predominant odor was the smell of the cow stable, which permeated the clothes of the cattle dealers in particular. Kurt Maier would cherish the whiff of cattle dung in the suit of his Uncle Siegfried as one of his favorite childhood memories.[31]

Geographically, Kippenheim found itself at a crossroads accentuated by the madness that had seized Germany during the six years of Nazi rule. To the west lay the Rhine River border with France, a seven-mile-wide plain bristling with military fortifications that had been the site of countless battles. To the north was the district capital Lahr and the oppressive bureaucratic apparatus of the Nazi dictatorship. All the torments that had been inflicted on Kippenheim Jews, including the bully boys unleashed at Kristallnacht, seemed to come from this direction. To the east rose the Black Forest, the fairy-tale Germany of quaint villages, bubbling brooks, and mythical monsters that had inspired generations of landscape artists and writers. The most obvious escape route from the Nazi evil lay to the south. The high Swiss mountains were a formidable natural barrier that offered at least a temporary refuge to the persecuted on their way to other lands.

Hitler passed through Kippenheim a second time in the spring of 1939.[32] He arrived, as before, from the north. His open Mercedes limousine swung past the elementary school and large church on Hindenburgstrasse that served both Catholics and Lutherans. The motorcade paused briefly outside the Rathaus so that the Führer could accept the pledges of eternal fealty from the village leaders. Rather than proceeding along Poststrasse, past the devastated synagogue, the convoy of cars turned right once more onto Adolf-Hitler-Strasse, toward the West Wall and the war that everyone suspected was coming.

As one of the oldest Jewish families in Kippenheim, and certainly the wealthiest, the Wertheimers took pains to remind others of their elevated status. Hailing from Wertheim in northern Baden, they could trace their German ancestry back to the thirteenth century.[33] When they married, it was often to distant cousins. The Wertheimer men dressed in the style of English country gentlemen, with waistcoats, starched wing collars, and gold watch chains. On High Holy Days, they attended synagogue in white gloves and bow ties to match their morning suits and top hats. They were influenced by the mores of Victorian England, which had spread to Germany. "The English *comme il faut* was the way we were brought up," recalled Pia Wertheimer, who immigrated to the United States in 1937. "Good manners, restraint, refinement, not letting go."[34]

Poorer Jews depended on the charity of Hermann Wertheimer, who owned the big metal equipment store opposite the Rathaus. In accordance with Jewish tradition, he distributed free food twice a week, with a serving of wine on Fridays. "Many other members of the Jewish community were beholden to him," said Pia. "He used his money in a way that made him perceived as the patron of the rest of the community." On his way to synagogue, he would occasionally hand out money to needy Christians as well, telling them, "You are going to pray, I am going to pray. You should get yourself a pastry."[35]

If Hermann Wertheimer the metal man was the undisputed patriarch of the Kippenheim Jews, the life and soul of the community was his namesake, Hermann Wertheimer the butcher. Although they had the same name, they were only distantly related. Like his butcher father before him, Hermann the butcher boasted a magnificent mustache. The oldest boy in a family of eight children, he was their acknowledged leader. According to Pia, his niece, Hermann was "highly intelligent, very funny, and full of anecdotes." A favorite anecdote from his childhood concerned a bedtime ritual. The young Hermann was permitted to sit on "the throne"—the toilet—while his brothers and sisters assembled in front of him on portable potties. When everyone was seated comfortably, Hermann recalled, "I told them a bedtime story."[36]

The butcher shop was on the other side of Poststrasse from the synagogue. Next to it was a restaurant, also owned by Hermann, called the Badischer Hof, the "Court of Baden," in honor of Grand Duke Frederick. A big room above the restaurant served as the meeting place for Jews after the Sabbath service, as well as weddings and other large parties. Jewish men would gather in the Badischer Hof in the evening to taste Hermann's sausages, play cards, and drink coffee with a shot of brandy. On holidays, there was dancing and singing. Since the Wertheimer family was musically gifted, there would often be impromptu piano recitals, interspersed with arias from German and Italian operas. One year, the young Wertheimers made up their own show about the village, featuring a song with the words "All this happens in Kippenheim, in no big city could life be more interesting."[37]

Hermann was on good terms with the only other butcher in the village, a Christian by the name of Karl Dorner. The two butchers had a long-standing arrangement to share meat. Karl would buy a cow. Hermann would slaughter it in accordance with kosher practices, and return the back half to his friend.[38] This practice continued even after the Nazis prohibited Jews and Christians from conducting business together. One day, in 1937, a neighbor informed the SS that Hermann was still buying meat from Karl. When an SS officer came to investigate, Hermann yelled at him to get off his property. The SS man left after warning Hermann to wind up his business. According to a family history, "It was at that moment that Hermann and his family decided they had to leave Germany as fast as they could."[39] The family traveled to New York on board the SS *Washington* in March 1938. He sold the inn and shop to Karl for 22,924 reichsmarks, a reasonable price at the time.[40]

Living a few doors up the street from the Badischer Hof was Hermann's older sister Fanny, a warm, generous woman who served as surrogate mother to the entire Wertheimer clan. Fanny was married to Max Valfer, the cigar distributor. Their living room boasted a well-stocked library and the first radio in Kippenheim, which became a gathering point for relatives and neighbors. While Fanny was not particularly religious, she attended synagogue regularly, and kept repeating a verse from the Torah; *Shema Yisrael!*, "Hear O Israel," became her mantra, the phrase with which everybody identified her.[41] She needed relief from the worries and responsibilities that had been heaped on top of her, first as the oldest child and then as the mother of a large and boisterous family.

Unlike the Wertheimers, the Valfers did not originally come from Kippenheim. Max Valfer traced his family's roots back to the medieval Spanish Inquisition. After being expelled from Spain in 1492, the Valfers had found refuge in the French wine region of Alsace. They lived for several centuries in a place called Valff, from which they acquired their surname. The Valfers crossed the Rhine amid the turmoil of the French Revolution, settling in Diersburg, a Black Forest village even smaller and more remote than Kippenheim.

Prior to his marriage to Fanny Wertheimer and his move to Kippenheim, Max Valfer had worked as a bookkeeper. He had served in the German army in World War I, rising to the rank of sergeant. After the war, he started a wholesale tobacco business, assisted by his oldest sons. The business expanded rapidly throughout the Black Forest, making

Valfer family, April 1937

the Valfers one of the wealthier families in Kippenheim. In contrast to his long-suffering wife, Max had the reputation of being impatient and often short-tempered.

Max ran his business out of the two front rooms of the house on Poststrasse, identified by a poster for Salem Gold cigarettes hanging on the outside wall. A photograph taken in the mid-1930s captures a bald-headed Max sitting in a dark, wood-paneled room beneath a long row of accounting binders. Dressed in a white shirt and gray waistcoat, he is squinting at the camera through rounded glasses, with a quizzical expression on his face. A still life depicting a large bowl of flowers hangs on the wall. Papers and tobacco paraphernalia litter Max's large, glass-covered desk. At the adjoining desk, closer to the window, sits his secretary, Berta Weil, a pretty, round-faced girl in a light summer dress, smiling broadly.

Another photograph, taken in April 1937, shows three generations of Valfers. Despite the strain of the Nazi years, the family is the image of bourgeois respectability. The oldest boy, Karl, dapper in a three-piece suit and white handkerchief, is standing next to his beautiful new wife, Trude. Next to him is his youngest brother, Erich, still a student at the Ettenheim Gymnasium. They are flanked by the three other unmarried children, Ruth, Hugo, and Else. The parents are seated in arm chairs in the front row, alongside their married daughter, Freya, who is juggling a two-year-old toddler, Sonja, on her lap. Freya's husband, Ludwig Maier, completes the contented-looking family circle.

Soon after this photograph was taken, the youngest daughter, Ruth, left for the United States. She simply told her parents one day that she was "getting out of Germany" because she could no longer stand the oppressive atmosphere. A cousin from a different village helped her find a distant relative to serve as her American sponsor. A sympathetic congressman from Mississippi pushed the required paperwork through the State Department.[42] Her brother Karl escorted her to the French port of Cherbourg and put her aboard the *Queen Mary* on April 14, 1937. She was seasick for the next five days. Ten days after leaving Kippenheim, she found herself in New York, virtually penniless, at the age of twenty-two. Fortunately, she had a network of relatives in the New York area and marketable skills as a nursery school teacher. She moved in with another family from Kippenheim and got a job as a nanny.[43]

By early 1939, the once closely knit Valfer family had effectively split apart. Hugo had joined his younger sister in America. Karl was back from Dachau, shattered by the experience and determined to get out of Germany as quickly as possible. Freya and Ludwig had moved to another village and were planning their emigration. The last Valfer child to leave home, Else, was desperately looking for a way out of the Third Reich after marrying a distant Wertheimer cousin. Her wedding in February 1938 turned out to be the last marriage ceremony performed in the Kippenheim synagogue.[44]

The Valfer parents were most concerned about their youngest son, Erich. Now twenty years old, he was known for his quirky sense of humor and talent for making friends. His cousin Pia would remember Erich as a boy sitting for hours on the eggs of a hen, trying to get them to hatch. Even though he was the lone Jewish student in his Ettenheim Gymnasium class, he had several good Christian friends. These friends earned Erich's ever-lasting gratitude by opposing an attempt to stop him from taking his final exams in March 1938.

Erich had always had a sense of wanderlust. Growing up, he had devoured the adventure novels of Karl May, renowned for his tales of the American West.[45] The writing was so vivid that it scarcely mattered that May had never set foot in America and that his fantasies bore little relation to reality. May's characters, particularly the Indian chief Winnetou and his German immigrant blood brother, Old Shatterhand, sparked the imagination of millions of Germans. The most widely read author in Germany, May also wrote a series of novels about the Middle East and Palestine, a part of the world in which Erich was becoming increasingly interested.

Erich knew there was no future for him in Germany. He had read *Mein Kampf* and attended compulsory lectures on Aryan racial superiority. Where he went was less important than getting out as quickly as possible. After graduating from the Gymnasium, he traveled to Switzerland. Since German passports were not yet being stamped with the letter "J" for *Jude,* he did not require permission to leave the country. From Switzerland, he moved to Italy. He hoped to study chemistry at Milan University, but his plans changed as the result of a meeting between Hitler and Benito Mussolini and a surge in Italian antisemitism. In September, Mussolini decreed that foreign Jews would no longer be permitted to attend Italian universities.

Back in Switzerland following his abortive trip to Italy in the summer of 1938, Erich heard about a group of young Czech Jews who planned to travel illegally to Palestine from Romania. A British naval blockade made the trip hazardous, but he decided to take a chance. To pay for his passage, he sold most of his possessions, including his camera, and a camera loaned to him by his sister. The rickety Greek cargo ship *Katina* had left the Romanian Black Sea port of Constanţa in January 1939 with more than six hundred illegal immigrants on board, packed together belowdecks.[46] Max checked at the Post Office every day for a letter from Erich, but months went by without any news. Fanny kept repeating her catchphrase, *Shema Yisrael!*

The Valfer family exemplified a general trend among German Jews: it was the younger people who were typically most eager to leave. They had fewer emotional and financial attachments than the older people and little to lose by emigrating. The comfortable middle-class lifestyle made it more difficult for the Valfer parents, and particularly Max, to leave Germany. Like many other successful German Jews,

TOP *Kippenheim photographed from the air during the 1920s. The church is visible on the left of the photograph, the Rathaus in the center, and the synagogue on the right.* BOTTOM *A postwar photograph of Poststrasse shows the stream running through the village, with the Post Office at the bottom of the street.*

TOP *Kippenheim synagogue, photographed in 1938.* BOTTOM *Hermann Wertheimer, shown with his wife, Zerline, was president of the synagogue and the richest man in Kippenheim, but was robbed of all his wealth after Kristallnacht. Hermann and Zerline immigrated to the United States in May 1940*

ᴘ *Freya Valfer is escorted to the synagogue by her brother Karl on her wedding day on January 12, 1933,* *hteen days before Hitler was appointed chancellor of Germany.* ʙᴏᴛᴛᴏᴍ *Nazi brownshirts gather* *ngside the Kippenheim firemen's band outside the home of Pia Wertheimer (whose mother, Berta, and* *nger brother Hans are visible in the window on the right) in 1935.*

TOP, LEFT *Max and Fanny Valfer on vacation in the spa town of Bad Neuenahr in 1934.*
TOP, RIGHT *Max and his secretary, Berta Weil.* BOTTOM *The identity card for Max Valfer (marked with a J for Jude), issued in 1939. A 1938 law required him to add "Israel" as a middle name.*

TOP *Hugo and Bella Wachenheimer in 1938, before Kristallnacht, with their fourteen-year-old daughter, Hedy.*   BOTTOM *A passport photograph of Hedy taken before she left Germany on a Kindertransport in May 1939.*

TOP *The Maier family grocery store and home in Kippenheim, in the early 1930s.*
BOTTOM *Siegfried and Charlotte Maier with their children, Heinz and Kurt, and a new car in 1935.*

TOP *Assistant Secretary of State Breckinridge Long in his State Department office in 1942.*

BOTTOM, LEFT *Assistant Secretary of State George Messersmith in 1938.* BOTTOM, RIGHT *Raymond ist, pictured leaving the White House in October 1939 after meeting with FDR, was acting consul general Berlin at the time of Kristallnacht.*

TOP *Adolf Hitler and his generals tour the West Wall defensive system against France on May 15, 1939.*
BOTTOM *FDR holds one of his twice-weekly news conferences in the Oval Office on August 25, 1939.*

Max had initially been reluctant to abandon the business he had built up over many years. He was proud of the company he had created from nothing, telling his children that "nobody can take away what we have built up."[47]

Despite all their troubles under the Nazis, Max and Fanny still had their own house and a decent income. Prior to Kristallnacht, everyday life continued with relatively few disruptions. Some of their Christian neighbors were hostile, but others did what they could to help. They quickly learned whom to trust and whom to avoid. If they went to America, they would be stripped of nearly everything.

Max and Fanny had applied for U.S. visas in September 1938 following the example set by their children. They had submitted their immigration papers to the American consulate in Stuttgart well before Kristallnacht, but after the first mass roundups in June that triggered a general panic among German Jews. As a result, they were in line behind many of their Kippenheim neighbors and relatives. Their registration numbers were 22,811 and 22,812.[48] The way the line was moving, they could expect to be summoned for an interview sometime in 1941.

Jews remained wary of the Stuttgart consulate, where the lines were long and the atmosphere unwelcoming. Consul General Honaker had fired six of his German clerks as a result of the bribery scandal. The visiting American students he hired to replace the Germans were eager to help, but knew little about visa regulations and administration. Suspicious by nature, Honaker stationed the students in "strategic places" around the office, such as the file room, adding to the general overcrowding. From his perspective, every link in the visa chain offered an opportunity for bribery. He even mistrusted his American consular staff. His experienced deputy, Herve L'Heureux, complained that a student was assigned to "spy upon him."[49]

Honaker spent much of his time writing lengthy memoranda in quadruplicate to Washington justifying his actions. One such missive, which continued for twenty-two pages with multiple attachments, exhausted the patience of his superiors. "No wonder Stuttgart is in hot water if they write such appallingly long despatches," a State Department official scrawled across the top.[50] Honaker had listed 151,939 "incoming communications" to the consulate in 1938 and 122,780 "outgoing communications," a fivefold increase from the previous year.

An American woman who visited the consulate in January 1939 criticized "the arrogant and almost sadistic way" in which some of the staff administered the required medical tests. "The physical examination is simply nerve wracking," reported Erna Albersheim, a New Yorker married to a German Jew. "As the Jews are so terribly intimidated, they dare not complain. The oculist has such a reputation that she is feared by all. I am quite sure that it would have been less difficult for her to ask my daughter to remove her glasses instead of jerking them off herself."

Much of the problem, Albersheim believed, stemmed from disorganization. Nobody seemed to know in advance when the consulate would begin receiving visitors or when they would be examined. Albersheim acknowledged that the consuls were desperately "overworked." Some clerks showed the "utmost patience" in attempting to answer questions. But overall, she concluded, "Jews fear Stuttgart [i.e., the consulate] more than they do the German police. A sad state of affairs."[51]

The consulate was now processing 860 visas a month, down from as many as 1,400 the previous summer. Erich Sonnemann, the young man who was turned down for a visa at the time of Kristallnacht, was finally approved in February after his hernia was removed. The chaos was sorted out, little by little. A Foreign Service inspector who visited the consulate in March reported that desks previously arranged "indiscriminately" had been turned around to face in a single direction. The revamped visa section, he noted with approval, was designed to function like "a belt line, as in mass production in industry. Once the belt is in movement, there is to be under no circumstances a halt."[52]

The larger problem was that there were simply not enough visas available to satisfy the overwhelming demand. By early 1939, half the Jews in the Third Reich had applied for an American visa. In Stuttgart, approximately ten thousand visas were available under the annual German quota for distribution to 100,000 applicants. More than half the applicants were typically rejected at the initial screening stage because of the lack of suitable affidavits or other problems with their documentation. The waiting time for an interview with the American consul for the remaining "qualified" applicants was around three years.[53]

At the same time, the Nazis were stepping up their pressure on Jews to leave. A February 25 Associated Press dispatch reported that the authorities had begun "a new, intensive drive to make Germany free of Jews." The Jewish community in Berlin was instructed to produce daily emigration lists of a hundred Jews from the German capital alone. If a Jew named on the list did not leave within two weeks, "dire consequences would follow."[54] The nature of the "consequences" did not have to be spelled out to people who had already experienced concentration camps like Dachau and Sachsenhausen.

And then, suddenly, a new possibility opened up. As usual, it initially took the form of a whispered rumor that spread rapidly through the visa lines and the bars and cafés around the foreign consulates. The director general of the Cuban immigration office, a man named Manuel Benítez González, was said to be selling tourist landing permits, no questions asked, for $160.[55] The permits did not specify how long the holder would be allowed to stay in Cuba, but at least they promised an exit from the Nazi nightmare.

FIVE

Flight

O NE DAY, in the middle of March 1939, Max Valfer arrived back home with a big smile on his face. He had just been to the Post Office to pick up his mail, normally an ordeal due to the hostility of the postmaster–Nazi spy, Herr Link. But this time, he had excellent news to bring back to his family. It had come in the form of a letter from his youngest daughter, Ruth, who had left for New York two years previously.

"Ruth is engaged!" shouted Max. His oldest son, Karl, later reported to Ruth that he had "just bathed and was still dripping when I received a whole heap of wet kisses from Papa."[1] Ruth's future husband was a Jewish boy from Laupheim in the Black Forest who had arrived in Manhattan around the same time as Ruth. Rudy Bergman was an aspiring comedy writer with a sharp, irreverent wit. His younger sister Gretel had achieved notoriety as a world-class high jumper excluded from the German team in the 1936 Berlin Olympics because of her Jewish origins. (She would later joke that she was Germany's "great Jewish hope" at a time when it was commonplace to see signs in German shops reading NO DOGS OR JEWS ALLOWED.)[2] Although Rudy lacked his sister's athletic prowess, he was tall, good-looking, and extrovert. All in all, he seemed an excellent choice.

Even better news followed six days later, when Max and Fanny received a letter from their youngest son, Erich. He had arrived in Palestine, surviving a traumatic two-month sea voyage that brought him face-to-face with death several times. After the shattering experiences of the last few months, the entire Valfer family finally felt that "we are born under quite a lucky star." Israel had listened to Fanny's prayers.

The trip from Romania to Palestine via the Black Sea, the Bosporus, and the Aegean would normally have taken five or six days. Erich had left Switzerland in the middle of December, and traveled by air to Brno in Czechoslovakia. There he had linked up with the party of Czech Jews belonging to a Revisionist Zionist youth movement known as Betar that dreamed of re-creating the ancient Jewish state of Israel. The Revisionists had taken the lead in promoting illegal immigration to Palestine, violating the strict quotas established by the British. Erich and his friends traveled by rail to Constanța on the Black Sea. Jewish villagers greeted them along the way with shouts of "Shalom, Shalom" and gifts of food pushed through the bars of the train windows.[3] After various delays, they finally boarded the *Katina* on January 18.

The ancient tub was more like a river barge than a proper seagoing vessel. The six hundred or so illegal immigrants were packed belowdecks on straw mats in three-tier wooden bunks. Since there were few toilets on board, most passengers had to relieve themselves over the side of the ship, hanging on to a rope in high winds. After passing through the Bosporus, they encountered violent storms in the Mediterranean, "making us seasick with no room to be seasick."[4] Food and water were in desperately short supply, forcing the captain to place the emaciated passengers on starvation rations.

Royal Air Force planes circled the *Katina* as she approached Palestine. The captain managed to put some of his passengers ashore by transferring them to a smaller vessel. The British disrupted the landing operation as the refugees were being ferried ashore in lifeboats, arresting seventeen of them.[5] The *Katina* was forced to retreat to Cyprus, where she was repainted in a different color.[6] The lightly armed Betar guards confiscated valuables from the passengers to pay for the necessary supplies. In the meantime, the poor sanitary conditions resulted in an outbreak of meningitis, a swelling of the membranes of the brain and spinal cord. Passengers were dying from the disease, which could easily turn into an epidemic. The ship doctor had no medicine to give them.

After almost eight weeks at sea, the *Katina* received an SOS from another boat crammed with refugees. A fire had broken out on board. The *Katina* picked up five hundred more illegals from the *Chepo* as she was sinking. The *Chepo* survivors were Polish Jews from a different Zionist faction, less disciplined than the Betar group. Shocked by the conditions on board the *Katina,* they demanded to be taken back to Europe.[7] The Betar commander, a strong-willed Latvian physician named Zelig Paul, was obliged to use an "iron fist" to put down the mutiny. He was supported by his Betar trainees in their berets and scruffy uniforms. Paul now understood that he had to land the illegal immigrants on the coast of Palestine "as fast as possible, under any circumstances, by any means."[8]

Paul was able to contact a Revisionist group on shore by flashing prearranged signals by torch. The final landings took place over two successive nights. A storm was raging and the seas were very rough, which made the operation more difficult but caught the British by surprise. On the first night, Revisionist volunteers carried women and children to the beach in their arms. The next night, the remaining men waded ashore in water rising up to their necks. Erich arrived in the Holy Land with no belongings at all, except for a water-soaked blanket wrapped around his shoulders. He made a note of his illegal immigration: March 21, 1939, three months after he left Switzerland on the first stage of his journey.[9]

While Erich Valfer was at sea, Europe had moved ever closer to war. After annexing the Sudetenland, Germany had marched into what was left of the Czech lands on March 15. Shaken by the violation of the promises made by Hitler at Munich, Britain and France pledged to support Poland militarily if she, too, was attacked. The takeover of the Czech provinces of Bohemia and Moravia added another 118,000 Jews to the pool of people seeking asylum in other countries.

The Nazis pressured German Jews to take whatever exit route was available to them and quietly encouraged the trafficking in visas for Latin American countries. The Gestapo sent a delegation of terrified Jewish leaders to London to plead for a big increase in immigration quotas. If nothing was done, the Jewish leaders warned, "the German authorities would return to the shock tactics which were so successful in ridding Germany of Jews in the past."[10] Back home, Jews were picked off the street at random and given a choice: get out of Germany or go to a concentration camp.

Faced with such dire threats, Freya Valfer and her husband, Ludwig, decided to go to Cuba with their four-year-old daughter, Sonja. As Ludwig explained in a letter to his sister-in-law Ruth at the end of March, "Things are very uncertain with England. It seems that there are harsher regulations over there. Life is very expensive."[11] Some of Ludwig's relatives had already succeeded in entering Cuba with visitor passes. They would make the necessary arrangements. A few weeks later, Ludwig and Freya received a typewritten letter from the Cuban Department of Immigration. It was not exactly a visa, but bore a large rubber stamp and was personally signed by the director general, Manuel Benítez González. The letter instructed immigration officials to allow the bearers into Cuba "for such time as the laws of this republic allow" for the purpose of onward travel to the United States.[12]

Encouraged by their relatives who were already in Cuba, two dozen Jews from Ludwig's hometown of Malsch booked passage to Havana on the MS *St. Louis*. The seventeen-thousand-ton ship was the pride of the Hamburg America Line, a luxurious vessel with seven passenger decks, ballrooms decorated with glittering chandeliers, wide staircases, and a swimming pool. It was hard to imagine a greater contrast with the decrepit *Katina* that had transported Freya's younger brother Erich to Palestine. Knowing that their money would otherwise be confiscated, Freya and Ludwig purchased first-class tickets for themselves and Sonja, at a cost of 800 reichsmarks per adult. To guard against the possibility of being refused entry to Cuba, they were also required to put down a deposit of 230 reichsmarks for the return journey. Since the shipping company was German-owned, they were able to pay for the tickets in German currency they had not yet been forced to surrender.

Before boarding the *St. Louis* at Hamburg, Freya made a final visit back to the Black Forest to see her parents. Ludwig had arranged for Max and Fanny to also receive Cuban landing permits, paid for by their American relatives. Fanny was desperate to follow her other children

Ludwig and Freya Maier board the St. Louis, *May 1939*

to America, or wherever else they ended up. She was already missing them terribly. Once her children had all left Germany, there would be no reason to remain in Kippenheim. "In every case, it was the mother who decided it was time to leave," noted her niece Pia. "The men were often resistant. The sense of protecting the family was burned into the women."[13]

In the end, Max and Fanny agreed to travel to Havana on the next available ship. They would try to come with Fanny's younger brother Siegfried, who had already purchased a ticket. Fanny looked forward to being reunited with her daughter and granddaughter very soon. The memory of Oma (Grandma) Fanny standing in the middle of the street in Kippenheim, waving not farewell but *auf Wiedersehen,* "until we see each other again," would remain with Freya for many years.[14]

Freya and Ludwig boarded the *St. Louis* on Saturday, May 13, with around nine hundred other passengers. A dockside photograph caught the smartly dressed couple striding up the gangway behind Ludwig's Aunt Berta. Freya has a big smile on her face. Her hat is cocked jauntily to the side. Not visible in the picture, because she was too small and therefore hidden by the gangway, is their daughter, Sonja. Both sides of Ludwig's extended Malsch family were represented on the *St. Louis*, including grandparents, uncles, aunts, cousins, and in-laws.

Prior to their departure, the Hamburg America Line had been notified of a new decree issued by the Cuban president, Federico Laredo Brú. Presidential Decree No. 937 stipulated that non-U.S. aliens wishing to travel to Cuba would need a visa authorized by the secretaries of state and labor. Obtaining the visas would require payment of an additional 500-peso bond, roughly equivalent to $500. Not to worry, insisted Immigration Director General Benítez. Visitor permits issued by his office prior to the publication of the decree on May 7 would continue to be honored. The decree would not be retroactive.[15]

For the first time in many months, Freya and Ludwig felt they could relax amid the luxury that enveloped them. Even though the *St. Louis* was a German ship, with a largely German crew, the atmosphere on board was unlike anything in their recent experience. The captain, Gustav Schröder, did all he could to make his Jewish passengers comfortable. He arranged for Orthodox services in the first- and tourist-class dining rooms without the mandatory portrait of Adolf Hitler staring down at the worshippers. The stewards, who included Nazi Party members, were polite and attentive toward people they had been taught to regard as "subhumans"—*Untermenschen*—back in Germany. Onboard shops were stocked with items impossible to acquire back home. The food, both kosher and non-kosher, was excellent and plentiful.

An old sea salt who had survived several run-ins with the Gestapo, Captain Schröder made sure that his passengers were well entertained. A busy ship was a happy ship. One evening, the crew decorated the social hall for a Bavarian beer festival. The ship's band played Bavarian folk songs, Tyrol yodeling music, and Viennese waltzes. People who had been hounded out of Germany just a few days earlier were suddenly nostalgic for the Fatherland. "If my old *lederhosen* had not been packed into the bottom of my luggage, I would have been tempted to wear them," seventeen-year-old Fritz Buff noted in his diary. "It was close to midnight when the band stopped playing. By then, the whirling of the waltzes had us on the edge of giddiness." A few nights later, passengers were invited to a Rhineland winegrowers' festival. "We danced, we drank wine, to excess I might add, and we did not go to sleep until the early hours of the morning," wrote Buff.[16]

Freya and Ludwig joined in the fun, leaving their four-year-old in the care of aunts and grandmothers. One evening, Freya attended a formal ball in a purple silk velvet gown that she kept for special occasions. Parties were also organized for the children, with noisemakers, streamers, and funny hats. For the first time in her life, Sonja tasted a banana and a pineapple. Freya told her daughter that the dark-skinned staff aboard the *St. Louis* were "good people—they are not Hitlers."[17] This comforted the little girl, who was haunted by memories of the Nazis barging into their home on Kristallnacht, smashing glasses and crockery, and ripping open the beautiful down quilts in her parents' bedroom. The most terrifying moment was seeing a photo of her father that had been torn into tiny pieces by the Nazi thugs. Freya had held the crying child in her arms, attempting to reassure her that Ludwig was still alive.

As the *St. Louis* entered tropical waters near Cuba, the death of an elderly passenger cast a pall over the upbeat mood. The Cuban government refused permission for the dead man to be buried in Cuba, so he was buried at sea. The ship's engines were shut down, crew members lined the deck for a final salute, and the body was slowly lowered into the ocean. The captain presented the widow with a map showing the location of her husband's final resting place. There was only one break with the usual maritime tradition: the body was draped not in the swastika flag of Germany but in the colors of the Hamburg America Line. Tragedy struck again a few hours later when a crew member committed suicide by jumping overboard in the darkness. After a fruitless search, the ship resumed course for Havana.

The *St. Louis* steamed into Havana at dawn on Saturday, May 27, two weeks after leaving Hamburg. The twin-funneled ship sailed grandly past the upscale villas of Vedado and the gleaming hotels along the Malecón, the famous seafront. The passengers had been instructed to leave their packed suitcases outside their cabins for immediate disembarkation. Crowded over the railings, they could see the palm-tree-lined streets of Havana coming to life in the early morning with cars and pedestrians. Many of the people ashore were waving. The big ship attracted a flotilla of small boats packed with relatives and loved ones of the new arrivals. They exchanged excited greetings.

As the ship entered the harbor, Freya and Ludwig lined up with other passengers outside the telegraph office to send a cable to Max and Fanny in Kippenheim. GUT GELANDET, they wrote, a little prematurely. LANDED SAFELY.[18] They also joined the lines for the required medical exam and inspection of boarding passes. Everybody expected to be off the ship by noon.

And then, mysteriously, the landing process came to a halt. Rather than docking at the berth reserved for the Hamburg America Line, the *St. Louis* remained anchored in the middle of the harbor. At first, passengers blamed the delay on a *"mañana* mentality which we believed was prevalent in tropical environments."[19] The comforting shipboard routines continued as normal. A blast on the horn at noon summoned the travelers to lunch. Another blast at 3:30 p.m. invited them to tea. At six p.m., they were called to dinner. "With every sounding of the horn, we expected it to be our last sitting on the ship," Buff recorded. "Our optimism was premature."

The ringing of the ship's bells and blasting of the horn became ever more monotonous. One *mañana* turned inexorably into another.

The *St. Louis* had sailed into a classic Latin American stew of wealth, power, and corruption incomprehensible to most outsiders. Stirring the pot was a motley crew of Nazi zealots, venal officials, rival politicians, cutthroat lawyers, and a Cuban strongman named Fulgencio Batista.

Although Cuba had a civilian president, real power lay with Colonel Batista as head of the armed forces. An impoverished laborer from eastern Cuba, Batista had led a "Revolt of the Sergeants" in 1933 against the Spanish-dominated elite that had ruled the island for centuries. U.S. officials were initially wary of the mixed-race Cuban, but soon embraced him as a man with whom they could do business. Always immaculately dressed, often in polished riding boots and spurs, Batista was naturally charming and affable. On a trip to Washington in November 1938, he was greeted with full military honors and granted a personal meeting with the president. Hoping to curry favor with FDR, the smiling strongman announced that Cuba would cooperate with the United States by providing a place of refuge for German Jews.[20] Initially at least, he made good on his promise. Cuba began admitting Jewish refugees at a rate of five hundred per month. By May 1939, the Jewish population of Cuba had doubled to more than five thousand.

Humanitarianism was far from Batista's only motive in admitting Jewish refugees to Cuba. Selling landing permits had become a very profitable business for his cronies, particularly Benítez. The immigration director was believed to have amassed a fortune estimated by U.S. officials at between $500,000 and $1 million, derived in large part from bribes and payments for the landing permits. Benítez had set up his own visa office alongside the office of the Hamburg America Line on the Havana seafront. The 160 Cuban pesos (roughly $160) that he charged for each typewritten "landing permit" was "an unofficial fee" that presumably went directly to Benítez.[21] A Jewish relief worker in Havana noted that the Cuban president and his aides were "getting very tired of having Col. Benítez get all the graft."[22]

The president, Laredo Brú, had long been considered a mere puppet of Batista. When the military chief returned from his visit to the United States, the president had declared a "national holiday" and personally led the welcoming celebrations. In recent weeks, however, he had been displaying some signs of independence. He was also under political pressure to crack down on Jewish refugees. The brazenness of the immigration director's greed had fired up Fascist sympathizers in Havana who were mounting a noisy press campaign against the "Jewish invasion." The mass-circulation *Alerta* conjured up lurid images of Cubans being subjected to "slavery by an alien race" that seemed straight out of Goebbels's playbook. On May 26—the day before the *St. Louis* arrived in Havana—*Alerta* issued a call to arms:

"OUT WITH THE JEWS!"

Twelve hundred Jewish families will arrive tomorrow in Havana. These false "tourists" will find bread and shelter in Cuba while thousands of native families have not even a crust nor a roof in the vilest slum.[23]

According to the American consul in Havana, the antisemitism was fanned by the arrival of fourteen Nazi agents, themselves disguised as refugees. The Nazis were spending freely. The consul reported that Jewish activists were raising funds "to persuade the newspapers in question to modify their attitude."[24] A planned counter-propaganda campaign would stress the benefits that Cuba derived from the Jewish refugee colony. So far, however, only the English-language newspaper *The Havana Post* had spoken out in defense of the refugees.

News of the plight of the *St. Louis* passengers quickly reached Jewish humanitarian organizations in New York, including the American Jewish Joint Distribution Committee. Widely known as "the Joint," the committee had played no role in arranging the voyage of the *St. Louis.* Nevertheless, Joint officials felt a responsibility to assist the passengers. On May 29, they dispatched a two-person team to Havana to help resolve the crisis. They assigned a social worker, Cecilia Razovsky, to work with the passengers and Jewish groups in Havana. Negotiations with Cuban officials were entrusted to a New York attorney named Lawrence Berenson, a former head of the Cuban-American Chamber of Commerce. Berenson was known to be on friendly terms with Batista and other prominent Cubans. Joint officials were convinced that he would be able to use his Cuban connections to find a solution to the crisis.

On their arrival in Havana, Berenson and Razovsky checked in to the historic Sevilla-Biltmore hotel, around the corner from the presidential palace. Berenson was disappointed to learn that he could not meet with his old friend Batista. The strongman was holed up in his military barracks at Camp Columbia, outside the city, with what was described as "a bad attack of the grippe."[25] The colonel could on no account be disturbed. Whether Batista was really ill, or simply wanted to distance himself from the whole affair, was unclear at the time. Many years later, Batista would tell Berenson that he was unable to intervene in the case for the simple reason that the landing permits were "invalid" and contravened Cuban law.[26] Berenson understood he had to deal directly with the suddenly not-so-figurehead president, Laredo Brú.

The president was also hard to reach, and was emitting confusing signals. First he sent word that the *St. Louis* was *"un caso cerrado"*—"a closed case."[27] Both Benítez and the Hamburg America Line needed to be taught a lesson. They had trafficked in illegal landing permits. Then he indicated, through a leak to the newspapers, that a "humanitarian" solution might be possible. Before any negotiations could begin, however, the *St. Louis* would have to withdraw from Cuban waters. The departure of the ship was set for June 1, and then pushed back to June 2.

Originally, there had been 937 passengers on board the *St. Louis*. Twenty-two passengers with the proper papers were allowed to disembark. One refugee had died at sea of natural causes. Another, a former Buchenwald inmate named Max Loewe, had jumped into Havana harbor after slashing his wrists in a suicide attempt. He was taken to the hospital, where he slowly recovered. His wife and children were not permitted to join him. That left 913 men, women, and children on board, none of whom had valid Cuban visas. Just as the *St. Louis* was about to sail, a further six passengers were escorted off the boat, causing a "panic" among the remaining refugees.[28] Nobody understood why these particular passengers were being accorded privileged treatment.

The mystery began to clear up after two Miami attorneys arrived in Havana by charter aircraft. They represented the millionaire businessman Walter Annenberg, a relative of the passengers permitted to disembark. One of the lawyers, James M. Carson, was particularly obnoxious. Drinking one highball after another, he boasted about his connections to the Cuban and American governments. The more he drank, the more antisemitic he became. He told Cecilia Razovsky that she and Berenson had no idea how to handle Cubans because of their "Jew psychology." Only someone with "American psychology," such as Carson himself, knew how to deal with them. He splurged on long-distance calls to Miami, saying "what do I care, Annenberg is paying for it."[29] He then pursued Razovsky to her hotel, where he ordered more drinks that he refused to pay for. He never did divulge how he got Annenberg's relatives off the ship, but the implication was that a significant amount of money had changed hands.

Razovsky eventually got rid of the insufferable Carson by introducing him to one of the many American reporters who had arrived in Havana to cover the *St. Louis* story. It was fast becoming a major international incident. The Associated Press reported on June 1 that Captain Schröder feared a "mutiny" or even a "collective suicide pact" among the passengers, who were terrified that they would be sent back to Nazi Germany. Weeping passengers lined the railings, calling out to relatives and friends assembled below on a flotilla of small boats. The following day, June 2, *The New York Times* reported that the *St. Louis* left Havana harbor at 11:30 a.m., escorted by the Cuban navy. The paper noted that attempts to reach Batista "to interest him in the plight of the *St. Louis* passengers have failed so far."[30]

As the *St. Louis* steamed slowly northeast toward Miami, Berenson opened his negotiations with the Cuban authorities. He started the bidding low, at $50,000, plus assurances that the Joint would ensure that the refugees did not become public charges. He quickly raised his offer to $150,000. The Cuban government repeated its demand of a $500 bond for each adult refugee. This sum was in addition to the $150,000 already offered by the Joint but was theoretically repayable if the refugees left Cuba. Back in New York, a Joint official complained that the organization was being "virtually blackmailed into ransoming one boatload of refugees," which would likely lead to similar ransom demands in the future.[31] Adding to the financial burden were a further 257 passengers aboard two smaller ships, the *Orduña* and the *Flandre*, who would be covered by any agreement reached with the Cuban government. Altogether, the Joint was being asked to put up nearly $600,000, the equivalent of over $10 million in 2019.

Laredo Brú set a deadline of noon on Tuesday, June 6, for reaching an agreement. Despite their concerns about ransom, Joint officials were willing to pay whatever was necessary. Berenson, however, was convinced he could get a better deal by holding out a little longer. He felt he had an ace up his sleeve: the Dominican Republic had offered to accept all the refugees for a landing fee of $500 per person. He told his nervous superiors in New York that he could save them "a considerable amount of money" if they would only "keep out of it" and allow him to conduct the negotiations.[32]

The departure of the *St. Louis* from Havana on Friday, June 2, was "heart shattering" for Freya and Ludwig Maier. They had been able to exchange greetings with Ludwig's relatives, the Löbs, who had arrived in Cuba on an earlier ship. The Löbs were on one of the small boats bobbing up and down in the harbor, before being chased away by the Cuban police. They had helped their friends and relatives purchase the landing permits signed by Benítez that now turned out to be useless.

Ever since arriving in Havana on May 27, Freya had been intrigued by the sights and sounds of Cuba. Havana seemed so full of life, so "large and beautiful." As the ship pulled out of the harbor, Freya saw cars, buses, and bicycles traveling along the palm-lined avenues. She gazed at the scene "until all we could see was sea and sky," but it no longer held any interest for her. The Maier family returned to their cabin around noon to get some sleep. "We had all had enough for one day," Freya reported to her parents in Kippenheim. She was greeted by a large matza and apple cake, a gift from one of Ludwig's aunts. "Just like home," Sonja shrieked delightedly.[33]

Over the next four days, the *St. Louis* meandered, seemingly aimlessly, between Cuba and Florida. On occasion, she seemed to go around in circles. The passengers assumed that the ship's movements were somehow connected with the ongoing negotiations in Havana about their fate. Their spirits rose whenever the ship headed back toward Cuba; they sank whenever she appeared headed for Europe. The changes in direction were interspersed with rumors about new places of refuge or, most alarmingly, a return to Hamburg. "The effect of this upon our nervous systems was as if an exploding bomb had been dropped," Fritz Buff noted in his diary. "This was just too much to bear. Any port other than Hamburg could be tolerated. The mere mention of the word brings back recollections. The resolve of most of the people aboard is to die rather than ever to see Hamburg again."[34]

On Saturday, Freya and Ludwig attended a Sabbath service in the ship's ballroom, which was "very comforting because the service is the same as at home." The following day, they sailed southward down the coast of Florida, anchoring for two hours some three miles off Miami Beach.[35] "We saw tall white buildings, hotels. Many ships and boats passed by us. We hardly believed that we could only sail by it all," Freya told her parents. Like most of the other passengers, the Maier family had registration numbers that would allow them to be admitted to the United States in one or two years. They could not understand why an exception could not be made that would allow them to reach "the land of our dreams" a little earlier.

As the *St. Louis* maneuvered between Fort Lauderdale and Key West, she was accompanied by a U.S. Coast Guard patrol boat as well as two Coast Guard planes. "We assumed that they had been dispatched to monitor our course, and prevent anyone from attempting to swim ashore," wrote Buff. "It was very hard to accept the disinterest of the American government."[36]

Preventing a mass suicide was very much on the mind of Captain Schröder. He organized some of the male passengers, including Ludwig, into a suicide watch.[37] He also posted a series of reassuring bulletins emphasizing the Joint's efforts to persuade foreign governments to accept the refugees. "Don't forget that the Joint has promised that you will land in a place outside Germany," he informed the passengers on June 4. "Please keep calm."[38] If the Cuba option failed, some other solution would be found. The captain established a passenger committee to represent the refugees and keep them up to date on the twists and turns in the negotiations.

Hopes soared on the morning of Tuesday, June 6, when the captain steered the ship back in the direction of Havana. He told the passengers that the Cuban government had agreed to intern them on the Isle of Pines. The refugees were "happy beyond words," even though they had never heard of the island, which lay off Cuba's southwestern coast. "We hugged and kissed each other. We rushed to the telegraph office to inform our dear ones around the world of the fortunate turn of events."[39]

The euphoria did not last long. Within hours, news arrived that the negotiations had failed. The Joint representatives in Havana had not met the noon deadline set by the Cuban president for agreeing to his demands. Laredo Brú insisted that there would be no more haggling. On the evening of June 6, the big ship changed course once again, this time for Hamburg.[40] That evening, the passengers' representatives sent a radiogram in German addressed to "President Roosevelt, Washington."

REPEATING URGENT DISTRESS CALL FROM THE PASSENGERS OF THE ST. LOUIS PLEASE HELP HERR PRESIDENT THE 900 PASSENGERS INCLUDING 400 WOMEN AND CHILDREN THE PASSENGERS.[41]

As the news flashed around the world that the *St. Louis* was headed back toward Germany, Freya received a two-word telegram from her sister Ruth in New York. SEID STARK, it read. BE STRONG.[42]

President Roosevelt was resting at Hyde Park, his childhood home in upstate New York, when news of the *St. Louis* incident first broke. He returned to the White House on May 31 with a bad head cold that caused him to cancel many of his appointments. Although the saga of the "wandering Jews" had grabbed the attention of the news media, it ranked low on the presidential agenda. Journalists did not bother to raise the subject with FDR at his regular press conferences.

"Anything new on the foreign situation?" a reporter had asked the president at the end of a May 30 briefing in Hyde Park that was devoted entirely to domestic matters.

"No, not a thing," FDR had replied cheerily.

At the next press conference, on June 6, the day the *St. Louis* turned back toward Europe, the discussion was dominated by the forthcoming visit of the king and queen of England. A reporter noted that American "wine people" were getting "quite agitated" about rumors that the president planned to serve imported wines to their majesties. Roosevelt sidestepped the question with his usual skill, saying he would not be "advertising any particular brands."[43] Again there was no mention of the refugee ship.

FDR had told the State Department not to interfere in the negotiations between the Cuban government and Jewish organizations over the *St. Louis*. He believed that the refugee burden had to be shared among all civilized countries. By filling the German immigration quota, his administration was already doing more than any other government to help the refugees. By law, 27,370 victims of Nazi tyranny could be admitted to the United States during the current quota year ending in June. That number could not be changed without the authorization of Congress. If the *St. Louis* passengers were allowed to jump the line, people still in Germany would have to wait even longer. If the Joint could persuade Cuba or some other country to accept the refugees gazing longingly at the Miami skyline, that would be a much better solution.

In refusing to get involved with the negotiations, Roosevelt was also guided by his "Good Neighbor Policy" toward Latin America that he had proclaimed in his first inaugural address. He had pulled U.S. Marines out of Nicaragua and Haiti, negotiated trade deals with Mexico, and no longer treated Cuba as an American colony. As FDR saw it, the policy of noninterference had been a great success. A source of trouble for decades, the region had become a bulwark for American foreign policy, at a time when Nazi Germany was seeking to win friends in the Western Hemisphere. Acting on behalf of the White House, the State Department instructed the American embassy in Cuba to treat the *St. Louis* negotiations as entirely "an internal matter of Cuba."[44]

As the *St. Louis* steamed up and down the Florida coast, Joint officials continued to hope for a successful outcome. They were still getting positive signals from their man in Havana, Lawrence Berenson. The Cuban ambassador in Washington assured the State Department that a solution would probably be found. The main problem was "financing."[45] In the last resort, there was always the offer from the Dominican Republic, even though it smacked of financial extortion on a religious basis. Joint officials noted that the $500 landing fee applied only to "Jews."[46]

The Roosevelt administration official who showed the most concern for the *St. Louis* passengers was Treasury Secretary Henry Morgenthau. The sole Jew in the cabinet served as the conduit between Joint officials in New York and Secretary of State Cordell Hull. When it seemed as if the Havana negotiations were about to break down on June 5, he called Hull to discuss "this terrible tragedy." Behind the scenes, Hull had explored the possibility of issuing the passengers tourist visas for the U.S. Virgin Islands.[47] This seemed like a viable option, as the legislative assembly of the islands had adopted a resolution in the wake of Kristallnacht offering "a place of safety for refugee peoples."[48] But State Department officials advised that such a step would run afoul of U.S. immigration law, and the idea was dropped.

Hull told Morgenthau that tourist visas could only be issued in cases where the applicants had "a definite home ... to return to." By definition, this did not apply to refugees.

Morgenthau could not conceal his disappointment.

"The Virgin Islands thing is out?"

"That's what my fellows tell me."[49]

As treasury secretary, Morgenthau had responsibility for the U.S. Coast Guard, which was a branch of his department. After hearing from the Joint on June 6 that they had lost track of the *St. Louis,* he called the Coast Guard to establish her location. The Coast Guard commander reported his men had stopped following the ship "somewhere down toward Key West," when she turned out to sea. Morgenthau instructed the Coast Guard to make another search. Even though the *St. Louis* had left American waters, the treasury secretary wanted to find out what had happened to her.

"I want you to treat it confidentially, see, so that nothing gets out that I'm interested.... Handle it so there's no comeback on it."

"All right sir."

"Thank you. I want to locate it."

"All right sir. We'll do all we can."[50]

News of Cuba's decision not to admit the refugees caused a change of approach by both the Joint and President Roosevelt. On June 7, the Joint announced that it had authorized the Chase National Bank to transfer the funds demanded by the Cuban government. After earlier instructing the American ambassador in Havana not to get involved, FDR now urged the State Department to do whatever it could to facilitate the financial transaction. Under Secretary of State Sumner Welles ordered the ambassador to seek the earliest possible meeting with President Laredo Brú and "stress the humanitarian considerations" of the case.[51]

It was too late. The normally obliging Laredo Brú could not be persuaded to change his mind yet again.

FDR'S hands-off approach toward the *St. Louis* was similar to the position he had taken on the child refugee bill, which had run into mounting opposition in Congress. He was acutely aware of the anti-immigrant sentiment in the country. Public opinion polls consistently reported that four out of five Americans were opposed to any expansion of immigration quotas. Less than one in ten favored an increase in the quota or exemptions for refugees. Four out of ten Americans informed pollsters that "Jews have too much power in the United States."[52] The president rejected a June 2 plea from a liberal New York congresswoman, Caroline O'Day, to express his views on the children's bill. "File, no action," he ordered his aides.[53]

As an astute analyst of public opinion, Roosevelt could tell which way the political winds were blowing. The previous day, June 1, the House Immigration Committee had heard testimony from various "patriotic societies" slamming the proposal to admit twenty thousand refugee children to the United States over two years. "Charity begins at home," insisted the widow of a Great War veteran. "In a world crisis these aliens are potential enemies of our children." Another witness noted that the United States had received "more refugees for permanent residence than all of the other countries put together."[54] This was true only for the most recent period. Prior to 1937, considerably more Jewish immigrants had been admitted to Palestine than the United States. (See chart on page 317.)[55]

As the *St. Louis* headed back to Europe on June 6, the House of Representatives was considering legislation to deport all "undesirable aliens."[56] The spokesman for the anti-immigration forces, Senator Robert Reynolds of North Carolina, denounced the child refugee initiative in a nationwide broadcast. His reasoning was simple to the point of being simplistic. The admission of the refugee children would mean "20,000 more boys and girls in the United States looking for jobs." Reynolds ended his talk with a ringing call to put "Our Citizens First."

Let's keep America for our boys and girls.
Let's give American jobs to American citizens.
Let's empty our prisons of alien criminals and send them back to
    their native lands.
Let's save America for Americans.[57]

Rather than block the Wagner-Rogers child refugee bill outright, opponents resorted to a parliamentary maneuver to circumvent it. On May 30, they introduced an amendment in the Senate that would give preference to child refugees, but count their visas against the overall

German quota.[58] For every unaccompanied minor allowed into the country, there would be one less place available for an adult who had already been waiting a long time for his visa. There would be no expansion in the overall refugee flow.

For Senator Wagner, the mutilated version of his bill was worse than no bill at all. On June 30, he announced that the changes were unacceptable and withdrew his proposal entirely. It was a bitter defeat for the progressives. They had earlier believed that the precedent set by the Kindertransport movement in Britain would stir "the humane instincts in all of us" and result in "the first relaxation of our immigration laws since 1924."[59] They had underestimated the strength of anti-immigrant feeling both in Congress and throughout the country.

The hostility to refugees went far beyond the anti-immigrant lobby that had mobilized around Senator Reynolds. A prominent Republican, William Castle Jr., even warned of anti-Jewish riots if the Wagner-Rogers bill was passed. Castle, who had served as under secretary of state during the Hoover administration, said he would "prefer to let in 20,000 old Jews who would not multiply" than 20,000 children.[60] FDR's sharp-tongued cousin, Laura Delano, who was married to Immigration Commissioner James Houghteling, expressed similar misgivings. She told a friend that she was worried that the "20,000 charming children would all too soon grow up into 20,000 ugly adults."[61]

The president did not want to waste his authority on a lost cause at a time when he was preparing for yet another battle with the isolationists over the Neutrality Acts.[62] Congress had blocked his earlier attempts to permit arms sales to Britain and France on a cash-and-carry basis. FDR believed that arming the European democracies was the best way to stop Hitler without sending American boys back to Europe. For him, the fight over the Neutrality Acts was much more important than either the children's bill or the destination of the *St. Louis*. His political base, both in Congress and in the country, would be undermined if he took an unpopular stand on the refugee issue.

FDR's handling of the *St. Louis* affair and the child refugee bill did not mean he was unmoved by the persecution of German Jews. He had been the driving force in the creation of the Intergovernmental Committee to coordinate international policy on refugee resettlement following the failed Évian conference of July 1938. He continued his efforts to find a solution to the refugee crisis even as the *St. Louis* was steaming up and down the Florida coast. In a June 8 letter to Myron Taylor, his representative on the Intergovernmental Committee, he conceded that his attempts "to stimulate concrete action by other governments" had met with little success so far. He now pinned his hopes on the creation of an "International Refugee Foundation," to be funded by "private corporations" that would be able to "negotiate more effectively" with Berlin than the ineffectual Intergovernmental Committee.[63] The refugee foundation would be made up of wealthy Jews such as the Rothschilds but also non-Jewish relief organizations.

In devising his new strategy, Roosevelt was influenced in part by the views of Raymond Geist in Berlin. The consul had taken over as America's senior diplomat in Nazi Germany in February following the unexpected death of the chargé d'affaires, Prentiss Gilbert. Geist had warned the State Department repeatedly that Nazi extremists were preparing to "handle the Jewish problem in their own way." He had spelled out what an "internal solution" was likely to mean in a prophetic April 4 letter to his patron, George Messersmith:

It will, of course, consist in placing all the able-bodied Jews in work camps, confiscating the wealth of the entire Jewish population, isolating them, and putting additional pressure on the whole community, and getting rid of as many as they can by force.[64]

In a May 3 cable, Geist urged his superiors to keep a line open to Nazi "moderates" around Göring. Geist believed that talks on an orderly emigration plan, which had been taking place intermittently in London with a Göring advisor named Helmut Wohlthat, were the best available option. They were certainly preferable to the probable alternative. "Otherwise I believe that the Radicals here will demand a free hand to handle the Jewish problems in their own fashion."[65]

The president took Geist's cable seriously. He told Jewish leaders on May 4 that "haste was essential." A State Department official noted that "the president was convinced that the warnings given by our Embassy in Berlin were sound and not exaggerated." Questions about how to raise the necessary funds were less important than saving "actual lives."[66]

Like the earlier Schacht proposal, the Wohlthat plan called on foreign Jews to bear a large portion of the resettlement costs of German Jews. Wohlthat linked the success of the talks to the willingness of foreign Jews to contribute to a proposed $100 million resettlement fund. Jewish leaders refused to commit to the fund as long as there was no guarantee that the Germans would permit Jewish assets to leave Germany. The problem was that neither side trusted the other to keep its side of the bargain.

The impasse came to a head at a meeting in London on June 6, just as the *St. Louis* was returning to Europe. Wohlthat's interlocutors included U.S. and British officials, and Jewish leaders like Paul Baerwald, the chairman of the Joint, and the British banker Lionel de Rothschild. The Jewish officials complained about Nazi concentration camps, antisemitic propaganda, and the confiscation of Jewish property. Wohlthat said that he, too, would speak frankly. He then went around the room asking the Jewish leaders in turn if they were prepared to finance the resettlement fund "either in whole or in part." The answer, to a man, was "no." At this point, the Nazi negotiator walked out.[67]

As was often the case, FDR preferred to think about the refugee crisis in sweeping geopolitical terms rather than concrete human terms. He wanted to solve the problem globally rather than piecemeal. Unlike his wife, Eleanor, he did not want to get personally involved in individual cases, even nine hundred individual cases. In the judgment of one of his biographers, he could "turn empathy on or off at will, as if it were water in a faucet." He was "like a physician who must daily operate in life-and-death situations." The president could not allow himself to feel the pain of others too deeply because that would only "impair his professional performance."[68]

Even though the London negotiations on a large-scale resettlement agreement had temporarily broken down, there still seemed a slim chance of success. Wohlthat insisted he had Hitler's support for an eventual deal that would allow the orderly emigration of German Jews.[69] FDR remained determined to press ahead. U.S. and British officials made a valiant attempt to bring the two sides together. With war becoming ever more likely, they knew that time was running out.

. . .

The mood on board the *St. Louis* had swung wildly between hope and despair over the previous four weeks. On the return journey across the Atlantic, the captain and the passenger committee sought to convince the refugees they would not be sent back to Germany. Slowly, morale began to improve. On June 10, a message arrived from the Joint in New York, saying it was working on "the possibility of admission to other countries, including England."[70] That same day, Freya sat down to write a long letter to her loved ones back in Kippenheim.

"We think there must be some sort of resolution, for we can't just sail here and there on the ocean for weeks on end," Freya wrote her parents. Personally, she was relieved that the negotiations with the Dominican Republic had led nowhere. She blamed the breakdown on the "climate there, which is reported to be unbearable. I was happy because one does not want to go just anywhere." She reported that the ship was "already half way to England." Sailing conditions were good. "The heat didn't bother me at all. On the contrary, it did me quite well."[71]

The telegraph office on board still functioned as normal, allowing the passengers to keep in touch with their friends and relatives. Radiograms arrived from Ludwig's family in London saying they were attempting to arrange a landing permit in England. "Keep head high," they cabled. From Kippenheim came news that Freya's Uncle Siegfried had "not departed" for Cuba as planned. Max and Fanny were also forced to cancel their plans, even though they now had the funds to purchase the landing permits.[72]

Freya was most concerned about the fate of her parents. "You prepared yourselves for Cuba and now what? I feel terribly sorry for you, dear parents, as well as for everyone else." Knowing that she would be unable to mail the letter until they reached a port, Freya kept adding more news at the end. The typewritten missive eventually resembled a diary. As the *St. Louis* neared Europe, she reported that she and Ludwig were attending English lessons. "Sonja goes to kindergarten . . . I take a nap after lunch. Then there is coffee and cake with a concert."

The hopes of the passengers were kept alive by the bulletins posted in the dining halls. On June 13, a telegram from the Joint reported that a solution was imminent. "All problems will be solved," the cable advised.

"Keep your courage." The decisive breakthrough came the following day in the form of a message from Morris Troper, the Joint's European representative.

> FINAL ARRANGEMENTS FOR DISEMBARKATION OF ALL PAS-
> SENGERS COMPLETED. HAPPY TO INFORM YOU GOVERNMENTS
> OF BELGIUM, HOLLAND, FRANCE, AND ENGLAND COOPERATED
> MAGNIFICENTLY WITH AMERICAN JOINT.[73]

"We are as good as disembarked," Freya exulted. "It is moving in a good direction." She noted that most of the passengers had seen Cuba only as a transit point to their final destination, the United States. That evening, the passengers held a big party to celebrate. The entertainment included singers, magicians, and comedians who joked about the delights of a "holiday cruise to Cuba." The passenger committee cabled Troper to thank him for his efforts. "Our gratitude is as immense as the ocean on which we have been floating since May 13."[74]

Troper had been working frantically with U.S. officials to persuade other governments to grant the *St. Louis* passengers a temporary haven, until they could go to America. After Britain agreed to admit several hundred refugees, other countries quickly followed suit. It was eventually decided that Britain would accept 288 refugees, France 224, Belgium 214, and the Netherlands 181. The passengers filled out questionnaires about their family ties and future plans to determine their most appropriate destination. When Troper boarded the *St. Louis* on June 17 shortly before it arrived in Belgium, he was greeted as a hero. Two hundred children lined up on either side of the ship's main hallway to cheer him. The daughter of the passenger committee leader, eleven-year-old Liesl Joseph, stepped forward to thank the Joint "for having saved us from a great misery."[75]

Since Freya and Ludwig already had family in England, they were taken by a smaller ship to Southampton. They were joined by Ludwig's parents. Various other relatives, including several members of the Löb family, remained in Belgium, whose neutrality had been "guaranteed" by Hitler in 1937.

.   .   .

The nineteenth-century Danish philosopher Søren Kierkegaard once observed that history is "understood backwards" but "lived forward." The voyage of the *St. Louis* is a prime example of this phenomenon. The *St. Louis* has come to be viewed as a symbol of international, particularly American, indifference to the tragedy of German Jews. At the time, however, the outcome was hailed as a success, most notably by the refugees themselves. The ultimate fate of the passengers was unknown and unknowable. What was known was that they had escaped from the country that had persecuted them.

"The jubilation was fantastic, indescribable, and spontaneous," wrote Fritz Buff, who also disembarked in Belgium. "Horizons have opened up. We were not forgotten after five weeks at sea, most of the time under severe duress and mental stress." The young man from Bavaria described the result as "a great, internationally coordinated accomplishment." He was particularly appreciative of Captain Schröder, who "managed to minimize the efforts of the known Gestapo plants aboard the ship."[76] After the *St. Louis* docked at Antwerp, *The New York Times* quoted a passenger as saying that "eighty per cent of us would have jumped overboard had the ship put back to Hamburg."[77]

It was left to Nazi officials to comment on the gap between American ideals—as represented by the welcoming arms of the Statue of Liberty—and the reality. The spectacle of the *St. Louis* sailing back across the Atlantic after being turned away from Cuba and America was tailor-made for German propaganda. "We say openly that we do not want the Jews while the democracies keep on claiming that they are willing to receive them—and then leave the guests out in the cold!" gloated the antisemitic journal *Der Weltkampf.* "Aren't we savages better men after all?"[78]

SIX

"Save Our Souls"

L IKE THE VALFERS, the Wachenheimers loved the Wild West adventure stories of Karl May. In good times and bad, Hugo Wachenheimer drew inspiration from May's world of make-believe to stage a family "pow-wow" whenever there was something important to discuss. He played the wise old Indian chief, with Bella as his "squaw." The headstrong Hedy was assigned the role of dutiful daughter.[1]

In the weeks after Hugo returned from Dachau, the family held a pow-wow to talk about leaving Germany. Seated around a pretend campfire, they grappled with the same agonizing choice faced by many Jewish families. Should the family stick together in all circumstances? Or would it be preferable for one of them to go to a foreign country if the opportunity arose—even if it meant leaving the rest of the family behind in the village on the edge of the forest?

They had been trying for a long time to find someone to sponsor their immigration to the United States. Back in 1937, Hugo had written to a distant relative in Chicago to plead their case. A few weeks later, Hedy picked up a letter with a Chicago postmark from their mailbox at the Post Office. She ran back home with the letter in her hands, fantasizing about skyscrapers and big American cars. Hugo employed his self-taught English to translate the letter into German. The relative explained that there was an economic depression in America and he was lucky to be employed. All his money went to supporting himself and his elderly mother. He was afraid to ask his employer for assistance as that might jeopardize his job. He also felt awkward about approaching the Chicago Jewish community. He encouraged the Wachenheimers to be patient. Life would surely get better in Germany.[2]

Hugo had re-registered with the American consulate in Stuttgart in the summer of 1938, but there was a two-year wait for an interview, even supposing that they could find an acceptable sponsor. By the time he held his family pow-wow, in early 1939, the options for escape were dwindling rapidly. The British government was sharply restricting legal immigration to Palestine. The Cuba route was oversubscribed. That left England, which had agreed to accept up to ten thousand unaccompanied Jewish children. Kindertransports were being organized every few days to evacuate as many youngsters as possible by rail and sea from German-controlled territory.

After discussing the matter thoroughly, the Wachenheimers reached a decision. Hedy would travel to England on a Kindertransport. Once there, she would try to help her mother find a job as a servant for a wealthy English family. Hugo would join his wife and daughter as soon as possible, but understood that it could be a long time before he was able to leave Germany. As he wrote to a potential sponsor in London, he was accustomed to "modesty and privation." He had spent "four and a half years in the trenches of the Great War," and had even been a prisoner of war. He was "ready to remain dignified."[3]

Like any fourteen-year-old, Hedy was excited by the thought of going to London, but also nervous. Her parents painted a picture of an exciting life in the big city, full of excursions on the Underground and visits to movie houses. She would be able to go back to school, learn English, and make new friends. It sounded wonderful at first, but then doubts crept in. Some Kippenheim Jews said it was better for families to stick together in difficult times. Hedy heard that the English were constantly drinking tea. She did not like tea. Most important, she hated the thought of being separated from her parents. She particularly looked forward to her weekly walks with her father in the Black Forest, which turned into seminars on growing up.

The weekly strolls all began and ended the same way, with a rousing rendition of a popular nineteenth-century song about a young man leaving home with "a happy heart." Hugo would link arms with Hedy as they belted out the refrain, *"Sing song, ding dong, a youngster sets out into the world."* Every week, Hugo would select a different topic for the walk, often revolving around their hopes for a new life. He expected his daughter to do the necessary reading in advance.[4]

During their final walk, the Sunday before Hedy's departure, Hugo asked his daughter if she had studied the survival techniques of the May bug, as he had requested.

"No," she replied stubbornly.

He tried a different approach.

"What does immortality mean?"

"They don't die off."

"Why not?"

"Because they lay eggs, have babies."

"Who takes care of the babies?"

"They burrow into the earth for two or more years. They nourish themselves on the roots of vegetables. Then they come out in May, which is why they are called May bugs."

"And then?"

"The species perpetuates itself. One generation follows the next. Because of the babies."

It was evidently the right answer. They walked for a long way in silence. As they neared the house, Hedy began to sing, this time alone.

> *A happy, desire-filled heart*
> *Full of love and full of song,*
> *Sing song, ding dong*
> *A youngster sets out into the world.*

There were numerous preparations to be made, and numerous forms to complete, before Hedy could leave Germany. It was necessary to surrender the family jewelry, and obtain a certificate showing that they had paid all their taxes. Packing lists had to be submitted to German customs for approval. Hedy was allowed to take only a few valuable mementos out of the country. These included a single place setting of silver flatware with her mother's initials, a silver sugar bowl, a watch with a silver chain, a small bracelet, and her mother's Oriental fan. Alongside these family treasures were a few photographs of her parents, a loden coat, a green knit dress with a polka-dot bow tie, and a navy blue suit with a Peter Pan collar. The dresses had been tailored from leftover fabrics from the now shuttered family store. Hedy was not permitted to take her beloved stamp collection with her. Stamps were considered items of value that could be sold.[5]

When everything was packed, a customs official came to the house to inspect the two small suitcases that now contained all Hedy's possessions. He bound the suitcases tightly together with wire mesh, sealing the ends with solder. Neither suitcase could be opened without clipping the wire.

Already upset about leaving home, Hedy began to wonder why her parents were so anxious to see her depart. It suddenly occurred to her that she was not their daughter after all. She imagined that she was the child of Gypsies who visited Kippenheim every year and set up camp on the outskirts of the village. Hedy had always been drawn to the brightly colored clothes of the Gypsies, their haunting, melodic music, and their seemingly carefree approach to life. She fantasized that she had been adopted by Hugo and Bella because her real Gypsy parents no longer wished to keep her. This led Hedy to accuse her parents of also wanting to get rid of her. They tried to calm her down, but she was not convinced.[6]

Hedy was determined to take her stamp collection with her to England. The night before she left Kippenheim, she crept up the stairs to the attic where the suitcases were stored. Her parents were asleep below. Using a flashlight, she discovered a tiny slit in the wire mesh large enough to push a stamp through. Risking a Gestapo investigation if she was caught, she slid her precious stamps individually through the opening.

Hugo and Bella accompanied their daughter as far as Frankfurt, the home of Bella's younger brother Max. The family stayed with Uncle Max and his new bride, Paula, for a couple of days before putting Hedy on the train. Like Hugo and Bella, Max and Paula were hoping to immigrate to America. Bella's other brother, Manfred, had already left. Posing for pictures on Hedy's last night in Germany, they promised each other that they would all be reunited on the other side of the ocean.

The train station was already packed on the morning of Thursday, May 18, when the Wachenheimers arrived to see their daughter off. There were five hundred children on the transport, ranging in age from six months to seventeen years. Behind the forced smiles, everybody was crying. "Please take good care of our babies," pleaded a young couple, as they surrendered their twin children to a stranger through a train window. Hugo put on his bravest Indian chief face as he marched Hedy down the platform to her compartment singing their song, *Sing song, ding dong, a youngster sets out into the world*. An identification tag hung around her neck: "Hedwig Wachenheimer, Permit Nr 5580, To London."[7]

The final whistle blew, and the train began to inch forward. Through the open window, Hedy noticed that tears were running down her parents' cheeks. They jogged alongside the train until they reached the end of the platform and could go no further. As the train picked up speed, "my parents became smaller and smaller until they were just two dots in the distance and I could no longer see them."

The click-clack of the wheels seemed to be telling Hedy, *You're going away, you're going away, you're going away*. As her parents disappeared from view, she instantly understood their motivation in sending her away. It was not that they did not love her. Quite the opposite. Their decision represented "a great act of love."[8]

Alone on the train to England, Hedy deeply regretted her outburst about being born a Gypsy child. Her eyes brimmed with tears as she wrote a letter to her parents, apologizing for her lack of trust. She remained wrapped up in these thoughts until she caught a glimpse of the imposing tower of Cologne's Gothic cathedral through the window. The train stopped in Cologne to allow additional children to board. Hedy used the opportunity to ask someone on the platform to put her letter in the mail. She wrote her parents another letter on the hour-long trip from Cologne to Aachen, the final stop in Germany. Once again, she handed it to someone on the platform to post.

As the Kindertransport crossed the border into Holland, the children were greeted by Dutch Jews, who passed cookies and fruit through the open windows. The train then headed northwest toward the Hook of

Holland through mile after mile of glittering, multicolored tulip fields, a contrast to the black and red uniformity of Germany. That night, the children took a ferry across the North Sea to Harwich in England.

At Liverpool Street station, the children were told to wait for their names to be called. Hedy fell asleep on her suitcase as refugee officials went through all the letters of the alphabet before reaching the letter "W." When she woke up, there was hardly anyone left in the reception area. She started to cry. A kindly refugee worker eventually tracked down the missing child and greeted her in a torrent of incomprehensible English. Using sign language, the woman instructed Hedy to follow her down a moving staircase into the Underground.

The village girl from the Black Forest had never seen an escalator before, and had no idea how to get on and off. Her knees began to shake. She put her suitcases on first, and jumped on after them, clinging to both sides of the strange contraption. She was terrified by the dark, echoing tunnels and the huge crowds of people. A roaring red train took them to a station named Edgware, at the end of the line. They then took a taxi through streets that all looked the same, stopping at the house of a family named Rose. The Roses had three daughters who burst into giggles when Hedy unpacked her suitcases, spraying loose stamps all over the room.[9]

The mail service between London and Kippenheim remained excellent, despite growing tension between England and Germany. It took one to three days for a letter to reach its destination, depending on whether the sender was willing to pay for air mail. Hedy's letters brought flashes of joy to the gloom and despair of Nazi Germany. *"Sing song, ding dong,"* wrote Hugo after receiving Hedy's first letters from the Kindertransport. "A youngster set out, and has given me great joy with her magnificent conduct and beautiful letters."[10]

"Keep on writing your beautiful letters," he instructed her a few weeks later as the war clouds gathered over Europe. "No matter how hard it rains or how much thunder and lightning there is, we feel as though the sun is shining when a letter arrives from the good little Hedy."[11]

Hugo and Bella wrote to their daughter two or three times a week. They lived vicariously through her experiences and insisted on knowing exactly what she was doing. "Every minute detail about you is of interest to us," Hugo told Hedy soon after her arrival in London. "Write to us how you spend your days, such as, At __ o'clock, I get up, wash my neck etc., until it is night and you say to your friend with whom you share the bedroom, 'I am very tired, good night, sleep well.' The letter has to read exactly the way you have always told stories. Don't forget anything."[12]

Hugo demanded to know whether his daughter had overcome her distaste for tea and what she ate for each meal. This question was difficult for Hedy to answer without alarming her parents. Her host family insisted that she follow a strict diet on the erroneous assumption that there had been little to eat in Germany. Meals consisted of a piece of toast with butter for breakfast along with a cup of tea, two pieces of toast and a cup of tea for lunch, and a cup of tea for dinner. On Sundays, she was given a cookie as a special treat. One day, after the Roses caught Hedy helping herself to a piece of roast beef from the pantry that they had reserved for themselves, they accused her of theft.[13]

After suffering in silence for two months, Hedy told the woman from the Kindertransport organization about her starvation rations. The woman arranged for her to move to another family in Edgware. In order to explain her change of address, Hedy felt obliged to tell her parents the truth. They were upset by the treatment of their daughter, but also disturbed that Hedy had failed to confide in them. They had suspected something was wrong from the tone of her letters, as well as gaps in her descriptions of life in London. "If there is ever anything again that bothers you, please share it with us," pleaded Bella.[14]

"Write us only the truth," her father admonished. "When we know the whole truth, we are at peace. Remember what you learned in French: *Rien que la vérité, toute la vérité.*"[15]

Back in Germany, rumors of war were growing ever stronger. After occupying most of Czechoslovakia, Hitler was threatening Poland, despite earlier promises to respect its territorial integrity. In the topsy-turvy world of Nazi propaganda, Poland was the aggressor and Germany the victim. By the beginning of August, Nazi newspapers were warning of a day of reckoning. The flashpoint was the Baltic port city of Danzig, which had been declared a "free city" under the protection of the League of Nations. The German population of Danzig wanted to "reunite" with the Fatherland, eliminating Poland's narrow corridor to the Baltic Sea. A Nazi propaganda sheet in Baden, *Der Führer,* accused the Poles of planning a surprise attack.[16]

WARSAW THREATENS BOMBARDMENT OF DANZIG!
UNBELIEVABLE POLISH ARCH-MADNESS

"The same tension for weeks, always growing and always unchanged," the Berlin diarist Victor Klemperer recorded on August 14. "*Vox populi:* he [Hitler] attacks in September, partitions Poland with Russia, England and France are impotent.... Jewish opinion: bloody pogrom on the first day of the war."[17]

For the beleaguered Jewish community in Kippenheim, a new war would mean the closing of potential escape routes. Both Britain and France had promised to help Poland resist an attack by Germany. If hostilities broke out, it would no longer be possible to travel to either country from Germany. Direct communications would be cut off.

As a politically aware person who followed current events closely, Hugo Wachenheimer understood that time was running out. Drawing on his ever-improving English, he had spent the last few months helping other Kippenheim Jews deal with foreign consulates and refugee organizations. He now needed to focus on his own escape from Germany. It no longer mattered whether he or Bella were able to find paid employment in England. As he told Hedy, "Of course we would be willing to accept a position in a village in primitive conditions. You know what my solution is—out at any cost."[18]

Hugo had mailed dozens of letters to potential sponsors and refugee organizations on both sides of the Atlantic. His hopes had been dashed again and again. Many of his correspondents did not even bother to reply. Others raised insuperable objections. But he still kept trying. In his laborious English, he compared himself to "the captain of a steamer forced to flash in the wide world the cry S.O.S.—Save Our Souls."[19]

In early August, Hugo received an air mail letter from the German

Jewish Aid Committee in London, informing him that it had been impossible to find a "guarantor" for his onward immigration to the United States.[20] The letter upset him greatly. He urged his daughter to find "an important person" who could plead their case directly with the Aid Committee. A few days later, he apologized for alarming her unnecessarily. "You can rest assured we are not nearly as sad as I sounded, and you don't need to worry about this."[21]

Hugo sprinkled his letters to Hedy with nuggets of news about Kippenheim. Cantor Gottfried Schwab was leaving for England with his family, depriving the Jewish community of its spiritual leader. He would bring "four pairs of nice white socks" for Hedy. The Durlachers were going to France with their children, Hansel and Gretel, named after the Grimm Brothers fairy tale. An Aryan neighbor was accused of embezzling money from the former Wertheimer metal business. "His wife tried to hang herself yesterday. However she is alive and has been hospitalized with a nervous breakdown."

The most disturbing news concerned Fanny Valfer's younger brother Siegfried, who lived in an apartment underneath the Wachenheimers on Bahnhofstrasse. On August 2, Hugo relayed the information that "Siegfried W" had been arrested for an unspecified crime. "He will not be back for a number of years. His case is not yet settled. It will be a few more weeks before we learn more."[22]

A dashing man in his youth with a flair for polka-dot ties, Siegfried Wertheimer was regarded as a "bon vivant" and a bit of "a rascal" by the rest of the family.[23] He had been married twice but never quite managed to settle down. The first marriage produced a baby girl but ended in divorce in 1932. His second wife, Erna, had died of cancer in October 1937, three days short of her thirty-sixth birthday.[24] Siegfried had tried to start his own metal company, in Cologne. But it had not worked out, and he had returned to Kippenheim to take a job as a salesman in the Wertheimer metal company.[25]

Uncertain about his future, Siegfried traveled to Palestine in the summer of 1938 to explore the possibilities of immigration. His younger sister Karolina had already moved to Tel Aviv from Kippenheim with her husband, Eugen, and their three children. Thanks to an immigrant investment program approved by Nazi Germany, Eugen had been able to rebuild his flour mill in Tel Aviv. Like many newly arrived German Jews, the Wertheimers were homesick for their native land. According to their son Stef, they both hated Germany and "longed for it at the same time. They spoke German, read German, and clung to the world of German culture that shaped them." Their friends were mostly émigrés like themselves, "uprooted from their natural surroundings." Their home was full of heavy German furniture.[26]

Siegfried found it even more difficult than his sister and brother-in-law to settle down in Palestine. He did not like the hardscrabble settler lifestyle. He missed his daughter, Yvette, who was living in eastern France, across the Rhine from Kippenheim, with his first wife, Alice. Also pulling him back to his home village was a budding—if dangerous—liaison with one of his co-workers from the Wertheimer metal business. Marta Bruder was a twenty-seven-year-old Christian girl from a peasant family, sixteen years younger than Siegfried, but already past the normal age of marriage in rural Baden. Sexual relationships between Jews and Christians were prohibited under the Reich citizenship law "for the protection of German blood and German honor," but Siegfried was "very lonely."[27]

After a few weeks in Palestine, Siegfried made the impulsive decision to return to Germany.[28] He still planned to immigrate, but to the New World, not the ancient world. He believed he still had time to make the necessary arrangements. He talked to his first wife about moving to America with their daughter.

Returning to Germany turned out to be a catastrophic mistake. Siegfried arrived back in Kippenheim just as the Nazi campaign against the Jews was entering a particularly ferocious stage. Less than three months later, he was swept up in the mass arrests of Kristallnacht. He spent a month in Dachau together with the other Jewish men from Kippenheim, before being released in early December 1938. The horrors of the concentration camp convinced him that he must leave Germany again as soon as possible. A plan to travel to Cuba fell through with the abortive voyage of the *St. Louis* and the change in Cuban visa regulations. His preferred destination was the United States, but that involved a multiyear wait for an immigration visa.

Siegfried's world fell apart after Marta informed her family that she was expecting a baby. Not only was she pregnant out of wedlock; she was pregnant by a Jewish man. They persuaded her to have an abortion. Someone—either a relative or a nosy neighbor—denounced Siegfried to the Gestapo. He was arrested and taken to jail in nearby Kenzingen, where he was investigated for the "crime" of *Rassenschande,* the Nazi term for "race defilement."[29]

The burden of hiring a lawyer to defend Siegfried, sorting through his affairs, and delivering care packages to him in jail fell primarily on Max Valfer. Max had little sympathy for his wayward brother-in-law. The family had warned Siegfried of the trouble that was likely to come from associating with an Aryan, but he had ignored their concerns. Max found it difficult to comprehend how a forty-four-year-old man could have been so foolish. "He who doesn't listen will suffer the consequences," he told his daughter Ruth in New York.[30]

In letters to his children, Max expressed a grim determination to ride out the latest family crisis. As he told Ruth, "Your dear Mama and I cannot do ourselves in because of it. We already feel like we are living in a darkened cell. Many people are against us." He comforted himself in the knowledge that other Jewish families were "also miserable, which makes us feel somewhat protected, even with a skeleton in the closet." Max was relieved to be able to tell Ruth that so far neither he nor Fanny had been "insulted or harassed" as a result of the scandal, even though "people here are very vocal."

Alone in jail, Siegfried wrote to his former wife, Alice, in France, fantasizing about their emigration plan. Alice wrote back immediately on August 18, 1939, urging Siegfried "not to despair." "Remain brave and strong. God will help you once more. Hopefully, we will be able to emigrate together very soon." Alice's letter reached Kenzingen on August 21. After being checked by the censor, it was returned to the sender with the handwritten notation, "Recipient is deceased."[31]

Siegfried had died earlier that morning. The official version was that he committed suicide after learning that he had been convicted of *Rassenschande.*[32] Some of his relatives suspected that he had been hounded to death by his captors. There was no way of knowing.

The hastily arranged funeral was a lonely, desolate affair. A few of Siegfried's relatives and neighbors, including Max Valfer and

Hugo Wachenheimer, escorted his coffin to the Jewish cemetery in Schmieheim. They laid him to rest in a hastily dug grave on a grassy slope beneath the towering firs, pines, and cypresses, next to his second wife, Erna. To avoid attracting Nazi vandals, they left the tombstone flat on the ground, in contrast to the erect grave markers all around.[33]

The mourners mumbled a few prayers, but were too absorbed in their own problems to shed many tears. "He did a number of not so nice things, and received four years of imprisonment as punishment," Hugo Wachenheimer reported to Hedy after returning from the cemetery. "To avoid that, he ended his own life, and perhaps it is just as well. His family is not too sad. With all the misfortune, there is perhaps one good thing: half of the house belonged to Siegfried, which poor Yvette will now inherit. There is no other news."[34]

The assumption in Kippenheim was that Siegfried had simply been "carousing" with Marta, in Max's phrase.[35] In fact, the relationship appears to have been more serious, at least from Marta's perspective. As punishment for her affair with a Jew, she was sent as a nurse to the Eastern Front, after Germany went to war with Russia in 1941. After the war, her family pressured her into marrying a disabled war veteran from Kippenheim, who was unable to give her any children. According to a family member who knew her story, she never got over the loss of her unborn baby. To the end of her life, in 1997, she kept a cradle in her house, with a baby doll wrapped lovingly inside.[36]

The person most affected by the Siegfried tragedy was probably his older sister Fanny Valfer. News of his death was the culmination of a series of shattering blows that included the departure of her remaining children and the collapse of her own plans to travel to Cuba. She and Max were now alone in Kippenheim, with no immediate prospect of escaping from Germany. "*Oma* is the most unfortunate person," Ludwig Maier wrote his sister-in-law Ruth in New York after learning of Siegfried's arrest. "All her children are gone, she has worried for them all, and now this torment."[37]

The last of the six Valfer children to leave Germany was twenty-six-year-old Else, who traveled to England at the beginning of August to join her husband, Heinrich. Freya and Ludwig were living in a Quaker boardinghouse in London, after their abortive trip across the ocean on the *St. Louis.* The oldest son, Karl, had left in April, and was now working in Glasgow as a radio mechanic. The other three children, Ruth, Hugo, and Erich, had all fled Germany before Kristallnacht. Fanny and Max were now among only forty-one Jews left in Kippenheim—down from 144 in 1933.

After finally getting out of Germany, Else attempted to provide her siblings with an "unfiltered picture" of life back home, without fear of her letter being read by Postmaster Link. She began by unloading on Hitler, but was still nervous about actually using his name. She used the family code to refer to the Führer as "the dog" and Germany as "Dogsland." "There is so much we have to suffer as a consequence of that dog. I ask myself where we get the strength to go through it all." Unfortunately, she had to acknowledge that "the wretched dog has some life in him yet."[38]

Next she complained about the theft or forced sale of the family's treasured possessions, including "fabulous rugs," "brocade quilts," and "a double sofa bed." "We have been swindled," she informed Ruth. "Nothing went as we thought it would. We had to pay for everything at twice the price." The "Reich flight tax" came to 35,000 reichsmarks; the "atonement fine" for the murder of the German diplomat was another 12,000 marks. Their remaining funds disappeared in exorbitant travel charges and currency conversion fees. "If only I knew how our dear parents will get by with money right now. I am so terribly heartbroken when I think of our Mama and Papa."

It had been particularly hard for Else to say goodbye to "our sweet Mama," who was "homesick for all of us" and "did not look her best." Fanny desperately wanted to join her children in England or the United States. So far, however, it had been impossible to arrange the necessary affidavits and offers of employment. With war approaching, it was becoming even more difficult to get to England. All applications had to be filtered through a Jewish refugee committee which passed them on to the British Home Office. Max and Fanny faced a wait time of more than two years before they could immigrate to the United States. This by itself was likely to disqualify them in the eyes of British officials.[39]

The escape plans of Max and Fanny were further complicated by Max's concern for his thirty-three-year-old secretary, Berta Weil. Berta lived a five-minute walk from the Valfers, with her mother, older sister, and brother. Her father had died three years previously. Whenever the topic of future travel plans came up, Max insisted that a way be found to allow the Weils to accompany him and Fanny. There was a problem, however: the Weils lacked a suitable American sponsor for their immigration application.[40]

Max's efforts on behalf of the Weil family upset his children and their spouses. They complained that he was paying too much attention to Berta, at the expense of his own family. "Your father is simply too fond of her, and doesn't understand that he must set aside the overly fond attachment," Ludwig Maier wrote his sister-in-law Ruth in New York in the summer of 1939.[41] By contrast, Max spoke of Berta as a source of comfort, particularly after his own children left Kippenheim. "We are very happy to have someone still around us who is good and honest in her words and deeds," he told Ruth. "We alone know what it means to have companionship in difficult times."[42]

The family drama was soon overtaken by stunning developments on the international front. On August 23, the day of Siegfried Wertheimer's burial, Nazi Germany announced a nonaggression treaty with its mortal enemy, Communist Russia. The German foreign minister, Joachim von Ribbentrop, traveled to Moscow to meet his Soviet opposite number, Vyacheslav Molotov. The full details of what came to be known as the Molotov-Ribbentrop Pact dividing up eastern Europe were kept confidential. It was clear, nevertheless, that the two totalitarian regimes had reached a cynical political accommodation that threatened the very existence of neighboring countries. A German attack on Poland seemed only days away.

Franklin Roosevelt was woken from a troubled sleep by the ringing of the telephone next to his bed. It was ten minutes to three on the morning of Friday, September 1. As he emerged from his dreamworld, he heard the White House operator say that his ambassador to France, William Bullitt, wanted to speak with him.

"Tony Biddle has just got through from Warsaw, Mr. President," said Bullitt, referring to the American ambassador to Poland. "Several German divisions are deep in Polish territory. Fighting is heavy. Tony said there were reports of bombers over the city. Then he was cut off."

"Well, Bill, it's come at last. God help us all."[43]

FDR spent the next two hours following the ever more alarming dispatches from Poland. Forty-two German divisions, including ten tank divisions, had crossed the Polish border at dawn with no warning. The Luftwaffe was bombarding Polish cities. At five a.m., Roosevelt telephoned Eleanor, who was in Hyde Park, and told her to turn on the radio.[44] Hitler was about to speak. Three hundred miles apart, they listened to the Führer accuse Poland of "intolerable" acts of oppression against ethnic Germans in Danzig. He depicted the invasion as a response to Polish aggression.

Having served as assistant navy secretary in the last war, Roosevelt was "startled by a strange feeling of familiarity—a feeling that I had been through it all before." After two decades of peace, he snapped back into the role of military commander, like someone "picking up again an interrupted routine."

"The days ahead will be crowded days," he warned his cabinet. "Crowded with the same problems, the same anxieties that filled to the brim those September days of 1914. For history does in fact repeat."[45]

In need of relaxation, the president stayed up late the following night playing cards with his cronies in his private study. The poker game was repeatedly interrupted by messengers bearing the latest news bulletins. It was still unclear whether Britain and France would keep their promise to defend Poland in the event of a German attack. After reading one such message, which arrived around eleven p.m., the president told his companions, "War will be declared by noon tomorrow." He then returned to the poker table, losing badly.

"One thing about playing with the President, we do not have to curry favor by letting him win," Interior Secretary Harold Ickes recorded admiringly.[46]

The outbreak of war put an end to the negotiations in London with the Nazi financial expert, Helmut Wohlthat, over the refugee crisis. Positions had hardened on all sides. Even so, Roosevelt refused to give up hope. The German government sent word to Washington that it remained ready to "cooperate with the Intergovernmental Committee," the international body that was attempting to facilitate Jewish emigration from Germany. A meeting of the committee had been scheduled for October 16 in Washington. The president insisted that it go ahead, overruling his advisors who felt the effort was now futile.

Addressing the delegates, FDR called for bold new thinking. He proposed the creation of "a supplemental national home" for the Jews following Britain's decision to halt immigration to Palestine. What was needed, said Roosevelt, was a massive project to resettle refugees in one of the "many vacant spaces of the earth's surface." He ended his address by adapting the words of Emma Lazarus etched on the base of the Statue of Liberty. "Let us lift a lamp beside new golden doors and build new refuges for the tired, for the poor, for the huddled masses yearning to be free."[47]

What had been intended as a stirring speech fell flat. Like many of FDR's visionary ideas, it failed to address the immediate problem. The United States Congress would not agree to any increase in American immigration quotas. Other receiving nations, such as Britain, were focused on the war.

The scope of the refugee calamity now went far beyond the travails of German Jews. Back in 1938, after the German annexation of Austria, FDR had created a body known as the President's Advisory Committee on Political Refugees to study the refugee issue and propose solutions. The crisis had only worsened since then. The chairman of the committee, James Grover McDonald, estimated that "over a million refugees" were wandering around Europe by the fall of 1939.[48] Half a million Spaniards had poured into France at the end of the Spanish Civil War. An equal number of Poles and Finns fled to neighboring countries in the first months of what would soon become known as World War II. Dwarfing all these refugee flows, but largely absent from the American political debate, were the ten million people dislodged from their homes as a result of Japan's invasion of China in 1937.[49]

Roosevelt's primary focus in the fall of 1939 was persuading Congress to permit arms sales to Britain and France. Polls showed overwhelming opposition to direct American involvement in the war. "I am almost literally walking on eggs," FDR told a British official.[50] When he traveled to Capitol Hill to urge revision of the neutrality laws, he was met by female protesters chanting, "We're mothers, we don't want our boys to go to war!" A group of twenty-four leading isolationist senators pledged to fight him "from hell to breakfast." Hoping to outmaneuver his opponents, the president co-opted their antiwar rhetoric. His plan, he told Congress, was guided by a "single hardheaded thought— keeping America out of the war."[51] On November 4, Congress accepted his logic, voting to allow arms sales to the democracies on a cash-and-carry basis.

The president found himself in a tricky position. Although he repeatedly expressed sympathy with the victims of German aggression, he could not come to their assistance too obviously for fear of the "warmonger" tag. He had long felt that America would be forced to confront the menace posed by the dictatorships. The challenge was to arouse the American people from their slumber without scaring them into thinking that he was dragging them into a new war. "What worries me especially," he wrote to a friend in December 1939, "is that public opinion over here is patting itself on the back every morning and thanking God for the Atlantic Ocean (and the Pacific Ocean). We greatly underestimate the serious implications to our own future."[52]

FDR's suspicions of Nazi intentions were confirmed by a reported conversation involving Joseph Goebbels. As relayed to Roosevelt, Hitler's propaganda chief had boasted that Germany would "quickly smash" both France and England after finishing off Poland.

"What next?" his interlocutor had asked him.

"You know what's next," Goebbels had purportedly replied. "The United States."

When the other man expressed astonishment that Germany could conquer a country on the other side of an ocean, Goebbels had a ready response.

"It will come from the inside."[53]

Roosevelt's caution in publicly articulating the Nazi threat frustrated many of his allies. His poker-playing friend Harold Ickes felt that the president should be much more outspoken in "pointing out the dangers of Nazism to such a country as ours." Ickes did not have any doubt that Hitler would eventually "turn his attention to the richest country in the world and therefore the greatest prize of a conqueror, the United States."[54]

FDR preferred to play a longer and more subtle game, hiding his cards behind a poker face. He concealed his ultimate objectives not only from his enemies, but also from his friends, and occasionally from himself. "You know I am a juggler, and I never let my right hand know what my left hand does," he would later confess. "I may have one policy for Europe and one diametrically opposite for North and South America. I may be entirely inconsistent, and furthermore, I am perfectly willing to mislead and tell untruths if it will help win the war."[55]

A similar dynamic applied to the biggest political question of all: whether Roosevelt would seek reelection. The countdown to the November 1940 election had already begun. If FDR ran for a third term, he would be breaking a two-term tradition dating back to George Washington. He refused to even hint at his intentions. At their annual winter dinner in December 1939, White House correspondents made fun of the president's inscrutability. They rolled out an eight-foot-high papier-mâché caricature of Roosevelt, complete with long cigarette holder and mischievous grin, in the form of the Great Sphinx of Egypt. Constructed entirely from newspaper clippings speculating on whether or not he would run, the sculpture became the centerpiece of an elaborate skit. Roosevelt laughed heartily at the joke but refused all comment.

In fact, he was genuinely of two minds about whether to run again. A part of him wanted to lay down the burdens of the presidency. He was already building a post-presidential library at Hyde Park. Although he was only fifty-eight, he was exhausted. In late February 1940, he suffered a mild heart attack. He complained about being confined to the Oval Office from morning to night. "People come in here day after day, most of them trying to get something from me, most of them things I can't give them, and wouldn't if I could." Other people could at least walk around when they got tired or irritated, but that was impossible for FDR. "I am tied down to this chair day after day, week after week, and month after month. And I can't stand it any longer. I can't go on with it."[56]

Another part of FDR was convinced that he was the man to guide the United States through some of the most perilous moments of its history. It was a challenge for which he had been preparing all his life.

The first few months of the war produced little change in the daily lives of Kippenheim Jews. Even though Germany was now officially at war with both France and Britain, there was hardly any fighting on the Western Front. The action was all in the east. This twilight period was termed "phoney war" by the English, *drôle de guerre* ("funny war") by the French, and *Sitzkrieg* ("sitting war") by the Germans. The most immediate impact of the war was the disruption in communications. To stay in touch with their loved ones in England, Kippenheimers had to communicate via a third party in a neutral country such as Switzerland or Belgium. It could take weeks to get a message back and forth.

The American immigration lines moved slowly forward. Since German Jews in "transit countries" such as Britain and France could travel more easily to the United States than Jews in Germany, they were now receiving priority for German quota visas.[57] The new system benefited nomads like Freya and Ludwig, who were spending their "waiting period" in London together with their daughter Sonja. Their American visas finally came through in early 1940, just as they were becoming accustomed to the daily routine of "air raids, shelters and gas masks."[58] The family caught their first, long-awaited glimpse of the Statue of Liberty on February 11, 1940.

Back in Kippenheim, meanwhile, Jewish families found themselves fending off ever more rapacious demands. A particular target of swindlers was Hermann Wertheimer the metal magnate, formerly the richest man in Kippenheim. The Aryan purchasers of his business refused to pay the sales price agreed with his wife while he was in Dachau. By haggling over the terms of the sale for more than six months, they delayed his planned departure to America. Once he had settled with the buyers, Hermann was obliged to pay a series of crippling fines and taxes. The various penalties came to around 90,000 reichsmarks, roughly twenty years' income for the average German.[59]

By the time he had paid all the fines and arranged for his four children to move to England, Hermann had no money left for his own emigration. He and Zerline were forced to depend on the charity of a Jewish relief organization, which paid for their transatlantic passage. The kindly Dr. Weber provided him with the medicines he needed to make the trip. The Wertheimer couple left Kippenheim on May 14, 1940, traveling to the Italian port of Genoa and from there, on board the SS *Washington*, to New York. They departed in the nick of time, as German armies swept into Belgium, Luxembourg, and the Netherlands. The "phoney war" had become a real war.

Siegfried and Charlotte Maier received their American visas a few weeks after Hermann and Zerline. The medical examination at the Stuttgart consulate left a big impression on their ten-year-old son, Kurt. "It was the first time I saw my father naked," he would later recall. Equally memorable for Kurt were the stone tiles of the examination room and his first attempt at using his schoolboy English. "My father's feet are cold," he told the consular official.[60]

The Maier family had tickets from Genoa to New York on an Italian ship, but were forced to cancel their plans. On June 10, news arrived that Italy had entered the war as an ally of Germany. The last reliable escape route from Nazi Germany to America—southward over the Alps to Switzerland and then to Italy—existed no longer.[61]

Four days later—on June 14—the Germans marched into Paris.

SEVEN

Fifth Column

T HE GERMAN ARMY was just fifty miles from Paris on the evening
of May 26, 1940, when President Roosevelt delivered his first "fireside chat" since the beginning of the war. It was titled "On National
Defense." He recorded the broadcast in the Diplomatic Reception
Room, an oval-shaped room on the ground floor of the White House.
On the desk in front of him were a sheaf of papers, a sharpened pencil,
a pack of Camel cigarettes, and a battery of microphones. There was
no actual fireplace in the room, but that did not matter to his millions
of unseen listeners. Through an intimate tone of voice and conversa-
tional turns of phrase, FDR persuaded ordinary Americans that he was
taking them into his confidence. He addressed them as "my friends"
and spoke frankly about common concerns and challenges. "You felt
he was there talking to you," a reporter recalled. "Not to fifty million
others, but to you personally."[1]

FDR reserved such broadcasts for special occasions, such as the
launching of his New Deal program or the outbreak of the war. His
goal now was to educate Americans about the Nazi threat and explain
how he would keep the country safe. He had shaken off his lethargy
of the previous winter and was determined to seize the moment. He
would use the international crisis as an opportunity to mobilize public
opinion to side with the victims of German aggression. The fighting in
Europe could no longer be viewed as "none of our business."

Norway, Denmark, and the Low Countries had already fallen. The French army was in full retreat. The British Expeditionary Force was trapped at Dunkirk. Civilians were fleeing Paris and other northern French cities. After describing millions of refugees moving in terror "over the once peaceful roads of Belgium and France," the president talked about "new methods of attack" designed to destroy nations from within.

"The Trojan Horse. The Fifth Column that betrays a nation unprepared for tragedy. Spies, saboteurs and traitors are the actors in this new strategy. With all of these we must and will deal vigorously."[2]

Ten days later, on June 5, the president explicitly linked Jewish refugees to the fifth column threat during a meeting with youth activists. Asked about the rising "suspicion of aliens," he said that "a number of definitely proven spies" had succeeded in infiltrating western European countries posing as refugees, including some who were "spying under compulsion." The German government was persuading refugees to serve as informants by threatening to shoot their "old father and old mother" if they failed to cooperate.

"Of course it applies to a very, very small percentage of refugees coming out of Germany," he added. "But it does apply and, therefore, it is something that we have to watch. Isn't it a rather horrible thing?"[3]

Fifth column fever swept America in the summer of 1940, in lockstep with the Nazi blitzkrieg sweeping across western Europe. Subversion by German agents provided an easily understandable explanation for the stunning collapse of the French army. Speculation about the "enemy within" increased with every German success, peaking with the fall of Paris on June 14. Tips to the FBI about fifth columnists reached three thousand a day by mid-June, up from a hundred earlier in the year.[4]

Conservatives and progressives alike were infected by the fifth column mania. Right-wing "vigilante groups" with names like "America for Americans" and "America's Minute Men" were hunting foreign spies. Even liberal commentators began to question the government's priorities. "Every American ship is bringing fifth columnists from

Europe, but a fighter for democracy is tripped up at every step," the columnist Dorothy Thompson cabled Secretary of State Hull on July 16. "A lot of us are getting very mad."[5]

Stories of German agents on subversive missions became a staple of American popular culture. Hollywood was scrambling to follow up on *Confessions of a Nazi Spy*, the first American movie "to call a swastika a swastika," in the phrase of the Warner Bros. publicity machine. The fifth column menace gave birth to pulp fiction characters like "Captain America" pledged to defend the country from "the threat of invasion from within." Soon Superman himself would be recruited to the anti-Nazi cause, dedicating his "tremendous powers" to the fight against "our most insidious foes... the hidden maggots, the traitors, the fifth columnists, the potential Quislings."[6]

The term "fifth column" went back to the Spanish Civil War. A Nationalist general, Emilio Mola, boasted in 1936 that he commanded four columns of troops advancing on Madrid plus a *"quinta columna"* made up of supporters inside the city. According to Mola, it was this "fifth column" that would ensure a Nationalist victory by undermining the Republican government from within. Ernest Hemingway used the term as the title of a play he wrote while living in the Spanish capital as a foreign correspondent during the siege. The play opened on Broadway in March 1940, shortly before the Nazis launched their onslaught against western Europe.

The beaters of the fifth column drum pointed to Norway, where the pro-Nazi actions of Major Vidkun Quisling had become synonymous with national betrayal. American intelligence officials believed that a similar process took place in France. "The masterpiece of the Fifth Column was unquestionably the French debacle," wrote FDR's intelligence advisor William Donovan. "Here everything that Hitler promised came to pass with almost mathematical precision." He blamed the French defeat on German agents who "went everywhere, saw everything, came to know everything" with the help of "scandalously venal French newspapers."[7] His analysis was echoed by the U.S. ambassador to France, William Bullitt, who claimed that "refugees from Germany" were responsible for more than half the spy operations against the French army.[8]

Despite such warnings, evidence that Jewish refugees from Nazi Germany posed a national security threat to America rested largely on hearsay. The FBI had recently penetrated a large German spy network based in New York with the help of a double agent, William Sebold. Every single member of the so-called Duquesne Spy Ring was either a naturalized American or longtime resident. Several were members of the German American Bund, a pro-Nazi group that had been formed in the mid-1930s. The internal threat from German Americans sympathetic to the Nazi cause turned out to be much greater than the external threat from refugees.

The European catastrophe, nevertheless, stirred huge concern about the security risks posed by insufficiently vetted refugees. From his new post as American ambassador to Cuba, George Messersmith warned that the United States was facing the "greatest national emergency" in its history. He claimed that some refugees had celebrated the fall of Paris, saying, "We are Germans first and Jews afterwards." He proposed a centralized screening of "so-called refugees" to determine their true loyalties and blackmail potential. Immigration restrictions had to be "considerably tightened" in the interest of "self-preservation." It was no longer wise to give "free play to the humanitarian impulses which have always animated our people."[9]

Messersmith's recommendations were put into effect by his successor as assistant secretary of state, Breckinridge Long. A former ambassador to Fascist Italy, Long was a senior Democratic party operative and ally of FDR. His ties to the president went back to their service in the Woodrow Wilson administration. A national security hawk, Long took a bleak view of the threats facing America. His diary entries for the summer of 1940 are peppered with comments like "The whole picture darkens everywhere. Destruction, disorganization, disintegration are rampant."[10]

Long set about the task of saving America from subversives with single-minded resolve, drafting a series of telegrams that greatly increased the bureaucratic obstacles facing refugees. A June 29 telegram ordered consuls to reject immigrant visa applications "if there is any doubt whatsoever concerning the alien." The cable acknowledged that the new regulations would lead to "a drastic reduction" in the number of visas issued to refugees. It was nevertheless "essential to take every precaution at this time to safeguard the best interests of the United States."[11]

"The cables practically stopping immigration went!" Long recorded in his diary that same day.[12]

The results were as predicted. The granting of immigrant visas in Germany plummeted almost overnight. For the previous two years, ending in June 1940, American consuls had almost completely filled the 27,370 slots in the German immigration quota. The Stuttgart consulate had issued between four hundred and six hundred visas a month for most of the previous year. That number dwindled to nineteen in July 1940 and two in August. While consulates in "transit countries" such as Britain increased their output, the overall number of new refugee visas decreased by nearly 50 percent.[13]

FDR did not need to be persuaded that fifth columnists posed a mortal threat, not only to France but to America. As assistant secretary of the navy during World War I, he had personal experience of German sabotage of American military installations. He had vivid memories of the July 1916 bombing of the ammunition depot on Black Tom Island in New York harbor that killed seven people and destroyed two million pounds of ammunition. The blast was so strong that it severely damaged the torch of the nearby Statue of Liberty, resulting in its permanent closure to visitors. Responsibility for the Black Tom explosion was eventually traced to the German secret service. A stream of dire intelligence warnings convinced the president that the Germans would attempt something similar again.

Emphasizing the threat from Nazi agents and saboteurs also served a political purpose for Roosevelt during a presidential election year. He could not allow himself to be outflanked by his political opponents when it came to protecting the United States from her enemies, both foreign and domestic. He framed the fifth column menace in a way that lumped his isolationist critics together with the Nazi foe.

By July, FDR had made up his mind. He would run again for an unprecedented third term. In his July 19 acceptance address to the Democratic National Convention in Chicago, the old poker player finally revealed his hand. Addressing the delegates by radio from the White House, he lambasted the "appeaser fifth columnists who charged me with hysteria and war-mongering." Americans faced "one of the great choices of history." The alternatives were stark: "the continuance of civilization as we know it versus the ultimate destruction of all that we hold dear." America's fate could not be entrusted to "untried hands."

FDR's reelection was by no means assured. His Republican opponent, a millionaire businessman named Wendell Willkie, was campaigning on the slogan that "a vote for Roosevelt is a vote for war." A Gallup poll taken soon after the political conventions predicted that Willkie would win the electoral college 304–227.[14] As Roosevelt saw it, this would be a disaster. Saving the country and winning a third term were closely connected. Everything else had to be subordinated to the overriding goal of leading America to victory.

Franklin and Eleanor Roosevelt occupied adjoining suites on the second floor of the White House that served as the head and the heart of the FDR administration. Eleanor's discovery, back in 1918, of Franklin's affair with her social secretary, Lucy Mercer, had put an end to their conjugal relations but helped launch a remarkable political partnership. Eleanor found fulfillment in public life, traveling tirelessly around the country on Franklin's behalf after he was paralyzed in 1921. As she emerged from her husband's shadow, she began to champion her own causes. One such cause was the plight of refugees.

Eleanor saw herself, and was viewed by many people around the world, as her husband's moral conscience. In contrast to FDR, who applied a political cost-benefit analysis to his every public utterance, she was happy to speak her mind. While their political views were similar, their approaches were very different. Franklin saw humanity in the abstract. He thought in terms of grand policy affecting masses of largely faceless people. Eleanor was moved by the stories of specific individuals who needed her help. As a child, she had spent hours by the bed of her invalid mother, gently rubbing her head to relieve her migraine. "The feeling that I was useful was perhaps the greatest joy I had experienced," she recalled later.[15] Helping others became her primary source of satisfaction.

A few months earlier, in the winter and early spring of 1940, Eleanor had experienced one of her recurring bouts of depression. She called these episodes her "Griselda moods," after the poor village girl in a Chaucer tale who sacrifices her children in order to demonstrate obedience to her powerful husband. Her dark state derived from the feeling that she had little useful to do, apart from her spousal duties. According to her friend Joseph Lash, she strove to exemplify "the medieval archetype of 'wifely obedience, all meekness, all yielding, all resignation.'"[16] In private, she "withdrew into heavy silence." In public, she maintained a brave face, but found it difficult to muster her usual enthusiasm or even get out of bed in the morning. Her loyal secretary, Malvina "Tommy" Thompson, was worried enough to share her concerns with Eleanor's daughter, Anna, "strictly between you and me." "Your mother is quite uncontented," Tommy wrote. "She has wanted desperately to be given something to do in this emergency and no one has found anything for her. They are all afraid of political implications etc."[17]

The refugee crisis in Europe proved the perfect outlet for Eleanor's humanitarian zeal, putting an end to her "Griselda moods." She was soon shuttling happily between Hyde Park and New York, where she served as honorary chair of a new relief organization, the U.S. Committee for the Care of European Children. The committee had plans to evacuate as many as twenty thousand children from "war zones," regardless of nationality and religion. Eleanor worked with government departments to simplify immigration procedures for the children. She also persuaded Franklin to personally sponsor the evacuation of two Jewish children who had escaped the German invasion of Holland by rowing a boat into the North Sea with their parents. After seven days and nights in the boat, the family was rescued by a British destroyer and taken to England. At Eleanor's urging, FDR wrote a personal check for $240 for transporting Ilay and Josephine Klein to the United States with one proviso: "OK, but *not* to live at H[yde] P[ark]."[18]

Offers to adopt refugee children soon poured in from across the country, together with donations for their transportation and accommodation. "I am thankful beyond words that it is going to be possible to do something for these children," Eleanor wrote in a June 26 column. Tommy Thompson rejoiced in her friend's fresh burst of energy. "Your mother is really enjoying her work with the refugee committee," she told Anna. "She looks very well and, of course, is always happier when she feels she is doing something constructive."[19]

In the event, however, plans for a large-scale evacuation of refugee children had to be scaled back because of the risks involved. Transports were suspended after a ship carrying ninety child refugees, the *City of Benares,* was torpedoed by a German U-boat on September 17. The Klein children and thousands of others on the committee's list never made it across the ocean.

In the meantime, Eleanor had found a new cause to embrace: the rescue of anti-Nazi politicians, intellectuals, and artists who had fled to southern France after the fall of Paris. Many of these people were now being hunted by the Gestapo. A clause in the armistice agreement obliged the rump French state based in the southern spa town of Vichy to "surrender upon demand" any citizen of the Greater Reich who was wanted by the Nazis. An American visa could mean the difference between life and death. The First Lady supported the creation of another privately funded organization, the Emergency Rescue Committee, to save prominent anti-Nazi intellectuals trapped in southern France.

Eleanor met with several refugee activists on June 24 at the suggestion of Joe Lash. After a relaxing dinner in Greenwich Village, the group returned to the modest two-bedroom apartment that Eleanor shared with Tommy Thompson on Eleventh Street.[20] The activists knew that Eleanor represented their best chance of bypassing the cumbersome government bureaucracy. As if to prove the point, the First Lady picked up the phone and called FDR in Washington. He was relaxing in his study with his aide Harry Hopkins after a long day dealing with the international crisis. As Lash noted in his diary, FDR was "somewhat impatient and irritated that it wasn't taken for granted he was already doing all that was possible. He kept bringing up the difficulties while Mrs. Roosevelt tenaciously kept pointing out the possibilities."

"Congress won't let them in," the president objected. "Quotas are filled. We have tried to get Cuba and other Latin American countries to admit them, but so far without success."

For a refugee trapped in southern France, the most practical escape route was over the Pyrenees to Spain and then to Portugal. When Franklin reported that Spain would not admit refugees in transit to America, Eleanor had a ready response. "You've always said that we can bribe the Spanish and Portuguese governments."[21]

According to the exiled Austrian Socialist leader Joseph Buttinger, who overheard Eleanor's end of the conversation, the First Lady ended the phone call with a warning. If Washington refused to authorize visas for the endangered refugees, their friends would charter a ship to bring them across the Atlantic. The ship would "cruise up and down the East coast until the American people, out of shame and anger, force the President and Congress to permit these victims of political persecution to land."[22]

"She was extremely sympathetic and voiced her inability to understand what had happened to us—the traditional land of asylum not being willing to admit political refugees," Lash recorded.[23]

Where FDR and the State Department sensed danger, Eleanor saw opportunities. In speeches and newspaper articles, she insisted that Americans should not allow themselves to be driven by fear in responding to the refugee crisis. She spoke out against the fifth column fever that had seized the country, calling on Americans to maintain a balanced perspective. "Are we going to be swept away from our traditional attitude toward civil liberties by hysteria about 'Fifth Columnists,' or are we going to keep our heads?"[24]

Far from constituting a threat, refugees could help the democracies win the war, Eleanor believed. "They know how Communists, Nazis, and Fascists work," she wrote in her "My Day" column. "They know how propaganda is spread, how young people are influenced. They are as good material as the political refugees who came with Carl Schurz the German [in 1848] or Kosciuszko the Pole [in 1776] whose statues we have taught our young people to honor because of their love of liberty."[25]

Eleanor had raised a question that was both topical and profound: how can a nation founded on the idea of freedom protect itself from an unscrupulous, totalitarian enemy? The First Lady and the guardians of America's gates had very different opinions on the appropriate response.

. . .

Events unfolded much as Eleanor had predicted. In August, a group of wealthy refugees chartered a Portuguese ship, the *Quanza*, to cross the Atlantic. When they reached New York, the passengers who possessed United States passports or visas were allowed to disembark. The ship then sailed to the Mexican port of Veracruz, where another thirty-three passengers were permitted to land. Mexican officials insisted that the visas of the remaining eighty-one passengers were invalid. They were either forged or had been obtained from corrupt consular officials for between $100 and $500 apiece.[26] The refugees would have to return to Europe. It seemed like a repeat of the *St. Louis* affair.

As the *Quanza* steamed back up the Atlantic coast, the passengers sent increasingly desperate telegrams to their friends and supporters in the United States. Refugee organizations lobbied the State Department and the Justice Department to allow the refugees to land. News of the impasse reached Eleanor on September 10 in the form of a cable from the "women passengers" of the *Quanza*. They informed the First Lady that the ship would be stopping at Norfolk, Virginia, to refuel. IMPLORE HELP, their telegram read. BEG POSSIBILITY LANDING.[27] Eleanor was at Hyde Park with her husband when she received the telegram. She took action immediately, pleading with FDR to find a way to allow the refugees to remain in the United States. She also cabled the State Department on behalf of the children.[28]

The *Quanza* arrived in Norfolk at ten a.m. on Wednesday, September 11, docking at Sewell's Point, where Union gunboats had exchanged fire with Confederate batteries in the Civil War battle of Hampton Roads. Waiting in the rain on the windswept coal pier were friends and relatives of the refugees, lawyers, journalists, and Jewish relief officials, such as Cecilia Razovsky, who had waged a losing battle on behalf of the *St. Louis* passengers. Armed guards kept the passengers from meeting their loved ones, but were unable to prevent a young mother with two children shouting to reporters, "I thought America was the land of the free."[29]

The previous night, a passenger had jumped overboard in the darkness and attempted to reach the shore. A conscientious objector who had refused to be drafted into the German army, Helmar Wolff knew he would be imprisoned, perhaps killed, if sent back to Germany. Swimming against heavy currents, he was in the water for a couple of hours before being intercepted and returned to the *Quanza*.[30]

The top priority for the refugee advocates was to prevent the ship from sailing back to Europe with the distraught passengers. The coal refueling operation would last eleven hours. Once the coal was on board, the *Quanza* would be free to leave. Alerted by telegram, friends and relatives had already hired local attorneys to stall her departure. They filed their first habeas corpus petition on behalf of a Romanian Jew at eleven that morning, alleging that he was being "unlawfully and wrongfully detained" on board the *Quanza*. In accordance with legal tradition that dated back to medieval England, a federal marshal ordered the ship's captain to produce "the body of Vladimir Zimmerman" to the local U.S. district court within twenty-four hours. Similar petitions were quickly filed for three other passengers.[31]

A lawyer named Jacob Morewitz adopted a different strategy. He was a specialist in the often arcane subject of admiralty law, involving civil actions against shipping lines. His typical day consisted of filing court orders to impound bags of corn or bales of cotton that had been improperly sold or shipped. Now he suddenly found himself at the center of a fast-developing international news story.

Morewitz's clients were a family of Czech Jews named Rand who had been prevented from landing in Mexico because their visas were invalid. Worried that there was insufficient legal basis for a habeas corpus case, Morewitz instead alleged a breach of contract. Instead of the Latin accusation "you have the body," he resorted to the admiralty term "libel," from the French *libelle*, meaning initiation of a civil action involving a ship. He claimed that his clients were the victims of a "diabolical scheme" on the part of the Portuguese shipping company designed to rob them of their wealth. According to Morewitz, the shipping company had colluded with various foreign officials to extract "exorbitant payments" from the passengers, knowing all along that they would not be permitted to disembark in Mexico. Alleging that his clients had been placed in a state of "abject fear," he demanded $100,000 in damages on their behalf.[32]

There was little to justify these allegations, but that was not the point. By libeling the ship, Morewitz could prevent her from leaving port until the master appeared in court to answer the charges. Morewitz filed his initial libel action at 3:38 on Wednesday afternoon, five and a half hours after the arrival of the *Quanza*. U.S. marshals duly attached an impressive-looking document to the ship temporarily impounding "her boats, tackle, apparel, furniture, engines, and freight" in the name of the "President of the United States of America." A Coast Guard vessel pulled up alongside to ensure that she did not leave the harbor. Guards were posted all along the pier.[33]

The impounding of the ship gave new hope to the despairing passengers. Just a few minutes earlier, it looked as if they would be sent back to Nazi-dominated Europe. Now they had a chance for a new life. "We laugh, we weep, we cannot believe it, we want to kiss the attorney," noted the French-Jewish actor Marcel Dalio, who had fled Paris ahead of the German invasion. "It seems to me that an enormous bible has appeared in the heavens, behind which stands God who has just winked at me."[34]

Morewitz's familiarity with the intricacies of admiralty law paid off. The district court judge rejected the writs of habeas corpus filed by the other attorneys, but allowed his libel suit to proceed. The *Quanza* would not be able to sail for at least the next three days.

While Morewitz shuttled back and forth between the *Quanza* and the Norfolk courthouse, a parallel drama unfolded at the Department of State in Washington. Assistant Secretary of State Long had his office on the second floor of the neo-Baroque building, adjacent to the White House. He had already received calls from the president, the First Lady, and numerous refugee organizations, expressing an interest in the fate of the *Quanza* passengers. Telegrams urging the State Department to admit the refugees were arriving by the hour, along with equally pressing demands to keep them out. A map of German-occupied Europe hung behind his desk, which was piled high with papers awaiting his signature.

A stickler for established procedure, Long was opposed to granting any exceptions to U.S. immigration law. He nevertheless agreed to allow the passengers to be screened on a case-by-case basis to see if any of them could be allowed into the country without a visa. There were only three admissible categories: children, people in transit to another country, and "political refugees" in mortal danger.

Immigration inspectors from the Department of Justice began interviewing the passengers on board the ship on Thursday afternoon. After concluding that there were no "fifth columnists" aboard, they cleared three children, two mothers, and thirty-five "transit passengers" for disembarkation. The task of determining who was a "bona fide" asylum seeker was entrusted to a representative of the President's Advisory Committee on Political Refugees, Patrick Malin. After listening to three days of legal arguments, he announced that the remaining forty-one passengers were political refugees admissible to the United States. He telephoned Long on Saturday evening to inform him of his decision.[35]

Long was furious. He recorded his strenuous objections in a State Department memo. "I told him I would not consent to it and would not agree to it; that I would not assume responsibility for it; that I thought it was a violation of the law; and that if it was done it would be on somebody else's shoulders and not upon mine." As Long saw it, the fate of the *Quanza* "did not constitute an emergency of any kind."[36]

The argument was partly semantic, partly an old-fashioned bureaucratic power struggle. Long understood the term "political refugee" to mean public figures "in danger of their lives." In his view, only two of the passengers qualified under this definition. One was Dalio, disdained by the Nazis as an archetypal Jewish character actor.[37] He was best known for his role as a Jew escaping German captivity in the 1937 Jean Renoir war film, *La Grande Illusion*. After fleeing Paris, Dalio had succeeded in reaching Lisbon with his young actress wife, Madeleine Lebeau. Like many of the other *Quanza* passengers, the glamorous movie couple had purchased Chilean visas, only to be refused transit passage via Mexico. (Dalio and Lebeau would both have supporting roles in the classic refugee movie *Casablanca,* alongside Humphrey Bogart and Ingrid Bergman.)

The presidential advisory committee had a much more expansive definition of "political refugee" that included anyone forced to leave their native country as a result of political persecution. The committee asserted its own right to determine who was in danger. By the time Malin telephoned Long, it was too late to reverse his decision. Joyous reunions were already taking place on the pier where the ship was docked. Fathers were being reunited with their children. Husbands were hugging wives they had not seen in months.

According to the Joint representative, Cecilia Razovsky, "Many of the passengers were exceedingly wealthy." The customs inspection revealed that two passengers had very valuable diamonds; one man arrived with two trunks of ostrich feathers; another man had a stash of gold wire.[38] There was no denying that wealth—which brought with it the ability to charter a ship across the Atlantic, hire attorneys, and mobilize public opinion—was a factor in the admission of these particular refugees. The typical Jewish refugee stranded in Holland or Belgium or France following the German invasion of western Europe did not enjoy the wealth or other advantages of the passengers of the *Quanza.*

Shortly after his phone conversation with Malin, Assistant Secretary Long received a telegram from Norfolk. "All the refugees of the SS *Quanza* want to voice their deepest gratitude for all you have done for them," the unsigned cable read.[39] Angered at being outmaneuvered, Long began plotting his revenge. He would take "the matter up some other way."[40] What had happened with the *Quanza* would never be allowed to happen again.

A couple of days later, a large vase of red roses arrived at the White House for Eleanor and Franklin. "With everlasting gratitude for your human gesture, from the refugees of the S.S. *Quanza,*" the card read.[41] Eleanor made sure that her husband saw both the card and the roses, which were prominently displayed outside his bedroom.

A breeder of racehorses in his spare time, Breckinridge Long boasted an impeccable pedigree of his own. He was the product of an alliance between two prominent political families, the Breckinridges of Missouri and the Longs of North Carolina. Known as "Breck" to his friends, he had attended Princeton when Woodrow Wilson was president of the university. When Wilson ran for president of the United States, Long contributed generously to his political campaign. He was rewarded with the position of assistant secretary of state, which brought him into close touch with the assistant secretary of the navy, Franklin Roosevelt. The two rising politicians belonged to the same social set. Long served as Roosevelt's floor manager at the 1932 Democratic Party convention. When FDR became president, he appointed his old friend ambassador to Rome.

During his first few months as ambassador, Long expressed admiration for Mussolini in personal letters to the man he still called "my dear Frank." He praised Il Duce for bringing order to the chaos of Italian life. Echoing a favorite theme of Fascist propaganda, he wrote that "the trains are punctual, well-equipped, and fast." He later revised his view of the Fascists, describing them as "obdurate, ruthless, and vicious."[42] His distaste for the dictators was nevertheless mingled with respect for their power. He considered Germans to be the only European people "with intelligence, courage, and obedience sufficient to bring order, system, and comparative peace" to the eastern half of the continent. "They need a strong leader—Führer, King, or Emperor," he confided to his diary after the annexation of Austria in March 1938.[43] After the fall of Paris in June 1940, he counseled against a premature military confrontation with Nazi Germany. "If we are not very careful, we are going to find ourselves champions of a defeated cause," he warned. "We may have war thrust upon us if we antagonize the military machine which is about to assume control of the whole continent of Europe."[44]

The defeat of France put an end to any illusions that Long might have harbored about a long-term accommodation with Hitler and Mussolini. The assistant secretary now saw himself as a man of destiny, responsible for protecting the United States against Fascists, Communists, and fifth columnists alike. "Of all the epochs of history to be alive this seems to be the most exciting," he told his diary on June 28, 1940. "No one knows what will happen next." He compared Hitler to the great conquerors of the past, such as Alexander, Caesar, Genghis Khan, and Napoleon. Two days later, he marveled that he was experiencing "the greatest moment in all history." He congratulated himself on his legal mind, calm head, and ability to think long-term. He was suspicious of people who were "too idealistic," a category that included his boss, Secretary Hull, and many of his government colleagues.[45]

Long's new responsibilities for refugee policy and other "special war problems" interfered with his life as a gentleman farmer. He lived outside Washington in a Georgian-style manse surrounded by five hundred acres of land ideal for hunting and horse-breeding. It was impractical to commute to the city from Montpelier Mansion, so he took a suite of rooms at the Mayflower Hotel, five blocks from the White House. He returned to the country at weekends to supervise his estate and race his thoroughbreds at nearby Laurel Park. He found himself taking "twenty five to fifty decisions a day on matters of real importance," in between dealing with the butler, looking after lame horses, and finding a new gardener. The stress was considerable. "No man can do all I have to do and do it well," he told his diary.[46] At times, he felt so tired he could barely stay awake.

The conclusion Long drew from his tactical defeat over the *Quanza* was that the power of the refugee relief committees must be curbed "so that the laws again can operate in their normal course."[47] His chosen terrain for the battle was national security. His foot soldiers were the consuls, who were on the front lines of the immigration war and traditionally had the final say on whether a visa should be granted. While the consuls were a motley group, with differing political views, many were suspicious of the crowds of visa seekers outside their doors. "Refugees are often dangerous," argued the American consul to Algiers in a September 28 memo. "They clothe themselves in misery and appeal, the better to carry on their nefarious work. The fact that any given applicant claims to have been, or actually establishes that he has been persecuted, does not necessarily prove the bona fide of his case."[48]

Long's determination to defend the interests of the State Department put him on a collision course with the chairman of the President's Advisory Committee on Political Refugees, James McDonald. A high-minded Midwesterner, McDonald had spent much of the previous seven years campaigning on behalf of victims of Nazi persecution. He had served as the League of Nations high commissioner for refugees from Germany and attended the ill-fated Évian conference. After a spell on the editorial staff of *The New York Times,* he had accepted

Roosevelt's invitation to serve as his advisor on refugees because he thought he could make a difference. Now, it seemed, his efforts were being systematically blocked.

The hyper-vigilant Long was quick to sense McDonald's hostility. "He looks upon me as an obstructionist and was very bitter," he noted in his diary following a meeting with McDonald at which "a few warm words" were exchanged. According to Long, McDonald "indicated that I had a superlative ego and a vindictive mentality."[49] For his part, McDonald accused the State Department of heartlessness. "Our doors are hermetically sealed against newcomers, no matter how tragic their individual positions may be," he complained.[50] Frustrated with his own lack of influence, he asked Eleanor to intervene on his behalf with the president. She was happy to oblige. "Mr. McDonald is so wrought up about it, he wants to talk to you for about 15 minutes," she wrote her husband. "I am thinking about these poor people who may die at any time. . . . I do hope that you can get this cleared up quickly."[51]

Eleanor frequently communicated with FDR by memo, even when they were both in the White House. Her secretary dropped her type-written notes into an "Eleanor basket" strategically placed next to the president's bed. Eleanor had a private understanding with Franklin that "any three things I put on top of his bedside table he will take care of first thing in the morning."[52] On this occasion, however, Long was confident that FDR shared his concerns about refugees. "I found that he was 100% in accord with my ideas," he recorded after a meeting with the president.[53] He welcomed the prospect of a showdown with McDonald.

Long prepared the ground carefully. He made sure that FDR saw an October 2 cable from his ambassador to Moscow, Laurence Stein-hardt, criticizing the organizations lobbying on behalf of the refugees. According to Steinhardt, such groups were "obviously more inter-ested in finding a haven for these unfortunates than in safeguarding the welfare of the United States at the most critical period in its his-tory." Steinhardt accused refugee advocates of misrepresenting the credentials of their clients in an effort to portray them as candidates for political asylum. "I still regard admission to the United States as a privilege, not a right," he concluded.[54] The fact that Steinhardt was himself Jewish made his arguments even more persuasive.

Roosevelt read the Steinhardt telegram out loud during his October 9 meeting with McDonald. He told Long the following day that he had instructed McDonald not to "pull any sob stuff."[55] At the same time, he urged the State Department to reduce delays in screening potential immigrants, and pay special attention to the recommendations of the President's Advisory Committee on Political Refugees. On balance, it was a victory for Long, whose control over visa policy was reaffirmed. Even Jewish leaders were reluctant to press the case for a more liberal refugee policy just weeks before a crucial presidential election.

With opinion polls showing a neck-and-neck race, the president's allies did not want to do anything that might tip the balance in favor of Willkie. They feared that the Republicans could exploit the refugee issue to claim that FDR was soft on national security. For men like Rabbi Stephen Wise, the president of the American Jewish Congress, it was essential that "the Skipper" remain at the helm. With France defeated, half of Europe under German occupation, and Britain struggling for her survival, this was not the time to rock the ship of state. For Wise, Roosevelt's reelection was "much more important for everything that is worthwhile and that counts than the admission of a few people, however imminent be their peril."[56]

FDR was at Hyde Park on Election Day, November 5. The early returns suggested that Willkie might have a chance, causing the president to lock himself in his study and sweat profusely. But the tide turned when the votes came in from big states like New York, Pennsylvania, and Ohio. By midnight, it was clear that he had won an unprecedented third term. "We are facing difficult days in this country," he told a crowd of cheering, torch-bearing neighbors, "but I think you will find me in the future just the same Franklin Roosevelt you have known a great many years."[57] The final result was 54.7 percent for Roosevelt, 44.8 percent for Willkie.

Now that the election was over, the progressives around Roosevelt felt it was safe to again press their cause. The secretary of the interior, Harold Ickes, revived the earlier plan to create a sanctuary for European refugees on the U.S. Virgin Islands. A draft proclamation allowed the governor of the islands to issue visitor permits to would-be immigrants in line for quota visas. The only proviso was that they must be able to support themselves without becoming a "public charge."[58] It seemed like a perfect humanitarian solution. The islands would provide a secure halfway house for refugees threatened with death if they remained in German-dominated Europe. The laborious bureaucratic routine of affidavits and background checks would be circumvented at a stroke. Instead of spending their "waiting time" in risky places like Portugal or southern France, the refugees would be under American protection.

When Long heard about the proposal, he threw a fit. "A tough day," he noted in his diary. His major objection to the plan was the lack of "consular investigation" of visitors to the Virgin Islands. He was convinced that there were "many German agents" among the estimated twelve thousand refugees stranded in Portugal alone. If Ickes and his allies got their way, these people would be free to come to the mainland with few formalities "after a short period of residence in the Virgin Islands." The scheme would constitute "a pipeline to siphon refugees out of Portugal into the United States without the precautionary steps of investigation and check."[59]

The alarmed assistant secretary called Ickes to outline his concerns. He defended the consular checks as "a sieve through which we can strain the applicants."

"The holes in the sieve are too small," countered Ickes. "They ought to be bigger."

"He was rather obdurate and a little sarcastic," Long recorded. For his part, Ickes described his bureaucratic rival as "this ignoramus."[60] Long appealed to the president to break the impasse. For FDR, it was a jurisdictional question. Foreign policy was the prerogative of the president and the State Department, not the Interior Department. He was also worried that the influx of large numbers of refugees would exacerbate social and economic tensions on the Virgin Islands.

"I yield to no person in any department in my deep-seated desire to help the hundreds of thousands of foreign refugees in the present world situation," Roosevelt wrote Ickes. He added, however, that the Virgin Islands was not the right place for a refugee camp. He urged

Ickes to look for "some unoccupied place" to shelter refugees that would not harm "the future of present American citizens."[61]

Ickes was obliged to back down, but did not surrender. An accomplished bureaucratic brawler, he knew there were other ways to continue the fight. Foremost among them was the media. He took every opportunity to privately brief sympathetic journalists, hoping for "enough favorable publicity to break down the intransigent position of the Department of State."[62] Articles identifying Long as the primary obstacle to a humane refugee policy duly appeared in progressive outlets such as *The New Republic, PM,* and *The Nation,* as well as *The Washington Post* and other mainstream media.

"Rich French Anti-Semite Admitted to USA While Gestapo Victims Are Barred" ran a typical *PM* headline in December 1940. "Long Is Responsible for Refugee Scandal" proclaimed another in February 1941.[63] The newspaper claimed that Long had failed to curb the discriminatory actions of consuls in Germany and Switzerland who were known to be "antisemitic."

A few days on a duck shoot in South Carolina provided the embattled assistant secretary with a temporary respite, but he returned to Washington to find himself the target of fresh newspaper attacks. "The wild-eyed elements have marked me out as their objective," he complained.[64]

The Long camp struck back with their own media leaks. In a syndicated December 1940 column, the conservative commentator Westbrook Pegler accused Ickes of "trying to pull a fast one" with his Virgin Islands proposal. He claimed that the pro-refugee campaign was "heavily charged with Communist influence, emanating mainly from New York and Hollywood, in which latter zone a group of mediocre Communist hacks of the writing craft and hams of the drama are posing as great liberal intellectuals."[65]

The issuing of visas picked up after the election, but remained well below the level of the previous year. The invasion of western Europe and German U-boat activity in the Atlantic exacerbated greatly the logistical nightmare confronting the refugees. Before being issued a visa, a refugee had to show that he had passage booked on one of the few ships crossing the Atlantic. Jews escaping persecution had to compete for berths with non-Jews and American citizens wishing to return to the United States.

A larger challenge was grabbing the attention of Washington policy makers. As the security threat to the United States increased, FDR focused his limited energy on a single goal: defeating Nazi Germany. Political allies like Ickes complained that it was difficult to get through to their old friend. "The tragic thing is that the President, as tired as he is, is isolating himself more and more," Ickes noted in his diary. "It is not either a happy or too hopeful situation, considering that the world is in such desperate straits for real leadership."[66]

Even Eleanor found it difficult to push her favorite causes. She continued to leave her nightly memos in the basket outside FDR's bedroom, but her influence was waning. At times, her husband was unable to conceal his impatience. A few weeks after his election victory, he complained to Ickes that "the Mrs came into my room yesterday morning before I was out of bed" to urge him to meet one of her friends. The irritated president had bluntly refused his wife's request.

"She is so strong herself that she does not seem to realize what a strain he is working under," Ickes concluded.[67]

EIGHT

Gurs

O N THE MORNING of Tuesday, October 22, 1940, uniformed policemen rapped on the front doors of the thirty-one Jews still living in
Kippenheim. They gave them two hours to pack and told them to bring
enough food for a journey that could last several days. Each person
was permitted no more than 100 reichsmarks, the equivalent of about
$30. There was no mention of the final destination.[1] Before leaving
home, the deportees were required to sign documents handing over
any remaining property to the Reich.

It was a cool, overcast day, normal autumn weather for the Black
Forest. The Jews were observing Sukkot, the Feast of the Taberna-
cles, in memory of their ancestors who had wandered in the desert for
forty years before reaching the promised land. The commandment
to "rejoice" for God's blessings in the midst of violent oppression was
more timely than ever, but more difficult than ever to fulfill. Religious
tradition called for the construction of huts out of tree branches to
symbolize the temporary shelters inhabited by the refugees fleeing the
"land of Egypt." But only a few families had built the *sukkah* this year.[2]
Most were too distracted by their own suffering to commemorate the
event properly. The evil described in the Bible had become part of
their daily lives.

There was scarcely enough time for everyone to assemble, let alone
prepare adequately for their departure from a place that had been

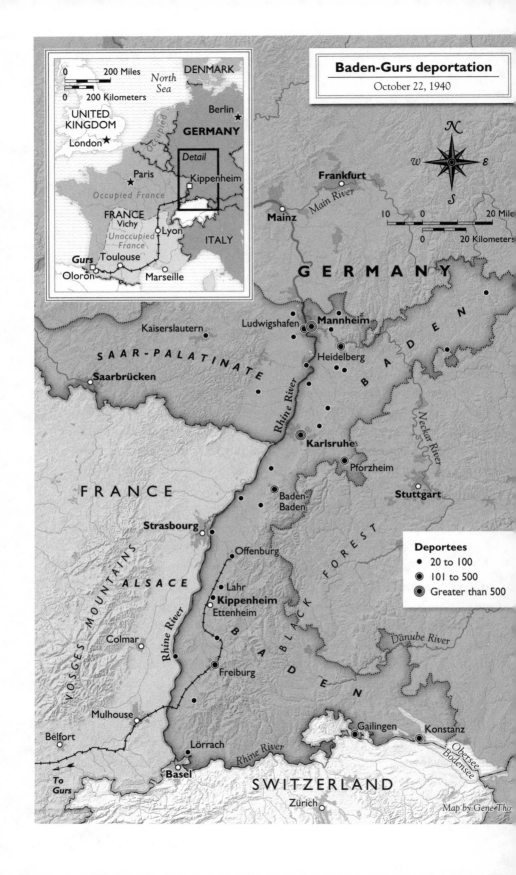

Baden-Gurs deportation
October 22, 1940

200 Miles
200 Kilometers

North Sea

DENMARK

UNITED KINGDOM
London ★

Berlin ★

GERMANY

Detail
Kippenheim

Occupied France

Paris

FRANCE
Vichy

Unoccupied France

Lyon

ITALY

Gurs
Oloron

Toulouse
Marseille

N
W   E
S

GERMANY

Frankfurt

Main River

Mainz

10   0   20 Mile

0   20 Kilometers

Kaiserslautern

Ludwigshafen Mannheim

BADEN

SAAR-PALATINATE

Heidelberg

Saarbrücken

Rhine River

Neckar River

Karlsruhe

Pforzheim

FRANCE

Baden-Baden

Stuttgart

Strasbourg

Offenburg

B L A C K   F O R E S T

ALSACE

Lahr

Kippenheim
Ettenheim

Deportees
● 20 to 100
◉ 101 to 500
◎ Greater than 500

Danube River

VOSGES MOUNTAINS

Colmar

Rhine River

B A D E N

Freiburg

Mulhouse

Gailingen   Konstanz

Belfort

Lörrach

Obersee Bodensee

To Gurs

Basel

SWITZERLAND

Zürich

Map by Gene Tho

home to at least five generations of Jews. Siegfried and Charlotte Maier had sent their two boys, Heinz and Kurt, to a Jewish boarding school in Freiburg, twenty-five miles away. They dispatched a taxi to retrieve their children and bring them back to Kippenheim.

By the time the boys reached home, their parents had stuffed some belongings into two suitcases and a couple of pillowcases. They had closed the wooden shutters of the two-story white house on Querstrasse, as if they were taking an extended vacation. Tattered advertisements for detergents still hung in the window of the shop at the side of the property, where Siegfried's father had founded a grocery store in happier times, during the reign of Kaiser Wilhelm II.

Siegfried made sure to wear his veteran's pin from the Great War on the lapel of his suit. The shiny piece of enamel emblazoned with the words *Ich hatt' einen Kameraden* ("I had a comrade") had once served as a talisman against Nazi fury. Its magical powers had become increasingly ineffectual since Kristallnacht, but Siegfried hoped it might still provide his family with a small measure of protection.[3]

The two boys found their parents in the family living room, together with their maternal grandparents. Hermann and Sofie Auerbacher had moved in to the house on Querstrasse after being forced out of their own home. Now they looked helpless and bewildered. Opa Hermann's hands were trembling, the result of a recent stroke. Everybody was waiting for the final knock on the door.

They knew it was time to leave when they heard the rumble of the canvas-covered police truck through the shuttered windows. Two police officers wearing heavy winter overcoats and shiny black boots let down metal steps on the side of the truck facing the Maier home. The policemen stood at either end of the truck, as if to block any attempt to escape. Charlotte left the house first, accompanied by twelve-year-old Heinz. They were followed onto the truck by Oma Sofie, bent over from age, and Opa Hermann, suffering from a wheezing cough. Ten-year-old Kurt followed, clutching his father's briefcase in his left hand. He wore a white workingman's beret that almost swallowed his head. Siegfried brought up the rear, with two bulging suitcases. As instructed, he left the house key in the lock.

As the Maier family lined up in front of the truck, a man from a

Deportation of Maier family

Deportation of Max and Fanny Valfer

nearby village snapped a photograph with his Agfa box camera. Standing in front of him in the autumn gloom was a young girl, a former playmate of Kurt's. She held her hands behind her back, watching the scene impassively. Her eyes were fixed on the same images as the photographer: the truck, the policemen, the suitcases, the Jews leaving the home of their ancestors. Other neighbors stole peeks of the sad procession from the windows and balconies of their homes.[4]

A carpenter turned aspiring Nazi propagandist, Wilhelm Fischer, took a total of five photographs that morning, documenting the "cleansing" of Kippenheim. On Adolf-Hitler-Strasse, he photographed the cattle dealer Marx Auerbacher leaving his house, followed by his wife, Minna, before being loaded onto the same truck as the Maiers. Marx was known in Kippenheim as the village jester. He had a nickname for everyone, and would entertain local children with scurrilous stories. Neighbors remembered him walking to the synagogue—before it was destroyed on Kristallnacht—with elbows thrust behind his back and thumbs clasped on his suspenders. Now, at the age of sixty-eight, Marx was too proud, and too resigned to his fate, to bother about a suitcase. He shambled, head down, toward the truck in an unbuttoned overcoat, watched by a few children on the sidewalk.[5]

The scene was more animated around the corner on Poststrasse. The street that led to the Rathaus from the Post Office was crowded with people from the surrounding countryside doing their business in Kippenheim. A farmer led his cow past the Valfer house, across the street from the vandalized synagogue. Max and Fanny had packed several suitcases full of clothes, shoes, and linens. According to the regulations, they were allowed to take one hundred pounds of luggage with them on their journey.[6] But "*die Herren,*" as the Kippenheimers referred to the Gestapo, decreed that there was not enough room in the truck. "I packed so much in two hours, but half of it '*die Herren*' threw back in the hallway of the house," Fanny informed her children a few days later. "No linen, no clothes, none of the things that your dear papa and I had acquired over the years. We have now become beggars."[7] The Agfa camera captured a hand reaching out to help Fanny climb aboard while Max waited impassively in the street.

Even though the deportation order theoretically made an exception for "Jews who are currently bedridden," no one was spared.[8] In the old Jewish quarter, on Friedhofstrasse, Cemetery Street, a wizened ninety-seven-year-old woman named Mathilde Wertheimer was declared "transportable," together with her two daughters, Rosa and Sofie.

The truck's final stop was Bergstrasse, a winding mountain road that led into the Black Forest, where several members of the extended Auerbacher family lived. By the time the truck reached Bergstrasse, there was no room left for luggage. Auguste Auerbacher helped her husband, Salomon, grab a couple of extra suits, which he put on one on top of the other. She attempted to do the same for herself, but time had run out. Unwilling to wait any longer, the policemen shoved the Auerbachers onto the truck by force.[9] Salomon's mother, eighty-three-year-old Mathilde Auerbacher, had been confined to bed in a home for aged and infirm Jews in Gailingen, near the border with Switzerland. She, too, was deported, along with all her fellow residents.

The Kippenheim Jews were taken to the railway station at Offenburg. This was one of a dozen collection points to receive the 6,504 Jews who were subject to the deportation order from the state of Baden and the neighboring region of Saar-Palatinate.[10] At the railway station, the deportees were ordered to list everything they owned, including houses, bank accounts, and personal belongings. Kurt Maier noted that the people around him seemed "well dressed." "The men had on fresh-looking shirts; all of them wore coats and a hat. The shoes were shined. The younger children had dolls and playthings in their possession. But in every face, one saw the anxious question: 'where are we being sent?'"[11]

After they had spent hours waiting in line, a train finally arrived. They were herded aboard with blasts of a whistle. "The first sound of my whistle means 'pick up your suitcase,' the second 'start walking,'" a Gestapo officer instructed.[12]

By the time the Kippenheimers boarded the train, it was already late in the afternoon. An SS man informed Siegfried Maier that he would be held responsible for any attempted escapes by the passengers crammed into his compartment. Noticing the veteran's pin in Siegfried's lapel, he added: "And you can take that off. It won't do you any good where you're going."[13]

The train moved agonizingly slowly southward, in the direction of Switzerland. This at least was a relief for the passengers, who were terrified by the prospect of being sent to the east, toward Poland. At Freiburg, the train headed west, toward Mulhouse, in occupied France. Here it stopped for several hours to allow the Jews to exchange their reichsmarks into French francs. SS men made their way through the train, threatening to shoot anyone who was discovered with more than 100 reichsmarks. As soon as the SS men disappeared, terrified deportees began destroying high-denomination bills they had been hiding. Many banknotes were burned. Others were torn into tiny pieces and flushed down toilets.

"There was never a search but, apart from a few who risked death to keep their money, the goal was achieved," reported an anti-Hitler German exile who interviewed the deportees after their arrival in France. "The Jews were now poor as beggars."[14]

Waiting for the trains packed with expelled Jews to arrive at the border between occupied France and unoccupied France was the Gestapo's specialist for "Jewish affairs," Adolf Eichmann. The thirty-four-year-old SS major had already made a name for himself overseeing the forced emigration of tens of thousands of Jews from Austria and Czechoslovakia. He had also helped organize the first large-scale expulsion of Jews from the Greater Reich to German-occupied Poland in 1939. He was responsible for ensuring that the operation went smoothly, overruling any objections from the French, who had not been informed in advance.[15]

According to Eichmann's later testimony, the initiative for the October 1940 deportation came from the gauleiter (regional Nazi Party leader) of Baden. After the defeat of France, Robert Wagner had been charged with incorporating newly conquered Alsace into the Third Reich. He had already cleansed Alsace of "undesirable elements," including Jews, Gypsies, criminals, and the mentally ill. More than three thousand Alsatian Jews were loaded onto trucks and dumped across the border in unoccupied France. Another seventeen thousand Jews, who had fled ahead of the German invasion, were barred from returning. The gauleiter of Saar-Palatinate, Josef Bürckel, took similar steps in the annexed French region of Lorraine.[16]

Having rid Alsace and Lorraine of "undesirables," the gauleiters turned their attention to their own territories. Their proposal to expel the entire Jewish population of Baden and Saar-Palatinate was formally approved by Hitler. The task of organizing the transports, and presenting the French with a fait accompli, was assigned to the Reich Main Security Office under Reinhard Heydrich. Eichmann traveled to the border crossing of Chalon-sur-Saône to supervise the transfer operation. If the French refused to accept the deportees, he would have to send them to a concentration camp in Germany.[17] Known after its capital, Vichy, the zone libre, or "free zone," had been granted at least nominal autonomy, in contrast to the remaining three fifths of France, including Paris and the entire Atlantic coast, which was fully occupied by Germany.

Soon nine passenger trains were backed up at the border, with five hundred to a thousand Jews on each train. Taken by surprise, Vichy officials were reluctant to admit the deportees. Eichmann negotiated with the French stationmaster, who agreed to declare the trains "German army transports."[18] This gave them the right to cross the demarcation line freely under the terms of the armistice. By his own account, the Gestapo's Jewish specialist feared that the trains would get stuck in a bureaucratic no-man's-land between the occupied and unoccupied zones, unable to move because of red signals in both directions. "It would have gone badly for me," he told an Israeli policeman decades later, "as well as for the Jews." Eichmann sat anxiously in his car "bathed in sweat" until the last train had crossed over into Vichy France.[19]

Heydrich was relieved to be able to report that the entire operation went "smoothly and without incident" and was "scarcely noticed by the population."[20] The regions of Baden and Saar-Palatinate were the first in the Reich to become officially judenfrei, or "Jew-free." French officials later said they believed that the trains contained French citizens expelled from Alsace. By the time they realized their mistake, it was too late.[21]

Overcoming its general unwillingness to challenge Berlin, the Vichy government of Marshal Philippe Pétain refused to become a dumping ground for the Jews of the Third Reich. A French protest note of November 18, 1940, asked Germany to repatriate the Jews, insisting that France could "no longer provide asylum to these foreigners."[22] Berlin rejected the protest, but did not attempt to carry out further large-scale deportations of German Jews to France. The French, meanwhile, were faced with the problem of what to do with people they termed *"indésirables."* Lacking suitable accommodation, they directed the trains toward an internment camp that had been created to house defeated soldiers of the Spanish Civil War. The camp was located near the village of Gurs, in the shadow of the Pyrenees Mountains.

It took three days and three nights for the deportees to reach their destination. They were packed together on wooden benches during the journey, with no room to stretch out. Many had to sit in the corridors of the unheated third-class coaches, squeezed between piles of suitcases. They received little to eat or drink. On the afternoon of the third day, after passing the French pilgrimage town of Lourdes, they arrived at a place named Oloron-Sainte-Marie. Rain was falling steadily, and a freezing wind was blowing off the mountains.

Trucks arrived to take the deportees the rest of the way to Gurs, some fifteen miles away along backcountry roads. Many trucks did not have tops, and the refugees were soon soaked. An American relief worker, Donald Lowrie, who happened to be visiting Gurs that day, was struck by the number of "gray-haired, fine-looking, well-dressed people, some in fur coats" perched on top of the open trucks. But the new arrivals also included invalids, cripples, and a scattering of "feeble-minded," herded along by soldiers speaking a language they could not understand. "There was a larger amount of baggage than one would have thought, most of it good-looking in ghastly contrast to the wretchedness toward which these people were bound. How quiet they all were! No chatter, no complaint."[23]

It was already dark by the time they reached Gurs. The camp consisted of a single gravel road, nearly a mile long, on either side of which stood collections of flimsy wooden huts, clustered into so-called *îlots,* or "islands." The term was appropriate, as each *îlot* floated on a sea of mud. To reach the huts from the central pathway, it was necessary to wade through a swamp of glutinous clay that sucked up everybody and everything.

The Baden expellees joined some three thousand existing inmates, including other foreign Jews, Spaniards opposed to Franco, and anti-Nazi Germans. Although they were accustomed to the rigors of camp life, the old-timers were "overwhelmed by the sight of such enormous misery." Hanna Schramm, an exiled Berliner who had been declared an "enemy alien" by the Vichy regime, watched the dazed newcomers being unloaded from the trucks.

> People of all categories and ages. Rich people, poor people, healthy ones, sick ones, and, alas, so many children. There were sick people who had to be carried into the *îlot* on stretchers, and old people aged seventy, eighty, even ninety. They looked like ghosts who had escaped the grave and were no longer of this world. They let themselves be led, saying a polite thank you when one gave them a hand. They were unable to comprehend what had happened to them.... These old people were not fighting any more. Their hands were still warm, their legs moved, but in actual fact they were already dead.

"Is this where the hotel is?" one of the new arrivals asked Hanna.

"I want to go home," cried another. "I am ninety-five years old."

"Watch out, there's a ditch," yelled Hanna, as a group of deportees stumbled through the camp with their suitcases. It made little difference. The new arrivals kept falling into the swamp. When they got up, they were so exhausted they barely noticed that they were covered in mud.[24]

Men and women were assigned huts at opposite ends of the camp, separated by long coils of barbed wire. There was room for about sixty people in each hut, lying next to each other in bunks. A few elderly internees were provided thin mattresses, but most had to make do with straw and a single blanket. Built out of uncured lumber that had "never known paint," the dark and gloomy huts lacked any kind of insulation.²⁵ Instead of windows, there were leaky wooden trapdoors in the roof that had to be closed during the frequent downpours. Wind and rain howled through the cracks between the plywood walls and the corrugated metal roofs. Rats and mice scampered along the muddy floors.

The first meal consisted of soup with hard peas and sweet potatoes, boiled in water. It was practically inedible, but the deportees were glad to finally have something in their stomachs. In the morning, they received a small piece of bread, followed by some watery soup for lunch, and a few chickpeas swimming in a murky liquid for dinner. The lucky ones were able to eke out their rations with some lard they had brought from Germany. By the end of the first month, as many as twenty inmates a day were dying of disease and malnutrition.

Simple matters, such as going to the toilet, were a major ordeal. In order to visit the makeshift latrines, the deportees had to leave the hut, brave the endless rain, and then climb up a ladder to a wooden platform suspended over a garbage can. Older people frequently got stuck in the mud, and were unable to extricate themselves because they were too weak. Rescue parties had to be sent to pull them out of the muck. Back in the huts, the constant wailing of children and stifled moans of the elderly made it impossible to get much sleep.

The population of the camp tripled overnight to nearly ten thousand. While the conditions were appalling, the newcomers were relieved to learn that there were no Nazi guards in the camp. A handful of French gendarmes assisted by relief workers in armbands maintained order. The inmates were permitted to communicate with the outside world, as long as they had sufficient money to buy stamps. They soon began writing letters describing their new situation to their loved ones in England and America.

"Our warm clothes and shoes are all at home in those parcels [the Gestapo] took away," Max Valfer wrote to family members soon after arriving in Gurs. "Hopefully we will have some heat in our barracks soon as it is very cold." He asked his children "to send money here immediately so we can buy something once in a while." He also urged them to follow up on the United States immigration application that he and Fanny had filed with the Stuttgart consulate more than two years previously. "Kind, sweet children, do not forget us," he pleaded. "Go to the Jewish committee over there and do all that is necessary so that we get some relief from the mess that we are in."

Fanny scrawled her own note at the end of Max's letter. "We are now, my dear children, in the Pyrenees as poor beggars. I still cannot grasp that we have become so poor and helpless. Often I cannot bear it. My eyes hurt from crying."[26]

Other Kippenheimers struck a more positive note. Gerda and Salomon (known as "Momo") Auerbacher had arrived in Gurs without any of their luggage, but were glad to be out of Germany. "Although we are destitute, I can breathe again now that we are away from home," Gerda wrote to her brother Hugo in New York. "Despite everything, I would no longer return to collect all our things even if I were allowed to do so." Gerda derived comfort from the words of one of her friends: "Those who have nothing have nothing to worry about." She was glad to hear about Roosevelt's reelection. "Perhaps now we will be able to come to you more quickly," she told her brother. "Don't worry about us too much. God will continue to help us."[27]

News of the mass deportation reached Western capitals within a few days. The American embassy in Berlin reported on October 25 that "some six or seven thousand" Jews had been expelled from southwest Germany to the south of France. A week later, the American chargé d'affaires in Vichy sarcastically described the transfer of the Baden Jews as "the first benefit for France in the new Franco-German collaboration policy." According to the diplomat, the Gurs camp commander was "upset" to have been given only "three hours notice" of the arrival of the deportees. "The local press here has of course been told to make no reference to this."[28]

Reports about the plight of the Gurs prisoners soon landed on the desk of Eleanor Roosevelt. "Situation in the French camp unspeakable," read a memo from a relief worker in southern France. "Nobody is at present doing anything for the thousands of poor devils in the camps." Another memo urged colleagues in the United States to "press just as hard as you can for visas" for the refugees. "Every day makes a difference," he wrote. "Visas mean lives."

Accompanying the memos was a cover note from the Austrian opposition activist, Joseph Buttinger, who had lobbied Eleanor on behalf of political refugees stranded in southern France following the fall of Paris. After thanking the First Lady for doing "everything possible to help," Buttinger wrote that "it looks again as if only your word" could resolve "this ghastly situation." Eleanor promptly forwarded the memos to the president with her own note. "FDR, Can't something be done?"[29] There is no record of a reply.

Firsthand accounts of the sufferings of the Baden deportees also appeared in the American press. "I am so terribly depressed," began one letter from Gurs, forwarded to *The New York Times* by a Red Cross official. "This is the greatest tragedy the world has ever witnessed."[30] The *Times* also published extracts from a devastating report on Gurs by Quaker officials under the headline "Misery and Death in French Camps."[31] The Quaker report described an "atmosphere of human hopelessness," with doctors fighting "overwhelming odds" to contain typhoid fever and other epidemics. A visit to a barracks revealed "sixty people lying on their mattresses, or standing, for there are no tables, no chairs. The children cannot play and the women cannot work."

According to the Quaker investigators, many of the older refugees exhibited "an intense desire to die.... They will not fight any more: apathetic, they lie on their straw mattresses, often refusing food and waiting for the end." An examination of corpses revealed numerous cases of malnourishment, with "skin sticking to the bones, the muscles hypertrophied, a state of thinness extreme." Nutrition experts estimated that Gurs inmates were receiving at most 850 calories per day, a catastrophically low amount for prisoners already enfeebled by a succession of "physical and moral sufferings."[32] The shocking reports from unoccupied France stirred memories of the horrific conditions in Dachau and other German concentration camps during the weeks after Kristallnacht.

Gaston Henry-Haye had been appointed ambassador of Vichy France to Washington following the fall of Paris on the strength of his excellent English and influential political connections. As a youth, he had worked as an elevator boy in a New York hotel and as an instructor to the U.S. Army. Elected mayor of Versailles in 1928, he belonged to the circle of right-wing French politicians who had advocated cooperation with Nazi Germany prior to the war. His double-barreled name, trim mustache, and fondness for pedigree Dalmatian dogs suggested an aristocratic background. He actually came from a poor peasant family, and had dedicated his political career to preaching a "national social revolution."

Henry-Haye was well regarded by the former U.S. ambassador to France, William Bullitt, but FDR's friend Harold Ickes "did not take a fancy to him. He struck us as being a smoothie." Ickes suspected that Henry-Haye—"a big, fine, good-looking man"—had been sent over to Washington to make trouble on behalf of Hitler.[33]

One of the new ambassador's first tasks in Washington was to urge the Roosevelt administration to admit Jewish refugees stranded in Vichy France. At the end of November, he presented Secretary of State Cordell Hull with a memorandum describing the arrival in Gurs of "several thousand Israelites" expelled from Germany. The memorandum noted that France was already providing shelter to "three and one half million aliens" including White Russians, Armenians, Germans, Spaniards, and Poles. It called for a "fairer distribution of the foreign refugees, particularly of the Israelites."[34] Henry-Haye wanted the State Department to facilitate the onward emigration of the Jews deported to Gurs.

His démarche posed a tricky problem for Roosevelt aides. While they had little regard for the pro-German government headed by Marshal Pétain, they had an interest in preserving at least the semblance of normal relations. Under the terms of the armistice, Vichy retained control of a powerful naval fleet as well as France's overseas colonies in North Africa and the Caribbean. These were important strategic assets that must not be allowed to fall directly into German hands. Furthermore, Henry-Haye had taken care to couch his note in the humanitarian language used by FDR himself in urging international action on behalf of political refugees. He praised the president's "noble initiative" in convening the 1938 Évian conference. His message was that it was up to the United States to live up to its own long-standing humanitarian ideals.

State Department officials detected a plot. They recalled previous attempts by Germany to expel Jews by driving them across the border at gunpoint at night into neighboring European countries. When "a weak point" was discovered, the process was repeated on a larger scale on subsequent nights. As the State Department saw it, the same tactic was now being deployed against the Americas. The French were "acting under German pressure" to force changes in U.S. immigration policy. The goal was to probe for "weakness" in the hope of encouraging "a backfire of humanitarian emotion" in democratic countries.[35] If the United States agreed to "rescue" the Baden deportees, the inevitable result would be more deportations.

Under Secretary of State Sumner Welles wrote a memo to the president advising him to resist the "blackmailing totalitarian tactics" of the Germans. He warned of "a reign of terror" against Jews who remained in Germany. "Hundreds of thousands of unhappy people will be dispossessed of their homes and their goods to be used as pawns in a German maneuver calculated to embroil opinion in the democratic countries."[36]

Welles drafted a reply to Henry-Haye and sent it to FDR for his approval. The document stressed that the United States was already doing everything possible "to relieve the pressure caused by the over-concentration of refugees in certain countries, including France." It claimed erroneously that the "maximum number of persons" allowable under the immigration quotas was already being admitted to the United States. This had been true for the German quota for the two years prior to June 1940. Since then, however, the German quota had been less than 70 percent filled. (See chart on page 296.) The much smaller French quota was also less than 70 percent filled.[37]

The president signaled his agreement with the State Department draft by scrawling "OK, FDR" across the top of the document.[38] If the Baden deportees were admitted to the United States, it would be on a case-by-case basis.

On November 28, just three days after Henry-Haye delivered his démarche to the State Department, a gleaming 1936 Buick pulled up outside the Gurs detention camp with two Americans.[39] One of the Americans was Donald Lowrie, the European representative of the Young Men's Christian Association, who had become a regular visitor to the camp. His companion was a tall, intense man with wire-rimmed spectacles, in his late thirties. He bore a letter of introduction identifying himself as Hiram Bingham Jr., vice consul of the United States of America.[40]

It was a cold, dreary, wet day, typical for this time of year. A former police commissioner from Alsace had just taken over command of the camp from a military officer. He was reviewing a ragtag honor guard of gendarmes and soldiers, assisted by rough young Spaniards in leather coats who served as camp messengers. The Americans did their best to keep warm as they waited to talk to the new commander. Some of the offices had an electric heater or a little coal stove, but it was impossible to keep out the cold and the damp. As Bingham recorded later, "The wind whistled through the cracks and the floors were dirty with tracked-in mud."[41]

The ostensible purpose of Bingham's visit to Gurs was to avoid much "useless correspondence" with inmates about their immigration to the United States. The American consulate in Marseille was already being flooded by letters from Baden deportees requesting urgent consideration of their visa cases. Vichy officials had informed the consulate that they were "anxious to facilitate the departure from France of all foreign refugees and non-French nationals." They proposed establishing an "emigration camp" closer to Marseille to house refugees with a good chance of immigrating to the United States. The consulate, however, lacked the support staff to handle more than twenty visa cases a day. Bingham had convinced his boss that a visit to the camps would help weed out the "hopeless cases" before they overwhelmed the consulate.[42]

In reality, Bingham wanted to focus attention on the plight of the refugees and help any way he could. He was making the trip at his own expense.[43] Since the fall of Paris, Bingham had earned a reputation among relief workers in Vichy France as the U.S. official most sympathetic to their cause. He had shown that he was willing to stretch the rules on occasion, and risk censure from Washington, to smuggle anti-Fascist refugees out of the country. He had helped organize the

escape from a French internment camp of the celebrated German Jewish novelist Lion Feuchtwanger, who was wanted by the Nazis for his
anti-Hitler writings. After sheltering Feuchtwanger in his own home
in Marseille, Bingham had issued him papers under an assumed name,
Mr. Wetcheck, an almost literal English translation of *feucht* (wet) and
Wange (cheek). Feuchtwanger had used the document to escape illegally across the border into Spain, one step ahead of the Gestapo.[44]

Known to his friends as "Harry," Bingham hailed from a long line
of Connecticut Yankees, distinguished by their stubbornness and
independence. His father, Hiram, had served as a United States senator from Connecticut, but was better known as an explorer who had
rediscovered the forgotten Inca city of Machu Pichu. His grandfather
and great-grandfather had been missionaries to Hawaii. Multiple generations of Binghams had attended Yale and Harvard. Typically, such
a bloodline would have led to a swift rise to the senior ranks of the
Foreign Service. Somehow, however, Harry did not quite fit into the
diplomatic old boys' club for which he had been trained and educated.
He had been repeatedly passed over for promotion. Superiors detected
an overly sensitive disposition, misplaced idealism, and lack of the
social graces expected from American diplomats.

An outspoken supporter of the Roosevelt New Deal, Bingham frequently got into arguments with more conservative colleagues. He
told a supervisor that his main aim in life was "to help people."[45]
Feuchtwanger described Bingham in his diary as "an awkward, friendly,
puritanical, dutiful, somewhat sad New Englander" who was "always
tired and exhausted."[46] At the same time, he acknowledged a huge debt
to Bingham for arranging his escape. In the opinion of the American
rescue worker Varian Fry, Bingham was "the one man at the Consulate"
who understood that his job was "not to apply the rules rigidly but to
save lives wherever he could."[47]

Bingham's humanitarian streak raised eyebrows among his superiors. "He is inclined to permit idealistic considerations to transcend
the letter of his instructions," noted the American consul general to
Marseille, Hugh Fullerton, in an annual efficiency report. "[He] sup-
ports his convictions with a stubbornness which, I understand, has at
times estranged former chiefs."[48]

As Bingham toured the Gurs camp with Lowrie, he was struck by

The bread surgeon in Gurs, a drawing by Karl Bodek and Kurt Löw

the appalling sanitary conditions and lack of food. The population had swollen to fourteen thousand because of the transfer of inmates from another camp ravaged by a typhoid epidemic. The primary source of sustenance was a twelve-ounce bread ration that was distributed in the morning and had to last all day. The division of the loaves was "the most important happening of the day" in the life of an *îlot*. Inmates hovered over the bread surgeon as he cut the loaf into six pieces. "That's too large," someone would cry, as the knife hovered over the loaf. "Now it's too small," shouted another. "Bigger, much bigger."[49]

The bread was supplemented by a thin vegetable soup which, Bingham observed, was "often cold or filled with sand and dirt" by the time it arrived in the barracks. Lacking dishes and spoons, inmates used "old sardine cans" to slop down the watery mixture.[50]

Alongside deep despair, the Americans also noted valiant efforts by the detainees to raise morale. They reported that teachers were already organizing classes for the children. In some camps, including

Gurs, adults could attend "theatrical entertainments," concerts, and lectures by university professors. Skilled craftsmen had set up small workshops where they turned discarded scrap materials into dominoes, chess pieces, and even model airplanes. There was a wealth of creative and intellectual talent. Bingham and Lowrie came across a young violinist who had previously worked as concertmaster for the Bremen opera. One of the Baden deportees told them he had once been a judge. Camp inmates used formal titles such as *Frau Professor* or *Herr Doktor* to address each other.

From his interviews at Gurs, Bingham estimated that there were approximately three thousand "prospective immigrants" to the United States in the camp.[51] Most were former Baden residents who had already filed their visa applications in Stuttgart and were waiting to be admitted under the German quota. To reduce the burden on the consulate, he suggested that relief officials conduct an initial screening to determine who should be given priority for transfer to Marseille.

Bingham's proposal delegated much of the preliminary work of interviewing visa applicants to Jewish relief organizations. The most prominent such organization was the Hebrew Immigrant Aid Society, known as HIAS, and its French affiliate HICEM. Initially founded to assist Jews fleeing pogroms in Russia in the nineteenth century, HIAS had been promoting German Jewish immigration to the United States since the early days of the Nazi regime. Its slogan was "Rescue Through Emigration." The organization raised funds from American Jews which were used to charter ships from Europe to the United States and help pay for tickets for refugees. A HIAS pamphlet claimed that the organization had helped a hundred thousand endangered Jews reach safety prior to the outbreak of the war.[52]

By the time Bingham arrived in Gurs, HIAS-HICEM was already well established in the camp. A HIAS press release dated November 19 warned that the Baden deportees faced a stark alternative: emigration or "death by starvation."[53] The vice consul met a group of deportees who had volunteered to handle visa-related correspondence from the camp, which would be channeled through the HICEM office in Marseille. He drove away impressed by their "willingness to cooperate" and understanding of the complexities of U.S. immigration law.[54] HICEM officials noted with satisfaction that their organization had become the officially approved intermediary between the refugees and the consulate. The consulate was so "overloaded with work" that it was unable to respond to individual letters requesting information.[55]

During the day the Americans were in Gurs and the following night, hospital workers recorded the deaths of thirteen inmates. They included seventy-three-year-old Hermann Auerbacher, who had been photographed being loaded onto a truck in Kippenheim less than a month before. He passed away at one in the morning in the camp infirmary, a few hours after Bingham's departure. The death certificate attributed his demise to "senility," the term used for the deaths of most elderly people.[56] In fact, Hermann was a victim of the rat-borne typhoid epidemic.

Sofie Auerbacher escorted the body of her husband to the cemetery at the far end of the camp, together with her daughter Charlotte and son-in-law Siegfried Maier. A rabbi mumbled Kaddish prayers over the grave. A few other internees observed the proceedings from a distance. A funeral was the one occasion when people could leave their *îlots* without prior approval from the camp authorities. Since men and women were separated into different *îlots*, burying the dead provided a rare opportunity for families to get together, whether or not they had known the deceased. Inmates would often pay their final respects to complete strangers, purely to socialize or get some exercise.[57]

Daily life at Gurs soon came to be dominated by the burial processions that proceeded down the central alleyway of the camp. During the exceptionally harsh winter of 1940, there were sometimes as many as twenty funerals a day. One of these funerals left a deep impression on ten-year-old Kurt Maier. He was standing by the barbed wire outside his barracks when a corpse passed by on a stretcher. The stretcher-bearers put down their load to rest, before proceeding to the cemetery. The deceased was an elderly woman with long white hair that tumbled onto the ground. When they picked up the stretcher, the hair of the corpse brushed against Kurt's pullover. He ran crying to his mother and begged her to wash the garment. Since there was no soap, she could use only cold water.[58]

Gurs was a coming-of-age experience for the youngest Kippen-heimer, a sudden and unwanted passage from childhood to adulthood. Kurt was old enough to remember the life of a German Jewish community before its destruction. He loved to accompany his father on his rounds of villages in the Black Forest largely unaffected by the Nazi madness, stopping in a Jewish-owned inn for a lemonade and a sausage sandwich. There had been dark times, too, of course. His father suffered a nervous breakdown around the time of Kristallnacht. His parents frequently quarreled about money, and whether they could afford to help their friends and relatives. After one such quarrel, his mother left the room in tears. A short time later, Kurt heard a cry from the attic. When he went up to investigate, he found her with a piece of fabric looped around her neck. She had attempted to strangle herself, but stopped when she saw her son.[59]

None of this, however, had prepared Kurt for the traumatic experience of being thrown out of his home and sent to a prison camp in a foreign land. In Gurs, he lived in the same hut—J17—as his mother and grandmother, close to the camp exit. Like everybody else, he wore his shoes to bed to prevent them from being nibbled away by rats. He slept in his overcoat to keep warm. There was a constant stench from dysentery and the failed attempts of old people to climb the ladder to the outdoor latrines. Gurs was a place where "everything was grey," from the flimsy huts to the bleak, wintery sky to the strained faces of the inmates. As he lay on the wooden planks, listening to the rats scampering across the floor and the rain pelting against the rooftop, Kurt felt a steady pain of anxiety in his stomach.[60]

Shortly before the death of Opa Hermann, Kurt was himself admitted to the quarantine barracks with diphtheria. In the next bed lay a pretty girl, a year or so older than Kurt, named Liesel Kling. Liesel had been a child movie actress back in Germany, and was well known in the camp. Fortunately, one of the doctors had a serum that was effective against an illness that would otherwise have killed them both. Kurt and Liesel slowly recovered. After they were discharged from the sick bay, they went for walks together to a small hill, above the sea of mud and flimsy wooden huts. As they sat in the sun, looking out at the majestic Pyrenees in the distance, Kurt desperately wanted to hold Liesel's hand and give her a kiss. But the shy ten-year-old did not dare.[61]

Hugo and Bella Wachenheimer took care to depict their deportation from Kippenheim in the most positive possible light in letters to their now sixteen-year-old daughter, Hedy. They missed her terribly. They avoided any mention of the atrocious conditions in Gurs or their confinement in a prison camp. "In the meantime, we have changed our address," Hugo wrote Hedy on November 20, four weeks after their arrival in France. "The main thing is that we are all healthy and the whole family is together."[62] Deported together with Hugo and Bella were Hedy's uncle and aunt, Oskar and Käthe, her maternal grandfather, Heinrich Eichel, and numerous other relatives.

Opa Heinrich had been living with Hugo and Bella, off and on, for the last four years. He was a semi-invalid who required a special diet that he was unable to receive in Gurs. Hedy was particularly fond of the gentle, bald-headed old man with the round eyeglasses. Hugo informed his daughter that he had arranged for "dear Opa" to enter a hospital, where he would "receive good care." Gurs camp records show that Heinrich Eichel died on December 29, 1940, soon after Hedy received her father's letter. He had been taken to the rudimentary camp infirmary, where there was little to be done for him.

Hugo and Bella saw each other only infrequently, as they lived at opposite ends of the camp. They needed special permission to visit each other's *îlot*. Passes were typically issued once or twice a month, or on special occasions, such as birthdays or anniversaries. In the middle of December, they were both allowed to attend a grand family reunion, in honor of the "Golden Wedding Anniversary" of Hugo's Uncle Julius. Three generations of Wachenheimers gathered outside one of the wooden barracks for a group portrait.[63] The fact that such a normally joyous moment was being celebrated amid the squalor of Gurs lent a macabre character to the event.

Half blind from a debilitating eye disease, Uncle Julius sat in the front row, arm in arm with his wife, Emma, squinting into the sunlight. He was dressed in a three-piece suit, tie, and silk hat. Except for his mud-splattered clothes, he personified bourgeois respectability. On either side of Julius and Emma were two of their grandchildren, ten-year-old Margot and seven-year-old Edith, their pant legs also covered

Julius and Emma Wachenheimer's "Golden Wedding Anniversary" in Gurs.
Hedy's parents are top right. For key, see page 282.

in mud. Standing behind Margot was her father, Max Strauss, who had been refused a visa to the United States because of a poor heart. Hugo and Bella stood on benches at the back of the group, alongside various aunts, uncles, and cousins.

Margot and Edith were both ill at the time the photo was taken. Their eyes were lifeless. They seemed dazed and almost half asleep. The day after the family reunion, Margot was examined by a nurse and diagnosed with scarlet fever. She was moved to a quarantine hut, soon to be joined by her sister and mother, who were also taken ill.[64]

Back in Germany, the Wachenheimer family had been riven by an inheritance dispute involving Uncle Julius and Hugo's father. The conflict resulted in the younger brother, Julius, leaving Kippenheim for the much larger town of Karlsruhe, where he established his own business. Although the details of the argument were soon forgotten, the two branches of the family had little to do with each other from that moment on.[65] The deportation to Gurs brought the estranged family members together once again. Rich and poor, young and old, healthy and sick, the twenty-two people in the photograph were now united in calamity and grief.

In his first letter to Hedy from Gurs, Hugo depicted the move to

France as temporary. "We hope we will only have to stay here a few weeks and can then come to the USA quickly." In a postscript, Bella also looked forward to the time when "we will all be happily reunited again. We will then gladly forget all the difficulties."[66]

Hugo provided a bleaker—and more accurate—account of his immigration prospects in a letter to a Jewish relief organization several weeks later. He and Bella had been unable to obtain the affidavits needed to support their visa application to the United States. They had no idea how they were going to pay for ship tickets across the Atlantic. "We are living here extremely depressed," Hugo informed HICEM officials. "Our only child was obliged to leave us two years ago. Because of this, homesickness weighs heavily on us both. We are also in mourning over the death of my wife's father [Heinrich], who died here."[67]

Still, Hugo refused to give up hope. Along with other Kippenheimers, he stood in line outside the HICEM office in Gurs to apply for an American immigration visa. He filled in a questionnaire optimistically titled *Demande de Voyage*, "Request for Travel," for himself and Bella. The most important questions concerned the names of the sponsors who would advance the money necessary to pay for their trip. Hugo gave the name of his brother-in-law Manfred, who had only recently arrived in New York, and the distant relative in Chicago who had already indicated that he was not prepared to help. He also provided the registration number issued by the American consulate in Stuttgart in August 1938. All this information would determine the Wachenheimers' priority for release from Gurs.[68]

The visa sweepstakes quickly became an all-consuming topic of conversation in the dimly lit barracks of the camp. As they debated their chances of escape, the prisoners were acutely aware that their fate depended on a higher power that operated on its own timetable, according to its own mysterious regulations. As a Gurs inmate remarked to an American consul: "To you, *we* are just numbers. To us, *you* are the god who has the right to open the gates of the promised land or keep shut that door and condemn us to despair."[69]

NINE

Marseille–Martinique

TOWARD THE END of February 1941, the Maier family received a summons to meet with the Gurs camp commander. They waited in his office as he slowly perused a file containing their request for emigration. The papers seemed to be in order, but *Monsieur le Commissaire Spécial* was taking his time making a final decision.

A policeman with combed-over hair and trim mustache, Georges Kaiser had been in command of the camp for less than two months. His predecessor had lasted only a few weeks, and had spent much of his time angling for a transfer to a less onerous position. To his critics, Kaiser seemed more "concerned about his personal welfare" than the welfare of the internees.[1] According to Donald Lowrie of the YMCA, the Gurs camp commander found himself "in the position of God-omnipotent" over the lives of more than ten thousand men and women, "most of them more cultured, more capable, more intelligent than himself."[2]

Running a refugee camp in Vichy France offered numerous opportunities for corruption. Wielding powers of life and death over his prisoners, the camp commander presided over an extensive black market system operated by the guards. While the daily food ration of 850 calories was inadequate for survival, bread, eggs, and even sausages were available for an exorbitant price. In Lowrie's words, the "second-rate men" who ran the camps came under "extraordinary temptation:

all purchasing, all supplies, involving sums of money a man had never dreamed of before, are completely in their hands."[3]

The dossier on Kaiser's desk noted that Siegfried and Charlotte Maier had been issued United States visas in Stuttgart in May 1940. The visas were valid for four months only and had expired in September.[4] Renewing the documents would require an interview with the American consul in Marseille. The Maier file also included a promise of a safe conduct pass from the local Vichy government prefect. German officials were reported to have raised no objection to the departure of the Maier family. Their relatives in New York and Texas had agreed to pay for their passage across the Atlantic. It seemed a fairly straightforward case.[5]

Watching the camp commander laboriously examine the file, Siegfried became impatient. Vichy bureaucrats might be more humane than their German counterparts, but they were also less efficient. Unable to contain himself, Siegfried murmured to his wife in German, "These Frenchmen don't kill themselves with work."[6]

"What was that you said?" the camp commander demanded angrily. Siegfried mumbled a hasty apology, encouraged by an alarmed glare from his wife. Evidently this Gallic blockhead understood some German. Or perhaps he did not like to be interrupted in his agonizingly slow perusal of the dossier. Internees were expected to be humble and respectful at all times.

Siegfried had spent much of the last three months studying possibilities for emigration from France. He carried with him a small black address book that included handwritten notes on how to obtain an American visa. One such note, in German, recorded a false report about U.S. consular procedures that was circulating among German Jews. "The American government is now willing to issue an unlimited number of visitors' visas to German emigrants who are in danger and are in France or Spain," the report stated.[7] It went on to claim that the American consul in Marseille would help the refugees cross the Atlantic on American steamers. U.S. officials traced the original report back to Nazi-controlled newspapers in Luxembourg and Belgium. While the authorship of the report was unclear, the overall effect was to raise unrealistic expectations among Jewish refugees about their emigration prospects.

The fact that the Maiers possessed expired U.S. visas meant that they had a much stronger case for release than other Gurs inmates. But even that chance now seemed jeopardized by Siegfried's inopportune outburst.

Kaiser was under pressure from his superiors to transfer detainees to "emigration camps" in the Marseille area. The Gurs camp was hopelessly overcrowded. Within days of the arrival of the Baden Jews, some three thousand mainly Belgian refugees had also been dumped in Gurs, bringing a typhoid epidemic with them from the camp of Saint-Cyprien. Death and a slow trickle of releases had reduced the camp population somewhat, but some twelve thousand people remained crammed into several hundred claustrophobic barracks.[8] For months, Vichy officials had been slow to issue exit visas to German Jews, for fear of releasing people on the Nazi wanted list. They were now determined to get rid of *"les indésirables"* as quickly as possible. They informed U.S. diplomats about the new policy in early February, stating that it would apply to all but a few German nationals specifically singled out by the Nazis.[9]

Despite his irritation with Siegfried, Kaiser signed the papers agreeing to the transfer of the Maier family. "Opening your big trap could have cost us our lives," Charlotte reprimanded her husband in her soft Black Forest dialect, when the family was safely outside the office.[10]

News of the Maier family's imminent release traveled rapidly around the *îlots*. Over the next few days, Siegfried was approached by many of his former Kippenheim neighbors with requests to contact their relatives overseas. Some asked for urgent transfers of money or assistance with an affidavit. Most simply wanted to remind their relatives that they were still alive and needed help. Siegfried scribbled dozens of names and addresses into his little black address book, promising to do what he could.[11]

Charlotte and her two children arrived in Marseille on March 2, after a day-long train journey across southern France. That same day, Siegfried was transferred to the Les Milles emigration camp, on a windswept plateau above the town, near the city of Aix-en-Provence.[12] They were a big step closer to their final goal, but men and women were still kept apart.

176 | THE UNWANTED

For much of its two-thousand-year history, the great port on the Mediterranean had served as a gateway to gentler European climes. Greeks, Romans, Phoenicians, and most recently Algerians had all passed through Marseille on their way north. Since the German invasion of France in June 1940, the human traffic had all been in the opposite direction. The city was packed with people focused on a single goal: to escape from Europe.

The fall of Paris had unleashed a wave of human misery that rolled across southern France. The refugees had fled the capital by any means available: car and train, bicycle and horse-drawn cart. Terrorized by German planes screaming overhead and tanks chasing them from the rear, they abandoned their broken-down buses and bombed-out trucks. When the roads became impassable, they had continued on foot, dragging their few possessions behind them. As one French town after another fell to the Germans, the crowds moved further south, toward the *zone libre*. Marseille was easily the biggest city in unoccupied France, even though Vichy was the nominal capital. The city of immigrants quickly became the gathering place for anyone on the run from Hitler.

In the words of a *Time* magazine reporter, the "agony of Europe was, for one delirious historical moment, crammed into a few square miles" of "a lecherous and filthy port."[13] Throngs of migrants ran from one foreign consulate to another in search of entry visas and transit visas. International relief workers established their committees in the Hôtel Splendide, interviewing potential "clients" under the watchful eyes of the French police. Anti-Nazi politicians held court in the cafés around the Old Port, alongside famous artists and intellectuals. Jewish families squeezed into tiny rooms in squalid hotels that had been transformed into makeshift internment camps. Long lines formed outside the offices of the steamship companies as refugees jostled for space on overcrowded boats.

In her autobiographical novel *Transit*, the German Jewish writer Anna Seghers called Marseille the place "where Europe ends and the sea begins." She depicted the city's main street, the Canebière, as a

TOP *Refugees line the deck of the* St. Louis *in Havana on June 1, 1939, and call out to their relatives on small boats in the harbor below.* BOTTOM *The actors Marcel Dalio and his wife, Madeleine Lebeau, were among eighty-one European refugees on board the* Quanza *admitted to the United States in September 1940.*

Senator Robert Reynolds (TOP) and newspaper columnist Dorothy Thompson (BOTTOM) represented opposite sides of the debate about admitting victims of Nazi persecution into the United States. Reynolds wanted to keep refugees out of the country, while Thompson agonized over "a piece of paper with a stamp" signifying "the difference between life and death."

TOP *Jews expelled from southwest Germany in October 1940 were sent to a French internment camp at Gurs, near the Pyrenees Mountains. Many died from disease and malnutrition.* ABOVE *An elderly refugee tries to make her way through the mud of Gurs, created by the endless winter rain.* LEFT *Refugees with a chance of receiving American visas were sent to Camp des Milles, an abandoned tile factory near Marseille.*

TOP *Prime Minister Pierre Laval and Chief of State Philippe Pétain review an honor guard in Vichy.* ABOVE *American vice consul Hiram Bingham Jr. on a boat overlooking Marseille harbor.* LEFT *Emergency Rescue Committee representative Varian Fry, in Marseille. Fry praised Bingham as the "one man" at the U.S. consulate who understood that it was his job to "save lives wherever he could."*

e Jewish rescue agency HIAS-HICEM produced the poster (TOP) as part of its fund-raising campaign
ring Jewish refugees to America.   BOTTOM *The "temporary" building constructed on the Mall in*
shington in early 1942 to house the new Interdepartmental Visa Review Committee.

The stark alternatives for many Jewish refugees trapped in southern France in 1942 were a boat to America or a train to Auschwitz. Ninety-nine-year-old Mathilde Wertheimer was aboard the Nyassa (TOP), which arrived in Baltimore in July 1942. A refugee worker took the clandestine photograph (BOTTOM) of Jews awaiting deportation from Rivesaltes to Drancy and Auschwitz in September 1942. The deportees included Bella Wachenheimer.

TOP, LEFT *The Valfer house in Kippenheim in the 1930s, with advertisements for cigarettes on the front wall.* TOP, RIGHT *A family of Kurdish refugees from Syria moved into the house in 2016 and opened a kebab shop.* BOTTOM *Max Valfer is expelled from his home in Kippenheim in October 1940, prior to his deportation to Gurs and later Auschwitz.*

TOP *After the war, the Kippenheim synagogue was used as an agriculture warehouse.* BOTTOM *The synagogue was fully restored in 2003 following a twenty-five-year campaign by former Jewish residents, local historians, and the mayor of Kippenheim. The photograph shows the renovated building.*

human sewer. Sloping gently downward, the arrow-straight, tree-lined avenue connected the hills rising on the edge of the city with the Old Port. In an ironic riff on Nazi propaganda, Seghers asked herself where "the defilers of all races, the deserters from all nations" would end up. Her answer: the Canebière. "This, then, was where the detritus was flowing—along this channel, this gutter, the Canebière, and via this gutter into the sea, where there would at last be room for all."[14]

Seghers drew on her own experiences as a refugee to describe the nightmare world of affidavits and permits that expired before they could be used. She became familiar with "the frizzy-haired bureau-cratic goblins" in the prefecture and the stone-faced consuls who "make you feel as if you're nothing, a nobody."[15] She grew accustomed to the "Godless emptiness" the French call *cafard,* a debilitating bore-dom associated with endless waiting. In the midst of general chaos, she was amazed to find the authorities "inventing ever more intricate drawn-out procedures for sorting, classifying, registering, and stamp-ing these people over whose emotions they had lost all power."[16] It was rule by permit and rubber stamp.

Everybody understood that the possibilities for flight were few, and liable to disappear at any moment. According to Varian Fry, Marseille representative of the New York–based Emergency Rescue Committee, refugees lived in a state of constant fear. "Every ring of the doorbell, every step on the stair, every knock on the door" could be a signal that the police were about to deliver them to the Gestapo. "They sought frantically for some means of escape from the net which had suddenly been dropped over their heads. In their eagerness to get away, they eas-ily became prey to every sort of swindler and blackmailer. Sometimes, under the incessant pounding of wild rumors and fantastic horror sto-ries, their already badly frayed nerves gave way altogether."[17]

The refugee world was governed by a hierarchy of misery that often determined the chances of escape. Most favored were writers with established anti-Nazi credentials like Lion Feuchtwanger, Heinrich Mann, and Franz Werfel whose names featured on lists of "endangered intellectuals" that had been drawn up by Fry's organization. On the next rung down were prominent artists such as Marc Chagall, Max Ernst, and André Breton. They, too, were eligible for "emergency" nonquota visas to the United States, effectively putting them at the front of the immigration line. Fry's rescue network smuggled some of its "clients" over the Pyrenees, and then on to Spain and Portugal, at a time when it was almost impossible to acquire French exit visas. Others waited, in relatively comfortable circumstances, for their paperwork to be completed. Breton and other Surrealist artists joined Fry in the Villa Air-Bel, a country house outside Marseille. Food was scarce but wine was plentiful. The artists found creative ways to ward off the *cafard*, from playing nonsensical games to singing ribald songs to designing a pack of Surrealist Tarot cards. They posted a sign at the entrance renaming the villa "Château Espère-Visa."[18]

At the other end of the refugee pecking order were the thousands of penniless Jews like the Maiers who had been robbed of everything. Arriving in Marseille at the Gare Saint-Charles, with its monumental, 104-step stone staircase, Charlotte Maier and her children were directed to a squalid, flea-ridden hotel next to the new port.

Requisitioned by the city authorities, the Hôtel Terminus des Ports now served as a "feminine emigration center" for Jews released from Gurs and other detention camps. According to Kurt Maier, "The rooms were so small that you fell on the bed as soon as you opened the door."[19] The residents did their own laundry, which they hung out to dry on the wrought-iron balconies facing the sea. In winter, they shivered from cold, as there was little heating. The plumbing leaked constantly, and the one rudimentary bathroom (for as many as 150 residents) was often out of order. The unpainted walls were black with grime and smoke. Social life revolved around the noisy central staircase, which was full of refugees exchanging gossip and bored children running up and down. Garbage piled up at the bottom of the stairs.[20]

From the windows of the hotel at the bottom of the Boulevard des Dames, the Maier family could watch the big steamships come and go. They could smell the invigorating sea air. The offices of the French shipping line, the Compagnie Générale Transatlantique, known for short as the "Transat," were just across the street. Their best escape route was tantalizingly close but at the same time frustratingly far away. Their relatives in the United States had deposited the money for their tickets across the Atlantic—but they still needed their American

Hôtel Terminus des Ports, Marseille, 1941

visas. Their days and nights were consumed by waiting. Waiting for a summons from a distant deity.

The consulate general of the United States of America was located in the Place Saint-Ferréol (now Place Félix-Baret), six blocks south of the Canebière. Day after day, a long line of neatly dressed visa applicants snaked around the square in front of the building. However desperate their circumstances, the asylum seekers always took care to arrive for their long-awaited appointments in their best clothes. Their carefully pressed suits and dresses and elaborately darned overcoats were intended to make the best possible impression on the bureaucrats who would determine their fate. As they waited patiently beneath the gnarled plane trees lining the sides of the square—a feature of the Provençal landscape—they caught up on the latest gossip. Rumors about changes in U.S. visa regulations and the arrival and departure of ships circulated freely.

Inside the four-story building with the classical stone façade, consuls and vice consuls struggled to make sense of a stream of confusing, sometimes conflicting, instructions from Washington. In theory, a consul had the final say on whether a refugee met the requirements of U.S. immigration law. In practice, he was guided by the wishes of his State Department superiors. Precisely what the department wanted was often difficult to determine. In the immediate aftermath of the fall of France, cables had arrived from Washington calling for "a drastic reduction" in the processing of immigration visas.[21] Now, six months later, it seemed that the department was heeding pleas by refugee advocacy groups to open the doors a little wider.

In a private letter to a colleague in Zurich, Consul General Hugh Fullerton attributed the new policy to the lobbying activities of the President's Advisory Committee on Political Refugees. "The Department seems obliged now to handle these visa cases in a most liberal way," he wrote. "Our office is endeavoring to accept the situation gracefully."[22]

The French decision to issue exit visas freely had added to the pressure on the consulate. The American embassy in Vichy estimated in mid-February that some twenty thousand predominantly German refugees had registered for American immigration visas in unoccupied France, including twelve thousand in Marseille.[23] There had been little point processing documents for these people as long as they could not also receive French exit visas. But that pretext for delay had now disappeared.

The arrival of the Baden deportees had created endless headaches for the consulate. "You may be sure that we heard of the six thousand odd Jews who were sent to the unoccupied part of France from the Stuttgart area in Germany," one of Fullerton's deputies, George Abbott, informed a colleague in Berlin. "We have been bombarded by cable and letter ever since they came." Like many of his fellow consuls, Abbott viewed the expulsions as "a feeler" on the part of the Germans.

"If they succeed in getting a visa without too much trouble, more will follow." But it was difficult "to do much holding back on these cases" given the pressure coming from Washington and various Jewish relief organizations.

"What can we do?" the consul complained. "The Department apparently wants them to be issued visas." According to Abbott, the work of the Marseille consulate was now consumed by answering inquiries from Washington "regarding the difficulties of Isaac Stein in getting a visa."[24]

Such complaints were disheartening for Vice Consul Harry Bingham, who detected a "defeatist," "antisemitic" atmosphere at the consulate. The idealistic Bingham felt that his efforts on behalf of refugees were being thwarted by the "dilatory tactics" of some of his superiors.[25] Rumors circulated that he was removed from his position as chief of the visa section at the end of 1940 for being too "generous" to asylum seekers. Transferred to a new post as head of the British interests section of the consulate, his visa-issuing responsibilities were sharply curtailed.[26]

Bingham blamed some of his troubles on a French consular clerk, Camille Delaprée, whom he later accused of being a German informer. A flirtatious, heavily perfumed lady with "bleached hair" and an "unnatural sparkle in her eyes," Madame Delaprée was the widow of a right-wing French journalist killed while covering the Spanish Civil War from the Nationalist side. As the consulate receptionist and "telephone girl," she occupied a strategic post that enabled her to observe anybody with business at the consulate. She performed her day job efficiently enough to gain the confidence of the senior staff. Bingham suspected that Madame Delaprée schemed behind his back for his transfer away from Marseille in April 1941—but was unable to offer any proof.[27]

Bingham's concerns were shared by some of the rescue workers, notably Varian Fry, who bombarded the State Department with complaints about recalcitrant officials. "The visa rigamarole here is inhuman," Fry wrote in a February 1941 memorandum. "It is almost literally killing the refugees. These poor devils not only have to go through a rigamarole with the French authorities to get their exit visas; they have to go through endless rigamaroles at the American consulate and a good deal too at the Spanish and Portuguese consulates. They have to wait in corridors and lines over and over and over again, until their very souls must be shriveled and shrunken by the experience."[28]

Other State Department officials defended the consul general from charges of antisemitism, and described the accusations of defeatism as "rot."[29] While Fullerton acknowledged that he took care to respect Vichy laws, and sought good relations with his hosts, he vehemently denied the charge of collaboration. He told the State Department that he had "to watch his step pretty carefully," as he was working "in enemy territory" under constant surveillance. Four policemen, two of whom were German, were stationed permanently outside the consulate entrance.[30]

While Bingham faulted his bosses for not doing enough to help refugees, others criticized them for being too liberal. Another Fullerton deputy, William Peck, felt the need to write a memorandum defending the consulate from charges of laxity.

"I do not subscribe to the school of thought which advocates refusing visas to all persons whose faces we do not like, on some flimsy pretext," Peck wrote. Nor was he in favor of turning down applicants whose paperwork was not entirely complete. The consul interpreted "humanitarian considerations" to mean favoring older refugees, "especially those in the camps." Peck saw little risk in granting visas to the elderly and chronically sick. "These are the real sufferers and the ones who are dying off," he wrote. "The young ones may be suffering, but the history of their race shows that suffering does not kill many of them. Furthermore, the old people will not reproduce and can do our country no harm, provided there is adequate evidence of support."[31]

The lack of support staff made it difficult for the overworked consuls to respond to the increased demand for visas, even if they were ready to be helpful. At the end of January 1941, a Jewish relief official complained that the number of visas available to refugees was limited by the "number of typists" in the Marseille consulate. A sympathetic consulate employee—possibly Bingham—urged the refugee organizations to lobby the State Department for additional staff. He suggested they make the approach through "non-Jewish" intermediaries.[32]

Word of the Marseille backlog reached Under Secretary of State Sumner Welles. A confidant of FDR's, Welles had the reputation of being the State Department official most sympathetic to the plight of the refugees. At his request, the consulate submitted a plan to hire more typists and stenographers and purchase additional typewriters. With the extra personnel, the consulate reported, it would be able to double its output of visas from four hundred to eight hundred a month.[33] By April, the HICEM rescue organization was happy to report that the consulate was "issuing visas much more liberally" than before.[34]

Prior to February 1941, the principal escape route from unoccupied France had been over the Pyrenees and then through Spain to Portugal. For those without the necessary permits, it was a dangerous option. Refugees were liable to be intercepted by the Vichy police, or sent back to France by Spanish border guards. Some refugees known as opponents of Hitler lost their nerve altogether. The German Jewish literary critic Walter Benjamin suffered from lung and heart disease; he had trouble climbing the rocky smugglers' path across the mountains. His friends feared he would have a heart attack, but he made it to the top of the pass. Pausing to rest, the party was rewarded with a view of the spectacular Costa Brava, which resembled "a glass sheet of transparent turquoise" lined by steep cliffs. "I gasped for breath," recorded one of his guides. "I had never seen such beauty before."[35]

Benjamin's relief at reaching Spain was quickly smothered. He was intercepted by the Spanish border police and told that he had entered the country illegally. Prior to being sent back to France, he was allowed to spend the night in a hotel on the Spanish side of the frontier. That night, he swallowed an overdose of morphine pills that he carried with him for precisely this eventuality. He died in the hotel.

Hints of a change in French policy came in late January with rumors of an escape route direct to the Americas. Refugees who had been waiting for months for exit visas reported that they had been offered passage from Marseille to the island of Martinique, in the French West Indies. From Martinique, there were plenty of boats to New York and other American ports. The new sea route offered obvious advantages over the previous overland route to Lisbon. It was no longer necessary to acquire Spanish and Portuguese transit visas, a process that could take weeks or months, or to make the dangerous trek over the Pyrenees. The fact that Martinique was a French possession made it easier to obtain the necessary travel documents.

One of the first people to sign up for a berth on a Martinique-bound ship was the Dadaist poet Walter Mehring. Known for his satirical ballads, Mehring had being stripped of German citizenship in 1935. The Nazis burned his books, banned his performances, and accused him of being a "Jewish subversionist." He had fled his native Berlin, only to be caught up in the German dragnet after the fall of France. After talking his way out of a French internment camp, he turned for help to Varian Fry, who included him on a list of "endangered political refugees." He was so small and inconsequential in appearance that Fry and his friends called him "Baby."[36] A sympathetic official in the Bureau des Passeports in Arles—known for its resistance to Vichy antisemitism—issued Mehring a special visa for Martinique and advised him to leave as quickly as possible.

The first available ship turned out to be the *Wyoming,* a rickety steamer that carried wine and perfumes to the West Indies and brought back sugar and spices. The *Wyoming* was scheduled to leave Marseille on February 4. Prior to boarding the ship, passengers had to line up to have their papers inspected. Under the terms of the armistice, the French were required to "surrender on demand" any German exile sought by the Nazis. Mehring had good reason to be worried that he was on the wanted list compiled by a commission headed by the German diplomat Ernst Kundt.

As he prepared to board the *Wyoming,* Mehring came face-to-face with a representative of the Vichy police, the Sûreté Nationale. The official checked his papers against a well-thumbed card index. He pulled out a card that read *"Walter Mehring, Interdit de sortir de France. Décision de la commission Kundt."* Mehring was banned from leaving the country on orders of the Kundt commission.

As Mehring waited in agony on the dock, the policeman disappeared to make a telephone call to his superiors. He returned some ten minutes later.

"*C'est peut-être un autre Walter Mehring,*" he announced with a smile. "*Partez!*"

"Perhaps it's another Walter Mehring. Leave."[37]

The journey across the Atlantic was blissfully peaceful. The poet celebrated his deliverance from evil by penning a "love song à la Martinique" that included a tribute to the ship that carried him to safety:

> *In uneventful faring over sea,*
> *With battle freight and Negro soldier lads,*
> *The staunch* Wyoming *bore us*
> *Through the oceanic muck.*[38]

News of Mehring's seemingly miraculous escape spread quickly among the anti-Nazi exiles in Marseille. Dozens of other Fry protégés bought tickets on Martinique-bound ships. Some twenty Emergency Rescue Committee clients, including several former denizens of the "Château Espère-Visa," were on board the *Capitain Paul Lemerle,* which left Marseille on March 25.[39] The passenger list included the avant-garde artists André Breton and Wilfredo Lam, the writers Anna Seghers and Victor Serge, and the French anthropologist Claude Lévi-Strauss. The intellectuals and artists kept apart from the remaining two hundred or so refugees sleeping in cargo holds that had been turned into communal dormitories. Many of these passengers had just been released from Gurs and other camps, and were accustomed to the most basic sanitary facilities.

"There were German Jewish refugees on board, but I cannot say how many," Lévi-Strauss recalled somewhat haughtily. "So as to overcome the promiscuity around us, we created small, inward-looking groups, rather than make outside contacts."[40]

A onetime Russian revolutionary who had known both Lenin and Trotsky, Serge depicted the *Paul Lemerle* as "a cargo boat converted into an ersatz concentration camp of the sea." He complained that many of his fellow passengers had "no thought except for flight." Serge recorded his delight at seeing "flying fish, the color of the sky, dart like dragonflies" from the ocean, prior to his first glimpse of the coconut trees and "green mountains of Martinique." His joy at escaping German-dominated Europe was marred by a stint in yet another internment camp "managed by thieves of policemen" on the French Caribbean island. The former Communist agitator wondered how long the ruling Martinique oligarchy of sugar growers and rum distillers could survive. "Perhaps for quite some time," he concluded sadly.[41] After a few weeks, he managed to arrange onward passage to the Dominican Republic and Mexico.

Vichy officials cited humanitarian concerns as the reason for dispatching unwanted refugees to "warmer climes." But there were other factors at play. The decision to open the Marseille–Martinique exit route reflected existing German policy. Expulsion, rather than systematic annihilation, remained official Nazi practice in western Europe up until October 1941, when Himmler issued a decree banning Jewish emigration from the Reich. Senior Vichy officials had been talking for months about getting rid of as many *"indésirables"* as possible. The minister of the interior, Marcel Peyrouton, complained that the refugees were "taking their fill of consumer goods without producing any themselves." He advocated a policy of "massive emigration" of foreign Jews, who could not be permitted to remain in their "current limbo." Martinique was seen as a temporary way station en route to any country in the Western Hemisphere willing to provide the refugees a permanent haven.[42]

Whatever the motivations for facilitating the exodus, the Martinique escape route offered a ray of hope to despairing refugees. At Les Milles, internees painted a mural of pineapples and seashells to symbolize their dream of liberation. In Gurs, cabaret artists entertained their fellow inmates with a ballad extolling the delights of the Caribbean.

> *Do you know the Antilles?*
> *You should go to live there with your family.*
> *What is the object of your dreams?*
> *The real paradise? Martinique.*
> *Where you can drink rum like milk . . .*
> *If only I could sleep on the beach,*
> *Far from the mud of this camp,*

How fortunate I would feel.
The sun would shine, and my heart would leap
Oh Martinique![43]

An escape to the tropics was not just a fantasy. By the beginning of April, ships full of refugees were leaving for Martinique every week, sometimes twice a week. Toward the end of April, rumors began circulating that at least three ships, carrying more than a thousand passengers, would depart for Martinique during the first half of May. The reports set off a new rush of refugees to the headquarters of the Transat shipping company and the American consulate on the Place Saint-Ferréol.

Kurt Maier's grandmother Sofie Auerbacher arrived in Marseille from Gurs on April 6.[44] Since she had not previously been issued a U.S. visa, her case had been considered separately from those of the rest of the family. She squeezed into the narrow single bed with Charlotte while the boys, Heinz and Kurt, slept on the floor.

The food in the Hôtel Terminus was better than in Gurs, and was served on plates rather than in rusty tin cans, but Kurt felt even hungrier than he had in the camp. He had been ill much of the time in Gurs and had not wanted to eat very much. Even when he was healthy, the filthy state of "the toilets took away my appetite."[45] In Marseille, his stomach expanded, and was never quite filled. Wine, by contrast, was so plentiful and cheap that even the children were allowed to drink. Kurt discovered that wine numbed his hunger and put him in a good mood.

The family scrounged for food wherever they could, to supplement the ersatz coffee and watery gruel provided by the hotel. One day, Kurt and Heinz came across a mountain of peanuts on the docks unloaded from a ship that had just arrived from North Africa. They filled a couple of bags with nuts, before retreating to the hotel in triumph. Since the Maiers had not been issued ration stamps, they were not permitted to buy bread in the stores. But a kindly Catholic nurse took pity on the children, and interceded with a saleswoman in the bakery. From then on, Charlotte was allowed to buy bread without the necessary stamps. During their visits to the bakery, Kurt was mesmerized by an elderly beggar who sat permanently across the street clothed in rags. The woman pushed a baby carriage that contained a tattered bag with all her possessions. For the ten-year-old Jewish refugee, the beggar became "the emblem of defeated France."[46]

On the first day of Passover, Saturday, April 12, the family went to the nearby Hôtel du Levant, where a local rabbi organized a Seder dinner.[47] More than a hundred bedraggled-looking women and children gathered to celebrate the liberation of the Israelites from the land of Egypt. When they were seated at the table, the children asked the questions that their ancestors had been asking for centuries. *Why is this night different from all other nights? Why is it that on all other nights during the year we eat leavened bread or matza, but on this night we eat only matza?*

In keeping with tradition, the adults explained that they ate unleavened matza "because our ancestors could not wait for their breads to rise when they were fleeing slavery in Egypt." They urged the children to taste bitter herbs symbolizing the "bitterness of slavery" and ponder what it meant to be a "free person," before ending with the prayer, "Next Year in Jerusalem!" The Seder ceremony was no longer just a ritual. The worshippers were describing their own predicament: They had left "Egypt," but had not yet arrived in "Jerusalem."

The long-awaited appointment at the American consulate was finally set for May 8. Siegfried received a leave of absence from Les Milles to join the rest of the family in Marseille. The Maiers had already booked passage to Martinique on the *Wyoming,* the same converted cargo vessel that Walter Mehring had taken back in February. The ship was due to depart Marseille in the middle of the month, leaving them little time to acquire their American visas. A French relative by the name of Salomon Lang, who had been wounded in World War I, came to Marseille to help the family with their papers.

When they reached the consulate, on the other side of the Canebière, they were greeted by a throng of visa applicants filling the Place Saint-Ferréol. Kurt wondered how long Oma Sofie "could wait on the street without being able to sit down."[48] She barely had the strength to stand for more than a few minutes. His father, Siegfried, was hardly in better shape. He was still suffering from swollen legs from his time in Dachau and Gurs. Salomon Lang was undeterred. He showed his war veteran's

American consulate, Marseille, May 1941

pass to the gendarme guarding the entrance to the consulate. The family was summoned to the front of the line.

Inside the consulate, they climbed the stairs to the office of one of the vice consuls, who questioned Siegfried on his political views and ability to earn a living. After satisfying himself that the Maiers were not "fifth columnists," the official agreed to renew their visas. He issued the family affidavits "in lieu of a passport," as their German passports had been confiscated by the Gestapo. The official stamped "German quota immigration visas" on the back of the affidavits, and punched a couple of holes through each document. Through the holes, he attached an impressive-looking red ribbon.[49]

Three years earlier, as the European refugee crisis mounted, the American journalist Dorothy Thompson had commented that "a piece of paper with a stamp on it" meant "the difference between life and death" for "thousands and thousands of people." The Maiers still needed a few more stamps on their precious piece of paper before they could get out of France, but they now had the key to the symbolic "golden door" guarded by the Statue of Liberty. Feeling a little guilty about jumping to the front of the visa line, they nonetheless went out to celebrate.

Salomon took them to one of the pizzerias celebrated by Anna

Seghers in her descriptions of the Marseille refugee experience as a "last haven in the old world."[50] Kurt would long remember the gleaming white tablecloth, the solicitous waiter who took their order, and the delicious spinach purée. The day's small miracles continued, even after the family left the restaurant. Sailors from the French navy were parading through Marseille, carrying the tricolor in front of them. A band was playing a sprightly march. As they looked on the flag of their defeated country, some of the spectators began to cry.

The Maiers spent the next week hurrying from office to office, collecting the stamps they needed to travel. Soon their travel papers were adorned with an assortment of stamps and permits and visas. Assembling the necessary stamps became a matter of intense anxiety and competition. For every berth on ships like the *Wyoming*, there were many people desperate to leave. Securing a passage across the Atlantic was like winning a lottery rigged in favor of those with the most resources and best connections.

It was a game of multiple traps and permutations in which success was never assured until the very last moment. Another Kippenheim couple, Gerda and Momo Auerbacher, had confirmed tickets on the *Wyoming*, paid for by Gerda's brother in New York. They had promises of American visas from the Marseille consulate, which had already determined that their affidavits were in order. Their French exit visas had been approved. There was one remaining problem, however. Momo had been transferred to the Les Milles "emigration camp," but Gerda was stuck in Gurs because of a lack of accommodation for female refugees in Marseille. If she was unable to reach Marseille in time to depart, she and Momo would forfeit their tickets on the *Wyoming*. Their emigration plans risked being delayed indefinitely.[51]

Also competing for berths on the aging freighter were a hundred or so "clients" of the Emergency Rescue Committee, including the family of Jacques Schiffrin, a leading French Jewish publisher. With the help of his close friend, the writer André Gide, Schiffrin had been placed on Varian Fry's list of two thousand "endangered" European intellectuals. This enabled him to bypass the long lines for U.S. visas. After fleeing Paris in advance of the Germans, Schiffrin had been holed up in an apartment in Saint-Tropez attempting to arrange his escape from

France. He moved his wife and five-year-old son to a Marseille hotel in early May after learning that places might become available on the *Wyoming*. They then underwent "a new kind of torture," described by Schiffrin in a May 11 letter to Gide:

> Arrangements are made and unmade several times the same day. That is to say: after one démarche succeeds and we have a chance of receiving everything we need to get on the boat (visas, tickets, passports etc.), we miss the next step and all is lost! To save what seems definitively lost or impossible, I drag myself through the streets in the hope of meeting someone who knows someone. Once or twice I have been lucky. Friends I have not seen for twenty years turn out to know someone in a consulate or a com- mittee or the prefecture. At nine this morning, all seemed lost. It is now eleven and I have just received a phone call to say that another telephone call will perhaps produce a solution tomorrow morning.[52]

The hours of waiting were agony for all concerned. On the day the *Wyoming* was meant to depart, Thursday, May 15, would-be passengers were still rushing back and forth between the shipping company, the American consulate, and the prefecture in frantic attempts to assem- ble the necessary documents and rubber stamps. Exhausted refugees besieged the offices of Fry's organization and other relief committees "to seek our advice or demand the impossible." The Schiffrins received a final stamp of approval from the Marseille harbormaster showing that they were "good to embark" a few hours before the departure of the *Wyoming*.[53]

Another Fry protégé, a doctor named Richard Berczeller, was struck by the atmosphere of excitement, mingled with extreme nervousness, in the departure hall. Every line has "its own personality," he observed later, depending "on what you are waiting for—a bread ticket, a bag of coal, a movie ticket, passage to the New World." Berczeller was sure that none of the people with tickets for the *Wyoming* had "ever been so close before to a ship that promised actually to put Europe behind us."[54]

The rabbi who had celebrated Passover with the Maier family was on the dock to see his congregants join five hundred or so other exhausted refugees climb aboard the decrepit freighter. "You can imagine the joy felt by these people at finally being able to leave," he reported.[55] Even more heart-wrenching was the despair of those left behind, including Gerda and Momo Auerbacher. French police records show that Gerda Auerbacher arrived in Marseille that same day from Gurs. Without sufficient resources of their own to overcome the bureaucratic delays, she and Momo missed their best chance of escape. A French official informed the Maiers that they "lacked a stamp."[56]

As the fortunate few boarded the *Wyoming,* their joy was marred by a final indignity. For weeks, Vichy propaganda had been depicting refugees as *"indésirable"* foreigners, leeching off honest French citizens. French longshoremen now lined the dock to yell abuse at the departing travelers. *"Sales youpins,"* they taunted. "Dirty kikes."[57]

The cargo holds of the *Wyoming* had been converted into communal dormitories, one for women, the other for men. Living space was severely restricted, as it had been in Gurs, but for the first time in months, the passengers felt free. After his son fell asleep, Richard Berczeller went up on deck to breathe the invigorating night air. His wife was already there. They stood "staring at each other, and then laughing for a long time, like children." Finally, they fell silent, looking back toward Marseille, "now a barely discernable glow on the black horizon."

Voices came out of the darkness, "deep and melancholy." Another couple was discussing whether they would ever return to Europe. The man was adamant. "No," he insisted. "Never, never let us go back."[58]

The old tub seemed to inch her way across the Mediterranean. "As long as we were in the Mediterranean, and as long as the coastlines of France, and later Spain, showed themselves, we all felt uncomfortably close to Europe," Berczeller recalled. When the *Wyoming* finally reached Gibraltar, at the entrance to the Atlantic, everyone breathed more easily. They started worrying again when they were required to put on emergency life vests because of suspected German U-boat activity in the straits.

Instead of heading westward, across the Atlantic, the *Wyoming* hugged the coast of Africa. Eventually she put into the port of Casablanca, in the French protectorate of Morocco, for refueling. At the entrance to the harbor, the passengers could see heavily damaged ships of the French navy that had been attacked by the British a few months earlier, to prevent their transfer to the Germans.[59]

"There we sat, aboard ship," recalled Berczeller. "One day passed, then another and another. No one would tell us anything, and rumors began to fly, none of them making much sense." The shipboard rations, previously barely adequate, became even more meager. Men in fezzes and barefoot children swarmed about on the dock, carrying baskets full of loaves of bread and bananas. Intense bargaining ensued as the almost penniless passengers attempted to negotiate a fair price for the food. When a sale was made, the passenger would lower a rope from the deck, pull the basket up, remove their purchases, and return the basket to the owner with the agreed amount of money.

After five days, the fruit sellers disappeared. Moroccan soldiers with fixed bayonets took their place on the pier. The refugees were escorted off the ship one by one, to be processed by plainclothes policemen.

"What are your plans?" they were asked. "Do you wish to return to France?"

"No, we want to go to America."

"Impossible. This ship is not leaving Casablanca."

"Why not?"

"An order from Vichy. That's all we can tell you."

The passengers were given a choice. They could either return to France, or they could be interned in a "camp" in the interior of Morocco. Without exception, they chose the camp.[60]

It took the Maiers and other refugees some time to learn what had happened. While the *Wyoming* was in Casablanca, her sister ship, the *Winnipeg,* had been intercepted by the British navy as it approached Martinique.[61] The *Winnipeg* had left Marseille nine days before the *Wyoming,* with more than seven hundred passengers on board, mainly Jewish refugees. While the *Winnipeg* was at sea, reports reached London that she was carrying unauthorized merchandise, undermining British attempts to choke off the trading routes between German-dominated Europe and the Americas. There were also reports that there were Nazi spies among the passengers.[62]

The interception took place in the early morning of May 26, as the wealthier passengers were celebrating their imminent arrival in Martinique with champagne. Operating under British orders, the Dutch gunboat *Van Kinsbergen* shone her lights on the *Winnipeg*. The Dutch ship then fired a warning shot across the bow of the French ship, in accordance with the classic rules of naval engagement. As the Dutch sailors stormed aboard with ladders and grappling hooks, the French crew threw bundles of documents into the sea.[63] Amid the general confusion, some of the refugees feared that they had been intercepted by a German submarine. The intruders wore steel helmets and spoke to each other in Dutch, which sounded very much like German to the frightened passengers.[64]

The captured ship was escorted to Trinidad as a "prize of war."[65] Many of the younger crewmen volunteered to join the Free French movement of Charles de Gaulle; the master and senior officers remained loyal to Vichy. The seven hundred passengers were taken in buses to an English internment camp on the island. "This time, everything was for the best!" recorded Yolla Niclas-Sachs, a photographer from Berlin who had been interned in Gurs along with her husband. "The British, always fair and correct, did not treat us like enemies, but as human beings."[66]

U.S. officials were unhappy about the seizure of the *Winnipeg*. They had no wish to foment trouble in the French West Indies or undermine the "economic stability" of Martinique. They believed that the Martinique authorities were abiding by the terms of an agreement with the United States that restricted imports and exports to bare essentials. They urged the British to release the ship.[67] The British, by contrast, regarded the *Winnipeg* as a "blockade runner." Her cargo included fine French wines and perfumes, in addition to nearly one thousand tons of Vichy mineral water, far in excess of the requirements of Martinique residents. "The French are callously hoodwinking the United States as they used to hoodwink us," a British naval officer complained. Releasing the *Winnipeg* was out of the question.

British intelligence officials were also deeply suspicious of the "cargo of Germans" aboard the ship. "Even if many of the Germans turn out to be genuine refugees, it seems very likely that some of them are German agents," the Foreign Office warned. "The fact that they are being dispatched to Martinique should make clear to the United States public the latest evidence of German machinations on their doorstep."[68] The British interviewed the refugees one by one to make sure that there were "no Nazis" hidden in their midst. Once they were satisfied, they allowed them to proceed to New York.

Unwilling to risk the loss of any more ships, the Vichy government immediately ordered the *Wyoming* and other Martinique-bound vessels to return to France. The episode marked the end of the Marseille–Martinique escape route. During the four months it had been in existence, French ships had carried several thousand refugees to safety and freedom. The men and women stranded in the internment camps of southern France would have to find another way to flee the Nazi terror spreading through Europe. The cabaret artists of Gurs and anti-Nazi intellectuals in Marseille would sing their love songs to Martinique no longer.

TEN

Les Milles

W HILE THE *Wyoming* was still at sea, headed for Casablanca, the State Department received a troubling report from the American consul on Martinique. Marcel Malige had been instructed to keep his eyes open for "German agents" infiltrating the Western Hemisphere. On May 20, 1941, he cabled Washington that two Germans traveling on French passports had recently arrived in Martinique. They were accompanied by a German official. All three men had been issued with "American visas" prior to leaving Europe.

The consul's cable set off alarm bells in an already jittery capital. "This telegram is very disquieting," Under Secretary of State Welles memoed Adolf Berle, the assistant secretary of state for security matters. "Are you satisfied that we are getting full and accurate information as to the situation in Martinique with specific reference to the arrival of German agents disguised as nationals of France and other countries?"[1]

Berle agreed that it was virtually impossible to keep track of refugees once they had been "turned loose" in Martinique. "The island schooners can, of course, take them pretty nearly anywhere." He, too, had heard rumors that "some of the people coming over as 'French' were in reality German." "I see no way of covering the situation adequately," Berle wrote Welles, "unless we are prepared to change our policy with respect to Martinique—which I, personally, strongly think we should do."[2]

The report from Martinique reinforced long-standing fears of Nazi agents and fifth columnists entering the United States, possibly disguised as Jewish refugees. While there was no evidence of a successful infiltration, that had not prevented the rumors from flying. Administration hard-liners seized on scraps of intelligence to call for a crackdown on all immigration. At a time of national emergency, the influence of the security establishment greatly outweighed the influence of the refugee advocates.

Similar reports from American consulates in Britain and Switzerland had already led to a comprehensive review of U.S. immigration practices. A January 1941 memo from London claimed that it was difficult, even impossible, to distinguish Nazi agents from genuine refugees. The consulate lacked both the time and manpower for detailed investigations. Jewish refugees were often "as Teutonic in their appearance and character as one of the so-called pure Aryan Germans" and equally loyal to "the Fatherland."[3] A February 27 cable from the Swiss city of Basel reported that German agents had offered to fund refugees who were willing "to work secretly for the German government in the United States."[4]

A prominent New Deal liberal, Berle had previously worried that America's moral standing in the world would be undermined by curbing the refugee flow. "Probably our greatest safeguard at this minute is the curious and mystic feeling in Europe that the United States is something great, powerful, and just," he wrote on February 11. He believed that refugees were being required "to jump through a set of hoops that oftener than not sift out the good ones and let in the ones we want least."[5] After reading the Basel telegram, Berle promptly reversed himself. "From now on every visa application will have to be referred to Washington," he told his State Department colleagues.[6] He suggested an additional change in procedure: FBI background checks on all visa applicants.

J. Edgar Hoover was happy to oblige. Citing "a confidential source," the FBI director claimed that "Germans desiring to enter the United States for subversive purposes" had little difficulty acquiring quota visas. He provided no evidence for this assertion beyond a vague report citing statements by "Germans on the West Coast."[7]

Other U.S. officials believed that the hunt for Nazi agents supposedly concealed among the refugees was largely pointless. Consul Malige in Martinique soon became exasperated by the repeated requests from Washington to investigate rumors about German spies. Previous leads had all proven false. "Germans here?" he asked a State Department colleague ironically. "We are amused by such stories—except when we have to devote overtime to gathering actual proof that they are wrong."[8]

The new system centralizing "alien visa control" in Washington was nevertheless approved by FDR on April 21, 1941.[9] From July 1 onward, all visa applications would be reviewed by an "interdepartmental committee" made up of representatives of the FBI, military intelligence, and naval intelligence, in addition to the State Department and the Immigration and Naturalization Service. The State Department would hire hundreds of extra staff to handle the increased paper flow. The regulations inserted an entirely new layer of bureaucracy between asylum seekers and the land of their dreams.

Enforcing the new visa regulations was the responsibility of Breckinridge Long, the bête noire of refugee advocates. The assistant secretary of state had long believed that the Gestapo was manipulating the refugee flow for espionage purposes. He viewed private relief agencies like HIAS-HICEM and the Quakers as unwitting tools of German policy. Their rescue operations were "sinister because the German government only gives permits to persons they want to come to the United States. It is a perfect opening for Germany to load the United States with agents."[10]

War by press leak intensified. On June 5, the anti-immigration senator from North Carolina, Robert Reynolds, publicly disclosed the confidential cable from the U.S. ambassador to Moscow, Laurence Steinhardt, criticizing the activities of the refugee advocates. In a Senate speech, Reynolds claimed that "Nazi and Communist agents" had infiltrated "every boatload of refugees" arriving in American ports. The only way to stop America becoming "a cesspool of revolutionary activities" was to erect an impenetrable barrier. "If I had my way," the senator thundered, "I would today build a wall about the United States so high and so secure that not a single alien or foreign refugee from any country upon the face of the earth could possibly scale or ascend it."[11]

Long's rivals struck back with their own leaks to sympathetic newspapers. On June 19, *The New York Times* reported that the State Department had introduced a new rule barring the entry of anyone with "close relatives" in German-controlled territory.[12] A front-page headline summed up the likely consequences:

U.S RULING CUTS OFF
MEANS OF ESCAPE
FOR MANY IN REICH

——

*Curb on Refugees Who Might
Be Spies Here to Save Kin
Drastically Interpreted*

——

MANY VISAS TO BE VOIDED

——

Thousands Who Have Booked
Passage from Lisbon Now
Face Rejection

Human rights advocates in the administration feared that the new visa regulations would severely compromise their rescue efforts. A HICEM report that somehow made its way to the White House estimated that more than 26,000 foreign Jews were languishing in internment camps in unoccupied France and northern Africa. "Emigration remains for all these wretched people the only alleviation of their fate," the report stated. *"The hope to be able to leave is the only moral strength which keeps them alive."*[13]

The controversy over the new U.S. immigration system was soon overwhelmed by momentous developments in the war. On June 22, Americans woke up to learn that Nazi Germany had invaded the Soviet Union. Hitler's fellow dictator Joseph Stalin was transformed overnight from an adversary to a potential ally. In August, Roosevelt traveled to Placentia Bay, Newfoundland, for a secret meeting with British prime minister Winston Churchill. Sitting side by side on the deck of a British battleship, HMS *Prince of Wales*, the two leaders agreed on an "Atlantic Charter" that would set the stage for a formal alliance.

At FDR's insistence, the statement of postwar goals included references to his cherished "Four Freedoms": freedom of speech, freedom of worship, freedom from want, and freedom from fear.

The refugee champions were reluctant to disturb the president while he was preoccupied with grand strategy. They finally managed to present their concerns at a White House conference on September 4. The meeting brought together Long and some of his most determined opponents, including Rabbi Stephen Wise; the newly appointed attorney general, Francis Biddle; and the head of the President's Advisory Committee on Refugees, James McDonald. The human rights activists urged the president to relax the "close relatives" rule and simplify the proposed review system. McDonald came away with the impression that Roosevelt was sympathetic to their concerns although, as usual, "he did not commit himself definitely."[14] While FDR could act decisively on occasion, ambivalence had become his preferred method of handling the refugee crisis.

"I got a little mad and fear I betrayed it," Long confided to his diary afterward. He detested the "sanctimonious air" of men like Rabbi Wise, who talked about the need to rescue "intellectuals and brave spirits, refugees from the tortures of the dictators." Long believed that only an "infinitesimal fraction" of the refugees met these criteria. Some were "certainly German agents"; others were Nazi "sympathizers."

"Each of these men truly hate me," wrote Long, referring to McDonald and his allies. "They would throw me to the wolves in their eagerness to destroy me."[15]

In New York and Casablanca, meanwhile, Joint officials were doing their best to rescue former Gurs inmates stranded in Morocco following the interception of the *Winnipeg*. Like most of the other Martinique-bound passengers, the Maier family possessed four-month immigration visas to the United States that would expire in early September. If they failed to reach an American port by that time, their paperwork would become invalid. They would be returned to bureaucratic limbo once again.

After leaving the *Wyoming* at bayonet point, the Maiers and other families with young children had been loaded into trucks and driven toward the Sahara Desert. Their destination was an abandoned French Foreign Legion camp at Sidi el-Ayachi, some fifty miles southwest of Casablanca. The camp consisted of rows of "stable-like wooden barracks" between desolate sand dunes. The exhausted travelers felt they had arrived "at the edge of, or perhaps a little beyond, the boundary of Nowhere."[16]

Their arrival was inauspicious. They were greeted by the "almost awe-inspiring appearance" of the camp commander, towering above them on horseback. His suntanned face gleaming beneath his helmet, the commander delivered a short speech that was the very opposite of a message of welcome. "You are *indésirables*," he told the intimidated refugees. "We didn't ask you here, and we don't want you here. You will have to behave yourselves and have discipline. You will work with your hands, not with your money."[17]

The refugees were put to work immediately, carrying straw into the barracks to serve as bedding. They ate their first meal in almost twenty-four hours: dark, coarse bread washed down with soup. During the night, huge rats scampered across the floor of the huts. In the morning, the commander organized the male prisoners into work crews, to make the camp more inhabitable. Some were sent to the nearby town of Azemmour to fetch supplies and a modest milk ration for the youngest children.

After a few days, the *Wyoming* refugees were joined by passengers from another ship that had turned back to Casablanca while en route to South America. The already crowded barracks became even more crowded. Soap disappeared completely. Laundry, "when it could be done at all, had to be done in water the color of mud." The rat population seemed to increase in direct proportion to the human population. Within three weeks of their arrival in Sidi el-Ayachi, a "raging epidemic" had broken out. Hundreds of people lined up outside the latrines day and night, "caught in the agonies of diarrhea," according to Richard Berczeller, the doctor whose son Peter hovered on the verge of death for several days.[18]

Gradually, the epidemic abated and conditions improved. The camp commander proved more humane than his initial appearance had suggested. After establishing his authority over the refugees, he did his best to make their life more tolerable. One day, still mounted high on his horse, he led the children on an outing to a glorious sandy beach on the edge of the Atlantic. After swimming in the sea, the children picked potatoes from a nearby field, and roasted them over an open fire on the beach. The experience left an indelible impression on Kurt Maier, who had just turned eleven. "It was a good day," he recalled later. "Is there another example in the history of World War II internment camps of a camp commander taking children on an excursion?"[19]

One day, in the middle of July, the commander announced that arrangements had been made to transport most of the internees to America. The Marseille–Martinique route was still suspended, but the Joint had succeeded in finding space on board a Portuguese steamer still making the run from Lisbon to New York. The *Nyassa* would put in at Casablanca to pick up the refugees from Sidi el-Ayachi.

The Maiers spent the night of July 25 in a cheap hotel in Casablanca. The following day, they were taken to the port in a horse-drawn cab.[20] Some six hundred passengers had already boarded the *Nyassa* in Lisbon, including a Polish princess and the widow of a Nobel prize laureate in physics. The Maiers shared a tiny cabin in the bow with several other third-class passengers. Their companions included a young lady who spent most of her time "amusing herself with the sailors," to the dismay of Kurt's straitlaced Oma Sofie.[21]

Crossing the Atlantic had become a hazardous undertaking. Passengers and crew were on constant lookout for German U-boats. They also ran the risk of being intercepted by the Royal Navy. Sure enough, five days out of Casablanca, they were halted by a British warship. The English sailors conducted a perfunctory inspection before allowing the *Nyassa* to proceed. The grateful refugees showered the boarding party with cigarettes and chocolates as they withdrew.

At dawn on Saturday, August 9, the Maier family caught their first glimpse of the Statue of Liberty. The *Nyassa* anchored beneath the outstretched arms of Lady Liberty for four hours, waiting for a high tide that would allow her to navigate the East River. Unfortunately, the tide rose a little too high. As she passed under the Brooklyn Bridge, the mast of the ship crashed into the bridge, shearing off a ten-foot section of the hollow steel structure. The passengers heard a "resounding crunch," and saw the top of the mast hanging precariously at a right angle. They rushed away from the forward deck of the ship, which was decorated with large American flags to celebrate her safe arrival in New York.

By the time the *Nyassa* docked at Pier 28, off Market Slip, a throng of reporters had gathered to make fun of the seamanship of her crew. "Liner Breaks Tip of Topmast in Tilt with Brooklyn Bridge" was the front-page headline in the *New York Herald Tribune* the following day.[22] "*Nyassa,* coming up river for first time, finds it's just ten feet too tall." The story mentioned, in passing, the arrival of "two hundred refugees from Casablanca" who had been engaged in "a race against time" to reach America before their visas expired.

The Maier family had made it to the promised land. Their Kippenheim friends, Gerda and Momo Auerbacher, were much less fortunate. After missing the chance to leave on the *Wyoming,* Gerda and Momo were back in visa purgatory. They had spent years collecting police records and affidavits testifying to their "moral and political character." Their relatives across the ocean had filed employment records and bank statements to prove that they would not become a burden on American taxpayers. Although the Auerbachers had been promised U.S. visas in April, they had been unable to pick them up prior to the change in regulations.[23]

"The consulate has not issued us a visa, and we anticipate new requirements," Gerda wrote to her brother Hugo in New York on June 25. "We have not advanced a step since April 19, and there is always some reason to complain." A few weeks later, she added a despairing postscript. "Now one has to receive permission from Washington. There are always new regulations and challenges. May God help us to withstand it all."[24]

Hugo wrote to the State Department on July 17 to "request new forms" for Gerda and Momo.[25] Among other hurdles, it was now necessary for him to convince the visa review committee that his sister and brother-in-law were not susceptible to Gestapo blackmail threats. Like many of the other Baden deportees, Gerda and Momo still had "close relatives" in "Nazi-controlled territory" who could become potential hostages.

"The work is becoming more and more difficult," the head of HICEM's Marseille office complained. "We now have to start again all necessary formalities for cases that we considered already settled."[26] To further complicate matters, the price of tickets on the few boats that were still crossing the Atlantic was constantly rising. A second-class ticket from Lisbon to New York that previously cost $250 now cost $450, nearly $8,000 in 2019 dollars.

Momo Auerbacher joined half a dozen other men from Kippenheim in the Les Milles emigration camp, near Aix-en-Provence. His companions included Max Valfer and Hugo Wachenheimer, who both arrived at the end of May.[27] The camp was housed in a disused tile factory, set against a classic Provençal landscape of olive groves, vineyards, old farmhouses, and a distant aqueduct. The contrast between the beautiful countryside and the "indescribably ugly" tile factory left a lasting impression on Les Milles inmates. According to the German writer Lion Feuchtwanger, "It was a strange sensation to gaze out from there upon the lovely, rolling, soft green fields, so near yet so far beyond our reach."[28]

There was a guard post at the entrance, where papers were checked and names registered. New arrivals were then escorted across a large courtyard where internees with nothing to do milled about, exchanging rumors. From the brilliant sunlight, they entered what seemed like "a huge black hole" leading into a murky darkness. Narrow corridors twisted around abandoned brick kilns, reminding Feuchtwanger of "a catacomb." The floor above was more spacious, with higher ceilings, but almost as dark. The windows were either boarded up or painted dark blue because of the danger of air raids. "At night there were a few very feeble electric bulbs that served rather to emphasize the darkness than to relieve it."

If life in Gurs had been dominated by mud and rain, the defining characteristics of Les Milles were dust and gloom. A fine red dust permeated the entire edifice, stirred up by the mistral, the strong northwesterly wind that whistled through the cracks in the roof and the walls. The dust settled on everyone and everything, including the vats of watery soup served to the inmates. "Dust, dust everywhere!" wrote Feuchtwanger. "Thick layers trodden hard underfoot made the floor difficult to walk on; bricks that seemed to be crumbling to dust lay about in piles."[29]

Internees fashioned chunks of broken brick into makeshift seats and tables that quickly fell apart. They scattered straw between the bricks to serve as beds, laying claim to precious slices of private space. Feuchtwanger estimated that each man had "a breadth of some thirty inches at his disposal. There was no passageway between our straw piles, so that we lay not only side by side, but head to head."[30]

The toilet facilities were completely inadequate, as bad as at Gurs. At times, as many as a hundred men waited outside one of the half dozen latrines in the courtyard. "There was no flushing. There was no avoiding the muck, no escape from the thick swarm of flies.... Many men were ill; all became so. If one failed to succumb to the food, infection from the toilet was inevitable."[31] Many inmates suffered from dysentery, made even more unpleasant by the long wait for relief.

The purpose of the Les Milles camp was to assist refugees in their emigration efforts by moving them closer to Marseille. The camp director issued passes to allow detainees to answer summonses from foreign consulates and meet with their wives and children in the Terminus and Bompard hotels. A day trip to Marseille took at least two hours in each direction: an hour-long hike from Les Milles to the village of Saint-Martin, followed by an equally long tram ride to the center of the city. If they could demonstrate a pressing need, internees were occasionally permitted to stay overnight in Marseille, before making the trek back to the tile factory.[32]

Les Milles operated primarily as a transit camp while the Martinique route was open and the American consulate was still issuing visas on a regular basis. But that changed in July 1941, when the new visa regulations came into force. For a few bleak weeks, it seemed as if immigration to America had been halted indefinitely. If that happened, Les Milles would revert to being an ordinary detention camp. "A mistral of pessimism blew through the brick factory that sheltered us," wrote the journalist Hans Fraenkel.[33] The hope of early release gave way to a "black despair" and "growing tension" that threatened to plunge the entire camp into a prolonged *cafard*. Rumors circulated that Les Milles would soon be closed, and the inmates used as forced labor in North Africa or occupied France. Or perhaps they would be sent back to Gurs.

The change in U.S. immigration policy plunged many Les Milles residents into "a state close to hopelessness," according to an August 1941 HICEM report. As bad as conditions were in Les Milles, the alternatives were much worse. HICEM arranged for a delegation of internees to express their concerns directly to the American consul. The consul gave them a sympathetic hearing, but made clear he was no longer the decision maker on visas. He advised them to get their supporters in Washington to lobby the President's Advisory Committee on Political Refugees.[34]

It was at this point that one of the inmates had the idea of turning Les Milles into a "work camp," dedicated to the spiritual and intellectual development of his comrades. To combat the dreaded depression, the refugees organized lectures and sports tournaments and concerts. Teachers offered courses in history and foreign languages; artists painted the walls of the guards' cafeteria with humorous frescoes; photographers built a darkroom with materials supplied by the camp director; there was even a book-binding workshop. The catacomb-like ground floor became a backdrop for cabaret shows and theater performances. The *cafard* did not disappear, but life became a little more tolerable "even for those who still did not know when they would be able to depart."[35]

The camp authorities encouraged the cultural activities at Les Milles in the belief that fully occupied internees were easier to control. The guards were mainly local farmers, who were friendly enough, as long as they could profit from the thriving black market. Paintings and sketches by inmates depict beret-wearing guards pushing huge sausages and barrels of wine through the camp, cigarettes dangling from their lips. Lion Feuchtwanger recalled the time when his fellow inmates were playing soccer and the ball flew over the fence. The players asked a guard for permission to retrieve the ball. That was strictly forbidden, replied the guard. He could not allow it, but "if someone would hold his gun for him, he would climb over the wall and bring it back. And he did."[36]

After saying goodbye to his wife, Fanny, in Gurs, Max Valfer spent much of his time at Les Milles writing beseeching letters to unknown officials. Getting his paperwork in order was a full-time occupation for the bald-headed cigar distributor and former Great War veteran. He had to interact with half a dozen different bureaucracies: the State Department, consulates in Marseille, HICEM and other refugee assistance organizations, the camp authorities, the prefecture, foreign shipping lines. Each bureaucracy had its own institutional quirks and regulations, which frequently conflicted with the rules of a rival bureaucracy. To leave France and make it to America, all the stars had to be perfectly aligned.

His immediate priority was to arrange for Fanny to be released from Gurs. Moving his wife to one of the cheap hotels reserved for refugees in the Mediterranean port city would represent a tangible step forward to their eventual escape from France. Conducting business at the American consulate would be greatly simplified. Unfortunately, obtaining permission to leave Gurs was becoming increasingly difficult. Camp officials would allow Fanny to travel to Marseille only if she had a confirmed passage on a ship across the Atlantic.[37] The shipping company made issuance of a ticket conditional on possession of a visa. In order to acquire a visa, she first had to get to Marseille. And so on. The circular logic, or illogic, of the emigration/immigration process was exasperating.

In addition to dealing with the bureaucrats, Max kept up a steady stream of correspondence with his children, who were scattered across the world. He depended on them for affidavits, food packages, and money for steamship tickets. By the summer of 1941, four of his six children (Karl, Hugo, Freya, and Ruth) had made it to the United States. Else was living in England with her husband, Heinrich, while the youngest, Erich, was making a new life for himself in Palestine. The burden of assembling the necessary affidavits fell primarily on the children in America, particularly Hugo and Ruth, who had been there the longest.

There were constant ups and downs. Max was frustrated to report in the middle of July that "things are going slowly with regard to our emigration," because of the new procedures in Washington.[38] He was happy to learn that Hugo and Ruth had made an initial deposit of $600 with a Jewish relief agency in New York to pay for transatlantic tickets for him and Fanny. However, it took months for the money to reach Europe, leading to another flurry of telegrams across the Atlantic. Max was still waiting for "written confirmation" of the transfer at the end of July, when he had an interview with the HICEM representative in Les Milles.[39] Without such confirmation, it would be impossible to secure Fanny's release from Gurs.

Letters written during this period reveal a profound difference in temperament between Max and Fanny. The serene, long-suffering Fanny was much better equipped to withstand the stresses of camp life than her stern, sometimes short-tempered husband. In letters to her children, Fanny made little mention of her own troubles, and constantly asked after the health of her loved ones. "The journey [to America] does not go quickly, but one must be patient and persevere," she wrote Else that summer. "I have such longing for all of you, my dear children, in particular for my dear Erich [her youngest son, now in Palestine]. When will I see my golden boy again?" She took pains to reassure her children that she was doing fine. "Every day I prepare good fruit and vegetables, and I am still your old Mama," she told Else. After Max left Gurs for Les Milles, Fanny found solace in the company of other Kippenheimers, including Berta Weil. "It is good that we are together," she wrote.[40]

Max's former secretary lived in the same hut in Gurs as Fanny, together with her mother and sister.[41] Max continued to attach great importance to helping Berta and her family reach the United States. "It is the wish of the Weil family, as well as ours, that we undertake the journey to New York together, in the same ship, if possible," Max wrote HICEM. "We came to Gurs together and have spent many months together since then. God willing, we will also undertake this next stage together."[42] Writing to his daughter Else from Les Milles, Max expressed relief that "our dear Mama" was "together with Berta" and her sister and mother in Gurs. The company of the Weil family was "as good as one's own folks," he added.

The children, and their husbands, still viewed Berta with suspicion. Ruth's husband, Rudy Bergman, was worried that his parents-in-law had "passed up quite a few opportunities" to get out of France on account of the Weils. "When they are here *zu gutem* [for good], we will take the proper steps," he told Else.[43] A careful examination of the sequence of events suggests, however, that the visa tribulations of Max and Fanny had nothing to do with the Weils. Their fate lay in the hands of the shipping lines and the State Department.

HICEM officials sought to finesse the competing demands for documents with bureaucratic sleights of hand. They issued vaguely worded certificates designed to persuade the American consul in Marseille that their clients were ready to travel. "We have the honor to confirm that our Lisbon office has reserved two places for Mr. Max Valfer and his wife on a ship leaving Lisbon for New York around December 31" read one such letter.[44] In the meantime, they assured relief officials in Lisbon—erroneously—that "the people concerned are already in possession of their visas and will leave in the near future."[45] The system depended on creating piles of impressive-looking paperwork, complete with rubber stamps, that no one would check.

Toward the end of October, the Valfers received the news for which they had been longing. Their visa applications had finally been approved in Washington. Armed with a summons from the American consulate general, Fanny was able to obtain permission to leave Gurs.[46] She made the long train ride to Marseille on November 14, reporting to the women's internment center at the Hôtel du Levant, around the corner from the Hôtel Terminus.[47]

On November 28, Max notified HICEM that he and Fanny expected to receive their visas from the American consul on Monday, December 8. Once they had their U.S. visas, they would immediately apply for transit visas through Spain and Portugal. "I respectfully ask you to arrange everything else, so that our tickets will be reserved in time [and] our departure will not be delayed."[48]

After more than a year in French internment camps, it seemed that the visa gods were finally smiling on Max and Fanny Valfer.

Franklin Roosevelt was having lunch in his private study on the second floor of the White House on Sunday, December 7, when the telephone rang. Seated next to him at his heavy oak desk—made out of timbers of the nineteenth-century British exploration ship HMS *Resolute*—was his confidant Harry Hopkins. Known to its first inhabitant, John Adams, as the "upstairs oval parlor," the nautically themed room was filled with model warships and other symbols of America's naval might. The two men were gossiping "about things far removed from war" when the White House operator patched in an urgent call from the secretary of the navy.[49]

"Mr. President," Frank Knox reported, "it looks like the Japanese have attacked Pearl Harbor."[50] The brass ship's clock on Roosevelt's desk showed 1:47 in the afternoon.

Hopkins was sure there must be some mistake: bringing the United States into the war would prove suicidal for Japan in the long run. The president felt intuitively that the report was accurate. He had boxed Japanese militarists into a corner by imposing an oil embargo on Japan in response to their invasion of Indochina. Intercepted cables indicated that the Japanese government intended to break off negotiations with Washington on a diplomatic settlement. A surprise attack on the American Pacific Fleet at Honolulu seemed quite logical to FDR, at least in retrospect.

The devastation wrought by two waves of Japanese planes, launched from aircraft carriers, was sickening. Moored side by side in the harbor, eight American battleships, three light cruisers, and three destroyers were damaged in the first few minutes of the raid. Hundreds of sailors were trapped inside the burning ships. By the time the attack was over, ninety minutes later, 3,500 Americans had been killed. The only good news was that half the U.S. fleet, including all three aircraft carriers, was out at sea, their location unknown to the Japanese.

As news spread of the attack, some senior officials talked of "unmitigated disaster" and an imminent Japanese assault on America's Pacific coast. At the center of the storm, by contrast, FDR remained "deadly calm" as the news flashes arrived from Hawaii, each "more terrible than the last." "His reaction to any event was always to be calm," marveled Eleanor Roosevelt. "If it was something that was bad, he just became almost like an iceberg, and there was never the slightest emotion that was allowed to show."[51]

The president understood that his moment in history—the moment for which he had been preparing the last four years—had finally arrived. To some of his aides, it seemed that he had been relieved of a tremendous burden. There would now be no more debate about whether the United States should join the war on the side of the democracies. The isolationists had been defeated. "I think the boss must have a great sense of relief that this has happened," Postmaster General Frank Walker whispered to a cabinet colleague. "This is a great load off his mind. I thought the load on his mind was just going to kill him.... At least we know what to do now."[52]

Roosevelt tinkered with the wording of his message to Congress until it expressed his thoughts as succinctly as possible. Aides urged him to make a major address, but he preferred to keep it short. His original draft described December 7, 1941, as "a date which will live in world history." In the final version, he struck out "world history" and substituted "infamy."[53] The speech was greeted by prolonged standing ovations. Congress approved his request for a war on Japan with only one dissenting vote.[54]

It was clear to FDR that war with Japan also meant war with her Axis allies, Germany and Italy. For political reasons, however, he was determined to avoid the impression that he had initiated hostilities. He preferred to wait until Germany declared war on the United States before declaring war on Germany. Adolf Hitler duly obliged on December 11, with an abusive rant against "the man who likes to make his chats from the fireside." As the Führer saw it, Roosevelt was the leader of the "Anglo-Saxon-Jewish-Capitalist world" allied with Soviet Bolshevism. "The full diabolical meanness of Jewry rallied around this man, and he stretched out his hands."[55] Congress responded by declaring war on Germany later that same day.

Eleanor had accompanied her husband to the Capitol for his speech to Congress. She left immediately afterward for a long-planned trip to California, which had become "a zone of danger," in the phrase of the *Los Angeles Times.* Warning of "the enemy within," the paper urged "keen-eyed civilians" to be on the alert for "spies, saboteurs and fifth columnists."[56] Anyone of Japanese, or German, or Italian ancestry was immediately suspect, however long they might have lived in America. Within forty-eight hours of the attack on Pearl Harbor, the FBI reported to FDR that 1,212 "Japanese aliens" and 620 "German aliens" had been "taken into custody."[57]

Eleanor was alarmed by the renewed fifth column hysteria. She acknowledged in her daily newspaper column that "German and Italian agents" had been active in the United States, but stressed the need for tolerance of minority groups. While she was on the West Coast, she made sure to have her photograph taken with smiling Japanese Americans.[58] "This is, perhaps, the greatest test this country has ever met," she wrote. "Perhaps it is the test which is going to show whether the United States can furnish a pattern for the rest of the world for the future."[59]

Max and Fanny Valfer reported, as instructed, to the American consulate in Marseille on the morning of December 8. Since they had an appointment, they were able to push their way through the usual throng of visa seekers beneath the plane trees in the Place Saint-Ferréol. Their interview did not go as expected, however. The consul refused to grant them the all-important "piece of paper with a stamp." Instead he demanded additional documents. The overland border between France and Spain had been closed to "aliens *en route* North America" following the outbreak of hostilities with Japan.[60] The consul asked the Valfers to explain how they would reach Lisbon by the end of December, even supposing that their ship reservations remained valid.[61]

Immediately after leaving the consulate, Max and Fanny walked around the corner to the HICEM office on Rue Paradis, which was packed, as usual, with nervous refugees. After they described what had happened at the consulate, they were issued a new piece of paper, pushing back their departure to January 31. Surely the border would reopen by then. Max returned to the consulate with the reissued certificate but this, too, was rejected. The consul wanted to know the name of the ship on which the Valfers would travel and the precise date of departure. If they were planning to travel via Lisbon, he wanted evidence of transit visas through Spain and Portugal.[62]

Hundreds of other former Gurs internees found themselves in a similar situation. Rumors soon began to fly about a further tightening of U.S. visa regulations. "At the moment, the consulate is on Christmas vacation," Gerda Auerbacher informed her brother Hugo in New York on December 24. "One hears so much gossip. The day before yesterday, we heard that we would have to get something else from Washington. Those who still do not have their papers are better off than those who do."[63]

The closure of the border with Spain trapped many refugees who already possessed U.S. visas. One elderly Kippenheimer "already had her hat on, and was about to leave, but word came through that the border was closed," Gerda wrote. Others found themselves stuck near the border, "with nowhere to go." "It is all so difficult when everything is expensive. You are already struggling to get by, and then you are given a runaround with all these formalities."[64]

Gerda dealt with the constant rebuffs and disappointments by developing an attitude of "indifference to it all, which has helped me survive." By contrast, Max Valfer could not contain his anger at the way in which he and Fanny had been treated. He accused HICEM of showing favoritism toward other internees by issuing them with travel documents that passed muster with the consulate, even after Pearl Harbor. Alleging "a reckless injustice on your part," he threatened to hold the immigration service "responsible for all eventualities."[65]

HICEM officials were accustomed to such complaints. "We understand perfectly your impatience to leave," they wrote Max on January 8. Unfortunately, the Valfers would now need "special authorization from the American authorities" before they could receive their visas.[66] German Jews who had been chased from their homes by Hitler were now considered "enemy aliens," in the same category as their persecutors.[67]

The problem lay not in Marseille, but in Washington.

ELEVEN

"Enemy Aliens"

B UILT LIKE A BULLDOG, with a heavy torso, spindly legs, and pugnacious visage, J. Edgar Hoover was the public face of American law enforcement. From his wood-paneled office on the fifth floor of the Justice Department building overlooking Pennsylvania Avenue, he controlled an investigative apparatus made up of tens of thousands of agents and informers. A row of electronic push buttons on his desk provided instant communication with top officials in the "Seat of Government"—Hoover's term for Washington, D.C.—and FBI field offices around the country. An ingenious filing system allowed him to keep tabs on a vast array of suspected spies and saboteurs.

Fanatically hardworking with an obsessive eye for detail, Hoover had created the Federal Bureau of Investigation in his own image. He insisted that his agents wear dark suits, white shirts, sober ties, and snappy hats. They could be neither too short nor too heavy. They were all men and, with very few exceptions such as his personal driver, all white. They had to conduct themselves professionally at all times. They were expected to be energetic, incorruptible, and totally loyal to the Bureau, in other words to Hoover himself. Hoover viewed his agents as America's first line of defense against subversives. He wanted them to be both respected and feared.

One of the keys to Hoover's power was a genius for public relations. He made sure that the exploits of his "G-men," or "Government men," were chronicled in newsmagazines, radio programs, movies, and even comic strips. Pulp detective books with titles like *Spy Smasher* and *G-Man vs. The Fifth Column* rose in popularity in direct proportion with the perceived threat from German or Japanese agents. By one count, Hollywood produced over seventy films in 1942 alone dedicated to the fight against foreign subversion, many lifted from FBI files.[1]

Hoover liked to peruse the scrapbooks of favorable editorial cartoons and news stories that he kept next to his desk. His scrapbooks from the weeks immediately after Pearl Harbor are filled with cartoons glorifying the FBI-led campaign against the "enemy within." Many of the drawings feature Hoover vacuum cleaners. A typical cartoon depicts an arm labeled "FBI" vacuuming up "enemy aliens" from a rug labeled "West Coast Defense Area." Another cartoon shows a G-man, wearing the standard fedora hat, shining a light on an "enemy alien" (depicted as a rat) caught in a trap. In a third drawing, a giant FBI agent is pushing a crowd of German- and Japanese-looking civilians into a "Reception Center for Saboteurs and Spies." "Safety First" reads the caption.[2]

Charged with protecting America's internal security, Hoover was constantly looking for ways to strengthen the nation's defenses. He mistrusted the State Department's visa application process. FBI reports emphasized the difficulty of compiling accurate dossiers on visa applicants when much of the vital information was "inaccessibly buried in Axis-occupied territory." Hoover rejected the notion that refugees were "oppressed people" who deserved the pity of the United States. In his view, the main beneficiaries of the quota system were "diamond merchants" and other "well-to-do people" who could bribe their way across Europe. The number of "little people" receiving U.S. visas was "regrettably small" compared to the number of "merchants and traders and members of the lunatic fringe of European radicalism."[3]

According to the FBI, the refugees had a "highly influential" network of supporters that included congressmen and senators in addition to the usual "self-styled liberals." Anyone attempting to bring large numbers of refugees into the country risked being labeled a "Red." Ingrid Warburg, a member of the Warburg banking dynasty, became the target of an FBI investigation because of her work for the

Emergency Rescue Committee sponsoring visas for European intellectuals. "In view of the intense interest this person has displayed in immigrants," Hoover memoed, "it is deemed advisable to determine her background, character, reputation, and organizational affiliations." Confidential informants reported that the committee—whose sponsors included Eleanor Roosevelt and Albert Einstein—was a "Communist Front organization."[4]

Hoover was also suspicious of HICEM, the organization most active in rescuing stranded Jewish refugees in France. He had written to the State Department in September 1941 to relay "strictly confidential" information that the Gestapo was "using HICEM" to infiltrate agents into the United States.[5] The State Department investigated the allegations, but was unable to find supporting evidence. The American consul in Marseille reported that he had yet to see "the slightest indication" of contacts between the Gestapo and HICEM, despite being in "almost daily contact" with the relief agency.[6] Nevertheless, the incident damaged the reputation of HICEM in the eyes of Washington officialdom. Its efforts on behalf of refugees were tainted by lingering suspicion.[7]

Among the "enemy aliens" swept up by the FBI in the immediate aftermath of Pearl Harbor was "a refugee from Hitlerism" by the name of Paul Borchardt. An expert on the Arab world, the former geographer and archaeologist had spied for Germany during World War I. He continued to instruct Wehrmacht officers in geopolitics up until 1938. Even though he had converted to Catholicism, Borchardt was of Jewish descent and therefore a "non-Aryan" in the eyes of the Nazis. Arrested twice by the Gestapo, he had spent a short time in Dachau before influential friends secured his release. After a year in England, he traveled to New York as an immigrant in early 1940. At his trial for espionage, in March 1942, his defense lawyer depicted him as "an unwilling servant of Nazism." The prosecutor accused him of hiding behind "the misery of thousands of others who really are refugees."[8] Borchardt was convicted of espionage and sentenced to twenty years in prison. Even though the case was exceptional, the resulting publicity bolstered Hoover's demands for an even more restrictive visa policy. " 'Refugee' Linked to Nazi Spy Ring" was the headline in *The New York Times.*[9]

For Hoover, the moral of the Borchardt case was obvious. Now that America was at war, the burden of proof for weighing up potential security threats needed to shift decisively. The onus should no longer be on the FBI to demonstrate that a refugee posed a threat to the United States. It was up to the refugee to prove the absence of a threat—a much more difficult, perhaps impossible, challenge.

One of the "self-styled liberals" in the Roosevelt administration who attracted Hoover's scorn was his nominal superior, Attorney General Francis Biddle. The scion of a long line of Philadelphia aristocrats, Biddle seemed to epitomize the notion of "noblesse oblige." His friends included writers, intellectuals, artists, and philanthropists. He was married to a distinguished poet, Katherine Garrison Chapin. A product of Harvard Law School, he agonized about the proper balance between national security and civil liberties. He was one of the main advocates within the government for a humanitarian refugee policy.

Some Roosevelt intimates regarded Biddle as effete and soft. The president himself enjoyed ribbing his attorney general for his earnest, somewhat self-righteous demeanor. On one occasion, a few weeks after Pearl Harbor, he casually announced that he had decided to suspend freedom of speech for the duration of the war. He wanted Biddle to draft a suitable proclamation. "It's a tough thing to do, but I'm convinced it's absolutely necessary." His other luncheon guests, who were in on the presidential joke, sat silently as the bow-tied Biddle rose to the bait. Pacing around the Cabinet Room of the White House, he urged FDR to reconsider. His passionate monologue went on for some five minutes before his audience burst out laughing.[10]

As attorney general, Biddle was in charge of a hydra-headed bureaucracy. In addition to the FBI, he also supervised the Immigration Service, a stronghold of New Deal progressives that had been transferred to the Justice Department from the Labor Department in 1940. When it came to refugee policy, the two heads were constantly sniping at each other. The Immigration Service stressed the contributions that refugees, including German Jews persecuted by Hitler, could make to the war effort. The Bureau was focused on the national security risks posed by "so-called refugees" serving as cover for enemy agents.

FBI agents assigned to background investigations of refugees lam-basted the "open door policy with respect to immigration" supposedly advocated by the attorney general and other "liberals." A March 1942 memo condemned the "crass stupidity" of the State Department in ignoring "exceedingly derogatory information" supplied by the FBI. Hoover signaled his approval with a scrawled "OK."[11]

Biddle took care to praise the spy-hunting zeal of the FBI while emphasizing the need for independent supervision. "A thorough inves-tigative job requires that every clue and bit of information be consid-ered in the most suspicious light," he wrote. The "evaluative function," by contrast, required the careful weighing of evidence, both "favorable and unfavorable." The fact that a refugee had displayed "leftist sym-pathies" in the past was insufficient reason to exclude him from the United States. Biddle pointed out that many refugees were "fighting the Nazis long before we were," and were then "persecuted and driven from their homes."[12] His aides complained that the security services preferred "to keep ten deserving persons out of the country rather than let one person in that is not deserving."[13]

Against his own better judgment, Biddle acquiesced to the mass internment of more than 100,000 Japanese Americans living on the West Coast. He initially resisted the relocation order on constitutional grounds, but dropped his objections after the army took responsibility for the "military exclusion areas." At the same time, Biddle contin-ued to deliver speeches warning against the persecution of foreign-born Americans and "loyal aliens." "The alien of today is the citizen of tomorrow," he told the Columbia Broadcasting System on Febru-ary 1, 1942. "Let us not be suspicious of them unless we have grounds for suspicion."[14]

Refugees posed a special problem in a time of war. German Jews no longer living in Germany had been stripped of their nationality on November 25, 1941, by an amendment to the Reich citizenship law.[15] Under German law, they were now stateless. As far as the United States was concerned, however, they remained "German natives" by virtue of their place of birth. After Congress declared war on Germany on December 11, all "German natives" who had not yet received U.S. citizenship automatically became "enemy aliens."[16] The same logic applied to "Japanese natives" and "Italian natives."

Under wartime regulations, the entry of "enemy aliens" into the United States was deemed "prejudicial to the public interest."[17] For a few weeks, virtually no new visas were granted to German Jews stranded in Europe.[18] Biddle and his supporters objected to such a blanket prohibition on the grounds that it excluded anti-Hitler refugees who did not pose a security threat.[19] A compromise was reached at the end of January, allowing for enemy aliens who would otherwise be admissible to appeal to the secretary of state for special consideration.

The appeals process was exceptionally cumbersome, involving multiple stages. Refugees whose visas had already been approved in principle before Pearl Harbor had to resubmit their applications to the State Department. The applications were examined by an interdepartmental committee composed of representatives of the State Department, the Justice Department, and the security services. A "primary" committee forwarded its recommendations to a "secondary" committee. The decisions of the secondary committee were in turn reviewed by a board of appeals, which made a final recommendation to the secretary of state.[20]

"The visa situation becomes more and more despairing every day," the American relief worker Varian Fry wrote to a French friend in early February. "It has now boiled down to a question of wire-pulling, as we say in America. In other words, about the only way to get a visa for anybody now, is to get some very important, influential person to bring pressure on the State Department."

The system reminded Fry, who had recently returned from Europe, of the times of the French monarchy. "If you can only get the ear of someone who has the ear of *le Roi Soleil,* perhaps you can get the favor you want. Otherwise there is no hope at all."[21]

As government agencies competed for a role in the "war effort," the Washington bureaucracy expanded inexorably. "Temporary" buildings—or "tempos" for short—appeared "almost overnight" on the green expanse of the National Mall. (The record construction time was thirty-eight days.) "The buildings were hideous," recalled broadcaster David Brinkley. "And they were everywhere." Tempos sprouted up next to the Lincoln Memorial, the Washington Monument, and the Tidal Basin. The Mall itself was lined with "row after row of dreary office block covering acres of what had previously been attractive parkland."²²

One such hastily erected office block housed the new Interdepartmental Visa Review Committee. Shaped like a monster comb with thick teeth, "Temporary Building U" occupied a prestigious corner of Constitution Avenue, sandwiched between the Washington Monument and the Smithsonian Museum of Natural History, a five-minute walk from the White House. The two-story edifice was home to multiple government agencies all dedicated to keeping enemy agents out of the United States but frequently at war with each other. Military intelligence officers focused on rebuffing "a frontal attack" by the Justice Department against their well-defended positions.²³ The War Department assigned "one Lieutenant Colonel, two Majors, and seven Captains," supported by six typists and four enlisted men, to full-time visa work but still complained about being outgunned by rival agencies.²⁴ The FBI was represented by twelve agents and a hundred clerks, the State Department by fifty officers and around 250 support staff.²⁵

Before a visa case could be considered, each agency had to search its files for derogatory information on the applicant or his sponsors in the United States. The primary committee rejected roughly 60 percent of the applications. This triggered a more detailed review, including interviews with sponsors and other witnesses. By early 1942, the State Department was reporting a backlog of more than 25,000 visa cases, which, it estimated, would take around fourteen months to clear.²⁶

The three security services generally took a more restrictive attitude toward granting visas than either the State Department or the immigration arm of the Justice Department. Many committee votes split 3–2 against admission. Representatives of the FBI, the War Department, and the Navy Department were continually pointing out risks involving the "hostage situation." They argued that any refugee with relatives in Nazi-controlled territory was subject to blackmail by the Gestapo. They were also unsympathetic to the "family reunification" argument sometimes made by State Department and Immigration Service representatives.

A typical case involved a sixty-one-year-old Jewish businessman from Baden-Baden named Theodor Köhler, who had been deported to Gurs with his wife, Auguste, in October 1940. With one exception, their siblings were all in the United States. As "German natives," the Köhlers were deemed "enemy aliens," even though no "derogatory information" had been discovered against them. The Immigration Service representative, supported by his State Department colleague, argued it was "desirable" to "remove them from the danger of further oppression abroad." It was difficult to believe that people who had been persecuted by the Nazis could have any remaining loyalty to Germany. The admission of the Köhlers to the United States would practically eliminate "the hostage situation which exists at the present time."

The representatives of the security services saw the case very differently. A naval intelligence officer pointed out that young Americans were preparing to go to Europe to fight a war "in the interest of democracy." They, too, would be separated from their families. "Millions of American homes" were being broken apart because of the war, "some of them forever." "Is it too much to ask the *enemy alien* to endure similar sacrifices to those Americans are making? We are sending American boys to the place where the *enemy alien* says it is too dangerous for him to remain." The review committee voted 3–2 against the granting of visas for the Köhlers, who were deported to Auschwitz three months later.[27]

For the security people, any refugee who was able to leave Nazi-controlled Europe was automatically suspect. "Vichy France is not a free nation," an FBI agent argued in a different case. "It is a Puppet Government, created by the Axis powers, with whom we are at war.... No person would be allowed to leave France unless it was to the benefit to the Axis Powers." By definition, any action that benefited the Axis powers "must necessarily be a detriment" to the United States.[28] It was a circular argument that the refugees could not win.

Military intelligence officers believed they were on strong ground in arguing for the exclusion of refugees, particularly enemy aliens. In a September 1941 memorandum, they claimed that "outstanding Jewish leaders" recognized that a large influx of Jews would "undoubtedly bring forth a strong native fascist reaction to the detriment of Jews in this country." According to the authors, public support for immigration control was "rapidly increasing." They called on the military to form "a united front" against "pressure groups" demanding less stringent regulations.[29]

The security representatives were upset to learn that the opinions of the visa review committees were merely "advisory."[30] Majority votes denying visas to refugees were frequently reversed by the board of appeals, composed of two presidential appointees with no intelligence background. In theory, the system was full of checks and balances that allowed favorable evidence to be considered along with the unfavorable. In practice, by the time a final recommendation was forwarded to the secretary of state, it was often too late.

By the time of Pearl Harbor, Hugo Wachenheimer had already spent seven months in the Les Milles emigration camp. His days and nights were consumed by a single dream: to reunite his family in America. His wife was still in Gurs, having failed to obtain permission to travel to Marseille. Hedy, now seventeen, was in London. She had left school and was working in a munitions plant.

Hugo had not seen his daughter in more than two and a half years. His lasting memory of her was the day they said goodbye at the Frankfurt railway station, when she boarded the Kindertransport for England. "It may seem silly that I repeat this so often, but I constantly see the image in front of me of how we walked arm in arm and sang the old *Sing song, ding dong*," he wrote her. "I can never forget the painful sight of your train getting smaller and smaller as I sang my song louder and more fervently, expressing my heart's highest wish: *A youngster has moved out into the world*."[31]

America's entry into the war gave Hugo reason to hope that the day of liberation was not too far away. "Already we can hear something like the distant ringing of bells announcing the coming of peace to the world. We count the hours until freedom can bloom again in this world, freedom whose most beautiful present will be your return to us."

Hugo's most precious possessions in the camp were four photographs of his daughter. On the nicest photograph, he inscribed a favorite Hedy expression: "Cheer up!" He thought of the photograph as a "good-luck charm" and carried it with him constantly.[32] At night, when he could not sleep because of the snoring and rumbling all around him, he would sneak a look at the images. "My fantasy enlarges them to life size. I inhale their breath and then I pretend that I am allowed to hold you, my grown-up girl, in my arms again like in the old days."[33]

Even as they pined for their only child, Hugo and Bella could not stop worrying about her. Vague references in her letters and post-cards to a boy named "Jimmy" disturbed them greatly. "Give us more detailed information about Jimmy, about the kind of person he is, about his parents, and also your relationship with him," Hugo insisted. "Do you remember how shortly before you left, dear *Mutti* talked to you about some important matters and gave you some valuable lessons? Now is the time to remember these lessons."[34] In another letter, he was a little more explicit. *"D'abord l'honneur,"* he wrote in French. "Honor first."[35]

Money was a constant concern. It was impossible to survive on the daily food ration at either Gurs or Les Milles. To help her parents buy food on the black market, Hedy sold the stamp collection she had smuggled out of Germany. But whatever money she sent was never enough. The Wachenheimers were on the verge of starvation. "Their situation is very bad," a HICEM official reported as early as August 1941.[36] By March 1942, Bella was down to ninety-four pounds, some thirty pounds below her normal body weight. She used her needle skills to "make alterations" to all her clothes and earn a few francs repairing stockings for her fellow inmates. "We have an extraordinarily long and difficult winter behind us," she wrote Hedy. "We were hardly able to protect ourselves from the cold." Bella reported that she was able to make some "soup out of bean flour and garlic" thanks to a money transfer from Hedy. The funds quickly ran out.[37]

Letters from Hedy provided both parents with their greatest joy. It could take up to six weeks for mail to reach France from London or New York. All mail was subject to censorship. Many letters never arrived at all. "Every morning when the mail is given out, we all wait," Bella wrote her daughter. "When mail arrives, the joy is great." The arrival of a food package was an even bigger event, necessitating a half-hour slog through the mud to the camp office to pick it up. "As soon as one returns, the questions start. What did you receive and from whom?

You should see how everybody here cooks, bakes, and fries the contents of the packages on the primitive stoves."[38]

Four hundred miles from Gurs, in the Camp des Milles, Hugo sought solace in the cultural and educational activities organized by relief agencies like the YMCA. He took French and English lessons, in addition to courses in "electrical engineering, photography, and last but not least, fashion designing." The professional courses allowed Hugo "to build castles in the air about our future."[39] Whenever he could, he also attended plays and concerts in the catacomb-like passageways of the former tile factory. He was comforted by the music of Beethoven, with its extraordinary "power to smooth every troubled forehead and open every clenched fist."[40]

One evening, at the beginning of March 1942, Hugo saw a performance of Goethe's play *Faust,* widely regarded as the greatest work in the German literary pantheon. He found himself "strangely moved" by a line spoken by God to Mephisto, the agent of the devil: "A good man in his darkest yearnings remains aware of the right path."

Hugo had recently taken the bold step of writing directly to a "big man" in the Vichy government to plead for Bella to be released from Gurs. He hoped they would be reunited in time for their twentieth wedding anniversary on March 29. If Bella could come to Marseille, they would be able to jointly plead their case with the American consul. Hugo decided to trust the words of Goethe.

"May my path be the right one," he told Hedy.[41]

Hugo's letter to the "big man" produced a brief flurry of activity on the part of the Vichy bureaucracy. A few days later, the Les Milles camp director received an official telegram inquiring about Hugo's chances of receiving a U.S. visa. "WACHENHEIMER Hugo will not be able to emigrate in the near future," he replied. "The transfer of his wife from Gurs is not required for the time being."[42]

The emigration prospects of Hugo and Bella were complicated by the lack of suitable sponsors. Hugo did not have any close relatives in the United States who were able to vouch for him. His distant Chicago cousin refused to get involved. Bella had two brothers in New York, Max and Manfred Eichel, but neither was an American citizen. They had only recently arrived in the United States, and were considered "enemy aliens" themselves. They had managed to scrape together $200 toward the cost of a steamship ticket for Bella, but HICEM was demanding more. "This sum is completely insufficient to meet the travel costs of two people," they had informed Hugo in a June 1941 letter. "Please let us know how you plan to make up the difference."[43] To pay for passage across the Atlantic, Hugo needed to find another $800 or so.

Still, both he and Bella refused to give up hope. Their spirits rose after Manfred Eichel reported that he had received a summons from the Interdepartmental Visa Review Committee in Washington in mid-April. "We now live in high expectation," Bella wrote Hedy on June 10, 1942. "God willing, things will finally work out and we will be able to see a future ahead of us again." She was sick of the "eternal sameness" of Gurs, the "sitting around without work or purpose," and the separation that "tears at the nerves."[44]

Their hopes received a further boost when Manfred wrote to say that the interview with the visa review committee had gone well. "We can expect the decision from Washington any day now," Hugo enthused. "When that day arrives, the colorful flags will be blowing in the wind for us."[45]

On July 2, the same day that Hugo imagined the flags fluttering in the wind, Bella was transferred to a different internment camp. The journey to Rivesaltes, at the eastern end of the Pyrenees, took twenty-four hours, including an hour-long march in the hot sun with her luggage. Approached on foot, Rivesaltes looked even more "forbidding" and desolate than Gurs. It was situated on a plateau that was "treeless, grassless, and tormented by strong winds."[46] Surrounded by barbed wire, clusters of low gray barracks extended as far as the eye could see.

Bella put a brave face on the move, telling Hedy she could buy fruit and tomatoes in the new camp, which was impossible in Gurs. A few days later, Hugo wrote to say that there was still no news on their visas. "Authorizations from Washington arrive almost daily," he told Hedy. "Unfortunately, ours is not among them."[47]

Unbeknownst to Hugo and Bella, their fate had already been settled.

On June 10, Max Eichel informed HIAS in New York that the State Department had rejected the visa applications of his sister and brother-in-law. HIAS relayed the heartbreaking news to HICEM in Marseille. "Mr. Eichel asks that you use discretion in breaking this information to Mr. and Mrs. Wachenheimer as he realizes that the news will be very disquieting and that they will worry greatly."[48]

It was still possible in 1942 to reach the United States from unoccupied France, but the journey was both hazardous and circuitous. The closure of the border between France and Spain prevented refugees from traveling via Lisbon. Instead, they had to take a ship across the Mediterranean from Marseille to Oran in Algeria. From Oran, they traveled six hundred miles overland to the Moroccan port of Casablanca. From Casablanca, they could take another ship to the New World. Only a few ships were still making the increasingly dangerous run across the Atlantic, however.

To obtain a U.S. visa, refugees had to provide proof of promised passage, including the name of the ship and date of departure. Consular officials checked with the shipping companies to make sure that the promised boat was actually leaving. The refugees found themselves in a bureaucratic trap. According to a February 1942 HICEM report, "The greatest obstacle preventing a rapid granting of an American visa is the necessity of proving a reserved passage on a specific ship." Ships left Casablanca at irregular intervals, with little advance notice. By the time HICEM heard about a departure, it was often too late to arrange transport from Marseille.[49]

Despite these obstacles, HICEM recorded 1,190 departures in the first three months of 1942.[50] Many of the refugees were headed for Cuba, which had resumed issuing visas to Jews following the *St. Louis* incident. Others had received their U.S. visas before Pearl Harbor. The fortunate few included two elderly Kippenheimers: Auguste Wertheimer and Rosa Auerbacher. Holding U.S. visas that had been issued back in November, Auguste and Rosa were able to travel via Oran and Casablanca. They arrived in New York on February 20 on the *Serpa Pinto*, together with three hundred other refugees.[51] Since their visas expired in early March, it was probably their last opportunity to escape.

Visa authorizations from Washington picked up slowly after March, as the visa review committees began tackling the lengthy backlog. Varian Fry became slightly less pessimistic. But even in the best-case scenario, he reported, it still took "four to six months to get any visa application through."[52]

The review committees tended to look more favorably on applications from older refugees with children already in the United States. In the ugly phraseology of the American consul in Marseille, these were people who "will not reproduce and can do our country no harm."[53] Refugee advocates could argue for their admission on humanitarian grounds. By reuniting families in the United States, the "hostage threat" would also be removed.

The committees' idea of a "desirable" refugee—to the extent they could agree on such a concept—was personified by Mathilde Wertheimer. The matriarch of the Kippenheim Jewish community was now ninety-nine years old. She had a daughter and son-in-law and granddaughter in New York. Two other unmarried daughters, aged sixty-nine and sixty-three, had been deported with her from Kippenheim to Gurs. She was so frail and small—just four feet four inches tall—that she looked "lost in ordinary furniture."[54] Even to the most suspicious bureaucratic mind, the white-haired grandmother could hardly be viewed as a security risk. She obviously did not have very long to live. Since she had close family in America, she would not become a "public burden."

Some relief workers had initially doubted the value of bringing Mathilde and her daughters to the United States. "They are so old it does not seem worth while," the Quaker representative in Marseille, Marjorie McClelland, had commented when asked to help. The Philadelphia office agreed. "It seems almost criminal to try to transport her," noted a January 30 message to McClelland.[55]

Others viewed the near-centenarian as a testament to the power of human endurance. HICEM officials annotated her case file with exclamation points in admiration of her longevity and toughness in the face of terrible hardships.[56] She had survived years of Nazi persecution, Kristallnacht, expulsion from her Kippenheim home at the age of ninety-seven, the horrors of Gurs. Promises of a U.S. visa had been made to her on at least two occasions—only to be snatched away at the last moment.[57]

Mathilde and her daughters had arrived in Marseille from Gurs three days before Pearl Harbor in response to a summons from the United States consulate.[58] The outbreak of war transformed them, automatically, into "enemy aliens" subject to extra scrutiny. It took six months for their visas to be reauthorized by Washington. They then had to go through the cumbersome process of assembling the required affidavits, birth certificates, judicial records, and medical reports for approval by the consul.

The Wertheimers had the good fortune of being examined by a Marseille physician known to be sympathetic to persecuted Jews. George Rodocanachi routinely ignored medical conditions that raised red flags for other doctors, such as rheumatism, arthritis, poor eyesight, digestion problems, and varicose veins. In addition to helping refugees, he also allowed his apartment to be used as a safe house for English soldiers and spies on the run from the Germans. His medical certificate for Mathilde Wertheimer showed a clean bill of health. Responding to a question about "the ability of this person to make a living," he stated laconically, "99 years old."[59]

The three women received their visas from the consulate on June 25, 1942, just in time to catch the ferry from Marseille to Oran.[60] They made the first leg of the overland journey between Oran and Casablanca on a reasonably comfortable passenger train. At the border between Algeria and Morocco, they were switched to a slow-moving freight train. They arrived in Casablanca on July 8 along with forty other refugees, mainly elderly women, exhausted from their "very tiring journey." Because of their advanced age, the women were put up in a maternity home while they waited for the ship to take them across the ocean.[61]

Mathilde and her companions won the hearts of rescue workers in Casablanca with their humble expressions of gratitude. "HICEM has been like a mother for us," they told their hosts. HICEM officials had become accustomed to complaints—even insults—from their clients.

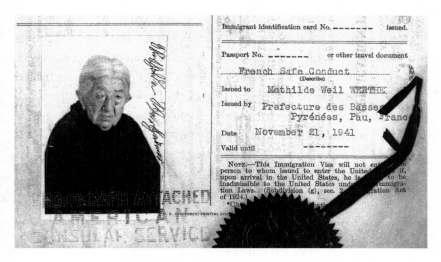

Immigrant identification card No. _ _ _ _ _ _ _   issued.

Passport No. _ _ _ _ _ _ _   or other travel document

_____French_Safe_Conduct_____
(Describe)

Issued to   Mathilde Weil WERTHE

Issued by   Prefecture des Basse
Pyrénées, Pau, Franc

Date   November 21, 1941

Valid until   _ _ _ _ _ _ _

NOTE.—This Immigration Visa will not en
person to whom issued to enter the Unite   if,
upon arrival in the United States, he is   to be
inadmissible to the United States und   immigration Laws. (Subdivision (g); sec. 2   ation Act
of 1924.)

Extract from U.S. visa for Mathilde Wertheimer

Every time a ship departed from Casablanca, there were furious arguments about accommodations on board, and who should be in first or
second class. There were often heartbreaking scenes as refugees were
prevented from boarding at the last moment due to some paperwork
problem or because their visas had expired.[62] But Mathilde was happy
simply to have survived. Her greatest wish, she told her family later,
was "a whole slice of bread that she could break up herself."[63] In Gurs,
the carving-up of the bread had been a humiliating daily ritual. There
was never enough to go around.

The three Wertheimers left Casablanca on July 13 aboard the
Nyassa, the same ship taken by the Maier family. Their fellow passengers included a party of thirty-five refugee children sponsored by the
Quakers. Relief officials had instructed the parents to remain "calm
and unemotional" as they bid their children goodbye in Marseille, perhaps forever. "The dignity and restraint which these unhappy people
showed was more dramatic and more touching than any emotional
scene could have been," Marjorie McClelland recorded. "It moves me
almost to tears even to recall it." One father explained that he was
sending his two children to America so they could be free and happy.
"We had a family life of rare happiness and contentment," he wrote.
"Unfortunately it was too short."[64]

It took the *Nyassa* seventeen days to cross the Atlantic, steering clear of shipping routes that had been mined. When she finally reached Baltimore, local newspapers devoted front-page headlines to the rescue of the child refugees. The *Baltimore Sun* also recorded the arrival of the "oldest passenger," a "Mrs Mathilde Wertheimer, 99, a native of Germany," who came over with her daughters, Sofie and Rosa.[65]

Mathilde's hundredth birthday the following April was marked by an article in *The New York Times* celebrating her escape from Europe:

2 OF HER 100 YEARS
IN DREAD NAZI CAMP

—

But It Would Take More Than
That to Crush the Spirit of
This Woman Refugee

—

SAFE WITH FAMILY HERE

—

A Whole Slice of Bread Still
Is Luxury and That Is What
She Wants on Birthday

"She is a tiny woman with a large sense of humor," the reporter noted. "One can understand how she withstood Nazi-imposed hardships. She never wants to go to bed before midnight. She refuses to use the wheelchair her son-in-law bought for her. She walks, instead, along the Hudson or goes window-shopping on Broadway. For her the most entrancing windows hold displays of fresh fruit, eggs and—more rarely now—poultry and meat."[66]

Back in France, meanwhile, Max Valfer was doing his best to overcome the shattering setback of being refused a U.S. visa in the aftermath of Pearl Harbor. An impatient man by nature, he was learning the value of patience from his wife. "We were the very first to be affected by the [changes in immigration] policy brought about by the clash between America and Japan," he wrote his children at the end of February. "Our fate has already been determined by God, and that is why we must continue to trust in Him. If and when we will be able to depart is not something we are able to know at this moment. We must continue to have patience and, God willing, remain healthy."

His greatest comfort came in the form of visits from "our sweet Mama." Every two weeks, Fanny was allowed to make the two-hour trek by tram and on foot from Marseille to Les Milles. She brought with her food that she had cooked herself, supplementing Max's meager camp rations. Such visits left them "happy as small children," he reported. "Although my hunger is never sated by these meals, I can feast until I am full on the joy that they bring. As long as I am in prison, nothing tastes as good as when our dear Mama sets the table." Max admired his wife's ability to produce small miracles out of virtually nothing through "her diligence and hard work." In a subsequent letter to his daughter Else, he wrote that Fanny's visits "strengthen us both. Mama looks in good health, if slim, and as beautiful as a young woman. I would not trade places with any Kaiser in exchange for a single moment of happiness with her."[67]

In her letters, Fanny made clear she was happy to no longer be in Gurs. The squalid, overcrowded hotel in Marseille was a vast improvement on the camp. Adversity had taught her to be "self-reliant." At the same time, she was frustrated by the constantly changing signals from Washington. "When I first arrived here, we expected to leave for the United States after four weeks. It did not work out that way. Now we must wait until it is our turn. In this difficult time, we have nothing to do but suffer."[68]

The Valfers were better off financially than the Wachenheimers. Their children had scraped together enough money for their transportation across the Atlantic. They also transferred smaller amounts via the Quakers and other relief organizations to pay for food and Fanny's hotel accommodation in Marseille. But the money was never enough, and frequently went astray. "Our dear children write that they have wired us money, but God only knows how and when it will reach us," Max complained toward the end of June. His "sense of honor" made it humiliating for him to have to constantly ask for money but, without money, it was difficult for him and Fanny to survive.[69]

As the weeks of waiting turned into months, Max felt increasingly lonely and abandoned. His children in America and Britain had either stopped writing as regularly as before or, more likely, their letters were not getting delivered. "Your prolonged silence is completely incomprehensible to us," he wrote his daughter Else in England toward the end of May. "We have received no letters, cards, or telegrams from you in many weeks. This troubles us greatly."[70] He sought support instead from his fellow prisoners. One of his most treasured possessions at this time was a poem that another Les Milles detainee wrote in honor of his sixty-second birthday, on April 12, 1942. Max shared it proudly with his children:

> *Helpful to the utmost*
> *In spite of quarrels and disputes,*
> *Always kind, quiet, and peaceful . . .*
> *Straight, sincere, free, and open,*
> *In short an honest man.*[71]

In early June, a letter arrived from daughter Ruth in New York that promised a resolution to the visa logjam. The first of the Valfer offspring to arrive in America announced that she had been summoned to Washington to testify before the visa review committee. "Hopefully, she will have good luck, and we will be freed from our fate here," Max wrote Else in England. "It is about time."[72] A subsequent message from Ruth reported that the interview had gone well. By the middle of July, Max was again urging HICEM to make the necessary travel arrangements.[73]

The longed-for breakthrough finally came on Saturday, August 1. The State Department announced that the Valfer visas had been approved. "I can hardly work at all from the joy," the oldest Valfer son, Karl, wrote his parents from Chicago. "I see you, my dears, trying to keep the tears from your cheeks. Keep your heads high. God willing, you will soon be able to set foot in this wonderful country."[74]

For their loved ones on the other side of the ocean, it seemed that Max and Fanny were already on their way. They might even reach the promised land in time for Rosh Hashanah, the Jewish New Year. "Once you are with us, we will be the happiest people in the world," Karl told his parents. "Do you think you could sail on August 15?"

TWELVE

"To the East"

T HE DAY AFTER Mathilde Wertheimer left Casablanca for the United
States, one of the Gestapo's "specialists in Jewish affairs" arrived in
Marseille on an "information-gathering" tour. Tall and thin, Theodor
Dannecker was dressed in the uniform of an SS captain. Prior to join-
ing the SS, he had worked as a textile dealer. His main qualification
for dealing with Jewish matters was his ideological zeal, extreme even
by Nazi standards. Vain, thin-skinned, and exceptionally ambitious, he
"lived in permanent conflict" with both subordinates and superiors.[1]
A senior Vichy official would later describe the twenty-nine-year-old
Eichmann associate as "a frenetic Nazi who went into a trance every
time the word Jew was mentioned."[2]

Dannecker had traveled to the *zone libre* from Paris with the mission
of conducting a census of "deportable" foreign Jews. His department
was responsible for implementing the new Nazi policy on Jews, which
had shifted from expulsion to annihilation. He had already overseen
the transport by rail of some five thousand Jews from occupied France
to Auschwitz in German-occupied Poland. As an initial step toward
a "final solution" of the Jewish question, Dannecker demanded that
Vichy France hand over another ten thousand Jews.[3] German and
French officials had jointly decided that foreign-born Jews—rather
than French Jews—would be sent to Auschwitz first.

The SS captain arrived in Marseille on July 14, Bastille Day. He
was shocked to witness the first large-scale demonstrations against

Vichy and Germany. As he recorded in his official report, the famous Canebière "was packed with an enormous crowd" chanting Gaullist slogans and singing the "Marseillaise." "The police formed barricades but it was clear they did not have the situation under control." Similar incidents took place in other towns, including Aix-en-Provence, where Jews joined the protests and "the police remained completely passive."[4]

Dannecker visited Les Milles the following day. He was displeased to learn from the camp commander that some ten thousand foreign Jews had succeeded in leaving France in 1941. Emigration had become "very difficult" but "remained possible" via Casablanca. Dannecker was also unhappy about the inadequate security arrangements at the camp. He noted with disgust that inmates often received passes to travel to Aix and Marseille "to prepare their emigration." In reality, the Jews spent much of their time "standing in line outside bakeries ahead of French housewives, buying the best merchandise." A French police officer who accompanied the SS man on his tour informed the camp commander that Vichy had "agreed to the deportation of foreign Jews." Their hopes for emigration would soon "become illusory."[5]

It did not take long for Vichy to deliver on its promise to Dannecker. On July 17, the French police chief secretly ordered his subordinates to annul exit visas for foreign Jews.[6] No new visas would be issued without special permission. The last Jewish escape route from Europe had effectively been closed.

As he toured the "Jewish concentration camps" of unoccupied France, Dannecker was disappointed to hear that there were not enough internees to fill his quota. He had been expecting to find twenty thousand Jews in Gurs alone. Instead he counted 2,247 "deportable persons" in Gurs, 1,192 in Les Milles, and 361 in the "female emigration centers" of Marseille. In the case of Les Milles, most of the inmates were Jews deported from Baden who were waiting for their U.S. visas. To satisfy his Gestapo superiors, Dannecker would have to take additional measures.[7]

Rumors of a new, even more vicious, phase in the anti-Jewish campaign soon began to circulate. From Paris came reports of massive *rafles*—"roundups"—of Jews conducted by the French police under German supervision. It seemed that on the night of July 16, some sixteen thousand foreign-born Jews had been taken to an indoor sports stadium near the Eiffel Tower known as the Vélodrome d'Hiver. Earlier raids had targeted adult males, but this one included many women and children. According to a Red Cross report, they were given "no time to prepare their affairs" and were not even permitted to carry basic toilet articles. "Everything is taken from them down to personal items including wedding rings." From the stadium, French police took the prisoners to an internment camp at Drancy, on the outskirts of Paris. Here they separated parents from their children, before herding them onto freight cars for a voyage to an "unknown destination."[8]

For a few days, it looked as if the new measures were confined to occupied France. "Terrified Jewish refugees" fled southward across the demarcation line. Max and Fanny Valfer continued to hope for the best. Toward the end of July, Max wrote an optimistic postcard to his daughter in England. "We look forward to a little peace once we are all together," he scrawled in his spindly, almost indecipherable hand. Fanny added a few sentences of her own from the Hôtel du Levant in Marseille. "I want so much to be with you again, my dear children. Dear father too. We must be patient." She added cryptically that she was "not lacking in worries," before signing the card "your loving Mama."[9]

Hopes that the *zone libre* would be spared were quickly dashed. Relief officials in Marseille learned about the Vichy police order canceling exit visas for Jews on July 21. They were also able to confirm that a "detailed census of the camp populations" had begun. All internees had to re-register. They were "asked in particular to give complete information on the composition of their families," reported Roswell McClelland, a senior Quaker official. "The compiling of this data went on day and night, the results being entered on master lists which apparently had to be handed into the various prefectures by various deadline dates."[10] In the meantime, camp officials refused all requests for temporary leave, even for interviews with foreign consulates.

On July 30, relief workers obtained the text of a secret Vichy police order to deport any foreign Jew who had arrived in France after 1936.[11]

Four days later, the police cleared out the Marseille hotels that had served as "emigration centers" for women and children transferred from Gurs. "The poor people were routed from their beds at four in the morning, given just time to dress, advised to take a blanket and supplies for a day's journey," recorded YMCA representative Donald Lowrie. "Loaded into trucks, they were taken to the railroad station, packed into box cars and transported to Les Milles."[12]

Among those arrested in the predawn raids in Marseille was Fanny Valfer. When she reached Les Milles, she was greeted by a menacing sight. A paramilitary force known as the Groupes Mobiles de Réserve had replaced the easygoing camp guards. Wearing black uniforms with steel helmets, the new guards reminded the terrified refugees of the German SS. They now surrounded the perimeter of the tile factory, a "disproportionate display of armed strength" that "contrasted almost ludicrously" with the "ill-clothed, undernourished, half-sick" internees.[13]

"The atmosphere was heavy with foreboding," recalled McClelland, who visited Les Milles on Monday, August 3, as the women and children arrived from Marseille. The only glimmer of hope lay in the fact that a few days remained before the transports to Drancy were scheduled to begin. There was still time to appeal to the "savior of France," Marshal Philippe Pétain.

A spa town renowned for its mineral water and Oriental baths, Vichy had become the capital of unoccupied France largely because of its luxury hotels. No other town in France had as many empty hotel rooms to house the politicians and bureaucrats who fled Paris in June 1940. The patronage of the emperor Napoleon III had endowed Vichy with grand boulevards, landscaped parks, and even an opera house big enough to accommodate the National Assembly. The population had swollen from 35,000 to more than 100,000 during the last two years.

Marshal Pétain and his immediate aides occupied a suite of offices on the third floor of one of Vichy's grand hotels, the Hôtel du Parc. It was here that he signed decrees, received foreign ambassadors, and addressed his people over the radio. Propaganda posters depicted the mustachioed soldier gazing across an idealized image of *la France éternelle,* complete with Catholic church, beautifully cultivated fields, happy workers, and cherubic children. *"Travail, Famille, Patrie"* the posters proclaimed, a deliberate rebuff of the Republican slogan, *"Liberté, Égalité, Fraternité."*

By the summer of 1942, real political power in Vichy had effectively passed from the third floor of the Hôtel du Parc to the second floor. The offices of Prime Minister Pierre Laval were directly below those of the chief of state. Dismissed as foreign minister in December 1940, Laval had returned as head of government in April 1942 on the strength of his Nazi connections. Known to French voters as "the horse dealer" for his bargaining skills, Laval was rude and unkempt, with a lock of hair that kept falling across his forehead. His influence rose in direct proportion to the tightness of the Vichy government's collaboration with Berlin. While he was not exactly a Nazi puppet, he depended on German support to outmaneuver his political rivals. The price for this support was acquiescence to German demands on matters that were of greatest importance to Hitler, including the anti-Jewish campaign.

"I wish for the victory of Germany," Laval had said in a June 22 radio broadcast. "Without it, Bolshevism would tomorrow be installed across Europe."[14]

Rumors that Laval was determined to deport the foreign Jews had been circulating for weeks. The Quakers had learned, from a source in the French government, of a conversation in early July between the prime minister and a senior German official. The German wanted to know when Vichy would implement the anti-Jewish measures that "we are using in occupied France." Laval replied by referring to the Jews expelled from Baden almost two years previously. "The only Jews we have are your Jews. We will send them back to you any time you say."[15]

Any remaining doubts about who was in charge vanished as soon as the Americans arrived at the Hôtel du Parc. Pétain's close aide and personal physician Bernard Ménétrel appeared "deeply distressed" by the planned expulsions. He made clear, however, that the aged marshal had little say in the matter. The man to see was Pierre Laval.

The Quaker officials were skeptical of claims that the Germans were creating a "Jewish reservation" in southern Poland where "families could be reunited." They had heard alarming reports of Jews being divided into different categories: able-bodied, old and ill, young girls, children. "Family reunification" seemed to be the last thing the Nazis had in mind.

"We fear the true purpose is physical annihilation," Roswell McClelland told Ménétrel bluntly.

The doctor brushed aside these fears as a "hysterical exaggeration," McClelland later recorded. At the same time, he seemed "visibly shaken."[16]

The following day, August 6, Ménétrel succeeded in arranging an impromptu meeting between the prime minister and the Quakers in the Hôtel du Parc. The haggard-looking Laval was dressed in his usual crumpled suit and trademark white string tie. He was "clearly impatient and harassed" and full of venom against foreign Jews. He described the refugees as "an undesirable element, a source of anti-government agitation, and black market activity." They had shown themselves to be *ingrats,* "ungrateful" for France's generous hospitality.

"We did not want them to come here in the first place. We ask nothing more now than to get rid of them," Laval continued. His information was that the Germans had decided to establish *une réserve ethnique*—"an ethnic reservation"—in Poland where "the Jews would live and work together."

Ménétrel mentioned the Quaker belief that "the real purpose behind the German policy is extermination."

"Preposterous," exclaimed Laval. "Pure fiction." He then launched into a diatribe against the United States. If the Roosevelt administration was so concerned about Jews, it should have admitted more of the refugees who were begging to go to America, "instead of merely criticizing." Laval made clear he would not be deterred by the inevitable "hue and cry" from overseas. "Words do not concern me, only actions."

Since the prime minister was clearly unwilling to stop the deportations, the Quakers focused their effort on persuading him to grant a few exceptions. They cited the cases of some six hundred refugees who were ready to travel immediately to the United States. That matter was "under consideration," Laval replied. The Americans then urged him to at least spare the children. If this happened, American relief organizations would do everything in their power to persuade Washington to grant the children asylum. At this point, Laval was called away "urgently." The fate of the children hung in the air.[17]

Later that same day, Ménétrel arranged for another foreign delegation to be received by Pétain. This one was led by Donald Lowrie of the YMCA, who chaired a committee of the principal relief agencies. The American was struck by the "bloodless, almost waxen color" of the face familiar from Vichy propaganda posters. The marshal seemed "physically well preserved" but "not altogether aware of all that goes on around him." He also had trouble hearing.

"What gives me the honor of your visit?" the eighty-six-year-old hero of Verdun asked with grave formality. Lowrie expressed concern over the reported deportations. The first transport—from Gurs—was due to depart that very day.

An aide explained that the deportees would be taken to "a sort of Jewish state" in southern Poland. "There, it appears, they will enjoy a certain liberty."

"Yes, I know, near Kraków," said Pétain.

"We cannot believe, Monsieur le Maréchal, that this has been done with your knowledge."

Pétain made a gesture of helplessness. "You know our situation with regard to the Germans."

By prior agreement with the Quakers, Lowrie again pleaded for exceptions to be made on behalf of the children and refugees whose U.S. visas had been approved.

"I will speak of this to Laval."[18]

Desperate for a concession, Lowrie told Pétain that the deportations would leave a most "unfortunate impression" on international public opinion. The marshal waved a dismissive hand in the air. He then stood up. The interview was over.

Gerda and Momo Auerbacher waited with the other internees beneath the broiling afternoon sun in the great courtyard of the Les Milles tile factory. They had been there since morning, under the gaze of the black uniformed police, automatic rifles slung across their backs. The guards had checked their names against a master list and then divided the internees into smaller groups, according to the letters of the alphabet. There were around twenty prisoners with surnames beginning with the letter "A."

It was now Monday, August 10. Just a few days earlier, it had seemed that Gerda and Momo were on the verge of emerging from their long bureaucratic nightmare. They had an appointment with the Marseille consulate for an interview on August 8. After months of delay and conflicting signals, the State Department had approved their immigration applications. Their passage across the Atlantic was booked and paid for. If all went well, they would travel to America on a Portuguese ship, the *Serpa Pinto,* scheduled to depart Casablanca at the end of August.[19]

The Auerbachers had been promised U.S. visas at least twice before. In May 1941, they had been left on the dock in Marseille as their Kippenheim neighbors, the Maiers, sailed away to freedom. A change in U.S. immigration procedures dashed their hopes of catching the next boat. Their visas were reauthorized in November only to be revoked once more after Pearl Harbor. In January, they had said goodbye to Momo's elderly Aunt Rosa, who had received her visa before the outbreak of war. Another six months of waiting ensued, followed by yet another summons from the American consul. For the third time in succession, the Auerbachers were unable to collect their visas. Four days before their scheduled interview, Gerda was rousted from her bed in Marseille and transported to Les Milles.

In the office of the camp director, overlooking the parade ground, French officials and foreign relief workers were poring over lists of "deportables." The cramped room resembled a "courtroom gone frantic" as arguments raged over the fate of individual detainees. HICEM officials pleaded on behalf of people who had been promised American visas; a Protestant pastor produced baptismal certificates of newly converted Jews; the Quakers begged for exemptions for children. In the midst of the mayhem, "police inspectors came and went, camp clerks brought in new telegrams from Vichy and protests from all sorts of Frenchmen." In theory, the power of selection lay with the camp director, "but behind his chair stood a police captain representing Vichy."[20]

Word came from Vichy that young people under the age of eighteen would be spared for the time being. Relief workers rushed from the director's office to the parade ground, asking parents whether they were willing to part with their children. All agreed, with the exception of one family that refused to be separated. The other fathers and mothers did their best to smile and murmur a few encouraging words as they hugged their sons and daughters goodbye. As soon as the convoy of cars disappeared through the camp gates, the distraught parents broke down in sobs. Some fainted while others had to be "half-led, half-carried away" by their friends.[21]

"We have to hold the fathers and mothers back as the buses leave the courtyard," the head of the main French Jewish organization, Raymond-Raoul Lambert, wrote in his diary. "Mothers are screaming in despair and the rest of us cannot hold back our tears."[22]

When McClelland returned to Les Milles late that afternoon, he was reminded of a scene from Dante's *Inferno*. Dust swirled above the sun-drenched courtyard in front of the dilapidated tile factory. Stretcher-bearers were "plying back and forth from the camp infirmary with the limp figures of the weak and old who had fainted in the heat and confusion."[23] A camp official was yelling out names of internees selected for deportation, one by one.

"Ascher, Herbert."

"Auerbach, Pinkas."

"Austein, Samuel."

"Austein, Dora."

"Axelrad, Schulin."

The first list included 260 people, reaching down to the letter "H." The names of Gerda and Salomon ("Momo") Auerbacher were missing—at least for now.[24]

As each name was called, the person selected for deportation was escorted back to his dormitory in the tile factory. After collecting a few meager possessions, the deportees had to pass through a narrow gauntlet of Groupes Mobiles to a holding pen near the camp gate. Amid the general chaos, the guards robbed many of the deportees of their remaining valuables.[25]

Piles of suitcases, bags, and bundles of clothes were scattered across the ground in the area reserved for the deportees. Despite the blistering heat, many people had put on heavy winter overcoats, believing they might need them in the months ahead.

"The spectacle was indescribably painful to behold," wrote Daniel

Bénédite, a French relief worker, in a letter smuggled to Varian Fry in New York in a toothpaste tube. "All the internees had been lined up with their pitifully battered valises tied together with string. Most of them were in rags, pale, thin, worn out with the strain, which had dragged on for more than a week. Many of them were quietly weeping.... There was no sign of revolt: these people were broken. Their faces showed only hopeless despair and a passive acceptance of their fate."[26]

Aware that many deportees had been promised U.S. visas, Bénédite went to a nearby café to telephone the American consulate in Marseille. He was unable to reach his regular contact. He finally got through to a junior official who listened with weary resignation to his pleas for prompt American intervention. The U.S. chargé d'affaires in Vichy, Pinkney Tuck, had already protested the deportations, to no avail.

"It's most unfortunate, sir," the consular official told the distraught young Frenchman, "but we can't do anything about it."[27]

A line of cattle wagons, "black like hearses" in Lambert's phrase, was drawn up in the little railroad siding opposite the main entrance to the camp. A foot of fresh straw had been laid across the floor of each wagon, but the only ventilation consisted of "barred, rectangular openings" near the roof.

As the evening wore on, people called out through the vents of the loaded cattle cars with last-minute messages for the children. Hands appeared through the bars with notes and urgent requests to "telegraph my relatives in the United States." Crumpled banknotes and pieces of jewelry were pushed through the vents with the simple remark, *"Für die Quäker."* "For the Quakers." "The hot smell of hay and closely packed human bodies struck your face as you got as close to the vent as possible," recalled Roswell McClelland. "One would catch a glimpse, for the last time, of a strained familiar face in the light of your flashlight."

The cattle cars remained in the siding for the rest of the night. Old people begged the guards to let them out to urinate. The guards ordered them to use the metal buckets that had been placed inside the wagons. The relief workers were permitted to empty the buckets and distribute supplies. They handed out pieces of soap, cans of sardines, condensed milk, and fruit donated by a Jewish organization in Marseille.

The relief officials continued to plead for exemptions. McClelland was appalled to see a woman who had just received a summons from the American consulate being loaded into a cattle wagon. After appealing to the camp director, he was able to extricate her. In the meantime, suicide cases were arriving at the infirmary. One couple had taken poison. It was too late to save them: the doctor did not have a stomach pump. Two others had slashed their wrists. The doctor stitched them back up again. "They have been bandaged and will be sent off nevertheless," Lambert recorded in his diary.[28]

At dawn, soup was ladled out from a large cauldron, and passed through the partly opened wagon doors. McClelland was struck by the nobility of a twenty-three-year-old violinist, Richard Freund, whom he had come to know well. The young man had been named *chef de wagon* of his cattle car. He took his duties very seriously: "helping the old people, cajoling the faint-hearted, trying to establish some order within his small and special domain, counting the number of parcels to ensure that everyone got one." The Quaker official noticed "his high-laced, black, old fashioned shoes that probably once belonged to some bygone, fastidious relative" in middle-class Berlin. The violinist reacted serenely to the sudden change in his circumstances. Perhaps he even welcomed the release from "the drab and crowded boredom of over two years of camp life," from being "half-sick and constantly hungry," from "the eternal waiting and hoping that a visa would finally come."[29]

Around 6:30 a.m., an antiquated steam engine was coupled onto the wagons. The engine pulled the train slowly out of the siding. McClelland and his fellow relief workers "stood watching it go, and then turned away, heartsick, and walked back into the camp."[30]

The five-hundred-mile journey to Drancy took nearly twenty-four hours. The train traveled via Chalon-sur-Saône, the same crossing point between occupied and unoccupied France that had been used for

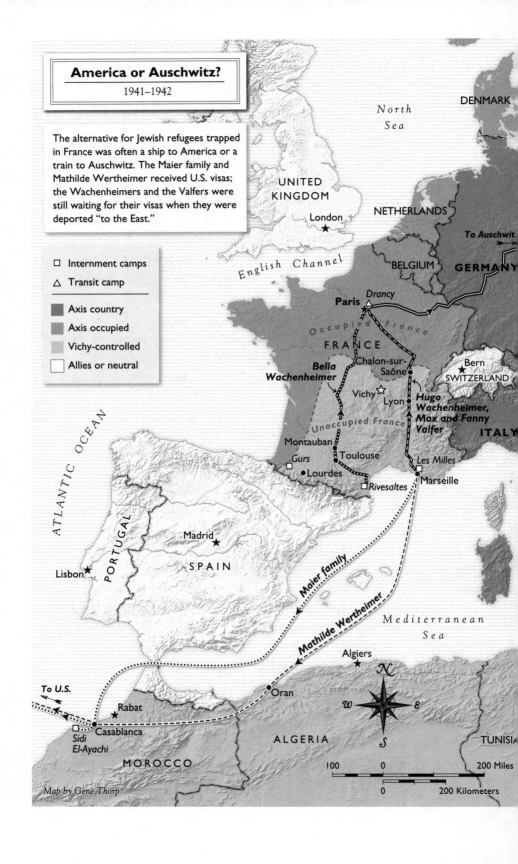

America or Auschwitz?
1941–1942

The alternative for Jewish refugees trapped in France was often a ship to America or a train to Auschwitz. The Maier family and Mathilde Wertheimer received U.S. visas; the Wachenheimers and the Valfers were still waiting for their visas when they were deported "to the East."

□ Internment camps
△ Transit camp

Axis country
Axis occupied
Vichy-controlled
Allies or neutral

North Sea

DENMARK

UNITED KINGDOM

NETHERLANDS

London ★

BELGIUM

GERMANY

To Auschwit

English Channel

Occupied France

FRANCE

Paris

Drancy △

Chalon-sur-Saône

Bern ★

SWITZERLAND

Bella Wachenheimer

Vichy ☆ Lyon ★

Hugo Wachenheimer, Max and Fanny Valfer

Unoccupied France

ITALY

Montauban ●

Gurs □ Toulouse ●

● Lourdes

Les Milles □

Marseille □

□ *Rivesaltes*

ATLANTIC OCEAN

PORTUGAL

Madrid ★

SPAIN

Lisbon ★

Maier family

Mathilde Wertheimer

Mediterranean Sea

Algiers ★

To U.S.

Oran ●

Rabat ★

Casablanca ●

□ *Sidi El-Ayachi*

ALGERIA

TUNISIA

MOROCCO

N
W   E
S

100   0   200 Miles

0   200 Kilometers

Map by Gene Thorp

the October 1940 deportation from Baden to Gurs. In Drancy, French policemen counted and sorted the deportees before loading them into different boxcars, bound this time for Auschwitz.

In Les Milles, meanwhile, the same sad scene repeated itself. Vichy officials assembled the remaining internees in the courtyard of the tile factory on August 12. It was another blazingly hot summer day. There were ten attempted suicides. The relief workers made the same desperate appeals to exempt certain categories of deportee, with less success this time. In the afternoon, a German officer appeared in the camp to confer with the Vichy police chief. According to the Protestant pastor Henri Manen, the visit resulted in "a real manhunt."[31] Internees excluded from the first transport were included in the second. The roll call of deportees began again with the letter "A."

"Abzug, Alfred."

Momo and Gerda waited to see if their names would be called.

"Auerbacher, Salomon."

"Auerbacher, Gerda."[32]

As the first group of deportees stumbled toward the waiting boxcars, the Groupes Mobiles beat those who did not walk fast enough. "The scene in the courtyard has become even more tragic," noted Lambert. "To think that none of these unfortunates has committed any crime except to be born non-Aryan!" The police action was "so brutal" that the relief workers felt compelled to protest. The police chief reminded the guards that they were dealing with "deportees, not detainees."[33]

The relief officials were coming to realize that pleading "special cases" was largely futile. If they convinced the camp authorities to spare someone from a transport, a replacement was immediately chosen. It became obvious that "possession of an American immigration visa, even one already stamped in a person's passport, would not exempt Jewish refugees from deportation." Such was the "inexorable logic" of the earlier Vichy decision to annul all exit visas for foreign Jews.[34] The German demand to Vichy to deliver an initial quota of ten thousand Jews overwhelmed all other considerations. Sooner or later, all foreign Jews would be deported. It would then be the turn of French Jews.

The roll call continued until it reached the end of the alphabet.

"Valfer, Max. Valfer, Fanny." Their papers, like those of Momo and Gerda, had been marked "Immigration to the United States pending." But that was no longer a sufficient reason for exemption from the transports.

There were two other Kippenheimers among the more than five hundred people taken from Les Milles that day: Julius Weil and Hugo Wachenheimer.[35] (Julius was the brother of Max's secretary, Berta.) Hugo had only recently learned that he would not be permitted to immigrate to the United States. In the end, it had mattered little whether his visa was denied or endlessly delayed. His fate—and the fate of thousands of others dreaming of the promised land—was already determined.

As he waited for his name to be called, Hugo thought mainly of his daughter, Hedy, in London and his wife, Bella, in Rivesaltes. He scribbled a brief note to Bella, dated August 9, the day before the first transport. He said he expected to be sent eastward very soon and hoped they would meet "somewhere *en route*." If that happened, Bella subsequently told Hedy, they would carry their burden, "however difficult it might be, with dignity and courage."[36]

The deportations caused widespread revulsion, even among Vichy officials who had previously shown little sympathy for foreign Jews. "I never thought I should live through scenes like those in our camp," the Les Milles camp director, Robert Maulavé, told Donald Lowrie. "Having responsibility for a crime like this, even purely executive, is heart-rending."[37] Lowrie reported that "transport to the East" was widely understood to be a euphemism for "either forced labor or slow extermination [from starvation and illness] in the Jewish 'reservation' in Poland."[38] It was still unclear how the people herded aboard the cattle cars of the French railway system would meet their doom. What was clear was that official German explanations for the urgent need to "resettle" tens of thousands of Jews made little sense.

Some of the regular camp guards were so appalled by the deportations that they assisted in escape attempts. A guard named Auguste Boyer hid a mother and her three children in the attic of the tile factory. As the second transport was waiting to depart, he led them to an old freight elevator, where he slid down a rope with the children on his back, one at a time. He then escorted the family through a hole in the perimeter fence that he was responsible for guarding. After hiding in his farmhouse, the family eventually reached safety in Switzerland.[39]

Similar incidents took place at other camps. When the commander of Rivesaltes learned that children would be included in the transports— despite an earlier order to exclude them—he handed them over to the Quakers. *"Faites-les disparaître!"* he instructed. "Make them disappear!" Individual policemen approached foreign aid workers to tell them they were disgusted by the deportations, which they described as a national shame.[40] According to a September 1942 report from Lowrie, "The markets and queues buzz with horror stories about the deportations and the disgrace thus brought upon France."[41]

Among the children who "disappeared" during this period were two members of the Wachenheimer family. Margot and Edith Strauss had sat in the front row of the Gurs "Golden Wedding Anniversary" photograph of December 1940 on either side of their grandparents Julius and Emma. A year later, the two girls were placed in a children's home run by the Children's Aid Society, known by its French initials, OSE. At the beginning of August 1942, Margot and Edith, now aged thirteen and ten, went to stay with relatives in the Alps, close to the border with Switzerland. Officially, OSE had granted them a "two-week vacation." They never returned.

Their parents, Max and Meta Strauss, remained in the camps, attempting unsuccessfully to organize their immigration to the United States. Max Strauss was transported to Drancy from Les Milles on the same day as Hugo Wachenheimer. Two days before he left, he sent a despairing letter to his children via their new foster parents. "Will I ever see them again?" he wrote. "Everything went so fast, and no one can help."[42] Meta was deported from Rivesaltes a few days later.

The list of exemptions changed almost every day, always getting shorter. Toward the end of August, the police raided the Hôtel Bompard in Marseille to arrest many of the children who had been spirited away from Les Milles with the consent of their parents. Several boys and girls succeeded in escaping with the help of the Quakers. "We gave them whatever we could in the way of money, foodstuffs and ration tickets," recalled McClelland. "But what could one really advise them to do except go into hiding?"[43]

In some quarters, disgust with Vichy was accompanied by bitterness toward the United States. The head of the Marseille office of HICEM, Wladimir Schah, complained about the hypocrisy of American refugee policy. "Representatives of the great North American Republic... protested against the deportation of alien Jews to the East, without giving them the possibility to go to the West." The discrepancy made it easy for Pierre Laval to argue that he was sending "alien Jews" to the one country that was prepared to accept them, namely Nazi Germany.

"It is difficult to protest against the deportations towards the East when everybody knows that it would have been possible to send the unfortunate refugees to the West, provided that the United States had opened their doors a little wider," Schah reported to his superiors. "What harm would two or three hundred thousand Jewish refugees threatened with deportation have done to the United States, with its 140 million inhabitants?"[44]

In claiming that "two or three hundred thousand" Jews might have been saved, Schah was referring to the four years since the Évian conference on refugees. Led by the American delegation, speaker after speaker had expressed sympathy for the victims of Nazi persecution. An "Intergovernmental Committee" had been created to deal with the refugee crisis. There had been much well-intentioned talk about creating Jewish homelands in Africa, South America, or even Alaska. But little substantive had been achieved.

By the summer of 1942, mass escape was no longer feasible. The borders of Germany, and occupied countries such as Poland, Belgium, and the Netherlands, were sealed. Even supposing that a refugee was able to reach Marseille or Casablanca, obtaining passage across the Atlantic was increasingly difficult. Without the right connections and a lot of money, it was next to impossible.

Even so, Schah refused to concede defeat. HICEM had managed to charter two ships from Casablanca at the end of August—one to New

York, the other to Mexico. Schah believed it might still be possible to send up to "thirty thousand persons" to the United States. He urged his American colleagues to persuade President Roosevelt to waive entry formalities for the threatened Jews. "Upon their arrival, they might be placed in concentration camps until investigation is made concerning each of them."[45]

It did not take long for reports on the deportations to reach America. At the end of August, Eleanor Roosevelt received a letter from Varian Fry describing the frantic attempts of the Vichy government to satisfy German demands. "Men, women and children are being arrested in the streets of Marseille, Toulouse, Lyon and other population centers to make up the quota. In the unoccupied zone children over five years of age are being deported with their parents, in the occupied zone some children of two years and more."[46]

Eleanor forwarded the Fry memorandum to her State Department friend, Sumner Welles, who agreed that the information was "basically correct." He told her that the American embassy in Vichy had repeatedly protested "this inhuman program." Unfortunately, the American protests had made "no impression on Laval who is apparently determined to carry out his original plans to return these unfortunate people to their oppressors."[47]

The First Lady used her newspaper column to call for the admission to the United States of children "whose parents are in concentration camps."[48] As usual, she carefully avoided the term "Jewish children," referring instead to "European children."

Among the prominent Americans expressing revulsion at the events in France was the father of Treasury Secretary Henry Morgenthau Jr. As American ambassador to the Ottoman Empire during the First World War, Henry Morgenthau Sr. had witnessed the state-sponsored massacres of around one million Armenians. "I am confident that the whole history of the human race contains no such horrible episode as this," he had written in 1918.[49] The former ambassador feared that history was repeating itself. He urged Secretary of State Cordell Hull to do everything in his power "to prevent the perpetration of this fearful crime."[50]

Reports filtering out of Germany lent credibility to the rumors of a new, even more horrifying, genocide. The representative of the World

Jewish Congress in Switzerland, Gerhart Riegner, had learned that the Germans were planning to kill as many as four million Jews with poison gas. His source was a well-connected German industrialist. Riegner relayed the information to Rabbi Stephen Wise in New York on August 28. Wise immediately alerted the State Department.

Sumner Welles found it difficult to believe that the Germans would waste "valuable labor," but admitted that Hitler was capable of anything. "Who can tell, seeing that you are dealing with that madman," he told Wise.[51]

Bella Wachenheimer wanted to put her affairs in order before being sent "to the East." She had been preparing for the worst ever since she found out that Hugo had been deported from Les Milles. It was particularly difficult to say goodbye to Hedy in London, but "there is no use, it has to be done," she told her daughter in an ink-smudged letter from Rivesaltes on September 1.

"There is another transport leaving from here and this time I am on it," Bella wrote. "My dear good child, I will try in every way possible to remain in contact with you, but it will probably be a long time before we hear from each other again."

Since she had only enough energy to write one letter, Bella sent farewell greetings to her brothers in New York through Hedy. She thanked Manfred and Max for their attempts to obtain immigration visas "for us poor ones." She knew they had done what they could: they could not be blamed for the lack of success. Bella's final words were for her daughter:

> Continue to be always good and honest, carry your head high and never lose your courage. Don't forget your dear parents. We shall continue to hope that one day we will see each other again, even if it takes a long time.... My dear good child, let me greet you and kiss you heartily. I will never forget you and deeply love you. *Mutti.*[52]

By early September, Rivesaltes had become "a sorting station for people who pass into an unknown and unknowable oblivion."[53] As in Les Milles, relief workers tried to persuade the camp director to exempt children from the transports. When this failed, they did their best to sabotage attempts to compile lists of deportable children, including those now in homes run by OSE. "Go back to your barracks," they whispered to parents waiting in line to provide camp authorities with details of their children's locations. "You don't really want to see your children again now, do you?"

The relief officials phrased their advice delicately, to avoid sounding too alarmist. By September, however, they were under no illusions about the fate awaiting the deportees. "We already knew the truth," an OSE worker recalled later. Relief workers had accompanied the first transports to the demarcation line with occupied France. They had seen men "pitilessly separated" from their wives. They had also heard reliable reports about the confiscation of luggage and separation of children from parents in Drancy. Talk about "family reunification" was obviously "a farce."

A delegation of relief officials visited the local prefect in a "last-ditch" attempt to save the children. They made the argument that young people had not been deported from Les Milles.

"Yes, but that's provisional."

The relief workers pointed out the horror of children being sent to their "extermination" from the so-called free zone.

"What do you expect? France has been defeated and we no longer have an army."[54]

In the end, the relief officials persuaded the prefect to exempt twenty children who had been labeled "retarded." Scores of others "disappeared" with the help of OSE and the Quakers. Even so, a total of 150 children would be sent from Rivesaltes to Drancy during the month of September.[55]

In the early morning of Friday, September 4, Bella joined 620 other men, women, and children for the mile-long march to the Rivesaltes railway station. Relief workers took care to feed the deportees well before they left. At the railway station, the men were loaded into cattle wagons. There were third-class railway cars for the women and children, but they were even more cramped than the cattle cars.[56] A Quaker representative handed out "change of address" slips they could forward to the International Migration Service in Geneva.

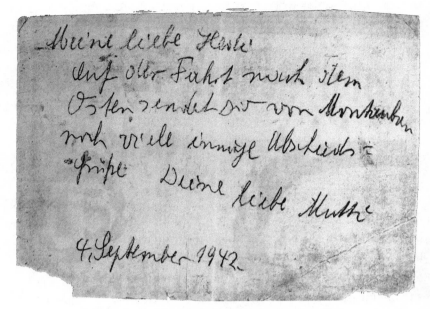

Bella Wachenheimer's final message to daughter Hedy

As the train rumbled slowly northward, Bella scribbled a postcard to *"Meine liebe Hedi"*—"my beloved Hedy"—in London. When the train reached Montauban, north of Toulouse, in the early afternoon, Quaker officials were waiting on the platform, hoping to comfort the refugees and relay messages to their loved ones. Bella handed her postcard to one of the relief workers shortly before the train pulled out of the station, en route to German-occupied France. Her farewell message to Hedy, mailed later that same day, was written in pencil in shaky hand-writing. Although the train was headed to Drancy, she had no illusions about her final destination.

> On the journey to the East, I send you again many intimate good-byes from Montauban. Your loving *Mutti*. 4 September 1942.[57]

Seated in his office on the second floor of the luxurious Hôtel du Parc, Pierre Laval was feeling increasingly isolated. Ordinary French citizens had reacted with dismay to the deportation of foreign Jews, particularly children. They were even more horrified by Laval's attempts to persuade French workers to "volunteer" for service in German factories. At least two attempts on the prime minister's life had been reported. Sabotage was "greatly on the increase."[58]

Laval had a standard tactic for dealing with criticism from foreign diplomats and humanitarian workers. He denounced the hypocrisy and "high moral tone" of "certain governments" who turned away Jewish refugees even as they censured Vichy. "Nothing can sway me from my determination to rid France of foreign Jews and send them back to where they originated," Laval told foreign journalists in mid-September. "I will take no lessons in humanitarianism from any foreign country."[59]

In private conversation, the prime minister used cruder language to describe his attitude toward foreign Jews. *"Qu'ils foutent le camp,"* he told U.S. chargé d'affaires Pinkney Tuck. "Let them get the hell out of here."[60]

Tuck disputed Laval's claim that the U.S. government had "shown little disposition in the past to admit people of the Jewish race into the United States." As ammunition for future discussions with Laval, Tuck asked Washington to provide him with the relevant immigration statistics. The State Department responded with a detailed breakdown for the years 1933 to 1942. The data showed that 162,575 "Hebrew immigrants" had been admitted to the United States since Hitler's rise to power in Germany. A hundred thousand had arrived in the three years following Kristallnacht. Adding visitor visas, the total number of self-identified Hebrew admissions for the decade came to 204,085. Although the United States could clearly have done more to help victims of Nazi persecution, the number of those admitted was scarcely negligible. The only territory that accepted more Jews than the United States during the same decade was British-administered Palestine. (See chart on page 317.) [61]

While under no illusion that he could stop the deportations, Tuck believed he might be able to persuade Laval to spare the children. True to his "horse-trader" reputation, Laval was anxious to maintain at least the appearance of normal relations with Washington to counterbalance his close ties with Berlin. The chargé urged the State Department to present "a concrete proposal" to Vichy for granting visas to children threatened with deportation. He believed that Laval might make a concession on this point, if only to "calm the storm of criticism which his inhumane policy has aroused throughout the country."[62]

Encouraged by Eleanor and her allies, FDR approved the granting of emergency visas to one thousand refugee children. He later increased the number to five thousand children, with the proviso that the program would remain confidential.[63] He did not want to stir up anti-refugee opinion in the United States or alert the Germans to the rescue plan.

At first, it seemed that Laval might be willing to cooperate. On September 30, he told Tuck that he agreed "in principle" to the rescue of the children. "I will only be too glad to be rid of them." Immediately afterward, however, he had a meeting with the German consul general that caused him to reverse course. The Germans were worried that the United States would use the children for "anti-German propaganda." Tuck suspected that the Germans had learned about the plan from an intercepted communication. He was furious, both with the State Department for failing to encrypt a sensitive telegram, and with the Germans for suggesting that the children might be exploited for propaganda purposes. "I had difficulty restraining my anger," he telegraphed Washington.[64]

The Quakers and other relief agencies pushed ahead with rescue preparations—but the political and military obstacles were insurmountable. It took another six weeks to make arrangements for an initial evacuation of five hundred children.[65] The transfer was canceled following the Allied invasion of North Africa on November 8. That same day, Vichy France broke off diplomatic relations with the United States. Two days later, German troops swept into the unoccupied portion of the country, taking full control of the borders.

On the other side of the ocean, the Washington visa bureaucracy was seemingly unaffected by the dramatic developments in France. It churned out approvals and rejections of immigration applications long after the people concerned were beyond all hope of rescue. There was a sudden upsurge in visa authorizations in the fall of 1942, both before and after the German army extinguished the last vestiges of the *zone libre.*

A typical case involved the family of Berta Weil, Max Valfer's secretary. On September 24, the Marseille consulate sent a letter to the Gurs internment camp notifying the Weils that their immigration applications had been approved by the State Department. They were asked to report to the consulate at their earliest convenience for a final interview and receipt of their travel documents. There was only one problem: Berta had been deported to Drancy, and then to Auschwitz, at the beginning of August, together with her mother and sister. The letters to the Weils were returned to the consulate as "undeliverable—no forwarding address," along with hundreds of similar notifications.[66]

Some visa cases went all the way up to the War Refugee Board, established by President Roosevelt in early 1944 to assist victims of Nazi persecution. On December 20, 1944, the head of the board received a letter from the Immigration Service approving the visa applications of Max and Fanny Valfer, of Kippenheim, Germany. It was the third time in three years that Washington had given the green light to their pleas for sanctuary across the ocean. The wheels of the U.S. bureaucracy continued to turn, disconnected from the tragic events that had set them in motion.

According to the letter from the Immigration Service, the "last known address" of Max Valfer, born 1880, was "Camp Les Milles, France." Fanny Valfer, born 1886, was reported to reside at "Hotel Levante, Marseille."[67] Like their Kippenheim friends, the Weils, Max and Fanny were no longer reachable. They had disappeared into the gas chambers and ovens of Auschwitz.

Memory

A LTHOUGH Hedy Wachenheimer had heard nothing from her parents since their transport "to the East," she clung to the hope they might still be alive. Perhaps they had somehow returned to Kippenheim, which was, after all, "east" of France. When the war ended, she would go back to Germany to find them. She got her chance in the summer of 1945 when she saw an advertisement for "exciting work in Europe." Her fluency in both German and English was sufficient qualification for a job with the Civil Censorship Division of the United States War Department. After a two-week training stint in Paris, she headed for Munich.

Six years after leaving Germany on a Kindertransport in her navy blue suit with the Peter Pan collar, Hedy was back in the land of her ancestors. She was now twenty-one years old and wearing an American military uniform. By her own account, she thought of all Germans as "Nazis." She hated them because of what had happened to her family. It took months before she could bring herself to give candy to impoverished German children who had nothing to do with Hitler's crimes. "That troubled me," she recalled later. "How can I live in a country with people I hate?"[1]

Her first job involved reading the intercepted mail of German civilians and reporting any anti-Allied sentiments. But she soon found more interesting work with the prosecutor's office at the trials of Nazi war criminals in Nuremberg. One day, during a recess, she found herself face-to-face with Hermann Göring. She stared at him intently. The former Nazi Party boss was obviously uncomfortable. "Who is this little one?" he asked his defense counsel, not knowing that Hedy spoke German. "What does she want?" The encounter in the corridor both amazed and gratified Hedy. "Here is Göring," she thought to herself. "Not long ago, I would have been mortally afraid of him. Yet here he is, afraid of me, little Hedy from Kippenheim."[2]

Hedy was assigned to the case of the "Nazi doctors." She spent much of her time in the captured German documents center in Berlin examining evidence of experiments on concentration camp inmates. When she found an incriminating document, she would flag it for translation and further review. She was repulsed by the "cold, unfeeling detail" of the descriptions of the "euthanasia program," which included lethal injections and gassing of the mentally ill. Reading about the experiments, Hedy found it difficult to eat and sleep. She thought how her parents might have suffered.

It took a long time to summon the courage to return to her home village. "On the one hand, I wanted to go to Kippenheim, on the other hand I was afraid," she wrote later. "As long as I was away from home, I could maintain the illusion that I would meet [my parents] again. But if they were not there, I would have to bury all my hopes."[3] The first time she went back, her resolution failed at the Kippenheim railway station. Instead of heading toward the village, she took the next train in the direction from which she had come.

She tried again in August 1947. Her American military uniform made her feel more confident. Even so, her nerves were "in tatters" as she walked along the familiar streets. Kippenheim had been assigned to the French occupation zone. All traces of Nazi rule had been eliminated. Adolf-Hitler-Strasse had reverted to its old name, Obere Hauptstrasse, "Upper Main Street." After a twenty-minute walk, Hedy passed her old home on Bahnhofstrasse, but barely glanced at it. She did not want to go in alone. Instead, she went to the Rathaus, around the corner, and asked to speak to the mayor.

News of Hedy's return spread quickly. A small crowd gathered outside the mayor's office, anxious to greet her. She did not feel like talking to them. Instead she went with the mayor to her former apartment. The mayor offered to take her inside, but she changed her mind at the last moment. She could not bear to see the familiar upstairs rooms with new occupants and new furniture. She wanted to remember everything as it had been when her parents were alive.

Next on her list of old childhood haunts was the old Wachenheimer textile trading business, up the street from the Rathaus. The inscription HEINRICH WACHENHEIMER LLC FOUNDED 1857 had been whitewashed out. On closer inspection, her great-grandfather's name was still faintly visible through the paint. Nobody was living in the house, which had been bombed during the war. The memories suddenly came flooding back. Hedy remembered the garden where she had grown wild strawberries, the hammock she had swung in as a child, the family car, the typewriter on which she had learned to type.[4]

Suddenly she remembered her father hiding some jewelry in the gutter high above her following his return from Dachau. She asked the mayor to help her look for the valuables. He summoned a workman with a ladder who searched the gutter thoroughly, to no avail. Eager to assist, the mayor suggested that her parents might have buried the jewelry in the garden behind the house. He ordered the workman to dig it up. Again nothing.[5]

Little by little, Hedy made contact with villagers who had behaved decently toward her parents, while avoiding the ones who had harassed them. She visited Anna Kraus, who had sold milk and eggs to the Wachenheimers. After her oldest son joined the Nazi Party, Anna was afraid she would be denounced for continuing to have contact with Jews. She asked Hugo and Bella to stop coming to her house. Nevertheless, she continued to secretly supply the Wachenheimers with food, visiting them late at night when the rest of the village was asleep. Tears ran down Anna's face as she apologized for not doing more for Hedy's parents.[6]

Hedy learned that the property of the Jews deported from Kippenheim in October 1940 had been put up for auction soon afterward. A neighbor arranged for her to meet a notary who had recorded the prices each item fetched. The notary's records would be helpful if Hedy decided to reclaim the belongings her parents had been forced to leave behind. As the time approached for the meeting, she was "suddenly overcome by fear and doubt." She did not know how she would react "when I found out who now owned the bust of Dante that had watched me gravely from the bookcase."[7] She canceled the appointment.

Hedy left Kippenheim with the certain knowledge that neither her father nor her mother, nor any of the other Jews deported with them to Gurs, had ever returned to the village. Nevertheless, she continued to hope that "somewhere, somehow, some day" she would be reunited with her parents.[8]

It took many years for Holocaust survivors from Kippenheim to establish what had happened to their loved ones. Hedy Wachenheimer was unsure about the fate of her parents until 1956 when she received two letters from a French government department dealing with war victims. The letters stated that Hugo and Bella Wachenheimer had been transported from Drancy to Auschwitz on September 11, 1942. In fact, as Hedy later discovered, her father had been deported the previous month.[9]

In the immediate aftermath of the war, the French had little interest in investigating the crimes of Vichy. Pierre Laval was found guilty of high treason and executed in October 1945. The former prime minister became "a symbol of evil incarnate," in the phrase of the American scholar Robert Paxton, "the ideal scapegoat" for the horrors of collaboration.[10] The Gaullist myth of widespread national resistance to the Nazis was not seriously challenged until the early 1970s when Paxton published his groundbreaking work on Vichy France. It was not until 1979 that the French Nazi hunters Serge and Beate Klarsfeld created an association to represent "the sons and daughters of Jewish deportees from France."

With the help of the Klarsfelds and other Holocaust researchers, the survivors were eventually able to piece together the full story of the transports to "the East." Hedy learned that her father had spent five days in the Drancy holding center, together with Max and Fanny Valfer and Julius Weil. They were dispatched to Auschwitz on August 19, 1942, on "Convoy number 21." Max and Fanny traveled together in "wagon number 14"; Hugo and Julius were in "wagon number 15."[11] The train journey took two days. On arrival in Auschwitz, the four Kippenheimers were gassed immediately, along with 440 other adults and 373 children. Of the 955 Jews in the convoy, only four survived the war.[12]

Vichy archives made it possible to document the fate of most of the 6,500 Jews deported from Baden to Gurs in October 1940. Roughly one in four of the deportees died in Gurs or other French camps, many from typhus or malnutrition. Four out of ten were deported to Auschwitz. Eleven percent found refuge overseas, mostly in the United States. A further 12 percent, mainly children and elderly women, succeeded in hiding out in France until the end of the war.[13]

The story of the Gurs deportees was reflected, in microcosm, in the "Golden Wedding Anniversary" portrait of Julius and Emma Wachenheimer. (See photograph on page 282.) Out of the twenty-two people in the photograph, only six are known to have survived the war. The older sister of Hugo Wachenheimer, Hilda Weil, immigrated to America with her husband, Theo, in late 1941. Escaping with them was Hugo and Hilda's mother, Lina Wachenheimer. Emma Wachenheimer obtained permission to join her granddaughters, Margot and Edith Strauss, in the town of Annecy in eastern France in late 1942. Aged seventy-three, she was excluded from the early transports. As long as Annecy was under Italian occupation, Emma and the two girls felt fairly safe. After the Germans replaced the Italians, they hid in a remote village in the Alps. They finally reached the United States in December 1946.[14]

In addition to Hugo and Bella, family members deported to Auschwitz included Oskar and Käthe Wachenheimer (Hugo's brother and sister-in-law) and Max and Meta Strauss (the parents of Margot and Edith). Julius Wachenheimer died in a French camp.

Compared with other German Jews, the Baden deportees were relatively fortunate. Despite the appalling conditions in Gurs and other French camps, they were at least afforded the possibility of escape. Had they remained in Germany, almost all would have been sent eastward, to Theresienstadt and Auschwitz. In France, they got a second chance at acquiring American visas, at a time when it was no longer possible to leave Germany. Many Jews living along the Rhine River in southwest

Germany had strong family ties in the United States, which simplified their immigration plans.

These factors help explain why the survival rate for Kippenheim Jews was a little higher than for German Jews in general, and much higher than eastern European Jews, who had fewer American connections and fewer opportunities for escape. Around 522,000 Jews were living in Germany when Hitler came to power in 1933. Roughly a third were killed in the Holocaust. By comparison, the Jewish population of Kippenheim in 1933 was 144. Thirty-one Kippenheim Jews died as a result of Nazi persecution, a death rate of just over 21 percent. Down the road, in Schmieheim, where the Jewish population was poorer and less well connected, the death rate was over 60 percent.[15]

Wealth, education, and family ties in the United States all contributed to the ability of Jews to organize their escape. The attitudes and prejudices of individual consuls and the visa review committees back in Washington also played a role. But there was another force at work whose importance should never be underestimated: plain, dumb luck.

Else Valfer filed for immigration to the United States on August 8, 1938, together with her husband, Heinrich. They were among tens of thousands of Jewish refugees admitted to Britain during the first eight months of 1939 on the strength of their low American registration numbers.[16] Else joined Heinrich in England less than a month before the outbreak of war on September 1, 1939. Had she not left Germany when she did, she would likely have been condemned to years of disappointment and heartbreak, ending in death.

Max and Fanny Valfer submitted their immigration paperwork to the United States a few weeks after their daughter. As luck would have it, the lines outside the Stuttgart consulate had become unmanageable by September 1938. A slew of anti-Jewish decrees had resulted in a huge spike in U.S. visa applicants. Max and Fanny were assigned high American registration numbers, which made them ineligible for asylum in Britain.[17] They were about to sail for Cuba when that escape route was shut down following the abortive voyage of the *St. Louis* in May 1939. They were promised U.S. visas in December 1941, only to see the promise snatched away in the wake of the Japanese attack on Pearl Harbor. A subsequent summons to the American consulate in

Marseille in August 1942 came a few weeks too late to save them from Auschwitz.

In Germany, as in France, the postwar years were a time of forgetting. After the Nuremberg trials of the top Nazi leaders, enthusiasm for bringing lower-level Nazis to justice declined rapidly. A new enemy had risen in the east, in the form of Soviet Communism, that quickly became much more threatening than the defeated ideology of National Socialism. The focus of both victors and vanquished switched from settling accounts with former Nazis to the Cold War and economic reconstruction.

Beginning in 1948, a series of trials of local Nazi officials took place. The results were often inconclusive and the sentences extraordinarily light. The Nazi Party leader for the Lahr district, Richard Burk, was cleared of "crimes against humanity." He managed to push responsibility for Kristallnacht and other anti-Jewish actions onto subordinates who had long since died or disappeared. The only charge proven against Burk was his order to tear down the tablets of Moses from the roof of the Kippenheim synagogue. The Nazi boss turned traveling salesman was sentenced to one month in prison for "destruction of property."[18]

The new West German government allowed Holocaust survivors to file legal claims for property either confiscated by the Nazis or sold at extortionately low prices. Some Jewish families from Kippenheim negotiated compensation directly with the new owners, frequently their former neighbors. Others hired attorneys to represent them in multiyear legal battles. Hedy Wachenheimer drew up a detailed list of the contents of her parents' apartment on Bahnhofstrasse at the time of her departure for England in 1939. She included such items as the bronze bust of Dante, a grandfather clock, a Mercedes typewriter, an antique Meissen candleholder "approximately 300 years old," and a collection of gramophone records, "including works by Beethoven, Mozart, and Schubert."[19]

Even when there was a successful outcome, the restitution process was fraught with frustration. No amount of money could bring back murdered loved ones. Hedy did not receive compensation for the theft of the Wachenheimer business and property until 1960. By then, she was living a middle-class life in Dayton, Ohio, married to a physicist working for Monsanto. She wanted to donate the money to charity but her husband insisted on buying a car. After much agonizing, Hedy gave in. "I hated that car," she recalled later. "For me, it would always symbolize the loss of my parents."[20]

The years of forgetting were epitomized by the fate of the Kippenheim synagogue. Following its desecration on Kristallnacht, the once splendid Moorish-style building was abandoned. The roof and windows were further damaged during the war, but the exterior structure remained intact until the late 1940s. With the exception of the missing tablets, it was still recognizable as a place where Jews had worshipped. That would soon change.

After the war, the building was returned to the South Baden Jewish Association as the legal successor of the Kippenheim Jewish community. Finding no use for a defiled synagogue in a village with no Jews, the association sold the building to the new mayor of Kippenheim, a war veteran named Anton Fritschmann. A stone mason by profession, Fritschmann turned the sanctuary into a workshop for producing hollow concrete blocks. He used the ritual bathing area as a private bathhouse. Wooden pews on which generations of Jewish congregants had said their prayers were turned into chicken coops. Stone columns and pediments from the sanctuary were incorporated into the mayoral wine cellar.[21]

In 1956, the mayor sold the building to a private agricultural supply company as a warehouse. The new owners pulled down the twin towers that had formed the western façade of the synagogue and bricked up the glorious rosette window. They converted the vestibule into a loading dock and ramp for trucks to pick up crates of animal feed and manure. The gallery where women and children had looked down on the men at prayer became an additional storage area, connected to the main hall by conveyer belt. A solitary testament to the building's original purpose was carved in stone above the wrought-iron entrance gates. Had the warehouse workers been able to decipher the Hebrew script, they would have recognized the biblical quotation that read: THIS IS NONE OTHER THAN THE HOUSE OF GOD.[22]

The destruction of the synagogue was omitted from the official history of the village, along with any reference to the persecution of Jews. A book celebrating the twelve hundredth anniversary of Kippenheim in 1963 referred only in passing to the former Jewish population. There was no mention of Kristallnacht, the deportation to Gurs, or the gassing of Kippenheimers in Auschwitz. The survivors were appalled. The son-in-law of Max and Fanny Valfer wrote a letter of protest to the mayor of Kippenheim. "It was not enough to kill the Jews," Rudy Bergman complained from New York. "It was also necessary to silence them."[23]

A couple of years later, a member of the once prominent Weil family became interested in the fate of the synagogue while passing through the village on vacation. Born in Switzerland, Leopold Weil had never been to Kippenheim before, but had heard about the village from his relatives. Parking his car on Poststrasse, he was dismayed to find that the former synagogue had been turned into a warehouse for storing animal feed. Indignant, he rushed to the Rathaus to lodge a complaint. Rebuffed by the mayor, he wrote letters to anyone he thought might help, including the local newspapers.

His protests attracted a flurry of media attention. Interviewed on German national television, Mayor Fritschmann accused Weil of stirring up an unnecessary controversy. He noted that the village council had voted to place a memorial plaque on the wall of the warehouse, describing the history of the building. When the TV reporter asked why the plaque was not yet installed, Fritschmann explained that it might attract antisemitic graffiti.[24]

On the national level, the 1960s witnessed a surge of interest in Germany's Nazi past. Student activists demanded a full historical accounting. Journalists unearthed disquieting evidence about the Nazi connections of prominent West Germans, including the chancellor, Kurt Kiesinger, who helped organize German foreign propaganda during the war. In late 1968, the Holocaust researcher Beate Klarsfeld slapped Kiesinger in the face at a political meeting. As she was dragged out of the room, she yelled in French and German, "Kiesinger! Nazi! Step down!"

There was a disconnect, however, between the largely abstract intellectual debates among student rebels and the conservative politics of rural Baden. The controversy over the Kippenheim synagogue rumbled on for a couple of years, only to become bogged down in practical considerations. Nobody was able to devise a workable plan for moving the warehouse to a new location. There were arguments over who would pay for the restoration of the synagogue. "They formed a commission and then forgot all about it," recalled Robert Krais, a community activist.[25]

Stef Wertheimer left Kippenheim with his parents and sister Doris in late 1937 at the age of eleven. His father, Eugen, who had lost a leg in the battle of Verdun in World War I, understood the threat posed by Hitler early on. "The man is crazy," he told his family. "We need to get out of here."[26] By immigrating to Palestine, Stef's branch of the Wertheimer family avoided the fate of his aunt, Fanny Valfer, who was murdered at Auschwitz.

In his autobiography, Stef would describe himself as "a rebellious child, a troublemaker."[27] He had been a mediocre student at the Etten-heim Gymnasium. Despite his limited education, he was good with his hands and had a strong business sense. From a small metal workshop in the backyard of his home in Israel, he created an extremely successful company, ISCAR, that manufactured industrial tools and blades for jet aircraft and gas turbines. By the 1970s, Stef had become one of the richest men in Israel.

The first time he returned to Kippenheim, in 1956, he "felt nothing but anger."[28] He walked past his former home on Bahnhofstrasse and the houses of his numerous relatives, but made no attempt to go inside or talk to anyone. Apart from a few close family members like his cousin Erich Valfer, Stef had "no pleasant memories" associated with Kippenheim and had "no sense of belonging."[29]

In 1977, he was elected to the Knesset, the Israeli parliament, as one of the leaders of a new centrist party. While he still thought of himself as primarily a businessman, he now had a political platform. He had never been religious, but was appalled by the willful destruction of the Kippenheim synagogue. He began writing letters of protest on Knesset stationery to his fellow parliamentarians in Bonn. He also sent a close aide to Kippenheim to lobby for the reconstruction of the synagogue.

In the meantime, Kippenheim had elected a new mayor. An engineer by training, Willi Mathis represented a new generation of Germans without emotional or political ties to the past. Just twenty-five years old, he was the youngest mayor in the new West German state of Baden-Württemberg. Like many rural administrators, he had no previous connection with the village and knew little of its history when he ran for office. Mathis learned about the synagogue controversy only after he was installed as mayor and began exploring the village archives. "It became clear to me that I had to deal with this topic," he recalled later. "The history of the Jews in Kippenheim was part of the history of our community."[30]

Spurred on by the letters from Stef Wertheimer, Mathis urged the village council to restore the synagogue as a memorial to Kippenheim's once vibrant Jewish community. Public opinion was split down the middle. A poll revealed that 50 percent of Kippenheimers supported his plan while 40 percent were opposed. There was also a generational split. Younger villagers were more likely to support the proposal than older villagers.[31]

As the new mayor saw it, the major obstacle was funding. The cost of restoring the synagogue was estimated at around 2.5 million West German marks, more than a million dollars. A village of two thousand people did not have the funds for that kind of project. If he could raise most of the money from other sources and find a new location for the warehouse, Mathis was confident that he could overcome the lingering opposition.

It took more than two decades to complete the restoration project. Stef paid 20,000 marks for the reconstruction of the synagogue towers. The village contributed 200,000 marks. The rest of the money came from state and national sources. A prominent regional politician, Wolfgang Schäuble, persuaded the federal government to declare the synagogue "a monument of national importance." Although it had been desecrated and severely damaged, it was one of the few surviving synagogue structures in Baden. Others had been torn down or transformed into office buildings, an arts center, and even a private home.

As arguments raged over how to fund the project, a local activist began contacting Jewish survivors. As a young athlete, Robert Krais had organized a German-Israeli friendship society following the massacre of Israeli team members at the 1972 Munich Olympics. He became "obsessed" with the Kippenheim synagogue after reading an article that mentioned the words carved into the stonework above the entrance: "This is none other than the house of God." His research revealed that most of the destruction had taken place not under the Nazis, but after 1945, under democratic rule.

By encouraging the former Kippenheimers to tell their stories, Krais hoped to dispel the historical amnesia that had settled over the village. The fact that he was not a Jew himself was irrelevant. The synagogue was a storehouse of local memory that was threatened with extinction. "This is not just Jewish history," he said. "This is *our* history."[32]

Both Mathis and Krais were shocked by the lack of support from what was left of the German Jewish community, now comprised mainly of immigrants from eastern Europe. The Jewish leaders considered the former synagogue "a house of God" no longer and therefore no concern of theirs. They showed no interest in creating a monument to Kippenheim Jews. A letter from the chairman of the Central Council of Jews in Germany stated that the Kippenheim authorities could do whatever they wished with the building. "We got no help from Jewish leaders," said Krais. "It was only through public pressure that we were able to achieve anything."[33]

Krais and Mathis were allies, but their personalities were very different. The mayor believed in tactful diplomacy; Krais was naturally confrontational. Mathis was a bridge-builder, Krais a loner. Mathis was patient; Krais wanted immediate results. In the end, it required both a sledgehammer and a wheelbarrow to dismantle the wall of denial, as well as a lot of pushing from outside.

A top priority for Mayor Mathis was to restore good relations with the former Jewish community of Kippenheim. Among the survivors who returned to Kippenheim regularly at his invitation was Hedy Wachenheimer, who had been packed aboard a Kindertransport at the age of fourteen. Over the years, she learned to distinguish between the Germans who had inflicted pain on her family and the Germans who sought to atone for the past.

One visit, in October 1997, proved particularly emotional. The interior of the synagogue was still only partially restored. As a child, Hedy had always dreamed of sitting downstairs with the men, rather than with the women in the gallery. Invited to meet with local students, she finally had the chance to stand in the place where her father had stood. After the talk, a member of the audience presented her with a torn-up piece of Torah scroll that had been hidden in an attic for half a century. Some of the Jewish men from Kippenheim had been wrapped in the Torah scrolls before being marched to the railway station. Other rolls were hung like curtains on the station platform for the men to see as they boarded the train for Dachau.

The villagers wanted Hedy to have the desecrated Torah roll, but she hesitated. She was unsure whether she should even touch a piece of the Torah that had been used to humiliate her father and the other Jewish men. She burst into tears as she considered what to do. Photographers crowded around, expecting her to accept the gift. Finally, she suggested that the fragment be given to a museum.[34]

There were other revealing moments during the visit. Hedy met with a woman who had bought her most treasured childhood possession—the bike she used to ride to school—at an auction of Jewish property. It turned out that the woman's older sister, Gertrud Strähle, had been a classmate of Hedy's at the Ettenheim Gymnasium. Hedy remembered her as a particularly zealous member of the Hitler Youth. Gertrud now wanted to be friends with the Jewish girl she had tormented sixty years earlier. She approached Hedy after an event at the school. She reminisced about the good old student days, sitting around campfires on school outings.

This was too much for Hedy, who had been ostracized by Gertrud and her friends and never invited on school outings. "Your reality and my reality are quite different," she told her former classmate. "You made my life a living hell." Gertrud kept insisting that she had been unaware of the indignities inflicted on Jewish children, before being asked to leave by event organizers.[35]

A historical accounting of a different kind was taking place across the ocean. At the center of the controversy was whether Franklin Roosevelt should—or could—have done more to save persecuted Jews. The debate about the American response to the Holocaust burst into the public consciousness at the very time that Kippenheim—and Germany—was rediscovering its Jewish heritage.

The case for the prosecution was presented by the historian David Wyman in a best-selling 1984 book titled *The Abandonment of the Jews.* Wyman argued that Roosevelt allowed the State Department to block visas for persecuted Jews and failed to respond adequately to credible reports of mass killing. Jewish advisors to FDR feared that "government aid to European Jews might increase antisemitism in the United States."[36] An honorable exception was Treasury Secretary Henry Morgenthau Jr., who persuaded FDR to authorize the creation of the War Refugee Board in January 1944. The board was credited with saving the lives of tens of thousands of Jews, a worthwhile effort but too little, too late, according to Wyman.

A rival historian, Arthur Schlesinger Jr., made the point that FDR had been viewed as "a hero" by most American Jews. They voted for him in overwhelming numbers in four successive elections. No previous president "had surrounded himself with so many Jewish advisers" or "condemned anti-Semitism with such eloquence and persistence." In Schlesinger's view, Roosevelt did all he could to persuade "an isolationist nation that Nazism was a mortal threat to the United States." The most effective way to stop the mass slaughter of Jews was to focus all efforts on "winning the war."[37]

The opposing sides came together for a round table debate on the Public Broadcasting System in April 1994. The occasion was the release of a PBS documentary titled *America and the Holocaust.* Wyman had served as a historical advisor for the program, which was subtitled *Deceit and Indifference.* The question, as framed by the host, Charlie Rose, was whether "Americans and the United States government turned their backs on the plight of the Jews in Europe during World War II."

To Wyman, the answer was clear. Both the president and the Congress had failed the test of leadership. The State Department was guilty of "outright obstructionism." The press was also complicit. The mass killings of Jews were "virtually never a front-page issue." That made it very difficult to build public support for concerted government action.

FDR's passivity in the face of the annihilation of European Jewry represented the "worst failure" of his presidency.

Schlesinger rejected the claim that America "turned its back" on the Jews of Europe at a time when "millions of American young men" were fighting their oppressors. He conceded that more refugees could have been admitted to the United States at the beginning of the war, but even that was "very difficult." If the administration had tried to increase the immigration quotas, Congress would have reduced them.

The historians differed sharply over the feasibility of large-scale rescue operations, including a proposal to bomb Auschwitz in late 1944. The plan was vetoed by the War Department on the grounds that the death camp was not a military target. For Wyman, this represented a missed opportunity to disrupt the machinery of mass murder. Schlesinger argued that railway lines could have been quickly rebuilt. The Allies did not want to run the risk of presenting the Nazis with a propaganda triumph by killing "a lot of Jews."

Another historian, Alan Brinkley, pointed to "a general failure of the American moral imagination in confronting the facts of the Holocaust as they became available." It was difficult for most Americans, FDR included, to conceive of evil on such a scale.

Wyman objected vehemently. "Maybe we weren't fully aware of the dimension of six million killed, but we were aware of Nazi atrocities of all types." From a briefcase stuffed with documents, he produced a long and complicated form dating from 1943 that refugees were required to fill out if they wished to immigrate to the United States.

"It's eight feet long, small print," he complained, waving the form in front of the television cameras. "It's an obstacle course to keep the refugees out."

"Come on, relax," Schlesinger shot back. He argued that the number of Jews who were excluded from America because of inadequate paperwork alone was "not very considerable." The idea that "millions of European Jews" could have been saved was preposterous.

"No one's ever said 'millions,'" Wyman countered.

"That is the implication."

"There's no implication."[38]

And so the arguments continued, with little hope of resolution.

There was, however, one matter on which the historians generally agreed. In a democracy, political decisions ultimately reflect the will of the people, as expressed through the ballot box. As Wyman noted in an earlier book, *Paper Walls,* most Americans "opposed widening the gates for Europe's oppressed" during the 1930s and early 1940s. U.S. refugee policy in the years leading up to the Holocaust, Wyman concluded, was "essentially what the American people wanted."[39]

A half century after the murders of Fanny Wertheimer and Max Valfer at Auschwitz, their descendants had "multiplied greatly," in the words of Exodus. They were now scattered all over the world—from North America to Britain to Israel to Australia. In 1990, 2005, and 2018, hundreds of Wertheimers and Valfers assembled for grand family reunions in the country that had become home to most of them, the United States. Each gathering was an occasion for mourning, but also cause for celebration. "All of us and our children are slaps in the face for Hitler" was how Marion Bloch, a grand-niece of Max and Fanny, summed up the attitude of the survivors.[40]

The reunions brought together a diverse, resourceful, and talented crowd. Stef Wertheimer had turned his backyard tool company into one of the most successful businesses in Israel. Stef's cousin, Pia Gilbert (formerly Pia Wertheimer), was an acclaimed pianist, dance composer, and professor at the Juilliard School in New York. Another cousin, Herta Bloch (Marion's mother), was celebrated in Jewish culinary circles for her authentic German *wurst,* sold from a Manhattan re-creation of the Wertheimer butcher shop in Kippenheim. A cousin once removed, Andrew Bergman, had made a name for himself in Hollywood as the writer of zany comedies such as *Blazing Saddles* and *Honeymoon in Vegas.*

One of the reunion organizers was Sonja Geismar, a granddaughter of Max and Fanny. As a four-year-old, Sonja had been a passenger on the *St. Louis* with her parents, Freya and Ludwig. After being turned away from Cuba, the family ended up in Britain, where they waited for their American quota numbers to be called. They finally arrived in New York on February 11, 1940, nearly ten months after leaving

Hamburg. The selection of Britain as their intermediary destination rather than the European mainland might have saved their lives. Many of their Löb relatives were trapped in Belgium after the German invasion of western Europe and transported to Auschwitz in the summer of 1942. Roughly a quarter of the 937 *St. Louis* passengers were killed in the Holocaust.[41]

The grande dame of the Wertheimer family was Pia Gilbert, who had immigrated to the United States with her family in 1937, settling in New York. She loved to tell stories about the shock of arriving in the big city after growing up in a tiny German village. Even in America, she was unable to overcome her fear of men in uniform. They reminded her of the storm troopers who had chanted, "When Jewish blood flows from the knife" outside her home in Kippenheim. It was a dread that gnawed at her during her first concert tour of the American Midwest at the age of eighteen. During a fifteen-hour train journey from Chicago to New York, she developed an irrational fear of the train conductor.

The conductor looked at her strangely as he inspected her ticket. Pia was "scared to death" by his uniform. Whenever he returned to the compartment, he would stare at her again, unnerving her even more.

After about five hours, the conductor asked Pia, "You from Germany?" The question startled her. There was a stigma attached to such an inquiry back in 1939, whatever the circumstances of one's departure.

"Yes."

"You from southern Germany?"

Her heart was pounding.

"Yes."

"You from Kippenheim?"

"Yes."

The conductor finally revealed the reason for his curiosity. "I'm from Kippenheim, too. My name's Herzog. You look just like your family. Wertheimer."[42]

Pia's uncles and aunts were on the platform in New York together with her parents to greet her back from her tour. The first to recognize the familiar face next to Pia as she descended from the train was Uncle Hermann the butcher.

"Look, that's Herzog," the former owner of the *Badischer Hof* told the assembled *Tantes* and *Onkels*. "From Kippenheim." Somehow it seemed perfectly natural that they should all meet up at Grand Central Terminal.

The great city by the Hudson obviously bore little resemblance to the village on the edge of the Black Forest, but in some ways it was simply a larger stage for the same actors, with similar dreams and passions to the ones they always had.

Of all the survivors, the one who felt the deepest nostalgia for the place of his birth was Kurt Maier. Ten years old when his family was deported to Gurs, Kurt returned to Kippenheim for the first time as an American G.I. stationed in West Germany in 1953. As a cataloguer of German books at the Library of Congress, and the author of a memoir about growing up under the Nazis, he remained steeped in the history and culture of his native land. Even after decades away from Kippenheim, he could still hear the ox-drawn hay wagons rattling down Poststrasse when he closed his eyes at night. He caught whiffs of Kippenheim barnyards in the crowds on the streets of American cities.

Along with other former Jewish residents of Kippenheim, Kurt was invited back to the village in 2003 to attend ceremonies marking the final restoration of the destroyed synagogue. For the first time in more than six decades, people named Maier and Wachenheimer and Auerbacher lit candles and intoned Hebrew prayers in the place their ancestors had worshipped. After welcoming them "home," Mayor Mathis promised to finally "break the seal of silence" surrounding the October 1940 deportation from Baden to Gurs.

Kurt replied to the mayor on behalf of the survivors. "We were country Jews," he reminded everybody. "We were close to the soil. This German soil was once ours as well."[43]

The boy who had huddled with his mother beneath an upturned bathtub on Kristallnacht as an enraged mob hurled rocks through the windows attempted to summarize two thousand years of Jewish history in a few sentences. "Jews settle in a community. They purchase land for a cemetery. Then they build a synagogue with a school and a ritual bath. Soon butchers and bakers open their shops. The community flourishes. The Jews feel safe. Then something happens. The government changes."

He was referring to events in Kippenheim, but he might have been talking about any number of threatened minority communities since the dawn of recorded history. He quoted from the Book of Exodus:

A new king, to whom Joseph meant nothing, came to power in Egypt. "Look," he said to his people, "the Israelites have become far too numerous for us. Come, we must deal shrewdly with them..."[44]

As the years went by, and other survivors passed away, Kurt came to be seen as a link to a way of life that had vanished forever. He accepted numerous invitations to return to Germany to give talks on Jewish life in Baden and his family's experience of Nazi persecution. His visits, and the publicity surrounding the restoration of the synagogue, encouraged Germans to search through their attics for forgotten photographs and letters. In 1995, a local man discovered a series of five photographs taken by his recently deceased father-in-law showing the deportation of Kippenheim Jews. When the photographs were published in the press, other villagers came forward to identify the victims and some of the onlookers. One of the photographs (reproduced on page 152) showed Kurt and his family being loaded aboard a police truck on the morning of October 22, 1940.

Inspired by the stories of the survivors, local historians began to meticulously document the almost three-century-long Jewish presence in Kippenheim and neighboring villages on the edge of the Black Forest. Mayor Mathis commissioned a beautifully produced two-volume memorial book listing the names of every person buried in the Schmieheim cemetery. Other publications included a book about the synagogue and a collection of essays on local Jewish history.[45] A guidebook to "Jewish Kippenheim" was published, identifying former Jewish homes and businesses. The homes of many of the murdered and deported Jews were commemorated with cobblestone-size tablets known as *Stolpersteine,* or "stumbling stones," embedded in the pavement outside. By 2019, some 70,000 *Stolpersteine* had been installed across more than twenty European countries, transforming what began as the private initiative of a German artist into the world's largest decentralized memorial project.

Kurt invited the author of this book to accompany him on one of his return visits to Kippenheim in October 2016, on the anniversary of the Gurs deportation. As usual, his hosts had arranged a packed itinerary that included talks in schools and churches, interviews with local historians and journalists, and ceremonies to commemorate the deportation. At each stop, Kurt summoned up memories of Kippenheim characters like the itinerant peddler, Ragman Jakob, who walked from village to village in a cloud of pipe smoke, with a bag of animal pelts and cast-off clothes on his back. The farmers' wives, all Christians, liked Jakob because he always knew the latest gossip: they would serve him a glass of wine as they listened to his stories. Since Kurt did not know Jakob's family name, he was unable to establish exactly what happened to him. All he knew was that the old peddler was "sent to the East," along with so many others.[46]

At the Anne Frank High School near the Rhine border with France, Kurt encouraged the students to reflect on the madness that seized Germans during the Nazi period. "How many Jews do you think there were in Germany when Hitler came to power?" he asked a group of students at the school. Hands shot up around the classroom.

"Six million?" guessed a sixteen-year-old girl. Several other students made other estimates, ranging upward from two million.

Kurt revealed the correct answer. "There were just over half a million German Jews in 1933. That was significantly less than one percent of the total population." A gasp could be heard around the room. To think that a tiny minority could become the object of so much hatred amazed the young Germans.[47]

Later, I joined Kurt for a walking tour of Kippenheim. It was a cold overcast morning, much like the day, three quarters of a century earlier, when his family was thrown out of their home. Now eighty-seven, Kurt was recognizably the same person captured in the grainy black-and-white image that recorded the deportation of the Maier family from Kippenheim. He clutched a briefcase in his left hand, just as he had done when he followed his grandfather Hermann out of the front gate and onto the police truck. He wore a gray workman's cap on his head, similar to the one in the photograph. The village too was little changed, at least in outward appearance.

As we walked around Kippenheim, Kurt reminisced about places associated with his childhood, including the Jewish bakery and butcher shop, "my favorite place because that was where we got sausages." He showed me the spot where he caught a glimpse of Hitler speeding through Kippenheim in his motorcade a few months before Kristallnacht. He recalled the cries of his aunt after she discovered the body of a Jewish neighbor who stabbed herself in the throat rather than suffer continued torments at the hands of her Nazi tormenters.

It was still painful for Kurt to walk past his boyhood home on Querstrasse. He did not want to talk to the present owners or have his photograph taken in the street where he had played hopscotch with Christian neighbors. He explained that he chose not to have a *Stolperstein* installed outside his former house for fear of rekindling bitter memories. Nevertheless, he pointed out the memorial tablets to other Kippenheim Jews, including those for Max and Fanny Valfer. The Valfer house, across the street from the renovated synagogue on Poststrasse, was now inhabited by a family of Kurdish refugees from Syria who had fled their homeland because of the brutal civil war. The front room, where Max ran his wholesale tobacco business, had been transformed into a take-away kebab shop. Apart from Kurt and me, no one paid attention to the two matching metal tablets discreetly cemented into the adjacent sidewalk. The *Stolperstein* for Fanny read simply:

Here Lived
FANNY VALFER
Née Wertheimer
Born 1886
Deported 1940
Gurs
Murdered 1942
Auschwitz

The memorials to Max and Fanny Valfer prompted Kurt to reflect on his family's good fortune in obtaining the "piece of paper with a stamp" that was "the difference between life and death," in Dorothy Thompson's phrase. In the case of the Maier family, there was more than just one stamp on the all-important piece of paper. The reverse side of their American visa was adorned with a multitude of stamps and signatures reflecting the family's roundabout odyssey from Kippenheim to Gurs to Marseille to Casablanca and finally, in August 1941, to New York. The absence of a single stamp condemned the refugees to endless bureaucratic purgatory, and often to death.

"This was the most precious document I ever possessed," said Kurt. "Those stamps saved our lives."[48]

Maier Family Visa

In Memoriam

(Victims of the Holocaust referenced in this book)

	Place of Death	Date of Death*
Siegfried Wertheimer	Germany	08.21.1939
Hermann Auerbacher	France	11.29.1940
Mathilde Auerbacher	France	12.06.1940
Joseph Auerbacher	France	12.27.1940
Heinrich Eichel	France	12.27.1940
Julius Wachenheimer	France	01.24.1942
Marx Auerbacher	France	01.29.1942
Theodor Köhler	Auschwitz	08.12.1942
Oskar Wachenheimer	Auschwitz	08.12.1942
Käthe Wachenheimer	Auschwitz	08.12.1942
Helene Weil	Auschwitz	08.12.1942
Gerda Weil	Auschwitz	08.12.1942
Berta Weil	Auschwitz	08.12.1942
Salomon ("Momo") Auerbacher	Auschwitz	08.17.1942
Gerda Auerbacher	Auschwitz	08.17.1942
Auguste Köhler	Auschwitz	08.17.1942
Max Strauss	Auschwitz	08.19.1942
Max Valfer	Auschwitz	08.19.1942
Fanny Valfer	Auschwitz	08.19.1942
Hugo Wachenheimer	Auschwitz	08.19.1942
Julius Weil	Auschwitz	08.19.1942
Gretel Durlacher	Auschwitz	08.26.1942
Meta Strauss	Auschwitz	08.28.1942
Bella Wachenheimer	Auschwitz	09.11.1942
Isidor Löb	Auschwitz	09.26.1942
Karolina Löb	Auschwitz	09.26.1942
Hans Durlacher	Auschwitz	10.31.1942

* Or date of deportation to Auschwitz. Date of death was usually two days later, on arrival.

Family Trees

Max Valfer
1880–1942
and
Fanny Wertheimer
1886–1942

Max and Fanny were
deported together

➔ *Gurs 1940*
➔ *Auschwitz 1942*

Karl	**Hugo**	**Freya** [Maier]	**Else** [Wertheimer]	**Ruth** [Bergman]	**Erich**
1907–1973	1909–1948	1910–2003	1913–1985	1915–2003	1919–2006
➔ *UK 1939* ➔ *US 1940*	➔ *US 1938*	➔ *UK 1939* ➔ *US 1940*	➔ *UK 1939*	➔ *US 1937*	➔ *Palestine* *1939*

Erich   Karl   Fanny   Freya   Hugo

Else   Max   Ruth

Heinrich ("Hershele") Wertheimer
Kippenheim Butcher
1850–1925

Fanny 1886–1942 ➲ Gurs 1940 ➲ Auschwitz 1942	**Therese** 1890–1969 ➲ Theresienstadt 1942 ➲ Australia 1952	**Richard** 1893–1958 ➲ US 1937 Daughter: Pia Gilbert	**Jeanette** 1897–1979 ➲ US 1938

Hermann 1888–1973 Butcher ➲ US 1938	**Leopold** 1891–1953 ➲ US 1936	**Siegfried** 1895–1939 Accused of Rassenschande Died in prison	**Karolina** 1899–1964 ➲ Palestine 1937 Son: Stef Wertheimer

Hermann   Richard   Leopold   Siegfried

Karolina   Therese   Hershele   Fanny   Jeanette

Heinrich Wachenheimer
Founded business in Kippenheim
1857

Max ——— **Lina**

Kippenheim
businessman
Died 1925

↪ *Gurs 1940*
↪ *US 1941*

Julius ——— **Emma**

↪ *Gurs 1940*
✡ *Camp Noé*
1942

↪ *Gurs 1940*
↪ *US 1946*

**Hilda &
Theo**

↪ *Gurs 1940*
↪ *US 1941*

**Hugo &
Bella**

↪ *Gurs 1940*
✡ *Auschwitz
1942*

Sophie &
Adolph

↪ *US
1939*

**Oskar &
Käthe**

↪ *Gurs 1940*
✡ *Auschwitz
1942*

Robert &
Ruth

↪ *US
1939*

**Meta &
Max**

↪ *Gurs 1940*
✡ *Auschwitz
1942*

Hedy

↪ *UK 1939*
↪ *US 1948*

Margot

↪ *Gurs 1940*
↪ *US 1946*

Edith

↪ *Gurs 1940*
↪ *US 1946*

Bold Family members deported to Gurs   ✡ Died in Auschwitz or French camps

"Golden Wedding Anniversary" photograph, Gurs, December 1940

Acknowledgments and a Note on Sources

The idea for this book originated with a long-neglected document and a photograph that remained hidden for more than fifty years. Dated December 21, 1940, the document was addressed to President Roosevelt and signed by Under Secretary of State Sumner Welles. It dealt with the expulsion, a few weeks earlier, of thousands of German Jews to unoccupied (Vichy) France. The French were requesting American help in arranging the onward migration of the "Israelites," now housed in a French camp, to the United States and elsewhere in the Americas. Welles advised the president to reject the French démarche, arguing that it would only invite further Nazi "blackmail." FDR scrawled "OK" across the top of the document (which is discussed in greater detail on pages 162–163).

The document, which has attracted little scholarly attention, intrigued me for several reasons. As part of my work for the U.S. Holocaust Memorial Museum, I had been helping out with an exhibition entitled "Americans and the Holocaust," researching the topic of American immigration policies during the Nazi period. It turned out that many of the people expelled from the Baden region of southwest Germany were on the waiting list for U.S. immigration visas. Here was a German story that was also an American story. When we talk about Nazi deportations of Jews, we tend to think about the deportations to the death camps "in the East" that began in 1942. This was an example of Jews deported not "to the East," but eighteen months earlier, "to the West." It seemed to me that the story of the Baden deportees could be an interesting case study of U.S. refugee policy during the period leading up to the Holocaust in the face of what we would now call "ethnic cleansing." I wanted to find out what happened to these "unwanted" people, and how their fate was bound up with the heated American debates about immigration that occurred under FDR.

As I researched the story of the 6,500 Baden Jews expelled from their ancestral homes on two hours' notice, I came across images of the actual deportation. There are dozens of photographs of this event, but only a few where it is possible to identify the victims by name. One, in particular, caught my attention. Published on page 152, it shows a family filing out of their home in the village of Kippenheim, prior to being loaded onto a police truck, as neighbors watch impassively. I soon discovered that the boy in the photograph, then aged ten, was named Kurt Maier. He was now aged eighty-six, and still working as a senior cataloguer of German books at the Library of Congress in Washington. I had found one of the principal subjects of my book a five-minute cab ride away, down the National Mall from my Holocaust Museum office.

Pride of place in these acknowledgments must go to Kurt and other former members of the Jewish community of Kippenheim, who spent many hours talking with me about their experiences, and shared precious family documents and photographs. I was fortunate to be able to interview Hedy Wachenheimer Epstein and Hans Wertheimer by phone and meet with Pia Wertheimer Gilbert before they passed away. Other interviewees with personal memories of growing up in Kippenheim included Sonja Maier Geismar, one of the last surviving passengers on the *St. Louis,* the prominent Israeli businessman Stef Wertheimer, and the writer Inge Auerbacher.

Researching a book like this can be compared to assembling a huge, multidimensional jigsaw puzzle, made up of thousands of different components. The jumbled-up jigsaw pieces include faded family photographs, oral histories, memoirs, and a vast array of documentation, from old court cases to immigration files to government records to letters from loved ones preserved in crumpled envelopes or flimsy shoeboxes. At first, it is difficult to connect the various pieces of evidence, but over time a detailed picture begins to emerge. You know you are on the right track when the disparate parts—a visa application, a police file, a diary entry, an old newspaper clipping, a seemingly obscure reference in a hard-to-decipher letter—begin to magically fit together. Dialogue in the book has been drawn from a wide variety of sources, including contemporaneous correspondence, newspaper accounts, official documents, personal memoirs, and interviews. Sources for all quotes are provided in the endnotes.

It would not have been possible to assemble the jigsaw puzzle without help from an extraordinary array of people, including fellow historians, archivists, and surviving eyewitnesses. I want to pay particular tribute to the local German historians who did much of the arduous legwork in rescuing the story of the Jewish communities of south Baden from decades of willful amnesia long before I came up with the idea of this book. I am especially grateful to Robert Krais, of the Deutsch-Israelischer Arbeitskreis, and Jürgen Stude, of the Förderverein Ehemalige Synagoge Kippenheim e.V. Krais is a one-man encyclopedia of Jewish life in Kippenheim. He spent much of the past three decades contacting former Jewish residents, now scattered all over the world, and lobbying for the restoration of the synagogue turned agricultural warehouse. He provided much of the detailed information for the town plan of Kippenheim that appears at the beginning of this book. Stude is the principal author of several well-researched historical studies on Kippenheim cited in the bibliography. He was exceptionally generous in sharing documents and photographs that he discovered during the course of his research.

To capture the experiences of the main characters of this book, I had to walk the streets of Kippenheim, Stuttgart, and Marseille and wander through the remains of former concentration camps like Dachau, Gurs, and the Camp des Milles. I made two visits to Germany and one to France. I incurred debts of gratitude and hospitality wherever I went. Kurt Maier suggested I accompany him on a trip back to Germany in October 2016. Robert Krais took me on walking tours of Kippenheim and the Jewish cemetery of Schmieheim. A retired English teacher, Ulrike Schumacher, introduced me to many people in Kippenheim, including the former mayor, Willi Mathis, who led the way in reconciliation efforts with the deported and their families. A teacher at the Ettenheim Gymnasium, André Gap, showed me the classroom where

Hedy Wachenheimer was ejected by the principal on Kristallnacht as a "dirty Jew." He also made available the school's Nazi-era records. Two linguistics students from the University of Freiburg, Julia Sofie Andreano and Julia Rosenfeld, served as my translator-assistants in Germany and guided me through the archives in Freiburg, Offenburg, and Karlsruhe. I was shown around Dachau by the dedicated volunteer guide Colinne Bartel. In France, I was given a private tour of Camp des Milles by the French historian Robert Mencherini, a leading authority on the Vichy period. Another historian, Sylvie Orsoni, helped me understand the operation of the family emigration centers in Marseille.

The personal impressions that I gathered during the course of my visits to Germany and France were grounded in archival research. This, in turn, would have been impossible without the assistance of numerous archivists and historians, both in the United States and Europe. I would particularly like to thank Ronald Coleman for guiding me to obscure corners of the voluminous collections of the Holocaust Museum in Washington, D.C., and providing valuable suggestions for further research. At the National Archives in College Park, Maryland, David Lambert provided similarly expert assistance to State Department records, indispensable for the understanding of U.S. refugee policy under FDR. State Department historian Melissa Jane Taylor generously shared personnel records of U.S. consuls, including Hugh Fullerton and Hiram Bingham Jr., that she gathered during the course of her own research into the operations of the U.S. consulate in Marseille. Gunnar Berg helped me locate important records at the YIVO Institute for Jewish Research in New York. Like other researchers, I would have been unable to navigate the records of the American Friends Service Committee in Philadelphia without the assistance of Don Davis. In Germany, I would like to acknowledge the assistance of Cornelius Gorka of the Offenburg Kreisarchiv, Walter Keck of the Kippenheim Gemeindearchiv, and the historians Norbert Klein, Uwe Schellinger, Ulrich Baumann, and Robert Neisen. I am also grateful to Amos Reichman for sharing his unpublished master's thesis on the escape of the Schiffrin family from Vichy.

Throughout my research, I kept in close touch with the families of former Kippenheimers. I enjoyed a memorable weekend with more than a hundred members of the far-flung Wertheimer-Valfer clan at a family reunion in the Pocono mountains of Pennsylvania in July 2018. My thanks in particular to Linda Kaplan and Sonja Geismar for inviting me, and Leslie Wertheimer, Fay Wertheimer, Doris Bergman, Michael Valfer, Marion Bloch, and Rachel McCarthy for providing documents, photographs, and other family information. My Wachenheimer family informants included Margot Walton and Edith Strauss, the two little girls from the "Golden Wedding Anniversary" photograph on pages 171 and 282, who subsequently immigrated to the United States, Harry Wachen, and Brenda Mandel. I am most grateful to Dianne Lee for sharing documents and photographs from the archives of her friend Hedy Epstein, after Hedy's death in 2016. Amy Wisnudel shared letters written from Gurs by her great-aunt and great-uncle, Gerda and Momo Auerbacher.

I undertook this book for the U.S. Holocaust Memorial Museum. It would not have been researched, written, or published without the friendship and support of my Holocaust Museum colleagues. It owes its origin to long conversations with Michael Abramowitz, the former director of the William Levine Family Institute for Holocaust Education, who has since moved on to become president of Freedom House. Museum director Sara Bloomfield and deputy director Sarah Ogilvie took a personal interest in the project from the start, and made many helpful suggestions, as did my immediate supervisors, Gretchen Skidmore and Greg Naranjo. I was saved from many egregious errors by a team of expert reviewers that included Richard Breitman, Peter Black, and the indefatigable Becky Erbelding, who provided many important documents. Needless to say, responsibility for any remaining mistakes, either factual or interpretive, rests with me. For translation help with German documents, including making sense of piles of seemingly indecipherable family correspondence, I owe a special *Dankeschön* to Kassandra Laprade Seuthe of the Museum's photo archives.

At Knopf, my publishing home for the last three decades, I want to thank my editor, Andrew Miller, for his encouragement and unerring sense for how to improve a long-form narrative. Andrew's assistant, Zakiya Harris, coordinated the production schedule. Copy editor Fred Chase caught more inconsistencies than I imagined possible. The team of Lisa Montebello, Maria Massey, Maggie Hinders, and Tyler Comrie performed their usual miracles. Cathy Dorsey produced a superb index under a very tight deadline. The lovely maps and graphics are the work of Gene Thorp. As with my previous five books, I am indebted to my agent, Rafe Sagalyn, for shaping and giving life to a half-thought-out idea. And last, but of course not least, I am grateful to my wonderful wife, Lisa, and daughter, Alex, for reading multiple versions of the manuscript, and supporting a frequently distracted author all the way.

Notes

ABBREVIATIONS USED IN NOTES

AFSC	American Friends Service Committee (Quakers)
AFSC-Ph	AFSC archives, Philadelphia
AJDC	American Jewish Joint Distribution Committee
AP	Associated Press
APP	American Presidency Project, University of California, Santa Barbara
CDF	State Department Central Decimal File, Record Group 59, NA-CP
CJH	Center for Jewish History, New York
FDRL	Franklin D. Roosevelt Library, Hyde Park, New York
F-BdR	Archives départementales des Bouches-du-Rhône, France
F-PA	Archives départementales des Pyrénées-Atlantiques, France
FRUS	*Foreign Relations of the United States* series
G-HSAS	Hauptstaatsarchiv Stuttgart, Germany
G-STAF	Staatsarchiv Freiburg, Germany
G-LAK	Landeskirchliches Archiv, Karlsruhe, Germany
IMT	International Military Tribunal (Nuremberg, Germany), *The Trial of the Major War Criminals*
IWM	Imperial War Museum, London
JTA	Jewish Telegraph Agency
LAT	*Los Angeles Times*
LC	Library of Congress, Washington, D.C.
M-UD	George S. Messersmith papers, University of Delaware
NA-CP	National Archives, College Park, Maryland
NA-DC	National Archives, Washington, D.C.
NA-Ph	National Archives, Philadelphia

NA-SL   National Archives, St. Louis
NYHT   *New York Herald Tribune*
NYT   *The New York Times*
OH   Oral History
OPF   Official Personnel Folders, NA-SL
RG   Record Group
SecState   Secretary of State of United States
UGIF   Union générale des israélites de France
UKFO   United Kingdom Foreign Office
UK-NA   United Kingdom National Archives
USC-SF   University of Southern California, Shoah Foundation, Los Angeles
USHMM   United States Holocaust Memorial Museum, Washington, D.C.
WP   *The Washington Post*
YIVO   YIVO Institute for Jewish Research, New York

All interviews are with author, unless otherwise stated.

CHAPTER ONE: NOVEMBER 1938

1. Hedy (Wachenheimer) Epstein interviews with the Shoah Foundation of the University of Southern California California on December 7, 1995, and the Imperial War Museum on December 12, 1991, and December 4, 1997. I have drawn extensively from Hedy's German-language memoir, Hedy Epstein, *Erinnern ist nicht genug* ("To Remember Is Not Enough"), referenced henceforth as Epstein, *Erinnern*. I also spoke with Hedy several times by phone in 2015, prior to her death in May 2016. These interviews are referenced as Epstein Dobbs 2015.
2. Selma Stern, *The Court Jew*, pp. 23–25.
3. Epstein USC-SF; Epstein Dobbs 2015.
4. Author visit to Ettenheim Gymnasium, October 2016. The school records include report cards on Hedy Wachenheimer and other Jewish students, as well as biographical and Nazi Party records for Walter Klein, Hermann Herbstreith, and other teachers. They show that Herbstreith joined the Nazi Party in July 1931, and had been an SS member since 1932.
5. Epstein, *Erinnern*, p. 40. Klein joined the Nazi Party in January 1932, and served as a regional propaganda leader.
6. Letter from Klein to Hugo and Bella Wachenheimer, April 14, 1937, Hedy Epstein papers, 1994.A.0117, USHMM.
7. Walter Klein and Edwin Fischerkeller testimonies, Ettenheim Kristallnacht case, "I.Str.S. gegen Seitz u.A.," May 1947, F179/1, G-STAF.
8. Jakob Reinbold testimony, Ettenheim Kristallnacht case, May 1947, F179/1, G-STAF; Epstein, *Erinnern*, p. 41.
9. Epstein, *Erinnern*, p. 41.
10. Epstein USC-SF.
11. *Hitler, Das Itinerar*, Vol. 3, entry for August 29, 1938, p. 1583; Kurt Maier interview and visit to Kippenheim with author, October 25, 2016 (henceforth Maier Dobbs 2016); "Hitler Sees Forts at Swiss Frontier," *NYT*, August 30, 1938, p. 6.

12. Adolf Hitler, *Mein Kampf,* Vol. 2, Chap. 14, "Germany's Policy in Eastern Europe."
13. "Hitler Inspects Nazi Forts," *WP,* August 30, 1938, p. 1; "German Army Massed at French Border," *LAT,* September 4, 1938, p. 1; "War or Peace?," *NYT,* September 4, 1938, p. 37.
14. Martin Gilbert, *Kristallnacht: Prelude to Destruction,* p. 23; personal letter from Raymond Geist to George Messersmith, November 7, 1938, M-UD.
15. Gilbert, *Kristallnacht,* p. 24.
16. "Tagebucheintrag vom 10. November 1938," Diaries of Joseph Goebbels Online, Institute of Contemporary History, Munich-Berlin.
17. "Estimate of Jewish population in Alte Reich," December 1938, Germany–Delegation to Germany file, November 1938, AFSC-Ph.
18. Heydrich to Gestapo, Criminal Police and SD offices, November 10, 1938, Nuremberg Document No. 3051-PS, IMT, Vol. 31, pp. 515–18.
19. Johannes Tuchel, *Konzentrationslager,* p. 171. See also Uwe Schellinger, ed., *Gedächtnis aus Stein,* p. 89.
20. Inge Auerbacher interview, July 2016; Maier Dobbs 2016.
21. Max Valfer to Ruth Valfer and Rudolf Bergman, undated letter but probably written in August 1939, Doris Bergman private collection.
22. Schellinger, ed., *Gedächtnis aus Stein,* pp. 79–80; Jürgen Stude et al., *Schicksal und Geschichte der jüdischen Gemeinden,* pp. 352–54.
23. Essay written by Ilse Wertheimer Gutmann for Rachel McCarthy, ed., *Wertheimer-Valfer Family Reunion August 2005,* a privately published family memoir. See also testimony of Kippenheim town clerk Otto Buggle, October 27, 1947, Lahrer Synagogenprozess, F179/1, Nr. 299, pp. 117–20, G-STAF.
24. Maier Dobbs 2016.
25. Robert Krais interview, October 2016. The photograph of the destroyed synagogue was donated to Hedy Epstein in 1999. Local historians have identified the SS officer in the photograph as Obersturmführer (First Lieutenant) Karl Rieflin, a subordinate of Heinrich Remmert. See Schellinger, ed., *Gedächtnis aus Stein,* pp. 84–86.
26. Otto Buggle testimony, October 27, 1947. See also Jürgen Stude, "Der Novemberpogrom in Kippenheim," in Stude et al., *Schicksal und Geschichte,* pp. 45–47.
27. Kurt Salomon Maier, *Unerwünscht,* p. 70.
28. Siegbert Bloch OH, August 20, 1996, USC-SF.
29. Siegbert Bloch later identified his tormentor as SA member Otto Lerch. See Schellinger, ed., *Gedächtnis aus Stein,* p. 91.
30. Ilse Gutmann essay.
31. Epstein USC-SF; Epstein Dobbs 2015.
32. Epstein, *Erinnern,* p. 43.
33. Epstein, *Erinnern,* p. 43; Epstein Dobbs 2015.

CHAPTER TWO: VISA LINES

1. Erna Albersheim letter to Assistant Secretary of State George Messersmith, March 9, 1939, CDF 125.8856/120.
2. Report of John. G. Erhardt, Foreign Service Inspector, March 27, 1939, Reports of Foreign Service Inspectors, 1927–1939, Entry 418, Box 2, RG 59, NA-CP.

3. Sections 9–12, 1917 Immigration Act.

4. Erhardt report, March 27, 1939.

5. Erich Sonnemann OH, 2014.34.1, USHMM. See also Toby Sonneman, "Why St. Patrick's Day Is My Jewish Family's Favorite Holiday," *Tablet,* March 14, 2014.

6. Honaker/Stuttgart to Wilson/Berlin, "Anti-Semitic Persecution in the Stuttgart Consular District," November 12, 1938, CDF 862.4016/2002.

7. Honaker/Stuttgart to Wilson/Berlin, November 12, 1938.

8. Honaker/Stuttgart to Messersmith, November 15, 1938, CDF 862.4016/2002.

9. Memorandum on "Percentage of Jewish visa applicants at the Stuttgart consulate," September 17, 1936, Stuttgart (1930s) I, Reports of Foreign Service Inspectors, 1937–1939, Entry 418, RG 59, NA-CP.

10. Honaker/Stuttgart to State Department, July 12, 1938, CDF 811.111 Quota 62/587.

11. Honaker/Stuttgart to State Department, July 12, 1938.

12. Rating Sheet, January 1, 1943, Samuel Honaker OPF, NA-SL.

13. Report by Inspector J. Klahr Huddle, February 18, 1937, Stuttgart (1930s) I, Reports of Foreign Service Inspectors, 1937–1939, Entry 418, RG 59, NA-CP. See also Herbert Lehman to FDR, June 15, 1936, OF 133, FDRL.

14. Correspondence of Maximilian Neubauer, 1938–1945, Otto Neubauer collection, CJH.

15. Roger Daniels, *Guarding the Golden Door,* p. 57.

16. President Herbert Hoover, Proclamation 1872, March 22, 1929, APP.

17. Mae M. Ngai, "The Architecture of Race in American Immigration Law," *The Journal of American History* 86, no. 1 (June 1999): 75.

18. Memoranda for SecState, March 14 and April 22, 1929, Box 145, CDF 811.111 Quota-National Origins/27.

19. Daniels, *Guarding the Golden Door,* pp. 47–48, 55.

20. According to data collected by the U.S. Census Bureau, the foreign-born share of the total U.S. population reached a peak of 14.8 percent in 1890. The Pew Research Center estimated the foreign-born share of the U.S. population in 2015 as 13.9 percent, projected to rise to 17.7 percent by 2065. This compared to a low point of 4.7 percent in 1970, according to Census Bureau data. Figures in chart on the next page reflect Census Bureau data and Pew Research Center projections.

21. Daniels, *Guarding the Golden Door,* p. 55.

22. The State Department reported "relatively little delay" in the processing of immigrant cases up until 1938. See letter from Warren/Visa Division to Malcolm Bryan, January 23, 1940, CDF 811.111 Quota 62/769. See also David S. Wyman, *Paper Walls,* p. 34, which states that the "refugee situation had been relatively stabilized" by the end of 1937. Wyman adds that, prior to the crises of 1938, "the problem of finding places for people who had the means and the desire to emigrate was met rather effectively."

23. "Freak letters" collection, October 20, 1938, CDF 811.111 Quota 62/619.

24. Honaker dispatch 1340, "Dismissal of Six German Clerks," January 17, 1939, CDF 125.8853/503. See also CDF 125.8853/497.

25. Honaker dispatch 1344, "Payment of Money to Germans Formerly Employed at the Stuttgart Consulate," January 24, 1939, CDF 125.8853/507.

26. "Preliminary Examination" form, cited in Honaker dispatch 1340, January 17, 1939.

27. Honaker dispatches 1340 and 1344, January 1939.

28. See, for example, profile of Geist, "Trouble-shooter in Berlin," *NYT,* July 23, 1939.

Foreign-born share of U.S. population

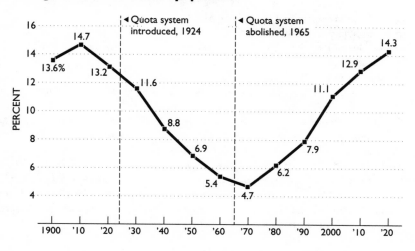

29. Geist to Assistant Secretary of State Messersmith, May 16, 1938, Messersmith collection, M-UD.
30. "Application for Appointment," Geist OPF, NA-SL.
31. Geist to Messersmith, October 21, 1938, M-UD.
32. Geist deposition, August 28, 1945, Nuremberg Document 1759-PS, IMT, Vol. 28, pp. 234–54.
33. David Glick, "Some Were Rescued," 1960 *Harvard Law Bulletin,* Glick collection AR 1239, CJH.
34. Geist to Messersmith, October 21, 1938, M-UD.
35. Geist deposition, August 28, 1945.
36. Geist to Messersmith, October 21, 1938.
37. "U.S. Asked to Bar Einstein as Radical," *WP,* November 30, 1932.
38. Messersmith to Oswald Villard, December 15, 1932, M-UD.
39. "Einstein's Ultimatum Brings a Quick Visa," *NYT,* December 6, 1932.
40. Messersmith to Oswald Villard, December 15, 1932, M-UD.
41. "Einstein Ridicules Women's Fight on Him," *NYT,* December 4, 1932.
42. Geist to Messersmith, December 12, 1938, M-UD.
43. Geist/Berlin to SecState, November 14, 1938, CDF 811.111 Quota 62/635.
44. "160,000 Germans Seeking Visas to Enter U.S.," *NYHT,* November 29, 1938.
45. Charles W. Thayer, *The Unquiet Germans,* pp. 162–63.
46. Geist to Messersmith, February 15, 1938, M-UD.
47. Geist to Messersmith, December 12, 1938, M-UD.
48. Geist to Messersmith, December 12, 1938, M-UD.
49. Geist to Messersmith, December 5, 1938, M-UD.
50. Geist to Messersmith, December 5, 1938. For Geist-Foley agreement, see British Home Office memo HO 213/100, UK-NA. See also Geist/Berlin to SecState, December 12, 1938, CDF 840.48 Refugees/1187.
51. Messersmith to Avra Warren, December 9, 1938, CDF, 811.111 Quota 62/662B.

52. Foley to British Home Office, January 17, 1939, HO 213/115, UKNA.

53. Geist to Messersmith, January 22, 1939, M-UD.

54. Geist to Messersmith, June 14, 1934, M-UD.

55. Messersmith to Geist, April 5, 1938, M-UD.

56. Messersmith to Geist, December 5, 1938, M-UD.

57. Messersmith to Geist, December 20, 1938, M-UD.

58. Messersmith to Geist, December 20, 1938.

59. Messersmith to Geist, November 30, 1938; Geist to Messersmith, January 4, 1939, M-UD.

60. Geist to Messersmith, October 21, 1938, M-UD.

61. Gilbert/Berlin to SecState, November 30, 1938, CDF 862.4016/1939.

62. Geist to Messersmith, January 4, 1939, M-UD.

63. Elizabeth Gray Vining, *Friend of Life,* p. 286.

64. Rufus M. Jones, "Our Day in the German Gestapo," *The American Friend,* July 10, 1947.

65. Vining, *Friend of Life,* p. 292. Schacht was dismissed from his position as president of the Reichsbank on January 20, 1939, just weeks after his meeting with the Quakers.

66. Elkinton to Pickett, November 24, 1938, Correspondence, Letters from Berlin, AFSC-Ph.

67. Honaker dispatch 1340, January 17, 1939.

68. "Report of Investigation of Alleged Visa Irregularities at Stuttgart Consulate," August 27, 1939, CDF 125.8856/125.

69. Honaker dispatch 1340, January 17, 1939.

70. Honaker dispatch 1340, January 17, 1939.

CHAPTER THREE: FDR

1. See, for example, editorial in *Washington Evening Star,* "America Protests," November 15, 1938, and front-page coverage in *NYT,* November 16, 1938.

2. "Roosevelt Coldly Serious as He Attacks German Persecutions," *WP,* November 16, 1938, p. 1.

3. William E. Leuchtenburg, *The FDR Years,* p. 13.

4. AP White House reporter Jack Bell, cited in Leuchtenburg, *The FDR Years,* p. 13.

5. John Gunther, *Roosevelt in Retrospect,* p. 135.

6. JoAnn Garcia, "Cherry Tree Rebellion," NPS.gov, March 15, 2012.

7. *WP,* November 16, 1938, p. 1; FDR press conference #500, November 15, 1938, FDRL.

8. PSF Diplomatic Correspondence, Germany 1933–1938, FDRL.

9. See, for example, Geist/Berlin to SecState, July 23, 1936, State Department CDF 811.111 Quota 62/505. Geist reported that 6,978 immigration visas were issued in the quota year ending June 30, 1936, 27 percent of the then German quota of 25,957. The quota was 48 percent filled for the year ending June 1937, and 71 percent filled for the year ending June 1938.

10. Charles Stember et al., *Jews in the Mind of America,* p. 145. See also "Fortune's Survey on How Americans Viewed Jewish Refugees in 1938," Fortune.com, November 18, 2015.

11. Hitler speech, Sportspalast, Berlin, September 26, 1938, BBC Monitoring Service.

12. Joseph Alsop and Robert Kintner, *American White Paper,* p. 15ff.

13. Samuel I. Rosenman, *Working with Roosevelt*, p. 167.
14. FDR letter to Emil Ludwig, November 15, 1938, PPF 3884, FDRL, cited in James MacGregor Burns, *Roosevelt: The Lion and the Fox*, p. 388.
15. Letter from Sara Roosevelt to Dora Roosevelt, cited in Jean Edward Smith, *FDR*, p. 25.
16. Inscription in FDR's copy of *Mein Kampf*, FDR book collection, FDRL.
17. FDR to Margaret Suckley, September 26, 1938, in Geoffrey Ward ed., *Closest Companion*, p. 125.
18. Ickes diary, November 15, 1938, LC, transcribed in Harold L. Ickes, *The Secret Diary of Harold L. Ickes*, Vol. 2, *The Inside Struggle*, p. 504.
19. Rosenman, *Working with Roosevelt*, p. 172.
20. Henry Morgenthau Jr. diary, November 16, 1938, FDRL.
21. Burns, *Roosevelt*, p. 320.
22. FDR message to Myron Taylor, January 14, 1939, contained in State Department telegram to U.S. embassy, London, 840.48 Refugees/1290B, reprinted in *FRUS*, 1939, Vol. 2, p. 66.
23. Morgenthau diary, November 16, 1938.
24. For maps of Jewish settlement possibilities prepared by the geographer Isaiah Bowman, see OS-053 PSF Maps, FDRL.
25. FDR to Taylor, January 14, 1939.
26. Morgenthau diary, November 16, 1938.
27. Morgenthau diary, December 6, 1938, FDRL.
28. Messersmith memorandum, October 25, 1938, CDF 811.111 Regulations/2175.
29. FDR press conference #501, November 18, 1938. See also Richard Breitman and Allan J. Lichtman, *FDR and the Jews*, p. 115.
30. Telegram to FDR, November 17, 1938, OF 76c, Church Matters Jewish, 1938, FDRL.
31. Correspondence regarding immigration, November 1938, CDF 150.626J.
32. Minutes of December 18–19, 1938, meeting, Non-Sectarian Committee for German Refugee Children, Marion Kenworthy papers, CJH.
33. Mark Jonathan Harris and Deborah Oppenheimer., *Into the Arms of Strangers*, p. 10.
34. Hoover news conference, White House, September 9, 1930, APP.
35. *Statistical Abstract of the United States 1933*, U.S. Census Bureau, Tables 87 and 96. The annual quota for Germany was reduced from 51,227 to 25,957 in 1929. Some immigrants admitted in 1930 received their visas under the previous quota.
36. Visa instruction to U.S. consuls, January 5, 1937, CDF 150.626 J/242.
37. "Quota years" ran from July to June. For annual summaries of German quota visas for the quota years 1932–1933 to 1936–1937, see General Visa Correspondence, 1914–1940, CDF 811.111 Quota, Box 165. For subsequent quota years, see tables contained in letter from Visa Division to Samuel Goldstein, April 15, 1943, CDF 150.001/4-1443. For overall German quota usage statistics see chart on page 296.
38. ER, "My Day," May 29, 1937.
39. ER letter to Justine Wise Polier, January 4, 1939, ER 100, 1939, Box 698, FDRL. Polier was the daughter of the American Jewish leader Rabbi Stephen Wise, a prominent family court judge, and the friend of both Eleanor Roosevelt and Marion Kenworthy. See also Polier OH, September 14, 1977, FDRL.
40. November 20, 1938, Coughlin broadcast, Holocaust Encyclopedia, USHMM.
41. Polier OH, FDRL.

German quota visas

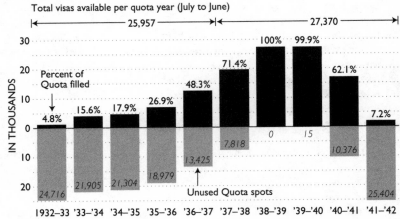

42. "Hoover Backs Sanctuary for Child Refugees," *WP*, January 16, 1939, p. 1.
43. "Children in the Dark," *NYT*, February 18, 1939, p. 7.
44. Julian Pleasants, *Buncombe Bob*, pp. 158–59.
45. Messersmith memorandum, January 23, 1939, CDF 150.01 Bills/99.
46. Stember et al., *Jews in the Mind of America*, 149; Frank Newport, "Historical Review: Americans' Views on Refugees Coming to U.S.," Gallup.com/opinion, November 19, 2015.
47. Mackenzie King diary, November 17, 1938, MG26-J13, Archives Canada.
48. Ickes diary, March 12, 1939, LC; Ickes, *The Inside Struggle*, p. 590.
49. Ickes diary, March 12, 1939.
50. "Roosevelt's Life Aboard Ship," *NYT*, February 19, 1939, p. 135.
51. "First Lady Backs Move to Open U.S. to 20,000 Exiles," *WP*, February 14, 1939, p. 1. See also Blanche Wiesen Cook, *Eleanor Roosevelt*, p. 26.
52. ER to Polier, February 28, 1939, cited in Joseph P. Lash, *Eleanor and Franklin*, pp. 576–77.
53. Exchange of telegrams between FDR and ER, February 22, 1939, Presidential Trip File, FDRL.

CHAPTER FOUR: KIPPENHEIM

1. Epstein, *Erinnern*, 44; Epstein Dobbs 2015.
2. Ilse Gutmann essay.
3. See, for example, postcard from Abraham Auerbacher in Dachau to his wife in Kippenheim, November 22, 1938, private collection.
4. Hugo to Hedy Wachenheimer, February 6, 1940, Hedy Epstein private collection, translated by Hedy Epstein. Hedy donated copies of the predominantly German-language correspondence to USHMM in 1994. See Epstein papers, 1994.A.0017, USHMM.

5. Author visit to Dachau concentration camp, November 2016.

6. Sigrid Schultz, "Berlin's Jews Seek Flight," November 15, 1938, *Chicago Tribune*, p. 1; Associated Press, "Berlin Preparing More Degrees of Ostracism," *NYHT*, November 15, 1938, p. 1.

7. Notes from meeting at Air Ministry, November 12, 1938, Nuremberg Document 1816-PS, IMT, Vol. 28, pp. 499–540.

8. See, for example, Ralph W. Barnes, "160,000 Germans Seeking Visas to Enter U.S." *NYHT*, November 29, 1938, p. 1; Louis Lochner, "Reich Papers Angrily Reply to Roosevelt," *Baltimore Sun*, November 17, 1938, p. 1.

9. Schellinger ed., *Gedächtnis aus Stein*, p. 81; Stude et al., *Schicksal und Geschichte*, pp. 352–54.

10. "Reich, Angered by Roosevelt, Waits for U.S. Reaction," *NYT*, November 17, 1938, p. 1.

11. "Nazi Restrictions, Special Taxes Strip Jews of Wealth," JTA, December 25, 1938.

12. OH interview with Pia Gilbert, 1988, Center for Oral History Research, University of California, Los Angeles.

13. Quoted by Amos Elon, *The Pity of It All*, p. 166.

14. Karl Kopp, *Das Kippenheimer Lied*, 57.

15. Naftali Bar-Giora Bamberger, *Der jüdische Friedhof in Schmieheim, Memor-Buch*, p. 936.

16. Schellinger, ed., *Gedächtnis aus Stein*, p. 68.

17. Jürgen W. Falter et al., *Wählerbewegungen zum Nationalsozialismus: Wahl- und Sozialdaten der Gemeinden Badens in der zweiten Hälfte der Weimarer Republik.* Statistical data collection provided by GESIS Institute, Cologne. Some of the electoral data is also cited in Schellinger, ed., *Gedächtnis aus Stein*, p. 75.

18. Kopp, *Das Kippenheimer Lied*, 64.

19. Epstein IWM 1991; Epstein, *Erinnern*, p. 25.

20. Stude et al., *Schicksal und Geschichte*, p. 347; Kopp, *Das Kippenheimer Lied*, 66.

21. Stude et al., *Schicksal und Geschichte*, p. 347.

22. Stude et al., *Schicksal und Geschichte*, p. 354.

23. Pia Gilbert OH 1988.

24. Pia Gilbert interview, January 17, 2017. See also Pia Gilbert OH 1988.

25. "Bericht über eine Predigt von Pfr. Kaiser," October 31, 1934, Adam Kaiser personal file, G-LAK.

26. Undated letter to regional bishop, Dr. Kühlewein, in Kaiser personal file, G-LAK.

27. Written statement by Pastor Kaiser, September 28, 1941, Kaiser personal file, G-LAK.

28. Ulrich Baumann interview, October 21, 2016. See also Baumann, *Zerstörte Nachbarschaften, Christen und Juden in badischen Landgemeinden, 1862–1940.*

29. Maier Dobbs 2016..

30. Kurt Maier OH, June 24, 1997, USC-SF.

31. Maier, *Unerwünscht*, p. 31.

32. Sandner, *Das Itinerar*, Vol. 3, p. 1692, entry for May 19, 1939.

33. Stef Wertheimer, *The Habit of Labor*, p. 5.

34. Pia Gilbert OH 1988.

35. Pia Gilbert interview, January 17, 2017; Schellinger, ed., *Gedächtnis aus Stein*, p. 80.

36. *Wertheimer/Valfer Family Reunion*, p. 60; Pia Gilbert interview, January 17, 2017.

37. Freya Valfer Maier memoir, *Wertheimer/Valfer Family Reunion*, p. 23.

38. Email from Marion Bloch, granddaughter of Hermann Wertheimer, July 1, 2016.

39. *Wertheimer/Valfer Family Reunion*, p. 25.

40. Sales contract between Hermann Wertheimer and Karl Dorner, November 12, 1937, Marion Bloch private collection.

41. Interview with Gunther Wertheimer, January 21, 2017.

42. See correspondence between Congressman William Whittington (D-Miss.) and State Department, CDF 811.III Valfer Gerhard.

43. *Queen Mary* passenger list, Cherbourg–New York, April 19, 1937, RG 85, NA-DC.

44. Emails from Fay Wertheimer, daughter of Else Valfer and Heinrich Wertheimer, June 15, 2016, and June 25, 2018.

45. Gunther Wertheimer interview, January 21, 2017; Pia Gilbert interview, January 17, 2017.

46. Erich Valfer letter, March 30, 1987, to Institute of Contemporary History, Munich.

47. Freya Valfer Maier OH, January 21, 1997, USC-SF.

48. The registration numbers for Max and Fanny are contained in family correspondence and their HIAS-HICEM case file at YIVO, New York (France III-462, RG 245.5). I have extrapolated the immigration registration dates from the wait numbers, which were issued in chronological order.

49. Report of John G. Erhardt, Foreign Service Inspector, March 27, 1939; Reports of Foreign Service Inspectors, 1927–1939, Entry 418, Box 2, RG 59, NA-CP.

50. Honaker dispatch, February 22, 1939, CDF 125.8853/510.

51. Albersheim to Messersmith, March 9, 1939, CDF 125.8856/120.

52. Erhardt report, March 27, 1939.

53. "Aryans Aid Jews Furtively in Reich," *NYT*, December 26, 1938, p. 9; "Half the Jews in Reich Beg for U.S. Visas," *NYHT*, March 9, 1939, p. 1. The State Department reported 240,748 outstanding requests for U.S. immigration visas under the German quota on January 1, 1939. In theory, this represented a nearly nine-year backlog. (See Avra Warren testimony to Senate subcommittee on immigration, March 23, 1939.) In practice, however, there were two different waiting lists. Visa applicants whose documents were deemed unsatisfactory were placed on an "inactive" waiting list. Qualified applicants were placed on an "active" waiting list. At Stuttgart, a "preliminary examination of documents" weeded out six of every ten would-be immigrants in the 1937–1938 quota year. (See Honaker/Stuttgart to SecState, July 12, 1938, CDF 811.III Quota 62/587.) The initial screening process reduced the wait time for qualified applicants to around three years in early 1939. (See note from Geist/Berlin, January 23, 1939, CDF 811.III Quota 62/670.)

54. AP, "100 Jews Each Day Must Leave Reich," *NYT*, February 26, 1939, p. 1.

55. Report by U.S. Consul General Coert du Bois, "Jewish Refugee Situation in Havana," June 7, 1939, State Department CDF 837.55/39.

CHAPTER FIVE: FLIGHT

1. Karl Valfer to Ruth Valfer and Rudolf Bergman, March 26, 1939, Doris Bergman private collection.

2. "Margaret Bergmann Lambert, Jewish Athlete Excluded from Berlin Olympics, Dies at 103," *NYT*, July 25, 2017. After vowing never to go back to Germany, Gretel (known by her married name, Margaret Lambert) accepted an invitation to visit her

hometown of Laupheim in 1999 after the sports stadium was renamed to honor her. She had been barred from competing in the stadium during the Nazi period.

3. Memoir of *Katina* passenger Michael Engel, in the form of a 1970 letter to Dr. Zelig Paul, the Betar commander. The Engel letter was supplied to the author by his daughter, Claudia Stevens. The details broadly coincide with those provided by Erich Valfer in his March 30, 1987, letter to the Institute of Contemporary History, Munich.

4. Engel letter.

5. For the British interception of the smaller vessel, the *Artemisia*, see February 16, 1939, report of the Chief Secretary of the Government of Palestine, FO 371/24088, UK-NA. The report states that the *Artemisia* was seized on February 6 "after she had successfully landed some 160 Jews illegally." The report was supplied to the author by Paul Silverstone.

6. Letter from *Katina* passenger Kalman Yardeni, August 17, 1999, Claudia Stevens private collection.

7. Yardeni letter.

8. Engel letter.

9. Erich Valfer letter, March 30, 1987; Claudia Stevens's conversations with her father. Stevens re-created the *Katina* voyage in a one-woman marionette performance, "In the Puppeteer's Wake."

10. Pell/London to SecState, May 18, 1939, CDF 840.48 Refugees/1617, reprinted in *FRUS*, 1939, Vol. 2, pp. 110–12. See also Henry L. Feingold, *The Politics of Rescue*, p. 65.

11. Ludwig Maier letter to Ruth Valfer Bergman, March 30, 1939, Doris Bergman private collection.

12. Maier family papers, 2004.515.1, USHMM.

13. Gilbert interview, January 17, 2017; Ludwig Maier letter to Ruth Valfer Bergman, March 30, 1939, Doris Bergman private collection.

14. Freya Valfer Maier OH, USC-SF.

15. Report by U.S. Consul Harold S. Tewell, "European Refugees in Cuba," June 8, 1939, CDF 837.55J/51. See also report dictated by Cecilia Razovsky, June 11, 1939, SS *St. Louis* folder, AJDC, reprinted in Henry Friedlander and Sybil Milton, eds. *Archives of the Holocaust: An International Collection of Selected Documents*, Vol. 10, part 1, pp. 264–74.

16. Fritz Buff diary, Fritz Buff papers, 2007.121, USHMM. An English translation has been published as Fred Buff, edited by Maryann McLoughlin, *Riding the Storm Waves*. See Buff, pp. 38, 44.

17. Sonja Geismar talk to B'nai Jeshurun, Yom Kippur, 2015.

18. Freya Valfer Maier to Valfer family, June 10, 1939, Maier family papers, 2004.515.1, USHMM.

19. Buff, *Riding the Storm Waves*, p. 52.

20. "Haven for Exiles in Cuba Planned," *NYT*, November 19, 1938, p. 3.

21. Du Bois report, June 7, 1939.

22. Paul Vincent, "The Voyage of the St. Louis Revisited," *Holocaust and Genocide Studies* 25, no. 2 (Fall 2011): 280, citing message from Laura Margolis, JDC Archives 33/44, file 378—*St. Louis*.

23. Tewell report, June 8, 1939.

24. Tewell report, June 8, 1939.

25. Du Bois report, June 7, 1939.

26. Batista letter to Berenson, December 4, 1967, Mirta Pérez-Benitoa collection, 2004.638, USHMM. Pérez-Benitoa is Batista's granddaughter.

27. Enclosure 4, Du Bois report, June 7, 1939.

28. Razovsky *St. Louis* report, June 11, 1939.

29. Razovsky *St. Louis* report, June 11, 1939.

30. Hart Phillips, "907 Refugees Quit Cuba on Liner," *NYT,* June 3, 1939. See also AP report, "Cuba Orders Refugee Ship to Go Away," reprinted in *NYHT,* June 2, 1939.

31. JDC Executive Committee minutes, June 5, 1939, JDC *St. Louis* file, cited by Vincent, "The Voyage of the St. Louis Revisited," p. 262.

32. Enclosure 13, Du Bois report, June 7, 1939.

33. Freya Valfer Maier letter, June 10, 1939, Maier family papers, 2004.515.1, USHMM.

34. Buff, *Riding the Storm Waves,* p. 62.

35. An AP photo shows the *St. Louis* anchored off Miami Beach on June 4. See, for example, "Home of the Wandering Jews," *Baltimore Sun,* June 5, 1939, p. 7.

36. Buff, *Riding the Storm Waves,* p. 63.

37. Schröder later wrote a letter to Ludwig Maier and other members of the committee, thanking them for their assistance. Sonja Geismar private collection.

38. *St. Louis* passenger bulletin, June 4, 1939, Karmann family papers, 2000.137, USHMM.

39. Buff, *Riding the Storm Waves,* pp. 63–64.

40. Some accounts have given a date of June 7 for the return of the *St. Louis.* However, a June 6 AP report stated that the ship notified Tropical Radio in Miami at 11:40 p.m. on June 6 that "she had set course for Europe." See, for example, "Denied Entry, Refugee Ship Heads Home," *Atlanta Constitution,* June 7, 1939, and "Cuba Recloses Door to Refugees," *NYT,* June 7, 1939.

41. Radiogram to FDR, June 6, 1939, State Department CDF 837.55J, Box 5969, Red Ink Letters folder.

42. Telegram from Ruth Valfer Bergman to Ludwig Maier, June 7, 1939, Maier family papers, 2004.515.1, USHMM; "Cuba Recloses Door to Refugees," *NYT,* June 7, 1939, p. 1.

43. FDR press conferences #550 and #551, May 30 and June 6, 1939, FDRL.

44. Messersmith memo, June 1, 1939, State Department CDF 837.55 J/36; Du Bois report, June 7, 1939.

45. Morgenthau diary, June 5, 1939, FDRL.

46. State Department Memorandum from Ellis Briggs, June 5, 1939, CDF 837/55J/44.

47. Morgenthau diary, June 5, 1939. The transcript shows that Hull explored the Virgin Islands option at the suggestion of the lawyer James Carson, who was looking for a temporary refuge for the Annenberg relatives.

48. AP, "Virgin Islands Willing: Legislative Assembly Would Open Doors to Refugees," *Baltimore Sun,* November 22, 1938, p. 10.

49. Morgenthau diary, June 5, 1939.

50. Morgenthau diary, June 6, 1939.

51. J. Butler Wright/Havana to SecState, June 8, 1939, CDF 837.55 J/43.

52. See, for example, "No Haven for Refugees," *Fortune,* April 1939, p. 102; Stember et al., *Jews in the Mind of America,* p. 121.

53. Annotation on memo to FDR, OF 3186 Political Refugees, FDRL.

54. "Admission of German Refugee Children," Hearings Before House of Representatives Immigration Committee, June 1, 1939.

55. For Jewish admissions to Palestine, see British government data cited in *American*

Jewish Year Book, Vols. 44–46. For U.S. admissions data, see SecState to Tuck/Vichy, October 2, 1942, CDF 851.4016/104.

56. Testimony on H.R. 3029, House Committee on Immigration and Naturalization, June 6, 1939, ProQuest.
57. Appendix to *Congressional Record,* June 7, 1939, pp. 2424–25.
58. "Poage Would Balance Child Exiles, Quota," *WP,* June 1, 1939, p. 2.
59. Cesar Saerchinger broadcast, May 5, 1939, CDF 150.01 Bills/138.
60. William Castle diary, May 26, 1939, cited by Breitman and Lichtman, p. 150.
61. Pierrepont Moffat diary, May 25, 1939, Houghton Library, Harvard University.
62. See, for example, "Hull Injects New Life into Neutrality Fight," *NYT,* June 4, 1939, p. E6.
63. FDR to Myron Taylor, June 8, 1939, OF 3186 Political Refugees, FDRL.
64. Geist to Messersmith, April 4, 1939, M-UD.
65. Geist/Berlin to SecState, May 3, 1939, CDF 840.48 Refugees/1597.
66. Pierrepont Moffat diary, May 4, 1939, Houghton Library, Harvard University.
67. Pell/London to SecState, June 7, 1939, Telegram 788, Myron Taylor papers, FDRL.
68. Kenneth Davis, *FDR,* 746–47.
69. Pell/London to SecState, June 7, 1939, Telegram 791, Myron Taylor papers, FDRL.
70. *St. Louis* passenger bulletin, June 10, 1930, 2000.137, Karmann family papers, USHMM.
71. Freya Valfer Maier letter, June 10, 1939. Although the letter was started on June 10, internal evidence suggests that it took several days to write.
72. Telegram from Kippenheim, June 12, 1939, Maier family papers, 2004.515.1, USHMM.
73. *St. Louis* ship bulletin, June 15, 1939, Karmann family papers, USHMM.
74. Gordon Thomas and Max Morgan Witts, *Voyage of the Damned,* pp. 281–82; Passengers' committee to Troper, June 14, 1939, Troper collection, 2005.27, Folder 4, USHMM.
75. Vincent, "The Voyage of the St. Louis Revisited," p. 272.
76. Buff, *Riding the Storm Waves,* pp. 68–70.
77. "907 Refugees End Voyage in Antwerp," *NYT,* June 18, 1939, p. 1.
78. Quoted by Arthur Morse, "Voyage to Doom," *Look,* November 28, 1967, p. 68.

CHAPTER SIX: "SAVE OUR SOULS"

1. Epstein IWM 1991; Epstein Dobbs 2015.
2. Harris, *Into the Arms of Strangers,* p. 40.
3. Hugo Wachenheimer to Robert Amias, June 4, 1939, Epstein papers, 1994.A.0017, USHMM.
4. Epstein, *Erinnern,* pp. 53–54.
5. Hedy Epstein private collection.
6. Epstein, *Erinnern,* pp. 56–57.
7. Epstein, *Erinnern,* pp. 55–56.
8. Epstein, *Erinnern,* p. 56.
9. Harris, *Into the Arms of Strangers,* p. 133.
10. Hugo Wachenheimer to Hedy Wachenheimer, May 20, 1939, USHMM.
11. Hugo Wachenheimer to Hedy Wachenheimer, July 12, 1939, USHMM.
12. Hugo and Bella Wachenheimer to Hedy Wachenheimer, May 23 and June 1, 1939, USHMM.
13. Harris, *Into the Arms of Strangers,* p. 134.

14. Bella Wachenheimer to Hedy Wachenheimer, July 28, 1939, USHMM.
15. Hugo Wachenheimer to Hedy Wachenheimer, August 9, 1939, USHMM.
16. William L. Shirer, *The Nightmare Years, 1930–1940*, p. 398.
17. Victor Klemperer, *I Will Bear Witness*, p. 304, August 14, 1939, diary entry.
18. Hugo Wachenheimer to Hedy Wachenheimer, August 5, 1939, USHMM.
19. Hugo Wachenheimer to Robert Amias, June 4, 1939, USHMM.
20. German Jewish Aid Committee to Hugo Wachenheimer, August 2, 1939, USHMM.
21. Hugo Wachenheimer to Hedy Wachenheimer, August 9, 1939, USHMM. See also letters of August 2, 4, and 5.
22. Hugo Wachenheimer to Hedy Wachenheimer, August 2, 1939, USHMM.
23. Ludwig Maier to Ruth Valfer Bergman, August 15, 1939, Doris Bergman private collection.
24. Kurt Maier interview, February 27, 2018.
25. "Dokumentationsstelle zur Erforschung der Schicksale der jüdischen Bürger," Kippenheim, EA 99/001 Bü 71, G-HSAS.
26. Wertheimer, *The Habit of Labor*, pp. 20–21.
27. Telephone interview with Lars Kindle, January 12, 2018; telephone interview with Stef Wertheimer, May 6, 2017.
28. Stef Wertheimer interview; email from Anett Daffan, December 13, 2017.
29. Stude et al., *Schicksal und Geschichte*, p. 355.
30. Max Valfer to Ruth Valfer Bergman, undated but evidently written in mid-August 1939, Doris Bergman private collection.
31. Alice Zivi to Siegfried Wertheimer, August 18, 1939, Robert Krais private collection.
32. Hugo Wachenheimer to Hedy Wachenheimer, August 24, 1939, USHMM.
33. Visit to Schmieheim cemetery with Robert Krais, June 30, 2017.
34. Hugo Wachenheimer to Hedy Wachenheimer, August 24, 1939, USHMM.
35. Max Valfer to Ruth Valfer Bergman, August 1939.
36. Kindle interview, January 12, 2018.
37. Ludwig Maier to Ruth Valfer Bergman, August 15, 1939.
38. Else Valfer Wertheimer to Ruth Valfer Bergman, undated but evidently written in August 1939, Doris Bergman private collection.
39. Heinrich Wertheimer to Ruth Valfer Bergman, July 20, 1939, Doris Bergman private collection.
40. Telephone interview with Steven Weil, December 29, 2017.
41. Ludwig Maier to Ruth Valfer Bergman, August 15, 1939, Doris Bergman private collection.
42. Max Valfer to Ruth Valfer Bergman, undated but evidently written in mid-August 1939, Doris Bergman private collection.
43. Alsop and Kintner, *American White Paper*, p. 1.
44. Eleanor Roosevelt, "My Day," September 2, 1939.
45. Notes taken by Acting Navy Secretary Charles Edison, reprinted in *F.D.R., His Personal Letters, 1928–1945*, Vol. 2, pp. 915–17.
46. Ickes diary, September 9, 1939, LC; Ickes, *The Inside Struggle*, pp. 712–13.
47. FDR address to Intergovernmental Committee, October 17, 1939, APP.
48. Breitman, Stewart, and Hochberg, eds., *Refugees and Rescue*, p. 183.
49. "Mrs. Roosevelt Charges Intolerance Drive Against Refugees," *NYT*, November 29, 1939, p. 1.

50. FDR to Lord Tweedsmuir, governor general of Canada, October 5, 1939, *F.D.R., His Personal Letters, 1928–1945,* Vol. 2, p. 934.

51. Front-page coverage of Roosevelt visit to Congress in *NYT,* September 22, 1939.

52. FDR to William Allen White, December 14, 1939, reprinted in *F.D.R., His Personal Letters, 1928–1945,* Vol. 2, pp. 967–68.

53. Ickes diary, September 9, 1939, LC; Ickes, *The Inside Struggle,* p. 720.

54. Ickes diary, September 9, 1939, LC; Ickes, *The Inside Struggle,* p. 721.

55. Morgenthau diary, May 15, 1942, FDRL.

56. Cited by Ted Morgan, *FDR,* p. 520.

57. German quota table for September–December 1939, State Department CDF 811.III Quota 62/860.

58. Sonja Geismar talk to B'nai Jeshurun, 2015.

59. Stude et al., *Schicksal und Geschichte,* pp. 352–53; Schellinger, ed., *Gedächtnis aus Stein,* pp. 81–82.

60. Maier, *Unerwünscht,* p. 75.

61. The Maier family received their U.S. visas, valid for a period of four months, on May 8, 1940. See "Demande de Voyage," November 9, 1940, Siegfried Maier refugee case file, France III-252, RG 245.5, YIVO.

CHAPTER SEVEN: FIFTH COLUMN

1. Betty Houchin Winfield, *FDR and the News Media,* p. 104.

2. FDR radio broadcast, May 26, 1940.

3. Meeting with American Youth Congress, June 5, 1940, Press Conference 649-A, FDRL.

4. "FBI Gets 3,000 Fifth Column Complaints Daily," *WP,* June 12, 1940, p. 3.

5. Dorothy Thompson cable, July 16, 1940, CDF 811.III Refugees/186.

6. "The Superman Creed," *WP,* March 10, 1942, p. 28.

7. William Donovan and Edgar Mowrer, "French Debacle Held Masterpiece of Fifth Column," *NYT,* August 22, 1940, p. 6.

8. William Bullitt, "America Is in Danger," *NYT,* August 19, 1940, p. 4.

9. Messersmith/Havana to SecState, June 21, 1940, State Department CDF 150.626J/798. For original report on refugees celebrating fall of Paris from U.S. naval attaché in Cuba Hayne Boyden, see attachments from Henry Stimson to SecState, December 15, 1942, CDF 811.III W.R. Committees/30.

10. Breckinridge Long diary, June 22, 1940, LC.

11. SecState to U.S. Consuls, June 29, 1940, CDF 811.III W.R. 108a.

12. Long diary, June 29, 1940, LC.

13. According to State Department data, the German quota was 100 percent filled in 1938–1939 and "99.9 percent filled" in 1939–1940. The failure to completely fill the 1939–1940 quota may have been due to an administrative error. The German quota was 62 percent filled in 1940–1941. See chart on p. 296.

14. Public Opinion News Service, August 4, 1940, Pathfinder Poll Data, Emil Hurja papers, FDRL.

15. Lash, *Eleanor and Franklin,* pp. 40, 133.

16. Lash, *Eleanor and Franklin,* pp. 157–58.

17. Doris Kearns Goodwin, *No Ordinary Time,* pp. 84–85, citing Malvina Thompson to Anna Roosevelt, June 17, 1940, Halsted papers, FDRL.

18. Undated September 1942 memo from ER to FDR, ER 102, Refugee Letters; letter from Muriel Martineau to ER, August 18, 1940, ER 100 Martineau, FDRL.

19. Goodwin, *No Ordinary Time,* p. 101, citing Thompson to Anna Roosevelt, July 12, 1940, Halsted papers, FDRL.

20. See *Life,* February 5, 1940, p. 74, for description of the Greenwich Village apartment.

21. Joseph Lash journal entry, June 25, 1940, retyped by his son, Jonathan Lash papers, FDRL.

22. Muriel Gardiner and Joseph Buttinger, *Damit wir nicht vergessen,* pp. 153–54. See also Buttinger report of meeting with ER, Holocaust/refugee collection, FDRL.

23. Lash journal entry, June 25, 1940.

24. ER, "My Day," June 21, 1940.

25. ER, "My Day," June 26, 1940.

26. Long diary, September 18, 1940, LC.

27. *Quanza* passengers' telegram to ER, September 10, 1940, CDF 811.111 Refugees/289.

28. ER telegram to Coulter/Department of State, September 10, 1942, CDF 811.111 Refugees 41/144; Coulter to ER, September 19, 1942, CDF 811.111 Refugees 41/92.

29. Associated Press, "War Refugees, Turned Back, Sob as Ship Coals at Norfolk," *WP,* September 12, 1940, p. 5.

30. Razovsky report on *Quanza,* September 16, 1940, Celia Razovsky papers, P-290, Box 5, CJH.

31. Habeas Corpus cases 6592, 6593, 6595, Records of U.S. District Court, Eastern District of Virginia, Norfolk Division, Admiralty Case files, 1801–1966, NA-Ph.

32. Case No. 6594, Records of U.S. District Court, Eastern District of Virginia, Norfolk Division, Admiralty Case files, 1801–1966, NA-Ph.

33. Case No. 6594; Razovsky *Quanza* report.

34. Marcel Dalio, *Mes années folles,* pp. 151–52.

35. Report by Patrick Malin, November 12, 1941, INS correspondence files, File 56 054/218, Entry 9, RG 85, NA-DC; see also Long diary, September 18, 1940, LC.

36. Long memo on conversation with Malin, September 16, 1940, CDF 811.111 Refugees/416.

37. Long memo on conversation with Malin.

38. Razovsky *Quanza* report.

39. Unsigned telegram to Long from Norfolk, Virginia, September 14, 1940, CDF 811.111 Refugees/414.

40. Long diary, September 18, 1940, LC.

41. Gift from *Quanza* passengers, received September 17, 1940, OF 3186 Political Refugees, FDRL.

42. Long to FDR, June 27, 1933, and September 6, 1935, cited in Fred L. Israel, ed., *The War Diary of Breckinridge Long,* p. xix.

43. Long diary, March 13, 1938, LC.

44. Long diary, June 13, 1940, LC.

45. Long diary, September 2, 1939, and June 28–30, 1940, LC.

46. Long diary, December 29, 1940, LC.

47. Long diary, September 18, 1940, LC.

48. Cole/Algiers to SecState, September 28, 1940, CDF 811.111 Refugees/608.

49. Long diary, September 24 and October 3, 1940, LC.

50. Breitman et al., *Refugees and Rescue,* p. 214.

51. Eleanor to FDR, September 28, 1940, OF 3186 Political Refugees, October–December 1940, FDRL.

52. Polier OH, FDRL.

53. Long diary, October 3, 1940, LC.

54. Steinhardt/Moscow to SecState, October 2, 1940, CDF 811.111 Refugees/397.

55. Long diary, October 10, 1940, LC.

56. Breitman et al., *Refugees and Rescue,* p. 210, citing Wise to Otto Nathan, September 17, 1940.

57. "Roosevelt Looks to 'Difficult Days,'" *NYT,* November 6, 1941, p. 1.

58. Memorandum from Department of State legal advisor, "Proposed proclamation by the governor of the Virgin Islands," December 16, 1940, OF 3186 Political Refugees, FDRL.

59. Long diary, November 13, 1940, LC. See also Ickes diary, November 17, 1940, LC.

60. Ickes diary, December 13, 1940, LC.

61. FDR to Ickes, December 18, 1940, OF 3186 Political Refugees, FDRL.

62. Ickes diary, December 13, 1940, LC.

63. Clippings from *PM,* December 15, 1940, and February 11, 1941, Long papers, LC.

64. Long diary, December 9, 1940, LC.

65. Westbrook Pegler, "Red Refugees May Suit Virgin Islands Official," *Philadelphia Inquirer,* December 20, 1940, Long papers, LC.

66. Ickes diary, November 23, 1940, LC; *The Secret Diary of Harold L. Ickes, 1939–1941,* Vol. 3, *The Lowering Clouds,* p. 375.

67. Ickes diary, December 21, 1940, LC; partially transcribed in *The Lowering Clouds,* p. 396.

CHAPTER EIGHT: GURS

1. Stude et al., *Shicksal und Geschichte,* p. 358; Schellinger, ed., *Gedächtnis aus Stein,* p. 94.

2. Maier, *Unerwünscht,* pp. 82–83.

3. Maier Dobbs 2016. See also Kurt Maier USC-SF.

4. Robert Krais/Deutsch-Israelischer Arbeitskreis photo archive. For a discussion of the photographs, see article by local historian Gerhard Finkbeiner in Stude et al., *Shicksal und Geschichte,* pp. 466–69, and *Unterbelichtete Erinnerung: Fotohistorische Zugänge zur Deportation der badischen Juden am 22.Oktober 1940,* minutes of Landeskunde am Oberrhein historical working group, December 13, 2001. Finkbeiner and Krais received the photographs in 1995 from the estate of the photographer, Wilhelm Fischer, who died in 1981.

5. Stude et al., *Schicksal und Geschichte,* pp. 466–67; Inge Auerbacher interview, July 21, 2016.

6. Document Nr. 437, Paul Sauer, ed., *Dokumente über die Verfolgung der jüdischen Bürger in Baden-Württemberg durch das Nationalsozialistische Regime, 1933–1945,* Vol. 2, pp. 236–37.

7. Undated Max and Fanny Valfer letter to children from Gurs following October 1940 deportation, probably written in November 1940, Doris Bergman and Leslie Wertheimer private collections.

8. Document Nr. 437, Sauer, ed., *Dokumente 2;* see also Stude et al., *Shicksal und Geschichte,* p. 358.

9. Auguste (Rosenfeld) Auerbacher to Poldi Auerbacher, December 27, 1940, Robert Krais private collection.

10. The number of 6,504 deportees comes from Heydrich report to German Foreign Ministry, October, 29, 1940, Document Nr. 440, Sauer, ed., *Dokumente 2*, p. 241.

11. Maier, *Unerwünscht*, p. 83.

12. Laure Wildmann diary, cited in "The Non-Emigration of the Wildmanns," www.wildmannbirnbaum.com.

13. Maier, *Unerwünscht*, p. 83.

14. Hanna Schramm and Barbara Vormeier, *Vivre à Gurs*, p. 80.

15. Trial of Adolf Eichmann, Jerusalem, Session 77, June 22, 1961.

16. Christopher Browning, *The Origins of the Final Solution*, p. 91.

17. Eichmann trial, Session 77.

18. Eichmann trial, Session 77; Browning, *The Origins of the Final Solution*, pp. 90–91.

19. Israeli police interrogation of Eichmann, tape number 4, reprinted in *The Trial of Adolf Eichmann*, Vol. 7, p. 144.

20. Heydrich report, Document Nr. 440, Sauer, ed., *Dokumente 2*.

21. Telegram from German delegation to Armistice Commission, October 28, 1940, Document Nr. 443, Sauer, ed., *Dokumente 2*, p. 244; Browning, *The Origins of the Final Solution*, p. 91.

22. Telegram from German delegation to Armistice Commission, November 19, 1940, Document Nr. 444, Sauer, ed., *Dokumente 2*, pp. 244–45; Browning, *The Origins of the Final Solution*, p. 92.

23. Donald A. Lowrie, *The Hunted Children*, p. 67. See also Donald Lowrie letter to friends, November 14, 1940, reprinted in Friedlander and Milton, eds., *Archives of the Holocaust*, Vol. 2, pp. 74–77.

24. Schramm and Vormeier, *Vivre à Gurs*, pp. 76–78.

25. Lowrie, *The Hunted Children*, pp. 61–62.

26. Max and Fanny Valfer letter to children from Gurs, ca. November 1940, Doris Bergman private collection.

27. Gerda Auerbacher letter to Hugo Auerbacher, November 6–8, 1940, EA 99/001 Bü 200, G-HSAS. Gerda and her brother Hugo were related by birth to Gerda's husband, Momo, and shared a common family name.

28. Morris/Berlin to SecState, October 25, 1940, CDF 862.4016/2173; Matthews/Vichy to SecState, November 3, 1940, CDF 862.4016/2176.

29. ER comment on letter from Joseph Buttinger with accompanying memos, November 15, 1940, OF 3186 Political Refugees, FDRL.

30. "Refugees Write of French Camps," *NYT*, February 23, 1941, p. 13.

31. "Misery and Death in French Camps," *NYT*, January 26, 1941, p. 24.

32. Camp Gurs report, February 1941, Internment Camps folder, AFSC-Ph.

33. Ickes diary, August 3, 1940, LC; Ickes, *The Lowering Clouds*, pp. 277–78; "France Puts Faith in New Envoy Here," *NYT*, August 11, 1940, p. 18.

34. For text of French note, and related correspondence, see CDF 840.48 Refugees/2317, reprinted in *FRUS*, 1940, Vol. 2, pp. 243–49.

35. Memorandum on "German refugees in France" by Robert Pell, November 22, 1940, CDF 840–48 Refugees/2317.

36. Welles to FDR, December 21, 1940, CDF 840.48 Refugees/2317, reprinted in *FRUS*, 1940, Vol. 2, p. 245.

37. Travers to Dickstein, April 15, 1943, CDF 150.001/4–1443. In contrast with the Ger-

man quota, utilization of the smaller French quota increased in the twelve months following the fall of France, from 25 percent to 68 percent.

38. Annotated note from FDR to Welles, CDF 840.48 Refugees/2352.
39. Photograph of car in Bingham family papers, 1991.240.8, USHMM.
40. ID reproduced in Robert Kim Bingham, *Courageous Dissent,* p. 19.
41. Hiram Bingham report on "Concentration Camps for Foreigners in the Marseille Consular District," December 20, 1940, CDF 740.00115 European War 1939/850.
42. Hugh Fullerton dispatch, "Concentration Camps in Southern France," December 20, 1940, CDF 740.00115 European War 1939/850.
43. Hugh Fullerton letter to Howard Kershner, December 13, 1940, CDF 740.00115 European War 1939/850.
44. Varian Fry, *Surrender on Demand,* pp. 11–12, 56–57.
45. G. Howland Shaw, memorandums of conversations with Hiram Bingham, June 14 and 15, 1938, Bingham OPF, NA-SL.
46. Feuchtwanger diary, July 22, 1940, translation from Bingham, *Courageous Dissent,* p. 138.
47. Bingham, *Courageous Dissent,* pp. 39–40, citing Varian Fry diary, May 7, 1941.
48. Annual efficiency report, 1941, Bingham OPF, NA-SL.
49. Lisa Fittko, *Escape Through the Pyrenees,* p. 34.
50. Bingham report, December 20, 1940.
51. Bingham report, December 20, 1940.
52. HIAS news release, November 19, 1940, OF 76c Church Matters Jewish, October–December 1940, FDRL.
53. HIAS news release, November 19, 1940.
54. Bingham report, December 20, 1940.
55. HICEM Marseille to HIAS New York, January 27, 1941, France C-4, RG 245.4.12, YIVO.
56. Hermann Auerbacher death certificate, November 29, 1940, 72 W 37, F-PA. Two other Auerbachers from Kippenheim died in Gurs in December 1940, according to the camp death register. Mathilde Auerbacher, eighty-three, who had earlier been living in the old people's home in Gailingen, died on December 6. Joseph Auerbacher, the seventy-seven-year-old father of Gerda Auerbacher, died on December 27. See 72 W 36, F-PA.
57. Bella Gutterman and Naomi Morgenstern, eds., *The Gurs Haggadah,* 30.
58. Maier, *Unerwünscht,* p. 87.
59. Maier, *Unerwünscht,* p. 20.
60. Kurt Maier USC-SF.
61. Maier, *Unerwünscht,* p. 89.
62. Hugo and Bella Wachenheimer to Hedy Wachenheimer, November 20, 1940, USHMM.
63. Photograph #07362, Hedy Epstein collection, 1994.A.117, USHMM.
64. Interviews with Margot and Edith Strauss, January 5, 2016.
65. Email from Hedy Wachenheimer Epstein, January 3, 2016.
66. Hugo and Bella Wachenheimer to Hedy Wachenheimer, November 20, 1940.
67. Hugo Wachenheimer to HIAS-HICEM Marseille, February 18, 1941, Wachenheimer HICEM file, France III-467, RG 245.5, YIVO.
68. "Demande de Voyage," December 12, 1940, Wachenheimer HICEM file.
69. Helen Lowrie letter to supporters, November 23, 1940, cited in *The Unitarian Register,* January 1, 1941. See also Lowrie, *The Hunted Children,* p. 102.

CHAPTER NINE: MARSEILLE—MARTINIQUE

1. Gurs inspection report, cited by Amicale du Camp de Gurs in "L'histoire du Camp," www.campgurs.com.
2. Lowrie, *The Hunted Children,* p. 63.
3. Lowrie, *The Hunted Children,* p. 63
4. Siegfried and Charlotte Maier Gurs file, 72 W 65, F-PA. For earlier U.S. visa, see "Demande de Voyage," November 9, 1940, Maier HICEM file, France III-252, RG 245.5, YIVO. For problems associated with early expiration of U.S. visas, see HIAS memo, November 1, 1940, CDF 811.111 Refugees/820.
5. Siegfried and Charlotte Maier Gurs file, 72 W 65, F-PA.
6. Maier, *Unerwünscht,* p. 90.
7. Siegfried Maier address book, Kurt Maier private collection; Hodgdon/Berlin to SecState, September 29, 1940, CDF 811.111 Quota 62/890; see also Stewart/Zurich, to SecState, December 20, 1940, CDF 811.111 Refugees/877.
8. Rapport Camp de Gurs, January 1941, UGIF, RG43–025M, Reel 27, Frame 173, USHMM. The USHMM collection is a microfilm version of the originals retained by the Archives départementales des Alpes-de-Haute-Provence, France.
9. Leahy/Vichy to SecState, February 12, 1941, CDF 811.111 Refugees/959.
10. Maier, *Unerwünscht,* p. 90.
11. Siegfried Maier address book, Kurt Maier private collection.
12. Charlotte Maier Marseille fiche, Hotel Terminus des Ports, 7 W 112, F-BdR; Siegfried Maier Les Milles fiche, 142 W 32, F-BdR; Sofie Auerbacher Gurs file, 72 W 57, F-PA. See also Maier, *Unerwünscht,* p. 90.
13. "End of a World," *Time,* May 24, 1948.
14. Seghers, *Transit,* p. 35.
15. Seghers, *Transit,* pp. 100, 153.
16. Seghers, *Transit,* p. 31.
17. Fry, *Surrender on Demand,* p. 13.
18. Fry, *Surrender on Demand,* p. 121.
19. Kurt Maier USC-SF; Charlotte Maier Marseille fiche.
20. André Fontaine, *Le camp d'étrangers des Milles,* p. 123.
21. SecState to U.S. Consuls, June 29, 1940, CDF 811.111 W.R. 108a.
22. Fullerton/Marseille to Stewart/Zurich, Marseille consulate, General Records 1941, 810–812.8, Box 43, RG 84, NA-CP.
23. Leahy/Vichy to SecState, February 12, 1941, CDF 811.111 Refugees/959.
24. Abbott/Marseille to Hodgdon/Berlin, February 26, 1941, Marseille consulate, General Records 1941, 810–812.8, Box 43, RG 84, NA-CP.
25. G. Howland Shaw, "Memorandum of Conversation with Hiram Bingham," October 9, 1941, Fullerton OPF, NA-SL.
26. "Strictly confidential" memorandum from Lisbon (probably written by Jay Allen), November 12, 1940, ER Warburg, FDRL; Bingham memorandum, Confidential annex to Fullerton OPF, NA-SL.
27. Bingham "strictly confidential" memorandum, undated but evidently written around April 1941, Fullerton OPF. See also Fry's description of a "coquettish" consular clerk in *Surrender on Demand,* p. 4, that is a clear reference to Madame Delaprée.
28. Fry memorandum, February 13, 1941, Varian Fry papers, Columbia University.

29. Shaw memorandum, October 9, 1941.

30. G. Howland Shaw, "Mr Hugh S. Fullerton," November 28, 1941, Fullerton OPF, NA-SL.

31. William Peck memorandum, March 6, 1941, Marseille consulate, General Records 1941, 851.2–869.2, Box 46, RG 84, NA-CP. For an overview on consular policy in Marseille and a more extended discussion of Bingham and Fullerton, see monograph by a Department of State historian, Melissa Jane Taylor, "American Consuls and the Politics of Rescue in Marseille, 1936–1941," *Holocaust and Genocide Studies,* August 2016, pp. 247–75.

32. HICEM Marseille to HIAS New York, January 27, 1941, France C-4, RG 245.4.12, YIVO.

33. SecState to U.S. embassy Vichy, February 4, 1941, 811.111 Refugees/909; Leahy/Vichy to SecState, February 12, 1941, CDF 811.111 Refugees/959.

34. HICEM Marseille to Max Gottschalk/New York, April 8, 1941, France C-4, RG 245.4.12, YIVO.

35. Fittko, *Escape Through the Pyrenees,* pp. 110–14.

36. Fry, *Surrender on Demand,* p. 48.

37. Eric T. Jennings, *Escape from Vichy,* pp. 70–71, citing Varian Fry papers. See also Fry, *Surrender on Demand,* pp. 173–74.

38. Walter Mehring, *No Road Back,* p. 147.

39. "Rapport administratif," November 6, 1941, Centre Américain de Secours, Marseille consulate, General Records 1941, Box 44, RG 84, NA-CP.

40. Eric Jennings, "Last Exit from Vichy France," *Journal of Modern History,* June 2002. See also Jennings, *Escape from Vichy,* p. 87.

41. Victor Serge, *Memoirs of a Revolutionary,* pp. 429–30.

42. Jennings, *Escape from Vichy,* p. 37, citing Peyrouton letter to Vichy Ministry of the Colonies, November 29, 1940.

43. Schramm and Vormeier, *Vivre à Gurs,* p. 137.

44. Sofie Auerbacher fiche, 7 W 112, F-BdR.

45. Maier, *Unerwünscht,* p. 91.

46. Maier, *Unerwünscht,* p. 91.

47. Reports by Rabbi Langer, April 15 and April 29, 1941, UGIF, RG43–025M, Reel 23, Frames 160–73, USHMM.

48. Maier, *Unerwünscht,* p. 91.

49. Kurt Maier donated the documents to the archive Kreisarchiv in Offenburg, Germany.

50. Seghers, *Transit,* p. 114; Maier Dobbs 2016.

51. Gerda Auerbacher Gurs fiche, 72 W 57, F-PA. For problems caused by lack of accommodation in Marseille, see Raymond-Raoul Lambert letter to HICEM Marseille, "Émigration du camp de Gurs," May 8, 1941, France II, RG 245.5, YIVO, and HICEM/Marseille to Chief Rabbi of France, July 16, 1941, France B-11, RG 245.4.12, YIVO. See also "Report on HICEM's Activities June–July 1941," Myron Taylor papers, FDRL.

52. André Gide and Jacques Schiffrin, *Correspondance, 1922–1950,* pp. 164–66. See also André Schiffrin, *A Political Education,* p. 30. After escaping France with his parents, the younger Schiffrin became one of America's leading publishers at Pantheon and the New Press. His authors included Noam Chomsky, Michel Foucault, Studs Terkel, and Marguerite Duras.

53. Amos Reichman, "Jacques Schiffrin, Aller Sans Retour," p. 51 (MA thesis, Columbia University, 2014).

54. Richard Berczeller, *Displaced Doctor,* pp. 107–8.

55. Rabbi Langer report, May 15, 1941, UGIF, RG43–025M, Reel 23, Frame 191, USHMM; Fullerton/Marseille to SecState, "Immigrants Sailing via Martinique," May 19, 1941, CDF 811.111 Refugees/1547.

56. Maier, *Unerwünscht,* p. 94. It is unclear whether Gerda reached Marseille before or after the departure of the *Wyoming.* Her Gurs fiche shows that she was transferred to Hôtel Terminus, Marseille, on May 15, 1941. Hôtel Terminus records (7 W 112, F-BdR) show that she registered there on May 16.

57. Schiffrin, *A Political Education,* p. 34.

58. Berczeller, *Displaced Doctor,* p. 108.

59. Maier, *Unerwünscht,* p. 96.

60. Berczeller, *Displaced Doctor,* p. 110.

61. The *Winnipeg* was intercepted twenty miles northwest of Martinique on the morning of May 26. Admiralty signal, May 26, 1941, FO 837/178, UK-NA.

62. Fullerton/Marseille to SecState, May 19, 1941; Jennings, *Escape from Vichy,* p. 220.

63. Contraband control service officer, Trinidad, to Director of Naval Intelligence, May 30, 1941, FO 837/178, UKNA. See also R. M. Sallé, *70,000 kilomètres d'aventures,* pp. 132–37.

64. Unpublished memoir of Rudolf Sachs, CJH.

65. "Dutch Navy Takes Germans Off Ship," AP report reprinted in *Baltimore Sun,* June 3, 1941.

66. Yolla Niclas-Sachs, "Looking Back from New Horizons," unpublished memoir, CJH.

67. British embassy Washington to UKFO, Telegram 2511, June 3, 1941, FO 837/178, UK-NA.

68. UKFO to British embassy, Washington, D.C., Telegram 2981, May 31, 1941, FO 837/178, UK-NA.

CHAPTER TEN: LES MILLES

1. Welles to Berle, May 21, 1941, CDF 811.111 Refugees/1447.

2. Berle to Welles, May 21, 1941, CDF 811.111 Refugees/1447.

3. Memorandum from Paul Reveley/London, January 8, 1941, Enclosure No. 1 to Stimson to SecState, December 15, 1942, CDF 811.111 W.R. Committees/30.

4. Blake/Basel to SecState, February 27, 1941, CDF 811.111 Refugees/1048.

5. Berle to Long, February 11, 1941, CDF 150.062 Public Charge/1352.

6. Berle to SecState, February 28, 1941, CDF 811.111 Refugees/1883.

7. Hoover to Berle, March 13, 1941, CDF 811.111 Quota 62/995.

8. Jennings, *Escape from Vichy,* p. 169, citing Malige to Department of State, July 12, 1941.

9. FDR to SecState, April 21, 1941, OF 20, Department of State 1941, FDRL.

10. Long diary, January 28, 1941, LC.

11. *Congressional Record*—Senate, June 5, 1941, p. 4753ff.

12. "U.S. Rulings Cut Off Means of Escape for Many in Reich," *NYT,* June 19, 1941, p. 1.

13. "Report on HICEM Activities," June–July 1941, Myron Taylor papers, FDRL. The italicized passage is underlined in original.

14. Breitman et al., *Refugees and Rescue*, p. 256, citing McDonald to ER, September 5, 1941.
15. Long diary, September 4, 1941, LC.
16. Berczeller, *Displaced Doctor*, p. 111.
17. "Liner Breaks Tip of Topmast in Tilt with Brooklyn Bridge," *NYHT,* August 10, 1941, p. 1.
18. Berczeller, *Displaced Doctor*, pp. 113–14.
19. Maier, *Unerwünscht*, p. 96.
20. Maier, *Unerwünscht*, p. 97.
21. Maier, *Unerwünscht*, p. 97; Hans Vogel diary, Accession # 2013.160.1, USHMM.
22. "Liner Breaks Tip of Topmast in Tilt with Brooklyn Bridge," *NYHT,* August 10, 1941.
23. Salomon Auerbacher Gurs fiche, 72 W 57 F-PA; Salomon Auerbacher HICEM file, France III-9, RG 245.5, YIVO.
24. Gerda Auerbacher to Hugo Auerbacher, June 25 and July 29, 1941, Amy Wisnudel private collection.
25. Hugo Auerbacher index card, CDF 811.111 Auerbacher, Solomon.
26. HICEM/Marseille to Chief Rabbi, July 16, 1941, France B-11, RG 245.4.12, YIVO.
27. Auerbacher Les Milles fiche, 142 W 30, F-BdR; Valfer and Wachenheimer Les Milles fiches, 142 W 33, F-BdR.
28. Lion Feuchtwanger, *The Devil in France*, pp. 24–25.
29. Feuchtwanger, *The Devil in France*, p. 25.
30. Feuchtwanger, *The Devil in France*, p. 30.
31. Feuchtwanger, *The Devil in France*, p. 51.
32. Visit to Camp des Milles, March 14, 1941; Frames 190–91, Reel 28, UGIF, RG43-025M, USHMM.
33. Hans Fraenkel report, October 27, 1941, quoted in Jacques Grandjonc et al., *Zone d'ombres*, pp. 260–63.
34. HICEM report, "re. Camp des Milles" August 12, 1941, France II-121, RG 245.5, YIVO.
35. Hans Fraenkel report, October 27, 1941.
36. Feuchtwanger, *The Devil in France*, p. 67.
37. Max Valfer to HICEM Marseille, July 28, 1941, Max Valfer HICEM file, France III-462, RG 245.5, YIVO.
38. Max Valfer to Else and Henry Wertheimer, undated but evidently written in July 1941, Leslie Wertheimer private collection.
39. Max Valfer to HICEM Marseille, July 28, 1941.
40. Fanny Valfer to Else and Henry Wertheimer, undated but evidently written July–August 1941, Leslie Wertheimer private collection.
41. Weil Gurs fiches, 72 W 70, F-PA. Helene, Gertha, and Berta Weil were in hut M16 with Fanny Valfer. They later moved to hut J2.
42. Max Valfer to HICEM Marseille, July 28, 1941.
43. Rudolph Bergman to Else and Henry Wertheimer, July 6, 1941, Leslie Wertheimer private collection.
44. HICEM to U.S. Consulate Marseille, November 21, 1941, Valfer HICEM file.
45. HICEM Marseille to HIAS Lisbon, October 31, 1941, Valfer HICEM file.
46. "Emigration de Madame Valfer Fanny," November 6, 1941, Valfer Gurs file, 72 W 321, F-PA. The consulate wrote letters to the Valfers on October 21 summoning them for an interview after receiving "initial authorization" from Washington. See Leonard Bradford to Fanny Valfer, August 1, 1942, Valfer HICEM file.

47. Fanny Valfer Gurs fiche, 72 W 70, F-PA.
48. Max Valfer to HICEM Marseille, November 28, 1941, Valfer HICEM file.
49. Robert E. Sherwood, *Roosevelt and Hopkins,* pp. 430–31.
50. Forrest Davis and Earnest K. Lindley, *How War Came,* p. 5.
51. Goodwin, *No Ordinary Time,* p. 289.
52. Frances Perkins OH, Columbia University Oral History Research Office.
53. Rosenman, *Working with Roosevelt,* 307. The original draft is in FDRL.
54. The lone dissent was Republican congresswoman Jeannette Rankin of Montana, who had also voted against the declaration of war on Germany in 1917.
55. Speech to Reichstag, December 11, 1941, as recorded by BBC.
56. "Death Sentence of a Mad Dog," *LAT,* editorial, December 8, 1941.
57. FBI reports, 1941, OF 10-B, FDRL.
58. *NYT,* December 15, 1941, p. 9.
59. ER, "My Day," December 16, 1941.
60. Hawley/Marseille to SecState, December 24, 1941, CDF 811.111 W.R./726.
61. Max Valfer to HICEM, December 31, 1941, Valfer file, YIVO.
62. U.S. consulate to Fanny Valfer, December 10, 1941, Valfer file, YIVO. See also Hawley/Marseille to SecState, December 24, 1941; and HICEM documentation, February 1942, France II-11, RG 245.5, YIVO.
63. Gerda Auerbacher to Hugo Auerbacher, December 24, 1941, Amy Wisnudel private collection.
64. Gerda Auerbacher to Hugo Auerbacher, December 24, 1941.
65. Max Valfer to HICEM, December 31, 1941, Valfer file, YIVO.
66. HICEM to Max Valfer, January 8, 1942, Valfer HICEM file; Hawley/Marseille to SecState, December 24, 1941.
67. For admission of refugees who were also "enemy aliens," see correspondence between Department of State and Senator Joseph Ball, September 1942, CDF 811.111 W.R./1030.

CHAPTER ELEVEN: "ENEMY ALIENS"

1. Francis MacDonnell, *Insidious Foes,* p. 136.
2. J. Edgar Hoover's Scrapbooks, Cartoons, Box 233, RG 65, NA-CP.
3. "History of FBI in World War II," FBI file 66-1723, RG 65, NA-CP.
4. Hoover to E. J. Connelley, June 25, 1941, FBI file 40-4538, RG 65, NA-CP.
5. Hoover to Berle, September 29, 1941, CDF 862.20200/37.
6. Hawley/Marseille to Everrett/Vichy, January 5, 1942, CDF 862.20200/53.
7. See, for example, Welles to U.S. Embassy Havana, March 28, 1942, CDF 862.20200/64.
8. "3 Spy Ringleaders Get 20-Year Terms," *NYT,* March 14, 1942, p. 1.
9. "'Refugee' Linked to Nazi Spy Ring," *NYT,* December 31, 1941, p. 1.
10. Rosenman, *Working with Roosevelt,* p. 321.
11. R. J. Lally memo, March 6, 1942, FBI file 40-6186-4, RG 65, NA-CP.
12. Biddle to SecState, November 27, 1942, CDF 811.111 W.R. Committees/31.
13. "Notes on Travel Control Conference," November 18, 1941, INS Subject and Policy Files, 1906–1957, 56114/398, Entry 9, RG 85, NA-DC.
14. Speech delivered via CBS, February 1, 1942.
15. Eleventh Decree to the Law on the Citizenship of the Reich, November 25, 1941.

16. For U.S. definition of "alien enemy," see Federal Register, December 17, 1941, p. 6451. "An alien who is a native, citizen, subject, or denizen of any country, state, or sovereignty with which the United States is at war, shall be considered an alien enemy." The terms "alien enemy" and "enemy alien" were used interchangeably.

17. Cordell Hull circular telegram, January 19, 1942, CDF 811.111 W.R./730.

18. HICEM documentation, February 1942, France II-11, RG 245.5, YIVO.

19. Biddle to Hull, December 27, 1941, CDF 811.111 W.R./730.

20. Hull telegram, January 19, 1942.

21. Fry to Daniel Bénédite, February 2, 1942, Varian Fry papers, Columbia University.

22. David Brinkley, *Washington Goes to War*, p. 120.

23. MID memo, "Present Status of Discussions Between the Department of State and Department of Justice," October 15, 1941, Correspondence relating to control of visas and passports, Box 900, Office of the Director of Intelligence, RG 165, NA-CP.

24. "Report Concerning Visa Control under Present Regulations and Procedure," October 1942, Box 900, Office of the Director of Intelligence, RG 165, NA-CP.

25. MID memo, "Visa Control," June 20, 1941, Box 900, Office of the Director of Intelligence, RG 165, NA-CP.

26. Visa Division memorandum, "Interdepartmental Committees," February 17, 1942, Visas Correspondence Folder, William Vallance papers, University of Rochester.

27. Theodor Köhler visa case, May 20, 1942, Vallance papers. Theodor and Auguste Köhler were deported to Auschwitz in August 1942.

28. Andre Szucs visa case, April 20, 1942, Vallance papers.

29. Memorandum for General Miles, September 19, 1941, Box 900, Office of the Director of Intelligence, RG 165, NA-CP.

30. "Report Concerning Visa Control under Present Regulations and Procedure," October 1942.

31. Hugo Wachenheimer to Hedy Wachenheimer, March 3, 1942, USHMM.

32. Hugo Wachenheimer to Hedy Wachenheimer, January 30, 1942, USHMM.

33. Hugo Wachenheimer to Hedy Wachenheimer, June 2, 1942, USHMM.

34. Hugo Wachenheimer to Hedy Wachenheimer, June 2, 1942, USHMM.

35. Hugo Wachenheimer to Hedy Wachenheimer, March 3, 1942, USHMM.

36. HICEM Marseille to HIAS NY, August 1, 1941, Hugo Wachenheimer HICEM file, France III-467, RG 245.5, YIVO.

37. Bella Wachenheimer to Hedy Wachenheimer, March 10, 1942, USHMM.

38. Bella Wachenheimer to Hedy Wachenheimer, March 10, 1942, USHMM.

39. Hugo Wachenheimer to Hedy Wachenheimer, April 27, 1942, USHMM.

40. Hugo Wachenheimer to Hedy Wachenheimer, July 9, 1942, USHMM.

41. Hugo Wachenheimer to Hedy Wachenheimer, March 3, 1942, USHMM.

42. Telephone message, March 27, 1942, Hugo Wachenheimer Les Milles file, 142 W 41, F-BdR.

43. HICEM to Hugo Wachenheimer, June 20, 1941, Wachenheimer HICEM file.

44. Bella Wachenheimer to Hedy Wachenheimer, June 10 and June 25, 1942, USHMM.

45. Hugo Wachenheimer to Hedy Wachenheimer, June 6 and July 2, 1942, USHMM.

46. "Visit to Rivesaltes," Quaker report, October 29, 1942, AFSC-Ph, reprinted in Friedlander and Milton, eds., *Archives of the Holocaust*, Vol. 2, Part 2, pp. 356–59.

47. Bella Wachenheimer to Hedy Wachenheimer, July 16, 1942; Hugo Wachenheimer to Hedy Wachenheimer, July 18, 1942, USHMM.

48. HIAS NY to HICEM Marseille, June 10, 1942, Wachenheimer HICEM file.

49. HICEM documentation, February–March 1942, France II-11, YIVO.

50. "Rapport annuel sur l'activité de la HICEM-France, 1942," France A-33, RG 245.4.12, YIVO.

51. *Serpa Pinto* passenger list, February 20, 1942, RG 85, NA-DC. Auguste was the mother-in-law of Else Valfer Wertheimer; Rosa was an aunt of Momo Auerbacher.

52. Fry to Daniel Bénédite, April 10, 1942, Varian Fry papers, Columbia University.

53. William Peck memo, "Immigration Policy at Marseille," April 11, 1941, Marseille Consulate General Records, 1941, CDF 855, Box 46, RG 84, NA-CP.

54. "2 of Her 100 Years in Dread Nazi Camp," *NYT,* April 11, 1943, p. 19.

55. Margaret Jones letters, January 30 and May 1, 1942, Case file # 7561, AFSC Refugee Assistance Case Files, 2002.296, USHMM.

56. Mathilde Wertheimer HICEM file, France III-490, RG 245.5, YIVO.

57. Mathilde Wertheimer index cards, CDF 811.111 Wertheimer. State Department records show that her visa was originally approved in June 1941, reapproved in November 1941, and finally issued in June 1942.

58. Mathilde Wertheimer Gurs fiche, 72 W 70, F-PA.

59. Medical certificate signed by George Rodocanachi, Mathilde Wertheimer file A-3127328, U.S. Citizenship and Immigration Services.

60. *Nyassa* passenger list, Baltimore, July 30, 1942, RG 85, NA-DC.

61. HICEM Casablanca to HICEM Lisbon, July 14, 1942, France II-154, RG 245.5, YIVO.

62. HICEM Casablanca to HICEM Lisbon, July 14, 1942. See also France II-153 folder, RG 245.5, YIVO, which contains numerous related descriptions of dockside confrontations.

63. *NYT,* April 11, 1943.

64. Marjorie McClelland to AFSC, July 20, 1942, Friedlander and Milton, eds., *Archives of the Holocaust,* Vol. 2, Part 2, pp. 301–5. See also research brief by Ronald Coleman on the U.S. Committee for the Care of European Children, USHMM.

65. "Lopez Family from Barcelona Arrives Here on Refugee Ship," *Baltimore Sun,* July 31, 1942, p. 24.

66. *NYT,* April 11, 1943.

67. Max Valfer to Else and Heinrich Wertheimer, February 29, 1942, and undated, probably May–June 1942, Leslie Wertheimer private collection.

68. Fanny Valfer to Else and Heinrich Wertheimer, undated but probably March 1942, Leslie Wertheimer private collection.

69. Max Valfer to Else and Heinrich Wertheimer, undated but probably June 1942, Leslie Wertheimer private collection.

70. Max Valfer to Else and Heinrich Wertheimer, undated but probably May–June 1942, Leslie Wertheimer private collection..

71. Sonja Geismar private collection.

72. Max Valfer to Else and Heinrich Wertheimer, probably June 1942, Leslie Wertheimer private collection.

73. Max Valfer to HICEM Marseille, July 15, 1942, Valfer HICEM file, France III-462, RG 245.5, YIVO; Hugo Valfer to Max and Fanny Valfer, June 21, 1942, Linda Kaplan private collection.

74. Karl Valfer to Max and Fanny Valfer, August 1942, Linda Kaplan private collection. See also U.S. Consulate Marseille to Fanny Valfer, August 1, 1942, Valfer HICEM file.

CHAPTER TWELVE: "TO THE EAST"

1. Claudia Steur, *Theodor Dannecker*, p. 157.
2. Commissioner General for Jewish Questions Xavier Vallat at his trial, December 1947, cited by Louis Saurel, *La Gestapo*, p. 106.
3. Dannecker report, "Further Transports of Jews from France," June 26, 1942, reprinted in Serge Klarsfeld, *Vichy-Auschwitz*, Vol. 1, pp. 215–16.
4. Dannecker report, "Tour of Non-occupied Zone," July 20, 1942, reprinted in Klarsfeld, *Vichy-Auschwitz*, Vol. 1, pp. 274–77.
5. Dannecker report, "Tour of Non-occupied Zone," July 20, 1942.
6. Telegram from Police Nationale, 7th Bureau, to *zone libre* prefects, July 17, 1942, cited by Klarsfeld, *Vichy-Auschwitz*, Vol. 1, p. 264.
7. Dannecker report, "Tour of Non-occupied Zone," July 20, 1942.
8. American Red Cross report, August 7, 1942, CDF 851.4016/90.
9. Postcard from Max and Fanny Valfer to Else Wertheimer, postmarked Marseille, August 21, 1942, Leslie Wertheimer private collection. The postcard is undated but was probably written toward the end of July 1942.
10. Unpublished memoir of Roswell McClelland, August 1942, 2014.500.1, USHMM.
11. Lowrie memorandum to Tracy Strong, August 10, 1942, CDF 851.4016/83, reprinted in Friedlander and Milton, eds., *Archives of the Holocaust*, Vol. 2, Part 2, pp. 312–17.
12. Lowrie, *The Hunted Children*, p. 204.
13. McClelland memoir, USHMM.
14. Laval broadcast, June 22, 1942, *Les Nouveaux Temps*, June 24, 1942.
15. Lowrie to Strong, August 10, 1942.
16. McClelland memoir.
17. McClelland memoir.
18. Lowrie to Strong, August 10, 1942.
19. Salomon Auerbacher HICEM file, France III-9, RG 245.5, YIVO.
20. Lowrie, *The Hunted Children*, pp. 208–9.
21. McClelland memoir. See also Hans Fraenkel eyewitness account, reprinted in Grandjone, *Zone d'ombres*, p. 385.
22. Raymond-Raoul Lambert, *Diary of a Witness*, p. 138.
23. McClelland memoir.
24. Serge Klarsfeld, *Les Transferts de juifs de la région de Marseille vers les camps de Drancy ou de Compiègne*, pp. 4–8.
25. Report of Chief Rabbi, Israël Salzer, reprinted in Grandjone, *Zone d'ombres*, p. 395.
26. Varian Fry, "The Massacre of the Jews," *The New Republic*, December 21, 1942.
27. Daniel Bénédite, ed., *Un chemin vers la liberté sous l'Occupation*, p. 268. For discussion of the role of Pinkney Tuck in protesting the deportations, see Yehuda Bauer, *American Jewry and the Holocaust*, pp. 175–76.
28. Lambert, *Diary of a Witness*, p. 139; Grandjone, *Zone d'ombres*, p. 395.
29. McClelland memoir. McClelland refers to Freund as "Richard F."
30. McClelland memoir.
31. Testimony of Henri Manen, "Au fond de l'abîme," reprinted in Grandjone, *Zone d'ombres*, p. 362.
32. Klarsfeld, *Les Transferts de juifs de la région de Marseille vers les camps de Drancy ou de Compiègne*, p. 8.

33. Manen testimony; Lambert, *Diary of a Witness,* pp. 139–40.

34. McClelland memoir.

35. Klarsfeld, *Les Transferts de juifs de la région de Marseille vers les camps de Drancy ou de Compiègne,* p. 17.

36. Bella Wachenheimer to Hedy Wachenheimer, September 1, 1942, Epstein papers, USHMM.

37. Lowrie, *The Hunted Children,* p. 214. Maulavé was later relieved of his duties.

38. Lowrie to Tracy Strong, August 22, 1942, reprinted in Friedlander and Milton, eds., *Archives of the Holocaust,* Vol. 2, Part 2, pp. 326–28.

39. Fontaine, *Le Camp d'étrangers des Milles,* p. 145.

40. McClelland memoir.

41. Lowrie memorandum to Tracy Strong, September 17, 1942, CDF 851.4016/83, reprinted in Friedlander and Milton, eds., *Archives of the Holocaust,* Vol. 2, Part 2, pp. 337–39.

42. Max Strauss entry, *Gedenkbuch für die Karlsruher Juden,* www.gedenkbuch.informedia.de.

43. McClelland memoir; Lowrie, *The Hunted Children,* p. 219.

44. Wladimir Schah to Édouard Oungre, August 1942, XII-France B-11, RG 245.4, YIVO.

45. Schah to Oungre.

46. Fry to ER, August 27, 1942, ER papers, Correspondence with Varian Fry, Holocaust/Refugee collection, FDRL.

47. Welles to ER, September 22, 1942, CDF 851.4016/105.

48. ER, "My Day," September 5, 1942.

49. Henry Morgenthau, *Ambassador Morgenthau's Story,* pp. 321–22.

50. Henry Morgenthau Sr. to Cordell Hull, September 4, 1942, CDF 851.4016/91.

51. Breitman and Lichtman, *FDR and the Jews,* p. 200.

52. Bella Wachenheimer to Hedy Wachenheimer, September 1, 1942, Epstein papers, USHMM.

53. "Visit to Rivesaltes," October 29, 1942, AFSC-Ph, reprinted in Friedlander and Milton, eds., *Archives of the Holocaust,* Vol. 2, Part 2, pp. 356–59.

54. Serge Klarsfeld, *French Children of the Holocaust,* pp. 58–61. See also Serge Klarsfeld, *Le Calendrier de la persécution des juifs de France,* Vol. 2, pp. 965–66, for August 30, 1942, police instruction rejecting exemptions for children.

55. Klarsfeld, *Le Calendrier de la persécution des juifs de France,* Vol. 2, pp. 990–92.

56. Vichy police order, August 30, 1942, cited by Klarsfeld, *Le Calendrier de la persécution des juifs de France,* Vol. 2, pp. 964–65.

57. Bella Wachenheimer to Hedy Wachenheimer, September 4, 1942, Epstein papers, USHMM. For other final messages transmitted through Quaker relief workers in Montauban, see Folder 82, Box 66, AFSC records relating to humanitarian work in France, RG-67.007M, USHMM.

58. Lowrie memorandum to Tracy Strong, October 7, 1942, CDF 851.4016/83.

59. Tuck/Vichy to SecState, September 11, 1942, CDF 851.4016/92 and September 12, 1942, CDF 851.4016/94; United Press International, "Laval Interns a Catholic Leader," *NYT,* September 18, 1942.

60. Tuck/Vichy to SecState, September 10, 1942, CDF 851.4016/114.

61. For Jewish admissions to Palestine, see British government data cited in *American Jewish Year Book,* Vols. 44–46. (Admissions for 1942 are available for the first seven months only.) For Jewish admissions to the United States, see Tuck/Vichy to/from

SecState, beginning September 24, 1942, CDF 851.4016/104. The U.S. data includes both self-identified "Hebrew" immigrants and non-immigrant visitors who were permitted to extend their visas after Kristallnacht. The twin sets of data can be summarized as follows:

Jewish admissions to U.S. and Palestine

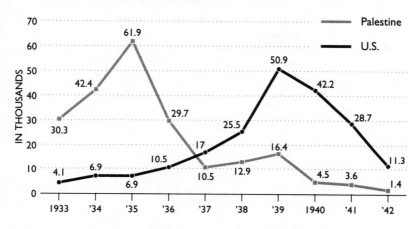

62. Tuck/Vichy to SecState, September 11, 1942, CDF 851.4016/92.
63. Breitman and Lichtman, *FDR and the Jews*, p. 202.
64. Tuck/Vichy to SecState, October 3, 1942, CDF 851.4017/108.
65. Lowrie, *The Hunted Children*, pp. 222–24.
66. List of Marseille visa notifications, November 4, 1942, CDF 811.111 W.R./1110 1/2.
67. Letter to J. W. Pehle, December 20, 1944, Records of War Refugee Board, General Correspondence, Issuance and Reissuance of U.S. Visas, FDRL.

EPILOGUE: MEMORY

1. Epstein IWM 1991.
2. Epstein IWM 1991.
3. Epstein, *Erinnern*, p. 137.
4. Epstein, *Erinnern*, pp. 139–41.
5. Epstein, *Erinnern*, p. 142.
6. Epstein, *Erinnern*, p. 144.
7. Epstein, *Erinnern*, p. 143.
8. Epstein, *Erinnern*, p. 144.
9. Letters from Ministère des Anciens Combattants et Victimes de la Guerre to Hedy Epstein, June 19, 1956, reprinted in Epstein, *Erinnern*, pp. 166–67.
10. Robert O. Paxton, *Vichy France*, p. 25.
11. French Deportation Lists Research Project, USHMM.
12. Klarsfeld, *Le Calendrier de la persécution des juifs de France*, Vol. 2, pp. 768–71.
13. Gerhard Teschner, *Die Deportation der badischen und saarpfälzischen Juden am 22. Oktober 1940*, p. 319.

14. Epstein Dobbs 2015; interviews with Edith Hausman and Margot Walton, July 2016.
15. Stude et al., *Schicksal und Geschichte*, p. 360. For names of Kippenheim and Schmieheim Jews killed in the Holocaust, see Stude et al., *Schicksal und Geschichte*, pp. 23–30.
16. Camp Commander, Isle of Man, to U.S. Consulate General, London, November 29, 1940, Henry Wertheimer private collection. For U.K. refugee policy, see Louise London, *Whitehall and the Jews, 1933–1948*, pp. 97–141.
17. Heinrich Wertheimer to Ruth Valfer and Rudolf Bergman, July 20, 1939, Henry Wertheimer private collection. According to the State Department, "total registered demand" for German quota immigration visas had reached 220,000 by October 1938. See "Demand Against German Quota," November 8, 1938, CDF 811.111 Quota 62/636.
18. Schellinger, ed., *Gedächtnis aus Stein*, p. 188.
19. "Hedwig Epstein gegen Deutsche Reich," F 166/3/2678, G-STAF.
20. Epstein, *Erinnern*, p. 168.
21. Schellinger, ed., *Gedächtnis aus Stein*, pp. 191–95.
22. Schellinger, ed., *Gedächtnis aus Stein*, pp. 209–15. A photograph of the inscription is on p. 213.
23. Schellinger, ed., *Gedächtnis aus Stein*, p. 217.
24. Schellinger, ed., *Gedächtnis aus Stein*, pp. 223–25.
25. Krais interview, July 2017.
26. Wertheimer, *The Habit of Labor*, p. 14.
27. Wertheimer, *The Habit of Labor*, p. 2.
28. Wertheimer, *The Habit of Labor*, p. 6.
29. Wertheimer, *The Habit of Labor*, p. 3.
30. Mathis interview, July 2017.
31. Schellinger, ed., *Gedächtnis aus Stein*, p. 239.
32. Krais interview, October 2016.
33. Mathis and Krais interviews, July 2017.
34. Epstein IWM 1997.
35. Epstein IWM 1997; Epstein, *Erinnern*, pp. 278–81.
36. David Wyman, *The Abandonment of the Jews*, p. 316.
37. Arthur Schlesinger Jr., "Did FDR Betray the Jews?," *Newsweek*, April 17, 1994.
38. Charlie Rose, *America and the Holocaust*, PBS, April 4, 1994.
39. David S. Wyman, *Paper Walls*, p. 213.
40. Wertheimer-Valfer family questionnaire, 2005, Sonja Geismar collection.
41. Sonja Geismar talk to B'nai Jeshurun, 2015. For an exhaustive study on the fate of the *St. Louis* passengers, see Sarah A. Ogilvie and Scott Miller, *Refuge Denied*.
42. Pia Gilbert OH 1988.
43. Ceremony with survivors, September 7, 2003, Kippenheim village archive.
44. Exodus 1:8–10.
45. Bar and Bamberger, *Der jüdische Friedhof in Schmieheim*, Vols. 1–2; Schellinger, ed., *Gedächtnis aus Stein*; Stude et al., *Schicksal und Geschichte*.
46. Memorial tablet unveiling ceremony, Lessing-Realschule, Freiburg, Germany, October 28, 2004.
47. Visit to Anne-Frank-Gymnasium, Rheinau, October 23, 2016.
48. Maier Dobbs 2016.

Selected Bibliography

Alsop, Joseph, and Robert Kintner. *American White Paper: The Story of American Diplomacy and the Second World War*. New York: Simon & Schuster, 1940.

Auerbacher, Inge. *I Am a Star: Child of the Holocaust*. New York: Puffin Books, 1993.

Bar-Giora Bamberger, Naftali. *Der jüdische Friedhof in Schmieheim: Memor-Buch*. Kippenheim, Germany: Gemeinde Kippenheim, 1999.

Bauer, Yehuda. *American Jewry and the Holocaust: The American Jewish Joint Distribution Committee, 1939–1945*. Detroit: Wayne State University Press, 2017.

Baumann, Ulrich. *Zerstörte Nachbarschaften: Christen und Juden in badischen Landgemeinden 1862–1940*. Hamburg: Dölling und Galitz, 2000.

Bénédite, Daniel. *Un chemin vers la liberté sous l'Occupation: Marseille-Provence, 1940–1944*. Paris: le Félin, 2017.

Berczeller, Richard. *Displaced Doctor*. New York: Avon, 1965.

Bingham, Robert Kim. *Courageous Dissent: How Harry Bingham Defied His Government to Save Lives*. Greenwich, Conn.: Triune Books, 2007.

Breitman, Richard. *U.S. Intelligence and the Nazis*. New York: Cambridge University Press, 2005.

Breitman, Richard, and Alan M. Kraut. *American Refugee Policy and European Jewry: 1933–1945*. Bloomington: Indiana University Press, 1987.

Breitman, Richard, and Allan J. Lichtman. *FDR and the Jews*. Cambridge, Mass.: Harvard University Press, 2013.

Breitman, Richard, Barbara McDonald Stewart, and Severin Hochberg, eds. *Refugees and Rescue: The Diaries and Papers of James G. McDonald, 1935–1945*. Bloomington: Indiana University Press, 2009.

Brinkley, David. *Washington Goes to War*. New York: Alfred A. Knopf, 1988.

Browning, Christopher R. *The Origins of the Final Solution: The Evolution of Nazi Jewish Policy*. Lincoln: University of Nebraska Press, 2004.

Buff, Fred, and Maryann McLoughlin, eds. *Riding the Storm Waves: The St. Louis Diary of Fred Buff*. Margate, N.J.: ComteQ Publishing, 2009.

Burns, James MacGregor. *Roosevelt: The Lion and the Fox*. New York: Harcourt, Brace, 1956.

Cook, Blanche Wiesen. *Eleanor Roosevelt: The War Years and After, 1939–1962.* New York: Viking, 2016.

Dalio, Marcel. *Mes années folles.* Paris: J.-C. Lattès, 1976.

Daniels, Roger. *Guarding the Golden Door: American Immigration Policy and Immigrants Since 1882.* New York: Hill & Wang, 2005.

Davis, Forrest, and Ernest K. Lindley. *How War Came: An American White Paper, from the Fall of France to Pearl Harbor.* New York: Simon & Schuster, 1942.

Davis, Kenneth S. *FDR, the War President, 1940–1943: A History.* New York: Random House, 2000.

Elon, Amos. *The Pity of It All: A Portrait of the Jews in Germany, 1743–1933.* New York: Picador, 2002.

Epstein, Hedy. *Erinnern ist nicht genug: Autobiographie.* Münster, Germany: Unrast, 1999.

Feingold, Henry L. *The Politics of Rescue.* New Brunswick, N.J.: Rutgers University Press, 1970.

Feuchtwanger, Lion. *The Devil in France: My Encounter with Him in the Summer of 1940.* New York: Viking, 1941.

Fittko, Lisa. *Escape Through the Pyrenees.* Evanston, Ill.: Northwestern University Press, 1991.

Fontaine, André. *Le Camp d'étrangers des Milles, 1939–1943.* Aix-en-Provence, France: Édisud, 1989.

Frank, Werner L. *The Curse of Gurs: Way Station to Auschwitz.* Lexington, Ky.: Werner L. Frank, 2012.

Friedlander, Henry, and Sybil Milton, eds. *Archives of the Holocaust: An International Collection of Selected Documents.* New York: Garland, 1990.

Fry, Varian. *Surrender on Demand.* Boulder, Colo.: Johnson Books, 1997.

Gardiner, Muriel, and Joseph Buttinger. *Damit wir nicht vergessen. Unsere Jahre 1934–1947 in Wien, Paris und New York.* Vienna: Wiener Volksbuchhandlung, 1978.

Gide, André, and Jacques Schiffrin. *Correspondance, 1922–1950.* Paris: Gallimard, 2005.

Gilbert, Martin. *Kristallnacht: Prelude to Destruction.* London: HarperCollins, 2006.

Gold, Mary Jayne. *Crossroads Marseille, 1940.* Garden City, N.Y.: Doubleday, 1980.

Goldstein, Alice. *Ordinary People, Turbulent Times.* Bloomington, Ind.: AuthorHouse, 2008.

Goodwin, Doris Kearns. *No Ordinary Time: Franklin & Eleanor Roosevelt; The Home Front in World War II.* New York: Touchstone, 1994.

Grandjonc, Jacques, ed. *Zone d'ombres: 1933–1944.* Aix-en-Provence, France: Alinéa, 1990.

Gunther, John. *Roosevelt in Retrospect: A Profile in History.* New York: Harper & Brothers, 1950.

Gutterman, Bella, and Naomi Morgenstern. *The Gurs Haggadah: Passover in Perdition.* Jerusalem: Devora, 2003.

Harris, Mark Jonathan, and Deborah Oppenheimer. *Into the Arms of Strangers.* London: Bloomsbury, 2000.

Ickes, Harold L. *The Secret Diary of Harold L. Ickes: 1939–1941,* Vol. 2, *The Inside Struggle;* Vol. 3, *The Lowering Clouds.* New York: Simon & Schuster, 1954.

Israel, Fred L., ed. *The War Diary of Breckinridge Long: Selections from the Years 1939–1944.* Lincoln: University of Nebraska Press, 1966.

Jennings, Eric T. *Escape from Vichy: The Refugee Exodus to the French Caribbean.* Cambridge, Mass.: Harvard University Press, 2018.

Kaplan, Marion A. *Between Dignity and Despair: Jewish Life in Nazi Germany.* New York: Oxford University Press, 1999.

Klarsfeld, Serge. *Le Calendrier de la persécution des juifs de France,* Vols. 2 and 3. Paris: Fayard, 2001.

———. *Les Transferts de juifs de la région de Marseille vers les camps de Drancy ou de Compiègne.* Paris: Association "Les fils et filles des déportés juifs de France," 1992.

———. *Vichy-Auschwitz: Le Rôle de Vichy dans la solution finale de la question juive en France.* Paris: Fayard, 1983.

Klarsfeld, Serge, Susan Cohen, and Howard M. Epstein, eds. *French Children of the Holocaust: A Memorial.* New York: New York University Press, 1996.

Klemperer, Victor. *I Will Bear Witness: A Diary of the Nazi Years, 1933–1941.* New York: Modern Library, 1999.

Kopp, Karl. *Das Kippenheimer Lied: Eine badische Volksschule und ihre israelitischen Kinder.* Ettlingen, Germany: Kraft Premium, 2017.

Lambert, Raymond-Raoul. *Diary of a Witness: 1940–1943.* Chicago: Ivan R. Dee, 2007.

Lash, Joseph P. *Eleanor and Franklin: The Story of Their Relationship.* New York: W. W. Norton, 1971.

Leuchtenburg, William E. *The FDR Years: On Roosevelt and His Legacy.* New York: Columbia University Press, 1995.

London, Louise. *Whitehall and the Jews, 1933–1948: British Immigration Policy, Jewish Refugees and the Holocaust.* Cambridge, U.K.: Cambridge University Press, 2000.

Lowrie, Donald A. *The Hunted Children.* New York: W. W. Norton, 1963.

MacDonnell, Francis. *Insidious Foes: The Axis Fifth Column and the American Home Front.* New York: Oxford University Press, 1995.

Maier, Kurt Salomon. *Unerwünscht: Kindheits- und Jugenderinnerungen eines jüdischen Kippenheimers.* Ubstadt-Weiher, Germany: Verlag regionalkultur, 2011.

Marino, Andy. *A Quiet American.* New York: St. Martin's Press, 1999.

McCarthy, Rachel, ed. *The Wertheimer/Valfer Family Reunion, August 2005.* Privately published, 2007.

Mehring, Walter. *No Road Back.* New York: S. Curl, 1944.

Morgan, Ted. *FDR: A Biography.* New York: Simon & Schuster, 1985.

Morgenthau, Henry. *Ambassador Morgenthau's Story.* Garden City, N.Y.: Doubleday, Page, 1918.

Ogilvie, Sarah A., and Scott Miller. *Refuge Denied: The St. Louis Passengers and the Holocaust.* Madison: University of Wisconsin Press, 2006.

Paxton, Robert O. *Vichy France: Old Guard and New Order.* New York: Alfred A. Knopf, 1972.

Pleasants, Julian M. *Buncombe Bob: The Life and Times of Robert Rice Reynolds.* Chapel Hill: University of North Carolina Press, 2000.

Roosevelt, Eleanor. *This I Remember.* New York: Harper, 1949.

Roosevelt, Franklin D., and Elliott Roosevelt. *F.D.R., His Personal Letters, 1928–1945.* 2 vols. New York: Duell, Sloan, & Pearce, 1947.

Rosenman, Samuel I. *Working with Roosevelt.* New York: Da Capo, 1972.

Sallé, R. M. *70.000 kilomètres d'aventures: notes de voyage: Indochine-France et retour.* Hanoi: Imprimerie d'Extrême-Orient, 1942.

Sandner, Harald. *Hitler—Das Itinerar.* Berlin: Berlin Story, 2016.

Sauer, Paul. *Dokumente über die Verfolgung der jüdischen Bürger in Baden-Württemberg durch das Nationalsozialistische Regime.* Stuttgart, Germany: Kohlhammer, 1966.

Saurel, Louis. *La Gestapo.* Paris: Rouff, 1967.

Schellinger, Uwe, ed. *Gedächtnis aus Stein: die Synagoge in Kippenheim, 1852–2002.* Heidelberg, Germany: Regionalkultur, 2002.

Schwertfeger, Ruth. *In Transit: Narratives of German Jews in Exile, Flight, and Internment During "the Dark Years" of France.* Berlin: Frank & Timme, 2012.

Schiffrin, André. *A Political Education: Coming of Age in Paris and New York.* London: Melville House, 2014.

Schramm, Hanna, and Barbara Vormeier. *Vivre à Gurs.* Paris: François Maspero, 1979.

Seghers, Anna. *Transit.* New York: New York Review Books, 2013.

Serge, Victor. *Memoirs of a Revolutionary.* New York: New York Review Books, 2012.

Sherwood, Robert E. *Roosevelt and Hopkins.* New York: Harper, 1950.

Shirer, William L. *Twentieth-Century Journey: The Nightmare Years, 1930–1940.* Boston: Little, Brown, 1984.

Smith, Jean Edward. *FDR.* New York: Random House, 2008.

Smith, Michael. *Foley: The Spy Who Saved 10,000 Jews.* London: Coronet, 2000.

Stember, Charles Herbert, et al. *Jews in the Mind of America.* New York: Basic Books, 1966.

Stern, Selma. *The Court Jew: A Contribution to the History of the Period of Absolutism in Europe.* New Brunswick, N.J.: Transaction Books, 1985.

Steur, Claudia. *Theodor Dannecker: ein Funktionär der "Endlösung."* Essen, Germany: Klartext, 1997.

Stude, Jürgen, et al. *Schicksal und Geschichte der jüdischen Gemeinden: Ettenheim, Altdorf, Kippenheim, Schmieheim, Rust, Orschweier.* Ettenheim, Germany: Historischer Verein für Mittelbaden, 1997.

Taylor, Melissa Jane. "'Experts in Misery'? American Consuls in Austria, Jewish Refugees and Restrictionist Immigration Policy." PhD diss., University of South Carolina, 2006.

Teschner, Gerhard J. *Die Deportation der badischen und saarpfälzischen Juden am 22. Oktober 1940.* Frankfurt: Lang, 2002.

Thayer, Charles W. *The Unquiet Germans.* New York: Harper, 1957.

Thomas, Gordon, and Max Morgan Witts. *Voyage of the Damned.* New York: Stein & Day, 1974.

The Trial of Adolf Eichmann: Record of Proceedings in the District Court of Jerusalem. Jerusalem: State of Israel, Ministry of Justice, 1992.

Trial of the Major War Criminals Before the International Military Tribunal. Nuremberg: International Military Tribunal, 1947.

Tuchel, Johannes. *Konzentrationslager: Organisationsgeschichte und Funktion der "Inspektion der Konzentrationslager."* Boppard am Rhein, Germany: Boldt, 1991.

Vining, Elizabeth Gray. *Friend of Life: The Biography of Rufus M. Jones.* Philadelphia: Lippincott, 1958.

Ward, Geoffrey C., ed. *Closest Companion: The Unknown Story of the Intimate Friendship Between Franklin Roosevelt and Margaret Suckley.* New York: Simon & Schuster, 2009.

Wertheimer, Stef. *The Habit of Labor: Lessons from a Life of Struggle and Success.* New York: Overlook Duckworth, 2015.

Wyman, David S. *The Abandonment of the Jews: America and the Holocaust.* New York: Pantheon, 1984.

———. *Paper Walls: America and the Refugee Crisis, 1939–1941.* Amherst: University of Massachusetts Press, 1968.

Index

ILLUSTRATION CREDITS

PAGE 14: Kippenheim synagogue: Robert Krais/Deutsch-Israelischer Arbeitskreis südlicher Oberrhein, Ettenheim/Hedy Epstein; PAGE 28: Lisl Weil self-portrait: National Archives; PAGE 51: Morgenthau and FDR: FDR Library; PAGE 78: Valfer family, April 1937: Sonja Maier Geismar collection; PAGE 88: Ludwig and Freya Maier board the *St. Louis*: Sonja Maier Geismar collection; PAGE 152: Deportation, October 1940: Förderverein Ehemalige Synagoge Kippenheim e.V./Robert Krais; PAGE 166: Bread surgeon: Harvard Art Museum; PAGE 171: Wachenheimer "Golden Wedding Anniversary": Dianne Lee/ Hedy Epstein Estate; PAGE 179: Hotel Terminus des Ports: Documentation Française/ Raymond Brajou; PAGE 189: American consulate, Marseille: USHMM/Hans Cahnmann; PAGE 229: Extract from Mathilde Wertheimer visa: USCIS; PAGE 252: Final message from Bella: Dianne Lee/Hedy Epstein Estate; PAGE 278: Maier family visa: Kurt S. Maier collection, edited by John Robert Bauer/Kreisarchiv Offenburg.; PAGE 280: Valfer family: Sonja Maier Geismar collection; PAGE 281: (top) Hershele Wertheimer: Sonja Maier Geismar collection; (bottom) Hershele Wertheimer and children: Marion Bloch; PAGE 282: Wachenheimer "Golden Wedding Anniversary": Dianne Lee/Hedy Epstein Estate

Insert 1

PAGE 1: (top): Gemeinde Kippenheim/Jürgen Stude; (bottom): Gemeinde Kippenheim/ Jürgen Stude

PAGE 2: (top): Haupstaatsarchiv Stuttgart; (bottom): Kurt S. Maier collection, edited by John Robert Bauer

PAGE 3: (top): Sonja Maier Geismar collection; (bottom): Hans Wertheimer

PAGE 4: (top left): Ruth Valfer Bergman Archives/courtesy Bergman family; (top right): Ruth Valfer Bergman Archives/courtesy Bergman family; (bottom): Archives Bouches-du-Rhône

PAGE 5: (top): Dianne Lee/Hedy Epstein Estate; (bottom): Dianne Lee/Hedy Epstein Estate

PAGE 6: (top): Kurt S. Maier collection, edited by John Robert Bauer; (bottom): Kurt S. Maier collection, edited by John Robert Bauer

PAGE 7: (top): Getty/Life Pictures; (bottom left): Library of Congress/Harris and Ewing; (bottom right): Library of Congress/Harris and Ewing
PAGE 8: (top): *Süddeutsche Zeitung;* (bottom): AP

Insert 2

PAGE 1: (top): AP; (bottom): Sargeant Memorial Collection, Norfolk Public Library
PAGE 2: (top): Library of Congress/Harris and Ewing; (bottom): Library of Congress/Harris and Ewing
PAGE 3: (top): USHMM; (middle): Troper Collection, Yaffa Eliach Collection donated by the Center for Holocaust Studies; (bottom): Documentation Française/Raymond Brajou
PAGE 4: (top): AP; (middle): USHMM/Hiram Bingham; (bottom): USHMM/Annette Fry
PAGE 5: (top): FDR Library; (bottom): National Archives
PAGE 6: (top): AP; (bottom): USHMM/Friedel Bohny-Reiter
PAGE 7: (top left): Ruth Valfer Bergman Archives/courtesy Bergman family; (top right): Michael Dobbs; (bottom): Förderverein Ehemalige Synagoge Kippenhein e.V./Robert Krais
PAGE 8: (top): Förderverein Ehemalige Synagoge Kippenheim e.V.; (bottom): Förderverein Ehemalige Synagoge Kippenheim e.V.

Michael Dobbs was born and educated in Britain, but is now a U.S. citizen. He was a longtime reporter for *The Washington Post,* covering the collapse of communism as a foreign correspondent. He has taught at leading American universities, including Princeton, the University of Michigan, and Georgetown, and is currently on the staff of the United States Holocaust Memorial Museum. His previous books include the best-selling *One Minute to Midnight* on the Cuban missile crisis, which was part of an acclaimed Cold War trilogy. He lives outside Washington, D.C.

A NOTE ON THE TYPE

This book was set in Janson, a typeface long thought to have been made by the Dutchman Anton Janson. However, it has been conclusively demonstrated that these types are actually the work of Nicholas Kis (1650–1702), a Hungarian. The type is an excellent example of the influential and sturdy Dutch types that prevailed in England up to the time William Caslon (1692–1766) developed his own incomparable designs from them.

Composed by North Market Street Graphics, Lancaster, Pennsylvania

Printed and bound by Berryville Graphics, Berryville, Virginia

Designed by Maggie Hinders